TEMPORARY WORK

The Gendered Rise of a
Precarious Employment Relationship

The first in-depth analysis of temporary work in Canada, this important
new book by Leah F. Vosko examines a number of important trends,
including the commodification of labour power; the decline of the full-
time, full-year job as a norm; and the gendered character of prevailing
employment relationships. Spanning the period from the late nineteenth to the late twentieth century, *Temporary Work* traces the evolution
of the temporary employment relationship in Canada and places it in
an international context. It explores how, and to what extent, temporary work is becoming the norm for a diverse group of workers in the
labour market, taking gender as the central lens of analysis.

Recent scholarship emphasizes that the nature of work is changing,
citing the spread of non-standard forms of employment and the rise in
women's participation in the labour force. Vosko confirms that important changes are indeed taking place in the labour market, but argues
that these changes are best understood in historical, economic, and
political context. This book will be invaluable to academics in a variety
of disciplines as well as to policy analysts and practitioners in government, industry, and organized labour.

LEAH F. VOSKO is an assistant professor of labour studies and political
science at McMaster University. She is also co-chair of the International
Working Group on Labour Market Regulation and Deregulation and
Co-chair of the Women, Work and Income Committee of the National
Action Committee on the Status of Women.

Temporary Work

The Gendered Rise of a Precarious Employment Relationship

LEAH F. VOSKO

UNIVERSITY OF TORONTO PRESS
Toronto Buffalo London

© Dr. Leah F. Vosko
Published by the University of Toronto Press Incorporated 2000
Toronto Buffalo London
Printed in Canada

ISBN 0-8020-4792-0 (cloth)
ISBN 0-8020-8334-X (paper)

Printed on acid-free paper

Canadian Cataloguing in Publication Data

Vosko, Leah F.
Temporary work : the gendered rise of a precarious employment
relationship

Includes bibliographical references and index.
ISBN 0-8020-4792-0 (bound)   ISBN 0-80208334-X (pbk.)

1. Temporary employment – Canada – History – 20th century.
2. Sexual division of labor – Canada – History – 20th century.
3. Women – Employment – Canada – History – 20th century.   I. Title.
HD5854.2.C3V67 2000   331.25'72   C00-930453-3

University of Toronto Press acknowledges the financial assistance to its
publishing program of the Canada Council for the Arts and the Ontario
Arts Council.

This book has been published with the help of a grant from the Humanities
and Social Sciences Federation of Canada, using funds provided by the
Social Sciences and Humanities Research Council of Canada.

University of Toronto Press acknowledges the financial support for its
publishing activities of the Government of Canada through the Book
Publishing Industry Development Program (BPIDP).

To Phyllis R. Vosko and in memory of Seymour H. Vosko

Contents

viii   Contents

Tables

Acknowledgments

Writing can be a solitary exercise. However, composing these acknowledgments is a reminder of the many people who supported me as I wrote this book, and diverted me from it at crucial moments.

This book began as a doctoral dissertation. I would like to express my deepest thanks to Judy Fudge, who was a model supervisor and continues to be an enthusiastic colleague and friend. I am similarly appreciative of Isabella Bakker and Pat Armstrong for their incisive comments on early versions of the manuscript.

Numerous academic colleagues provided encouragement and assistance at various stages of my research. From York University, I thank Kate Bezanson, Lynnette Boulet, Barbara Cameron, Marlea Clarke, Deborah Clipperton, Jane Couchman, Robert Cox, Patricia Evans, Karen Flynn, Amanda Glasbeek, Harry Glasbeek, Andrea Harrington, Jennifer Lund, Meg Luxton, Stacey Mayhall, Norene Pupo, Ester Reiter, Chris Roberts, Lisa Rosenberg, Christine Saulnier, Katherine Scott, Katherine Side, Rusty Shteir, Sandra Whitworth, Joanne Wright, and Feng Xu. I owe a special debt to Agatha Campbell, who skillfully helped me navigate the York bureaucracy while I was a graduate student. I also thank Jackie Druery, the York librarian who (through a string of happy coincidences) got me access to the ILO archives, and Mirka Ondrack and Ann Oram of the Institute for Social Research, who assisted me in preparing some of the statistics used in the book.

Colleagues and friends outside York were also helpful to me as I prepared the final manuscript. I thank Sylvia Bashevkin, Fay Blaney, Janine Brodie, Francoise Carré, Jacky Coates, Dorothy Sue Cobble, Marjorie Cohen, Michelle Dodds, the members of the Feminism and Political Economy Discussion Group, Marnina Gonick, Karen Hadley,

Daood Hamdani, Steve Herzenberg, Martha MacDonald, Kathy McGrenera, Lorraine Michael, Marni Norwich, Laurell Ritchie, Katherine Robertson, Jackie Rogers, Lisa Rothman, Jane Springer, and Jennifer Stephen. Thanks, too, to my new colleagues in Labour Studies and Political Science at McMaster University, who allowed me the time and space required to complete this book, and my colleagues at the Institute for Research on Women and the Center for Women and Work at Rutgers University, where I completed this project.

My deepest appreciation goes to all of the people and organizations that assisted me in my research. I thank the members of the Canadian delegation to the Eighty-Fifth Session of the International Labour Conference, and Sol Dobberstein, Bjorn Dolvik, Slava Egorov, Yves Malpart, N. Phan-Thuy, and Ann Trebilcock, who facilitated my archival research at the International Labour Office in Geneva. As well, I thank the temporary help agency staff who allowed me to observe their activities, and the agency managers, customers, and industry officials who agreed to be interviewed. Of course, my greatest debt is to all of the workers who participated in this study for generously giving me their valuable time and answering my questions so thoughtfully.

Financial support from the Social Sciences and Humanities Research Council of Canada, the Canada-United States Fulbright Foundation, the York Centre for International and Security Studies, CUPE Local 3903, and the Faculty of Graduate Studies at York University made the research for this book possible. The staff at the University of Toronto Press, especially Virgil Duff, Siobhan McMenemy, and series editors Stephen McBride, Michael Howlett, and David Laycock helped bring the project to fruition, and two anonymous reviewers commented on the manuscript with considerable care.

These acknowledgments would not be complete without thanking my family. Few scholars find in their families such encouragement as I have received. I am especially grateful to my mother and my sister for standing by me throughout this lengthy endeavour, to my late father for inspiring me on so many levels, and to Rachel Kernerman (whose intellectual friendship I treasure) and Morry Kernerman for their ongoing enthusiasm for my work. Finally, this book would not have been written without the support, encouragement, and love of Gerald Kernerman; it is to him that I owe my greatest thanks.

Abbreviations

AIP	Anti-Inflation Program
APPA	Association of Professional Placement Agencies
CAFE	Carolina Alliance of Fair Employment
CUPE	Canadian Union of Public Employees
EC	European Community
ECC	Economic Council of Canada
EUROSTAT	European Statistical Agency
ILO	International Labour Organization
IMF	International Monetary Fund
KWS	Keynesian Welfare State
NAFTA	North American Free Trade Agreement
NAIRU	Non-Accelerating Inflation Rate of Employment
NSS	National Selection Service
OECD	Organization of Economic Cooperation and Development
OLRB	Ontario Labour Relations Board
OPEC	Oil Producing and Exporting Countries
OPEIU	Office and Professional Employees International Union
RSA	Revised Statutes of Alberta
RRBC	Revised Regulations of British Columbia
RSBC	Revised Statutes of British Columbia
RSC	Revised Statutes of Canada
RSM	Revised Statutes of Manitoba
RSNS	Revised Statutes of Nova Scotia

RSO	Revised Statutes of Ontario
RSQ	Revised Statutes of Quebec
SEA	Single Europe Act
SEIU	Service Employees International Union
SER	Standard employment relationship
SIC	Standard Industrial Classification
TER	Temporary employment relationship
THI	Temporary help industry
TLC	Trades and Labour Congress
UI	Unemployment Insurance
UNITE	Union of Needletrades Industrial and Textile Employees

TEMPORARY WORK

Introduction

The research for this book began with the premise that the nature of work is changing, and that non-standard forms of employment are spreading rapidly to the point where the full-time permanent job – along with its typical package of benefits – is becoming something of an anomaly in the labour market. With the research complete, it became necessary to amend this premise. While there are indeed important changes taking place in the labour market, these changes are occurring on a bedrock of continuity. In the course of studying employment change, the underlying logic of capitalist labour markets comes into clearer view.

The object of inquiry in this book is the history and evolution of the temporary employment relationship associated with the Canadian temporary help industry. Its central argument is that, with the shift away from the standard employment relationship since the early 1970s and the coincident rise of the temporary employment relationship[1] – two trends that reflect the feminization of employment – workers situated at the expanding margins of the labour market are increasingly treated like commodities. This set of developments is significant since the first coordinated international effort to curb abuses by private employment agencies in the twentieth century revolved around the maxim that 'labour is not a commodity.'[2] Recent employment trends, specifically the rise of the temporary employment relationship, thus reveal the fragility of the balance that this maxim encouraged states such as Canada to achieve: labour power is inevitably a commodity under capitalism and its commodification intensifies with the erosion of security and freedom in the wage-relation.

Understanding Employment Trends

Scholars and analysts are increasingly preoccupied with examining the changing nature of employment. Depending upon their field of study, they pose a range of questions about the magnitude, direction, and character of employment change and posit a variety of hypotheses about the future of employment.

Some scholars concern themselves with outlining employment trends through in-depth statistical analyses that examine the scope of change both cross-sectorally and within individual sectors. The emphasis of these studies is normally descriptive rather than analytic; still, they provide important evidence of employment change at national and international levels, which indicates that while the rise of nonstandard forms of employment is indeed a global phenomenon, patterns and trends vary from region to region (ILO, 1996, 1997a; Krahn, 1995; Lipset and Reesor, 1997; OECD, 1995). At a more abstract level, other scholars use existing data to explore the shift away from the standard employment relationship, assessing its causes and its significance. Examining the relationship between prevailing employment trends and institutions such as the family, the state, unions, and firms, many scholars critically engage with theories such as Segmented Labour Markets Theory[3] and Regulation Theory[4] in investigating changing employment patterns. In contrast, scholars concerned with how gender relations operate in the labour market are in search of new understandings of the process of employment change. Many suggest that the feminization of employment is occurring on a global scale (Armstrong, 1995; Bakker, 1989; Cohen, 1994; Jenson, Hagen, and Reddy, 1989; Standing, 1989; Tiano, 1994; Ward, 1994). Drawing insights from a range of theoretical approaches, including scholarship positing a 'new international division of labour,' these scholars centre attention on the rise of a supply-side politico-economic agenda and its gendered impacts on global employment patterns. Still other scholars, preoccupied by the macrodynamics of employment change, reveal and investigate the persistence of various forms of unfree waged labour in late capitalist societies (Miles, 1987; Satzewich, 1991). These scholars attempt to understand why various forms of unfree waged labour continue to exist in contemporary capitalist labour markets given the widespread assumption that free waged labour will eventually become the dominant mode of organizing production as free market economies develop; ultimately, they have much in common with scholars probing the nature of labour power as a commodity.

Each of the preceding approaches to analysing shifting employment trends and norms merits attention. However, with the obvious exception of scholarship positing the global feminization of employment and early feminist interventions into the commodity status of labour power (Armstrong and Armstrong, 1983; Picchio, 1981), dominant explanatory frameworks lack a gender analysis. This absence is a notable shortcoming. Any thorough investigation of the changing nature of employment demands a synthesis of several approaches that is highly attentive to gender – and Chapter 1 undertakes this project.

Why Study the Temporary Help Industry?

For numerous reasons, ranging from its composition to the character of its associated employment relationship, the temporary help industry offers a highly instructive case study in describing the nature and direction of employment change and its gendered underpinnings. The temporary help industry emerged in Canada and other advanced capitalist welfare states in Europe and North America as a female-dominated industry (OECD, 1993; Statistics Canada, 1993: Cat. 63–232). Although the industry's roots lie in the history of labour market intermediaries – specifically private employment agents operating in the labour market in the late nineteenth century – temporary help agencies first situated themselves as autonomous labour market entities in the post-Second World War period with the explicit objective of drawing a particular group of married women, displaced from their location in the wartime division of labour, into the labour market. For three decades after its initial inception, the industry remained highly female-dominated, providing clerical workers to businesses requiring temporary assistance. Initially, firms used the services of temporary help agencies as a short-term measure to fill in for employees on vacation, maternity leave, or sick leave (Carré, 1992; Hamdani, 1996; Mangum, Mayall, and Nelson, 1985). Hence, the common image of the 'Kelly Girl.' To this day, women still dominate in the industry. However, women's representation is declining in the Canadian temporary help industry, partly as a consequence of the expansion of the industry into a wider range of sectors and occupations and its shift away from supplying stopgap workers to taking over the staffing of entire departments. The latter development reflects structural changes in the employment practices of firms using temporary help workers (Carré, 1992: 49; Statistics Canada, 1996: cat. nos. 63–232, 7100MGPE).

The shifting contours of the temporary help industry, especially its current expansion into new branches of the economy, make an historical investigation of the emergence of the temporary employment relationship particularly instructive. Numerous excellent studies examine the character of female-dominated industries and/or occupations (Gannage, 1986; Johnson and Johnson, 1982; Phizacklea and Wolkowitz, 1995), women's work in highly male-dominated sectors or industries (Sugiman, 1994), and the operation of gender in particular workplaces. Several outstanding studies also examine the transformation of a highly male-dominated sector into a more female-dominated one (Lowe, 1987). In sharp contrast, there is a dearth of scholarship investigating the transformation of female-dominated industries – or, more accurately, industries that initially arose to attract women – into industries where sex parity is emerging. In this respect, the temporary help industry is unique. Its post-Second World War history illustrates how and why an employment relationship, one that was originally crafted to fill an acute demand for temporary and part-time clerical workers and to target a narrow group of women confronting significant restrictions to their labour force participation, can become a norm for a wider segment of the population. It also reinforces the insight that gender itself is a crucial constituent element in the labour market (Scott, 1988). Labour market analysis can only go so far when it restricts itself to examining the biological category of sex without sufficient attention to how gender relations – that is, 'the entire system of relationships that may include sex, but is not [necessarily] determined by sex' – operate at the level of the labour market (Scott, 1988: 1057). What is of central concern in this book, then, is not the history of the temporary help industry as a labour market entity per se, but the evolution of the precarious gendered, or, more precisely, feminized employment relationship (the temporary employment relationship) upon which the industry is predicated.

The temporary help industry is not an 'industry' in the classic sense of the term since it engages workers with diverse skills to work in various sectors and occupations on a temporary basis. Indeed, its associated employment relationship, carefully crafted by the industry in the early 1950s, consolidates temporary help work as a domain of economic activity crossing traditional industrial lines. As demonstrated by its accelerated rise since the 1970s, and the growing prominence of the temporary employment relationship in an expanding cross-section of occupations and sectors beginning in the 1980s, the shape of the industry increasingly follows and capitalizes on the contours of the contemporary labour market. For example, temporary help agencies place workers ranging from scientists, lawyers, and managers to computer programmers, clerical workers, sewers, and assemblers. Furthermore, the temporary help industry remains sex-segregated internally and it is characterized by income polarization both between women and men and among women and men themselves, based largely on criteria related to race, immigration status, and age (Hamdani, 1996). While all temporary help workers are parties to a precarious model of employment that deviates considerably from the standard employment relationship, workers in the upper tiers of this increasingly polarized industry have significantly higher levels of remuneration and benefits than workers in the lower tiers. Thus, as an expanding sphere of economic activity, the temporary help industry mirrors growing dualism and persisting income and occupational polarization in the labour market, even in the face of shifting employment norms.

Analysing the Temporary Employment Relationship

While the temporary help industry first emerged as a formal entity in the Canadian labour market in the early 1950s, the notion of a temporary employment relationship is deeply rooted in the history of capitalist relations of production. Some analysts trace the origins of the contemporary temporary employment relationship to employment relationships involving so-called middlemen, employment agents, and/or labour market intermediaries supplying 'labour first to the workshops and then to the factories' during the Industrial Revolution (Gonos, 1994; ILO, 1994a: 4; Parker, 1994). However, this book limits itself to examining the shape of this employment relationship during the twentieth century and focuses on Canada in an international context. The examination formally begins in 1897, since the first set of regulatory measures pertaining to the employment relationship that prefigured the temporary employment relationship in Canada dates to this year, and it ends in 1997, when the International Labour Organization took unprecedented measures to legitimize the temporary help industry and its associated employment relationship, abandoning both its historic stance against labour market intermediaries and its unqualified support for the standard employment relationship (ILO, 1994a, b; ILO, 1997).

Complementary to its historical approach, the book examines the evolution of the temporary employment relationship through an interdisciplinary lens, infusing dominant disciplinary perspectives with a gender analysis. My objective is to capture the gendered evolution of the temporary employment relationship in Canada in the twentieth century from a wide range of angles. Indeed, a study of the evolution of the temporary employment relationship, both prior to the advent of the temporary help industry and since its inception, requires moving within and between disciplinary boundaries. It involves using a range of methodological tools and creating a framework where various analytical lenses overlap to expose the textured history of the temporary employment relationship.

Five distinct methodologies frame this study: historical/archival research, textual analysis, statistical analysis, observation and open-ended interviewing (see Appendices A and B). There is a strong rationale for each method, and I drew heavily on feminist approaches to methodology, such as those of Sandra Kirby and Kate McKenna (1989), particularly at the level of collecting, processing, organizing, and presenting the data derived from open-ended interviews and observation.[5]

In the Canadian context, the historical research involved examining federal, provincial, and municipal legislation and regulations dating from the late nineteenth century as well as parliamentary and extra-parliamentary debates and discussions on the temporary employment relationship and its forerunners. At the international level, I conducted extensive fieldwork at the International Labour Office in Geneva, where I examined texts dating from the International Labour Organization's formation in 1919 and its rich collection of national and regional labour legislation. A comparative historical investigation of legislation and regulations governing the temporary employment relationship, when taken on its own, provides a formalistic view of the temporary help industry. Thus, to develop a more complete understanding of the range of forces involved in constructing and legitimizing the modern temporary employment relationship, I attended the Eighty-Fifth International Labour Conference (June 1997), where national governments and organizations of labour and employers debated the revision of the Fee-Charging Employment Agencies Convention (No. 96), an international labour standard of central significance to this study. Within this tripartite forum, the groups designed and adopted a new convention concerning private employment agencies (Convention No. 181) that outlines a framework for regulating the operation of temporary help agencies in member states. The significance of the new convention is far-reaching because of the International Labour Organization's historic stance against labour market intermediaries, its sceptical view of nonstandard forms of employment, and its early advocacy for the creation of a public monopoly on placement in employment. Its adoption substantiates several central pillars of the argument in this book, specifically the state-sanctioned erosion of the standard employment relationship as a *normative* model of employment and the gradual abandonment of the sentiments behind the maxim 'labour is not commodity' at the supranational level.

A study of the temporary employment relationship also demanded a profile of the temporary help industry in operation as well as the three central actors involved in this triangular relationship: branch managers of temporary help agencies; representatives (usually human resource managers) of firms using temporary help workers; and temporary help workers themselves. Thus, I observed the daily activities and procedures at a local branch of a major international temporary help business in the fall of 1996. As well, I conducted open-ended interviews with temporary help workers, branch managers, representatives from firms using temporary help workers, and Canadian industry officials.

Another method used in conducting the research for this book is public policy analysis, which helps explain the role of the Canadian state in legitimizing the temporary employment relationship. Chapter 7 in particular relies on public policy analysis in examining the emergence of a provincially based policy initiative falling under the Ontario Works program. Known as Workfirst, this initiative requires 'employable' social assistance recipients to register with temporary help agencies in their job search. In the provincial context, analysing the design and delivery of this project is crucial in discerning the government's response to the temporary employment relationship, as well as in making informed predictions about the future. In studying this initiative, beyond examining its policy design, I also observed orientation sessions designed for participants and conducted interviews with key stakeholders in the program.

Statistical analysis, the final methodology, is used to address the Canadian industry's strategy from the early 1970s to the late 1990s, as well as the nature of the temporary employment relationship in operation.[6] Many of the national statistics are set in the context of comparable statistics obtained from three organizations: the United States Bureau of Labor Statistics, the Organization for Economic Cooperation and Development, and the International Labour Organization. Without these statistics, the starting premise of this book – that nonstandard forms of employment are spreading in Canada and abroad – would hold significantly less weight, as would the related claims that men are increasingly engaging in temporary employment relationships and that the occupational diversity in the temporary help industry is growing.

The Gendered Rise of the Temporary Employment Relationship

This book begins by setting out a theoretical framework based on three interlocking lenses of analysis: the character of the labour power as a commodity under capitalism; shifting employment norms; and the feminization of employment. Chapter 1 probes the relationship between the spread of the temporary employment relationship in the Canadian labour market and the growing economic insecurity among workers at its expanding margins. The central argument of the chapter (and the inquiry as a whole) is that the shift away from the standard employment relationship and the corresponding spread of the temporary employment relationship – two developments consonant with the feminization of employment – reveal the decline of security and freedom in the wage relation and its gendered underpinnings.

Chapter 2 initiates the investigation into the evolution of the temporary employment relationship in Canada by tracing the roots of early precursors and immediate forerunners to the 'classic' temporary help agency, describing the shape of their associated employment relationships and identifying the types of workers that these distinct labour market entities targeted. It relies primarily on materials detailing international, national, and provincial debates and developments (involving elected officials, representatives from organized labour, and business leaders) surrounding the role of intermediaries and employment agents in the labour market between the late nineteenth and early twentieth centuries. Focusing on the type of employment relationships that predated both the standard employment relationship and the temporary employment relationship, the discussion starts in 1897, when the first federal legislation on private employment agencies was adopted in Canada, and ends in 1933, when a relatively long era of prohibition at the supranational level and a shorter era at the national level began. In examining this period, it becomes apparent that the earliest forerunners to the 'classic' temporary help agency[7] were private employment agents (general labour agents and 'padrones'), many of whom acted abroad to encourage the temporary and permanent migration of workers to Canada. Equally significant, in the face of growing international disapproval of these agents, as well as national interventions on the part of immigrant communities, organized labour, and the state aimed at curbing the activities of the most unscrupulous actors, private employment agencies run by typewriter companies became immediate precursors to the 'classic' temporary help agency. This small but reputable segment of the private employment agency industry carved out a niche in the clerical sector where temporary help work was considered an acceptable type of employment for women, particularly those young, well-educated, and Canadian-born middle-class women who were perceived to be secondary breadwinners.

Building on the discussion of how private employment agencies operated by typewriting companies thrived in Canada in the early decades of the twentieth century even in the face of increasingly rigid regulations governing the conduct of private employment agencies as a whole, Chapter 3 addresses the period from 1933 to the late 1960s. This period is of central importance in revealing the profoundly gendered character of the temporary employment relationship, since, when the temporary help industry first arose after the Second World War, it targeted primarily white middle-class married women. The emergence of the temporary help industry in this period corresponded with two mutually reinforcing developments; namely, the ascendance of the standard employment relationship as a *normative* model of male employment that grew out of the capital-labour entente, and a particular manifestation of the ideology of domesticity. In this way, the temporary help industry played a crucial mediating role in the Canadian labour market. It upheld the standard employment relationship as a male norm, while still contributing to preserving labour market dualism, by catering to firms requiring temporary clerical assistance and targeting white middle-class women as its chief workers.

Chapters 4, 5, and 6 cover the period from the early 1970s to the late 1990s. They describe the temporary help industry's newest marketing strategy, the nature of the temporary employment relationship in practice and regulatory developments at the national, international, and supranational levels, which have been shaped in large part by the aggressive posture of the industry throughout this era, and by the limited coordinated opposition on the part of organized labour until the early 1990s.

Chapter 4 describes the new image advanced by the temporary help industry beginning in the 1970s, and the industry's accelerated growth from the early 1980s to the late 1990s, examining statistical data on employment change at the national level and analysing the new market-

ing strategy in the North American temporary help industry. It emphasizes the prevailing shift within the industry from supplying temporary
help workers to its customers as a 'stop-gap' measure to selling 'staffing
services' as a means of lowering labour costs by minimizing the payment
of benefits and other employment-related expenditures. Through its
investigation of the changing industry strategy, the chapter establishes
the temporary employment relationship as a triangular employment
relationship, and begins to examine this model in relation to the standard employment relationship by scrutinizing the long-term goals of
industry officials and the reasons that their customers use the temporary
help industry.

Chapter 5 examines the shape of the temporary employment relationship in operation, drawing on statistical data detailing the conditions of
employment associated with temporary help work, an analysis of the
legal arrangements surrounding the temporary employment relationship, and qualitative data probing how workers, branch managers, and
customers perceive it. Based on this investigation, it argues that the
modern temporary employment relationship is a highly precarious model
of employment, one whose growth reflects the feminization of employment. The chapter also points to the dualism inherent within the modern temporary help industry by showing how agency personnel and
customers deal with temporary help workers located in various tiers of
the industry, and by revealing how and to what extent they are treated
like commodities at the micro-level of the firm.

Shifting to the regulatory level, Chapter 6 examines the fundamental
challenge that the temporary employment relationship poses to the
framework of social protections for workers that grew up alongside
the standard employment relationship in Canada and elsewhere after the
Second World War – the challenge to preserve protections, benefits, and
security for workers in employment relationships where responsibility
does not rest squarely with one entity. Probing developments at the
provincial, national, and supranational levels, this chapter explores
the prospects for regulating the temporary employment relationship
in the twenty-first century. Even though many states recognize the depth
of the challenge posed by the spread of the temporary employment
relationship, partly as a consequence of organized labour's renewed
concern with regulating temporary help work and other forms of nonstandard employment, there is a growing movement among advanced
welfare states (including Canada) to legitimize temporary help agencies
without instituting a sufficient package of social protections for tempo-

rary help workers. Events at the supra-national level in June 1997, when the lengthy stalemate between workers, employers, and governments over how to treat private employment agencies ended with the International Labour Organization's adoption of a new international labour convention on private employment agencies, reflect this movement. The chapter devotes special attention to these developments since they point to the gradual breakdown of the original sentiments behind the maxim 'labour is not a commodity.'

Looking to the future, Chapter 7 examines the design and delivery of Workfirst, a controversial Ontario-based welfare-to-work initiative that requires 'employable' social assistance recipients to register with temporary help agencies in the job-search process, and to accept whatever forms of temporary help work are on offer. The chapter makes the argument that the policies and practices associated with Workfirst offer important insights into the provincial government's perception of the temporary employment relationship and the changing status of workers at the expanding margins of the labour market. The shape of this initiative also exposes the nature and direction of the Canadian state's broader policy response to prevailing employment trends – a movement away from welfare-oriented social policy and towards workfare-driven social policy that increases the compulsion for social assistance recipients and other segments of the unemployed and the underemployed to enter the low-wage labour market to fulfill their basic needs. The example of Workfirst provides the clearest evidence to date of the Canadian state's role in legitimizing the temporary employment relationship as a viable alternative to the standard employment relationship, thereby increasing the level of coercion in the labour market.

Chapter 8 returns to the questions posed at the outset of the book, synthesizing the central findings by sketching the shape of the early precursors, the immediate forerunners, and the current manifestation of the temporary employment relationship. However, it focuses most centrally on the challenges and prospects for organizing temporary help workers. The chapter argues that, beyond adapting outmoded modes of regulation, the only way to improve the substandard conditions of employment associated with temporary help work is through embracing broader-based bargaining initiatives that make collective representation possible. Still, it recognizes that building more inclusive representational structures is an enormous task, one that necessitates a shift in emphasis and priorities not only among state actors but among various segments of organized labour[8] and civil society as a whole.

'Labour Is Not a Commodity': Shifting Employment Norms and the Modern Labour Market Intermediary

It feels like you're supposed to conduct yourself like a regular employee with none of the advantages of it. It is a bit odd to be in a situation where you recognize that more than the work you do for the company, your real worth to them is your disposability. They don't want me because I am good at what I do. They want me because they can get rid of me easily.[1] (T7)

More than perhaps any other category of workers, temporary help workers have the appearance of being listed, bought, sold, and traded in the labour market. Given that temporary help agencies are 'labour suppliers,' temporary help workers are treated like commodities even though they freely enter into a relationship with a temporary help agency. Thus, it is worth probing labour power's commodity status under capitalism to locate and understand fully the situation of temporary help workers in contemporary Canadian society, how their status has changed over the twentieth century, and the gendered underpinnings of these changes.

This chapter introduces the three main lenses of theoretical inquiry in this book: the investigation of labour power's commodity status; the exploration of the rise and decline of the standard employment relationship (SER); and the examination of the gendered character of prevailing employment trends. To this end, it revises the large but gender-blind body of scholarship exploring the nature of labour power as a commodity by probing its status in capitalist labour markets at a conceptual level and describing the gendered ways in which states have dealt with it historically.

In the aftermath of the First World War, states involved in crafting the postwar settlement ushered in the modern labour market by, among other things, advancing the maxim 'labour is not a commodity' in the founding charter of the International Labour Organization (ILO). Responding to pressure from organized labour and other segments of civil society seeking to minimize the social and economic devastation that followed the war, many countries took direction from the sentiments behind this maxim by curtailing the activities of private employment agencies, establishing free public employment services, and introducing other measures aimed at protecting workers at the national level. Their efforts at neutralizing labour power's commodity status, which entailed introducing these and other social protections for workers, were particularly successful in the post-Second World War period when the SER rose to dominance as a *normative*[2] model of male employment. However, with the shift away from the SER since the early 1970s and the corresponding spread of the temporary employment relationship (TER) – two trends indicative of the feminization of employment – workers located at the growing margins of the labour market are increasingly treated like commodities. This most recent set of developments underscores the conflict-ridden attempt to limit the commodification of capitalist wage-labour in the ILO's founding charter. Labour power is inevitably a commodity under capitalism, and the decline of security and freedom in the wage relation accentuates its commodity status.[3]

Labour Power's Commodity Status

The notion of labour power as a commodity is highly contested among social scientists.[4] Many contemporary thinkers associate the commodity status of labour power with a central tension in capitalist labour markets, one that must be mediated to preserve their legitimacy (see, for example, Picchio, 1992). This tension revolves around the fact that capitalist labour markets require the circulation of labour power but the production of labourers (the embodiment of labour power), which differs from the production of *all* other commodities, requires constraints on the market circulation of labour power. The 'peculiar' (Polanyi, 1957) commodity status of labour power underpins this tension and gives rise to important contradictions in capitalist labour markets: on the one hand, the power to work is bought and sold but, on the other hand, the free person is attached to the commodity (Marx 1976).

Labour power's peculiar commodity status is central to the unique character of the capitalist labour market and the contradictions inherent within it. It lies at the heart of the profound conflict between the standard of living of workers, which is never determined by the market mechanism exclusively, but affected by historical, institutional, and moral forces (Marx, 1976: 275), and the drive for accumulation. This conflict makes capitalism perpetually unstable and requires mediation on the part of the state, and it is in the context of this instability that temporary help workers are treated like commodities by the agencies that place them on the market, as well as by the firms that use them to increase their 'labour flexibility.' It is thus instructive to describe the nature of labour power, examining its 'peculiar' character and its persisting 'commodity' status, as well as those features that distinguish it from other commodities and labour markets from other markets.

There is considerable debate over the most appropriate means of characterizing labour power. Yet most critical thinkers agree, following Marx (1976: 272), that under capitalism the sale and purchase of labour power does not imply the ownership of the worker but his or her capacity to work. They therefore concur that labour power is not of the same order as other commodities. According to Polanyi (1957: 73): '... the alleged commodity "labour-power" cannot be shoved about, used indiscriminately, or even unused, without affecting also the human individual who happens to be the bearer of this peculiar commodity. In disposing of man's [sic] labour power the system would incidentally dispose of the physical, psychological moral entity of "man" [sic] attached to that tag. Robbed of the protective covering of cultural institutions, human beings would perish from the effects of social exposure; they would die as the victims of acute social dislocation through vice, perversion, crime and starvation.' Such remarks suggest that it is the social character of labour power that makes it distinct from all other commodities. We see this in six basic ways. First, the labourer may sell his or her labour power, echoing Marx's crucial distinction between labour (the activity of work) and labour power (the capacity to work), but s/he has no price (Marx, 1976). Second, with the exception of other living commodities, labour power is unique in that it is impossible to separate the labourer from his or her work even though the sale of labour power often alienates the worker from his or her creative capacities. Third, in the case of the commodity labour power, sociodemographic processes control the volume of supply, processes that have their own logic: the only (indirect) means of controlling the labour supply is through political regulation, since, as feminist and other critical scholars demonstrate, the pure logic of capitalist relations cannot assure the production and reproduction of labour power (Barrett, 1988; Offe, 1985). Fourth, labour power is a perishable good. Fifth, the seller of labour power is always at a disadvantage, relative to capital, in the bargaining process because 'the supply side has no way of controlling its own volume in a market-strategic manner,' as Offe observes (17). Sixth, and finally, the extraction of labour from labour power creates numerous points of conflict between the buyer and the seller; in addition to negotiations over price (i.e., over wages), conflicts arise over intensity, pace, and conditions of work.

The central reason that labour power is a peculiar type of commodity under capitalism is because it is attached to the worker. The worker has agency, s/he has some capacity to resist oppressive conditions of work, and therefore the allocation and control of labour power has definitive limits, although these limits vary historically. Still, the fact that labourers are produced outside the labour market, normally through highly gendered divisions of labour, is frequently underplayed in discussions examining the commodity status of labour power. This omission is not surprising since Marx himself excludes the dimension of social reproduction in his examination of labour power's commodity status (Marx, 1976: 655). However, as feminist scholars demonstrate, if we are truly to understand labour power's commodity status as well as the gendered and racialized underpinnings of capitalist labour markets and the central tensions within them, it is essential to address this shortcoming.

The fact that labour power is produced outside the labour market through affective ties, usually in families and based largely on women's unwaged domestic labour, makes it subject to a very different logic than that of other commodities (Armstrong and Armstrong, 1983; Elson, 1995; Luxton, 1990; Picchio, 1992; Rubery and Humphries, 1984). Indeed, it reinforces the limits that employers confront in allocating and controlling labour power and workers themselves and it also affects the circulation of labour power that is so central to the smooth operation of the economic system. The means by which workers are produced also makes the labour market distinct from all other markets. Since labour power is produced in the nonmarket sector, the labour market must serve as a dividing line between the system of social reproduction and the market sector, where the production of goods and services for circulation in the market largely takes place (Picchio 1992). The labour market must also perform a twofold allocative function: distribute the labour power of individual workers among concrete production processes and provide monetary (income) and social (status) means of subsistence to people engaged in both the market and the nonmarket sectors (Offe, 1985: 14, 52–3; Picchio, 1992).[5] Thus, unlike commodity markets, the labour market is not a self-sustaining institution, whereby all labour power is produced, disposed of, and consumed. Nor does its existence make all workers free (i.e., as free as possible given that labour power is bought and sold) under capitalism.

The peculiar character of labour power as a commodity is certainly underpinned by a degree of freedom – what is unique about the capitalist labour market is that workers have a host of unprecedented politico-legal rights and entitlements – but its commodity status, and thus a degree of unfreedom, still remains. As Marx noted (1976: 415), 'It must be acknowledged that our worker emerges from the process of production looking different from when he entered it. In the market, as owner of the commodity "labour power," he stood face to face with other owners of commodities, one owner against the other owner. The contract by which he sold his labour-power to the capitalist proved in black and white, so to speak, that he was free to dispose himself. But when the transaction was concluded, it was discovered that he was no "free agent," that the period of time for which he is free to sell his labour-power is the period of time for which he is forced to sell it' [*sic*]. Here, Marx argues that free wage labourers lose access to the ownership of the means of production in gaining access to the labour market, and he, more generally, reveals the inherently unbalanced nature of labour market relations. He therefore shows that while free wage labourers possess their labour power as a form of private property, and are both free to dispose of it and to choose how their wages are spent, their arena of personal determination is severely constrained by market conditions as well as by the need to sustain themselves. Building on Marx's early insights, numerous scholars also highlight the central role of the state in providing (or witholding) various politico-legal rights to workers, thereby affecting the degree of freedom in the wage relation.[6]

As this examination of the TER will demonstrate, the means by which states have historically managed the wage relation have, in some instances, involved attempts to neutralize the commodity status of labour power. However, in other instances they have contributed to legitimizing labour market entities such as private employment agencies, which treat workers themselves like commodities. The fact that temporary help agencies belong to this group of labour market entities raises a central question: How do the experiences of temporary help workers differ from other categories of workers in the labour market? More specifically, is the commodification of the temporary help worker's labour power more pronounced than that of other types of workers, especially that of the standard worker? If it is, then a study of the evolution of the TER not only has potential to help establish the direction of current employment trends but to deepen our understanding of labour power's commodity status in the contemporary context.

In registering with a temporary help agency, temporary help workers surrender their right to choose both their worksite and their direct employer, even though they are not engaged in fixed-duration contracts that formally limit their mobility in the labour market. They also yield their right to select freely their place within the division of labour, because in signing an employment agreement with the temporary help agency, temporary help workers forfeit their ability to choose their preferred type of work. Indeed, the temporary help agency not only assigns workers to a specific worksite but also to a particular location within the occupational division of labour, frequently disregarding the skill set claimed by the individual worker (see Chapter 5). Additionally, the triangular shape of the TER prevents many temporary help workers from benefitting from standard labour protections (both minimum standards laws and collective bargaining legislation), such as notice of termination and severance pay, and social insurance coverage. While there is little doubt that most temporary help workers are free waged labourers, some of these workers also experience extreme forms of economic compulsion (e.g., Workfirst participants), even though the state *does not* actively curtail their mobility in the labour market.

These central facets of the contemporary TER, as well as others to be described in succeeding chapters, highlight the declining politico-legal freedoms amongst workers at the expanding margins of the labour market. They also reveal the persistence of outmoded customs, habits, and practices in the labour market and labour market entities, whose roots go back at least a century, as well as the decline of public employment services and other measures designed to neutralize (even minimize) labour power's commodity status.

Twentieth-Century Developments Flowing from the Maxim 'Labour Is Not a Commodity'

The maxim 'labour is not a commodity' underpinned one of the earliest collective attempts on the part of states to stimulate the emergence of the modern labour market. The origins of this declaration may be traced to the end of the First World War, when the Treaty of Versailles (Part XIII) entrenched seven core principles designed to delineate fundamental workers' rights in what became known informally as the Labour Charter. These principles included the right of association, payment of an adequate wage to maintain a reasonable standard of living, equal pay for equal work; an eight-hour day or forty-eight-hour week, a weekly rest of at least twenty-four hours, abolition of child labour, equitable economic treatment of all workers in a country, an inspection system to ensure the enforcement of laws and worker protections, and the principle that 'labour should not be regarded as merely a commodity or article of commerce' that led to the maxim that 'labour is not a commodity' (Lee, 1997).[7] The ILO became the guardian of these principles when it was founded in 1919 (ILO, 1994a: 6–7; Lee, 1997: 468). Although the charter as a whole contributed to the development of a host of core international labour standards, the idea that 'labour is not a commodity' was a particularly important theme in this period. Indeed, the international community first embraced this maxim at a time of tremendous social and economic turmoil and in an era when private employment agencies faced harsh criticisms for perpetrating abuses in the global labour market (ILO, 1994a).

In proclaiming that labour must not be treated as a mere commodity, spurred by pressure from several national governments, workers' organizations and social reformers alike, the ILO effectively called on national governments to extend formally to all workers the right to circulate freely in the labour market. In effect, the ILO sought to create a new type of labour market. But, beyond encouraging states to support the formation of modern (i.e., free) labour markets, the ILO had several more specific aims. It crafted this maxim as a first step in establishing a coherent set of international labour standards designed to minimize the degree of 'economic bondage' endured by workers by introducing rules that would more sharply distinguish the labour market from all other commodity markets.

When the ILO first became an international voice on labour issues, one whose mandate was to address workers' interests within the confines of the modern capitalist labour market, the leading maxim in its charter came to be interpreted narrowly as suggesting that 'workers should not have to pay for work' (ILO, 1997a). Therefore, beginning in 1919, the ILO acted on this sentiment by devising two specific types of regulatory measures that are of foremost importance in this inquiry: first, measures designed to regulate fee-charging employment agencies, and second, measures to encourage the establishment of free public employment services nationally (ILO, 1923; 1933a, 1949, 1994a). Later in the century, particularly in the aftermath of the Second World War, the maxim (and the charter to which it belonged) also became key to establishing a host of new measures designed to stimulate the creation of the modern welfare state, such as basic social programs ranging from medical care to maternity protections to education and training (Lee, 1997).

Origins of the SER

In serving as an emblem of the postwar welfare state, the maxim 'labour is not a commodity' also encouraged the emergence of the SER as a *normative* model of employment, albeit one that only extended to a narrow group of male workers primarily in core sectors of the economy. This *normative* model of employment was arguably the product of the most successful effort at brokering a central tension in capitalist labour markets (i.e., the tension between production for the market and social reproduction): the decline of the SER and the spread of the TER, an employment relationship which has its basis in the temporary help industry (THI) but increasingly extends beyond the bounds of this industry, signal the breakdown of this effort at mediation. Given the importance of these developments, it is instructive to examine the emergence of the SER, identifying the legal, social, and political institutions upon which it is based, and probe its recent erosion, isolating several common explanations for contemporary employment trends by critically engaging with the insights of Regulation Theory[8] and Segmented Labour Markets Theory.[9]

The origins of the SER may be traced to developments at the turn of the century. However, as a normative entity, it is largely a product of the post-Second World War reconstruction period. Various international and national developments helped precipitate its accelerated rise in the aftermath of the war, chiefly because countries were forced to recognize the link between unemployment and social and political ills pervading the postwar period, and to acknowledge that 'the interplay of blind economic forces' could not ensure the fulfilment of the social objectives deemed necessary for reconstruction (ILO, 1944: ii). Both these realizations were grounded in the lessons of the Great Depression, when the free market system had led to mass unemployment and poverty. Together, they contributed to a coordinated international effort, spearheaded by institutions such as Bretton Woods, the ILO, the United Nations, and the Roosevelt government in the United States, to stimulate sustained economic growth through the formation of the modern welfare state (Gill and Law, 1988: 127–58, 170–2; Gilpin, 1987: 132–3; Spero, 1990: 21–7). At the level of the nation-state, the goal of full employment was at the centre of the agenda; after all, the war had shown that full employment was possible given the unprecedented strength of core industries and the growth of mass production. But, even more important, after the war large segments of the populace viewed full employment as a moral imperative. The text of the official record of the International Labour Conference of 1949, which set the terms of the *Philadelphia Declaration* and re-affirmed the maxim 'labour is not a commodity,' communicates the depth of this sentiment: '... the right to subsist, the right not to die of starvation, can no longer be regarded as exhausting the claims of the individual upon the modern state. Men and women will no longer tolerate an organization of society under which those who are willing and anxious to work are obliged to forfeit their self-respect by remaining idle' (ILO, 1949: i).

At a domestic level, this moral imperative translated into a fundamental challenge to reintegrate Second World War troops into the economy, and, equally significant, to re-establish groups of workers that were formerly either part of the nonmarket sector or the marginal labour force, primarily women, young people, and the elderly, who took over adult men's jobs during the war. In the Canadian context, 're-establishment' involved creating new universal social programs that 'would help maintain demand [and hence consumption] while encouraging women to drop out of the labour force, leaving places for men demobilized from the armed forces' (Armstrong and Armstrong, 1989: 69). It also involved the creation of explicitly exclusionary policies that barred married women from entering specific professions, such as teaching, and large segments of the labour market, including the Federal Public Service (Cuthbert-Brandt, 1982: 247; Morgan, 1988; Pierson and Light, 1990: 260). Hence, the reference to full employment had a particular connotation in Canada and elsewhere: that is, full employment for men.[10]

Wartime devastation and the resulting cross-national desire to create effective reconstruction machinery forced a spirit of compromise internationally. Led by the increased power of the United States, with its postwar military and monetary strength, a series of bargains and repositionings was struck between two normally antagonistic actors in the capitalist labour market – corporate capital and organized labour – and arbitrated by nation-states. David Harvey (1989: 133) nicely sums up the character of this entente: 'The state had to take on new (Keynesian) roles and build new institutional powers; corporate capital had to trim its sails in certain respects in order to move more smoothly on the track of secure profitability; and organized labour had to take on new roles and functions with respect to performance in labour markets and in production processes.' To reach a rapprochement, the core of the organized working class had to exchange its historic attachment to craft-based production for the promise of greater security in the mass production system: this side of the compromise translated into real wage gains in exchange for factory discipline. Corporate capital had to accept steady rather than accelerated growth in investments brought about by enhanced efficiency: this side of the compromise translated into raised standards of living for a large segment of wage earners in exchange for more or less guaranteed growth for corporate capital (Gordon, Edwards, and Reich, 1987). Most centrally, however, the postwar compromise demanded that governments, through building social security, health care, education, and housing systems and policies, provide a reasonable social wage.

The postwar compromise is often associated with Fordist-Keynesianism. While the roots of Fordism may be traced to Henry Ford's deployment of Taylorist techniques as early as 1914, what made this bargain *Fordist*-Keynesianism was Ford's belief that mass production meant mass consumption, and hence a new means of reproducing labour. The notion of the SER, initially symbolized by the $5 eight-hour workday espoused by national corporate figures like Ford, international figures like Keynes, and institutions such as the ILO, arose out of this compromise. The SER was intended to provide a narrow group of male workers and their families with sufficient funds and leisure time to consume the mass-produced goods they were producing. Borrowing the term 'Fordism' from Antonio Gramsci (1971: 277–320), Michel Aglietta (1979: 154–9) demonstrated that for the first time Fordism created a *norm* of working-class consumption where individual ownership of commodities – specifically standardized housing (the site of private consumption) and the automobile (which allows for a separation between the home and the workplace) – governed the concrete practices of consumption. The SER, and its associated reference wage, served as the basis for this new consumption norm. However, as scholars such as Aglietta and other proponents of French Regulation Theory do not sufficiently acknowledge, this norm only extended to workers in high-wage and high value-added sectors where mass production techniques took hold. The SER was indeed a *norm*, but as Ann Porter (1996) argues, its benefits did not extend to workers in female-dominated sectors; her claim may also be extended to immigrant workers in a range of sectors. Since Fordism clearly involved increased polarization between the high- and the low-waged working class, the *norm* of working-class consumption to which Aglietta refers only reflected the consumption practices of workers in core sectors.

With the gradual, although partial, materialization of Ford's vision, specifically the idea that sustained economic growth could be achieved through the twin forces of mass production and domestic consumption, the SER came to be characterized as a lifelong, continuous, full-time employment relationship where the worker has one employer and normally works on the employer's premises or under his or her direct supervision (Butchetmann and Quack, 1990: 315; Muckenberger, 1989: 267; Schellenberg and Clark, 1996: 1). Its essential elements came to include an indeterminate employment contract, adequate social benefits that complete the social wage, the existence of a single employer, reasonable hours and full-time, full-year employment, frequently, but not necessarily, in a unionized sector. The high level of compensatory social policies, such as pensions, unemployment insurance, and medical coverage associated with the SER is particularly worthy of emphasis. According to Rogers and Rogers (1989: 1), this *normative* model of employment initially 'incorporated a degree of regularity and durability in employment relationships, protected workers from socially unacceptable practices and working conditions, established rights and obligations, and provided a core of social stability to underpin economic growth.' Thus, the SER operated most effectively within the framework of the postwar welfare state where workers successfully secured associational rights, where collective bargaining rights were becoming the norm, and where rates of unionization were relatively high. Notably, in the Canadian case, the SER first rose to normative pre-eminence in a period when organized workers' militancy was at a high point.[11] Workers' collective strength – evidenced by the fact that union membership quadrupled between 1940 and 1956 in Canada – and the fear of revolt that it generated clearly affected the SER's ascendancy (Galarneau, 1996: 43).

In examining the spread of Fordism (and the coincident rise of the SER) and evaluating it as a development model, many limitations within this model become apparent. Not only was Fordism geographically limited to advanced capitalist welfare states, only emerging in industrializing countries in so-called peripheral forms, and temporally isolated to the period preceding the early 1970s, the generalization of its social wage through the SER excluded many people within leading welfare states, particularly those outside core unionized sectors. Correspondingly, welfare states endorsed (or failed to endorse) the Fordist-Keynesian compromise and implemented its related commitment to full employment to varying degrees.[12]

The geographic and temporal limits of Fordism, and its apparent deficiencies as a sustainable economic development model where it took hold, justify characterizing the SER as primarily a *normative* model of employment. They also underscore an important critique of Regulation Theory, specifically its failure to acknowledge the significance of the balance-of-class-power, both at the national and the international level, in shaping the terms of the postwar entente (see, for example, Botwinick, 1993; M. MacDonald, 1991). Even more central for our purposes, they reveal a myth of the so-called Fordist period. After the Second World War, welfare state governments, like Canada, did not extend the social wage to *all* workers. Rather, they encouraged employers to differentiate among the labour supply. There have always been segmented labour markets: in the public sphere of production, Fordism relied on many types of production (small-batch and unit production, large-batch and mass production), many technologies, many workforces, and, most notably, many forms of employment that differed from the SER (Pollert, 1988: 58). In this sense, dualism, however masked by the *normative* pre-eminence of the SER, existed in the labour market under Fordism as in many other pre-existing capitalist social formations (Broad, 1991).

The understandings of Segmented Labour Markets Theory are particularly instructive here.[13] At a general level, they contribute to a thoroughgoing critique of several of the core claims of Regulation Theory, revealing the internal inconsistencies within so-called Fordist labour markets (Peck, 1996). At a more specific level, they contribute to an understanding of the means through which capital divides the labour supply.[14] Segmentation theorists examine, describe, and attempt to explain dualism in the labour market largely at the level of the firm. Their origins may be traced to the first generation work of Doeringer and Piore (1971) who developed the concepts 'primary' sector and 'secondary' sector and isolated the roots of these segments to technical imperatives and industrial structures while retaining classical frameworks. Of particular relevance to this study is the work of third-generation theorists, who place greater emphasis on the role of social forces and workers' organizations in seeking causes for segmentation,[15] and also critique early variants of Segmented Labour Markets Theory, such as dual labour markets analysis, for their ahistoricism and for positioning sex, age, ethnicity, and race as variables of the same order (see, for example, M. MacDonald, 1982: 187–9; Rubery, 1978: 18–19). Taking an historical approach, many of these theorists link dualism in the labour market to capital's use of ascribed characteristics to segment the labour supply. Some even focus on the important, but often ill-acknowledged, relationship between segmentation and social reproduction in identifying how employers, often backed by the state, use socially ascribed characteristics to create divisions in the labour market (M. MacDonald 1982; Picchio, 1981, 1992; Rubery and Humphries, 1984). For example, according to Jamie Peck (1996: 31): 'those social groups placed at a disadvantage in the labour market – young people, women, older workers, the disabled, migrant workers – also tend to be the bearers of characteristics which, in political and cultural spheres, are used in the granting of access to forms of unwaged subsistence. It is seen as both normal and legitimate for such groups to participate in the labour market on a discontinuous basis. The fact that the members of such groups supposedly have access to a socially-sanctioned alternative role outside the labour market tends to undermine their position in the waged sphere.' Peck's insights provide one important, although limited, explanation for why people belonging to marginalized groups did not benefit from the post-Second World War compromise through direct access to the SER package – that is, through the extension of the social wage – the capitalist welfare state's unprecedented success at using the wage to distribute subsistence to market, submarket and nonmarket groups (Offe, 1985).

On the basis of the claims of third-generation Segmented Labour Market theorists, we can see how, if only at an institutional level, employers (backed by the state) denied women, migrant workers, the disabled, the elderly, and other marginalized groups access to the SER, and instead made wage-earners in prototypically 'Fordist' sectors its classic beneficiaries (Hobson, 1990; Porter, 1996). Still, even third-generation Segmented Labour Markets Theory fails to provide a deep causal explanation for the shape of dualism persisting in any given post-Second World War labour market (or other pre-existing capitalist labour markets) or for the decline of the SER. Despite this important weakness, it is potentially useful to harness the work of third-generation theorists to feminist ends, following M. MacDonald (1982), Picchio (1992), and Rubery and Fagan (1994).[16]

The Decline of the SER and the Growth of Nonstandard Forms of Employment

Even in the face of these well-founded critiques of Regulation Theory, the strengths and weaknesses of specific variants of Segmented Labour Markets Theory and the questionable notion of 'Fordism' as a coherent economic development model, it is still instructive to reflect on Fordism historically and examine the extent of the 'golden age' of the SER.

Cracks and fissures in Fordism, and hence in the SER as a *normative* model of employment, first became apparent in the late 1960s when labour market rigidities were becoming obstacles to global economic growth and when nation-states began to use monetary policy as a tool to perpetuate the postwar boom in the face of rising inflation, slower growth, and the newly identified problem of 'stagflation' (stagnant output of goods and high inflation of prices) (Gill and Law, 1988: 171–4; Lee, 1997: 482). These fissures intensified between 1970 and 1973, a period which many scholars label the beginning of the end of Fordism and some associate with the rise of 'competitive austerity' (Albo, 1994: 144). Chief among the events signaling the end of Fordism were the world property crash, the decision by the Oil Producing and Exporting Countries (OPEC) to raise oil prices, and the Arab countries' decision to embargo oil exports to the West, which contributed to an increase in the cost of energy (Harvey, 1989: 145). The breakdown of the Bretton Woods Agreement, in favour of floating exchange rates, and emerging debt crises also contributed to these tensions. Almost simultaneously, a new monetarist ideology, which blamed supply-side factors for the lack of labour market flexibility, began to gain credence as countries abandoned the postwar objective of full employment. Welfare-oriented social policy became subordinate to demands for labour market flexibility,[17] and, in many advanced capitalist welfare states, workfare-driven policy initiatives began to emerge (Jessop, 1990: 15).

The mid-1970s, which were marked by several of the preceding features, have led some scholars to associate the period with the beginning of neo-Fordism (Aglietta), flexible accumulation (Harvey), or post-Fordism (Jessop).[18] Rejecting these labels, others suggest instead that the accelerated drive for 'flexibility' in the labour market neither represents a 'radical break' from the past nor a 'surprise development' because the labour market had shown signs of decay for decades (Broad, 1993; Gordon, Edwards, and Reich, 1987; M. MacDonald, 1991; Pollert, 1988). My findings largely confirm the insights of the latter group.

Indeed, as Chapters 2 through 7 illustrate, the history of the TER (and the set of actors involved in this employment relationship) highlights the importance of studying continuities in the evolution of capitalist labour markets. In the context of this work, Fordism is a useful historical label but post-Fordism and its emphasis on radical change has less salience. Rather, it is preferable to think in terms of 'continuity through change.' The history and evolution of the TER (and the SER) is very much about how states mediate *persisting* tensions and contradictions in capitalist labour markets, the means by which employers modify their practices to suit different regulatory environments and the ways in which labour resists coercive employment practices and continually attempts to neutralize the peculiar commodity status of labour power.

Still, while this work focuses on persisting dualism in the labour market, there is considerable evidence that the growth of nonstandard forms of employment began to outpace the growth of the SER in many advanced welfare states beginning in the late 1970s (Economic Council of Canada, 1990; Advisory Group on Working Time and the Distribution of Work, 1994; ILO, 1996; OECD, 1993, 1994). For example, while patterns and trends vary nationally and locally, most OECD countries have experienced substantial increases in at least one form of nonstandard employment since the 1970s (ILO, 1996). Self-employment grew considerably in the United Kingdom, Portugal, New Zealand, Canada, and Australia between 1973 and 1993. Similarly, temporary employment grew rapidly in France, the Netherlands, and Spain, and remained steady in the United Kingdom, Japan, and Germany, as a share of waged employment between 1983 and 1993. Most notably, the growth of part-time employment has been consistent across the OECD since the 1970s. With the decline, but not the disappearance, of the SER, greater income and occupational polarization also began to emerge as a product of deindustrialization in core male-dominated sectors and professionalization in the service sector in the late 1970s and early 1980s (Brodie, 1994: 50; Cohen, 1994: 112; Economic Council of Canada, 1990: 15; Shea, 1990: 5).

While they differ drastically in a number of respects, many nonstandard forms of employment demonstrate a common tendency: the absence of security. Not surprisingly, many also involve atypical employment contracts (ILO, 1996).[19] Thus, one of the fundamental questions first raised by Segmented Labour Markets theorists in the early 1970s is especially applicable here: namely, to what extent will the new forces of competition lead to changes in the terms and conditions of employment, particularly in the form of the labour contract? (Rubery, 1994: 5).

Unlike the SER, the features of which are easily discernible, nonstandard forms of employment are more easily defined by what they are not, than by what they are: in 1991 the Economic Council of Canada (1991: 12) defined nonstandard forms of employment as simply 'those which differ from the traditional model of a full-time job,' and further indicated that they include all forms of employment falling below a thirty-five hour per week threshold.

Perhaps because of the lack of coherence among nonstandard forms of employment, as well as the material and ideological force of the postwar welfare state's mediation of central tensions in capitalist labour markets, the SER remains a pivotal reference point in defining non-standard forms of employment and their associated entitlements (e.g., unemployment insurance, pensions, maternity and paternity benefits, and sick leave). In contrast to the core features of the SER, nonstandard forms of employment are structurally heterogeneous (Polivka and Nardone, 1989). Viewed collectively, therefore, nonstandard forms of work do not offer a new *normative* model of employment of the same order as the SER even though they seem to be replacing full-time, full-year employment as the norm.

Towards a Temporary Employment Relationship?

Undeniably, the SER only represented the *normative* model of employment in the postwar period, and many scholars argue quite convincingly that the degree of economic expansion in this period represents an exception rather than a rule (Broad, 1993; Pollert, 1988). However, the SER has played a central prescriptive role since the Second World War as the model for wages' policy, labour legislation, and social policy in Canada and abroad. It was, and in some respects still is, a template for the organization and regulation of the contemporary labour market. Therefore, given the apparent erosion of the SER as a norm, and, in real terms, the task of identifying what types of employment relationships will supplement and/or displace it at a *normative* level is increasingly important.

The TER, epitomized by the employment relationship associated with the contemporary THI,[20] represents a model of employment that is gaining increasing *normative* prominence in the current period for two distinct reasons. First, and most concretely, the THI, its sectoral reference point, has experienced considerable growth over the last two decades both in Canada and in other industrialized countries. While industry analysts attribute the THI's initial emergence to the mass entry of married women into the labour market in the 1950s and 1960s, with the arrival of labour-saving technologies in the home and women's displacement from their location in the wartime division of labour, they credit the THI's recent growth to firms' desire to abdicate responsibilities conventionally associated with the SER, such as those pertaining to hiring, administration of benefits, and dismissal (Carré, 1992; Hamdani, 1996; Mangum, Mayall, and Nelson, 1985). Consequently, the buoyancy of the THI does not translate into increased security for temporary help workers. In sharp contrast to the SER, and regardless of the revenues generated by the THI, the TER is based on a more precarious model of employment, partly due to its origins as a female-dominated industry.

Second, due to its triangular nature, the employment relationship typically associated with the THI contradicts *all* three core features of the SER: the worker establishes occupational connections with several employers rather than one, is rarely party to an indeterminate contract of employment, and often may be dismissed with little notice (Cordova, 1986: 641). In most advanced welfare states, workers engaged in TERs (e.g., temporary help workers) are also rarely unionized and/or covered by collective agreements, in contrast to many of their counterparts engaged in SERs. In Canada the virtual absence of unionization among temporary help workers and their relatively low rates of coverage under firm-based collective agreements reflect stagnating union density and the shifting demographic profile of unionized workers. Although Canada did not experience a decline in union density akin to the sharp decline in the United States in the last thirty years, with the shift in employment away from the goods-producing sector, union density has stagnated since the mid-1960s (hovering between 31 and 33 per cent from 1967 to 1997) (Akyeampong, 1997: 45; Galarneau, 1996: 43).[21] Behind the stagnation of union density lie a number of changes in the demographic and labour market characteristics of unionized workers over the last three decades. Chief among the variables stabilizing union density in Canada are (1) growing labour force participation rates among women, who have increased their presence in the unionized labour force in every decade since the 1960s, and (2) the growth of unionization in the public sector (Akyeampong, 1997: 47; Galarneau, 1996: 45). Still, a snapshot of the shape and composition of the unionized workforce in 1997 calls into question prospects for continued stability in union density in Canada. Three variables related to the shape of the unionized workforce substantiate this concern: age distribution, work arrangements and job tenure, and unionization rates in the public sector versus the private sector

TABLE 1
Union Membership and Density by Sex, Selected Years 1967–1997

	Union Membership (000s)			Union Density* (percentage)		
	Both Sexes	Men	Women	Both Sexes	Men	Women
1967	2,056	1,654	402	33.2	40.9	15.9
1972	2,355	1,780	575	31.9	37.9	21.4
1977	2,785	2,003	781	31.2	37.4	22.6
1982	2,997	2,016	981	31.0	37.8	24.0
1987	3,614	2,261	1,353	32.0	36.0	27.0
1992	3,803	2,216	1,587	33.2	36.1	29.8
1997**	3,547	1,949	1,598	31.1	32.4	29.6

Sources:
1. E.B. Akyeampong (1997), 'A Statistical Portrait of the Trade Union Movement,'
Perspectives on Labour and Income (Winter), 45.
2. CALURA (1967–1992).
3. Statistics Canada, *Labour Force Survey*.
*Union density: the ratio of the number of employees who belong to a union to the
number of paid employees.
**Average for January–September 1997.

(Tables 1, 2, and 3). Furthermore, prospects for organizing temporary
help workers and other nonstandard workers in the future also appear
quite bleak given the nature of the regime of collective bargaining
currently operating in Canada (see Chapters 6 and 8). In essence, the
rise of the THI, and the related spread of the TER, reflects profound
shifts in the balance-of-class-power,[22] specifically the uneven power of the
organized labour movement. It also signals the growing pressure that
employers are placing on workers to concede to their demands for
greater 'flexibility,' a development that contrasts sharply with the tenor
of struggles in the post-Second World War era when the SER rose to
dominance alongside the establishment of legal rights for organized
labour.

The notion of a TER fits nicely with the increasingly contingent nature
of employment in advanced capitalist labour markets. However, it is
important to emphasize that individual employment relationships reflecting the TER are not necessarily precarious. Nor is the TER inherently insecure since it cuts across a range of sectors and occupations,
making it of a different order than the SER. As Heidi Gottfried (1992:
447) notes, 'temporary [help] work occupies an institutional space that
spans multiple locations.' At one end of the spectrum, a small but

TABLE 2
Union Membership and Coverage of Employees by Selected Characteristics, 1997*

	Union Membership			Union Coverage **			Non-Union (000s)***
	Total employed (000s)	Total (000s)	Density (percentage)	Total (000s)	Rate (percentage)		
*Total Public/ Private Sector****	11,414	3,547	31.1	3,881	34.0		7,533
Public sector	2,070	1,501	72.5	1,604	77.5		466
Private sector	9,344	2,046	21.9	2,277	24.4		7,067
Sex							
Men	6,010	1,949	32.4	2,132	35.5		3,878
Women	5,404	1,598	29.6	1,749	32.4		3,655
Age							
15–24	1,888	202	10.7	244	12.9		1,644
25–54	8,640	3,029	35.1	3,297	38.2		5,343
25–44	6,350	2,019	31.8	2,214	34.9		4,137
45–54	2,289	1,009	44.1	1,083	47.3		1,206
55 +	887	317	35.7	340	38.4		546
Work Status							
Full-time	9,336	3,096	33.2	3,383	36.2		5,953
Part-time	2,079	451	21.7	498	24.0		1,580
Industry							
Goods-producing	3,003	957	31.8	1,043	34.7		1,961
Service-producing	8,411	2,590	30.8	2,838	33.7		5,573
Occupation							

(continued)

TABLE 2 (concluded)
Union Membership and Coverage of Employees by Selected Characteristics, 1997*

	Union Membership			Union Coverage **				Non-Union (000s)***
	Total employed (000s)	Total (000s)	Density (percentage)	Total (000s)	Rate (percentage)			
White-collar	8,248	2,361	28.6	2,604	31.6			5,644
Blue-collar	3,166	1,186	37.5	1,277	40.3			1,890
Job Tenure								
1–12 Months	2,641	340	12.9	410	15.5			2,231
1–5 Years	3,293	660	20.1	745	22.6			2,548
5–9 Years	1,883	676	35.9	735	39.0			1,148
9–14 Years	1,312	554	42.2	598	45.6			714
14 Years +	2,285	1,316	57.6	1,393	61.0			892

Sources:
1. E.B. Akeampong (1997), 'A Statistical Portrait.'
2. Statistics Canada (1997), Labour Force Survey.
*Average for January–September 1997 period.
**Includes both union members and persons who are not union members but are covered by collective agreements.
***Includes employees who are neither union members nor are covered by collective agreements.
****Public sector employees are those working for government departments or agencies, crown corporations or public schools, hospitals or other institutions. Private sector employees are all other wage and salary earners.

TABLE 3
Selected Job Characteristics by Union Status, 1995

Work Arrangements	Union Employees*	Non-Union Employees**
Percentage of employees:		
In full-time jobs	87.4	76.7
In permanent jobs	91.1	86.9
In temporary jobs	8.9	13.1
With flexitime arrangement option	16.7	27.1
Who work only Monday to Friday inclusive	65.8	58.2
Who work both Saturday and Sunday	5.8	8.4
Who do some/all of the work at home	8.9	9.1
In job-sharing arrangement	12.1	6.8

Sources:
1. E.B. Akeampong (1997), 'A Statistical Portrait.'
2. Statistics Canada (1995), Labour Force Survey.
3. Statistics Canada (1995), Survey of Work Arrangements.
*Employees who are union members only.
**Employees who are neither union members nor covered by a collective bargaining agreement.

significant percentage of workers engaged in TERs are high-paid 'consultants' in burgeoning fields such as computer programming where the demand for workers significantly outweighs the available supply. At the other extreme, reflecting the historic origins of the THI, a majority of temporary help workers are low-paid, part-time, or casual workers engaged largely in clerical or light industrial work (Rubery and Fagan, 1994: 157). Both sets of workers lack an indeterminate contract of employment, reflecting the erosion of job security across the labour market as a whole over the last several decades, yet they inhabit opposite poles of the income and occupational hierarchy. Thus, as a purely conceptual tool, the notion of a TER has the potential to capture growing dualism in the Canadian labour market evidenced by the diversity of nonstandard forms of employment, but, at the same time, to convey the expansion of precarious forms of employment at its base.

The Feminization of Employment?

While the SER and the TER are valuable analytic concepts, they are useful primarily in describing and identifying *normative* models of employment and periodizing employment change. At this juncture, therefore, it is useful to examine the gendered international and national labour market contexts in which the rise and spread of the TER is occurring. This involves describing and critiquing scholarship advancing the original global feminization of employment thesis and offering a revised conception of feminization by examining its central elements in relation to the rise of the TER.[23] What this examination reveals is that the shift away from the SER has the potential to take scholars beyond an understanding of the significance of sex-typing in the labour market to viewing gender as a necessary constituent element in labour market analysis (J. Scott, 1988: 1067). Both the SER and the TER represent gendered employment norms. But, while the material referent for the SER is clearly the (white) male breadwinner engaged in full-time, full-year employment in a core sector of the economy, the TER lacks an equivalent (unitary) reference point in the contemporary period. For this reason, the *process* of feminization is integral to understanding the rise and spread of the TER.[24]

The Conventional Global Feminization of Employment Thesis

Scholarship theorizing the 'global feminization of employment' is rich in both descriptive and explanatory potential. At the descriptive level, it captures the highly gendered nature of a wide range of international employment trends. At the causal level, it links prevailing employment trends to the macroeconomic policy outcomes of a supply-side politico-economic agenda first emerging in the early 1970s (Standing, 1989: 1079). In his article 'Global Feminization through Flexible Labour' (1989), Guy Standing presents one of the earliest,[25] most comprehensive and most widely criticized versions of the global feminization of employment thesis.[26] Standing's summarized version of global feminization is that 'women are being substituted for men and many forms of work are being converted into the kinds of jobs traditionally geared to women' (1989: 1077).

According to Standing, the global feminization of employment encompasses four core features. First, and least contested, it involves women's mass entry into the labour market on a global scale; more specifically, for industrializing countries, it means that women are entering into the formal labour market on an unprecedented scale, and, for both industrializing and industrialized countries, it means that women's unemployment rate is falling to the extent that 'their unemployment rate becomes lower than the male equivalent' (1989: 1086). Second, it entails women appropriating jobs traditionally occupied by men, such as those in primary manufacturing industries. Third, it involves a decline in the sex segregation of the labour force since many women are taking jobs formerly held by men (1084). Finally, it entails an increase in so-called static jobs with limited potential for mobility over so-called progressive jobs that encourage occupational mobility (1084, 1086). When scholars refer to the feminization of jobs, they are usually citing this last feature of the conventional thesis.

Standing ties the global feminization of employment to capital's desire for a more disposable labour force with lower fixed costs (Standing 1989: 1086). At the level of macroeconomic policy, he views this phenomenon as a direct consequence of the rise of a supply-side, politico-economic agenda. This agenda generally involves the introduction of structural adjustment and stabilization programs; accompanied by the decline of a 'social adjustment model,' these programs emphasize privatization, deregulation, trade liberalization, and export-led industrialization. Standing also suggests that the typical distinction between 'modern' and 'traditional' sectors is increasingly blurred on a global scale, both within and between nations, due to the growing prevalence of subcontracting and homework (1080). His assertions regarding the effects of global employment trends are less nuanced, however, since they imply a unidirectional shift in economic 'leadership' from industrialized to industrializing countries. According to Standing (1078), 'It is scarcely an exaggeration to say that *the leaders have become the led* [my emphasis]; international competition from low-income countries where labour costs and labour rights are least developed has been instrumental in weakening the rights and benefits of those in the lower end of the market of many industrialized economies.' This statement represents a clear articulation of a dominant position in the field of development studies in the early 1980s, whereby scholars argued that the *relocation* of production was occurring on an international scale (Frobel, Heinrichs, and Kreye, 1980; Sanderson, 1985). However, many scholars have since scrutinized, enlarged, and deepened this assessment of the changing nature of global production, suggesting that it is more appropriate to characterize shifts in production as amounting to the *reallocation* of production both within and across national borders; the service sector is a case in point since many jobs in this domain of employment cannot move (Fernandez-Kelly and Garcia, 1989; Mitter and Rowbotham, 1994). Some also question the causal connection between feminization and the rise of a supply-side, politico-economic agenda that Standing poses, tracing rising female labour force participation rates to the early 1900s.

A Critique of the Conventional Thesis

Scholarship examining feminization within industrializing countries and regions generates strong criticisms of three of Standing's initial claims and questions his general emphasis. First, it illustrates that the feminization of the labour force need not entail the substitution of women for men in formerly male jobs.[27] This facet of feminization often results when new jobs open up in regions where the majority of men are otherwise employed, and intensifies when families face difficulties in reproducing themselves.[28] Additionally, in contrast to Standing's second claim, scholars focusing on industrialized and industrializing nations also repeatedly demonstrate that declining sex segregation is not a *necessary* feature of feminization.[29] Third, emerging scholarship also challenges the notion that women's rising labour force participation rates necessarily lead to lower official unemployment rates for women than for their male counterparts. For example, in Turkey, when women's share of the urban labour force was at its highest level in 1989, women still constituted over one-third of the urban unemployed (Catagay, 1994: 132). Hence, Nilufer Catagay (133) incisively notes that 'The increase in urban women's labour-force participation rates supports Standing's feminization thesis. *But this increased participation contributed more to feminization of unemployment than feminization of employment* [my emphasis]: while Standing predicted a fall in female unemployment rates and a rise in male unemployment rates, in the Turkish economy the opposite occurred.'

More generally, studies examining feminization in industrializing countries also suggest that the emphasis of the conventional thesis is somewhat misplaced. It focuses too narrowly on women's rising labour force participation rates. While Standing is correct to suggest women's rising labour force participation rates are an important facet of feminization, what is perhaps more significant is women's so-called 'triple shift' (Tiano, 1994: 214; Ward, 1994: 6).[30] In many industrializing countries, women entering the formal labour market do not represent a 'new' category of workers but groups of workers whose primary location of work has shifted largely from the informal to the formal sector, and whose workload (paid and unpaid) is intensifying due to the increasing marketization of tasks associated with social reproduction and the absence of adequate state supports in this sphere (Tiano 1994).

Country-specific studies further substantiate criticisms raised by scholars focusing on industrializing countries. A recent study by Marjorie Cohen (1994) argues that the concept of feminization is only useful in the Canadian context if it incorporates the *entrenchment* of sex segregation in female-dominated sectors, 'the intensification of the feminized character of jobs that have always been important to women' (111). While she finds Standing's argument regarding the prospect for declining sex segregation provocative, Cohen maintains that '[i]t seems equally plausible to argue that intensified international competition could bring about a sufficient repression of wages in general so that the cost advantage of hiring women over men would not be sufficient to change the gender-typing of jobs' (105–6). Thus, her study demonstrates that when unemployment is widespread, declining sex segregation will not necessarily accompany rising female labour force participation rates.

Supplementing Cohen's macro-level analysis of gendered employment trends in Canada, other scholars explore the nature of feminization in particular sectors. Monica Boyd, Marianne Mulvihill, and John Myles (1991: 412) define feminization rather loosely as the increase of women in the labour force, and associate it with the shift to a postindustrial economy. Using the example of the service sector, like Cohen, Barron, and Catagay, they also illustrate that sex-segregated labour markets and the feminization of employment can be potentially mutually reinforcing developments. They further indicate that an economy can respond to women's increased labour force participation in one of two ways: 'by a decline in the number of sex-segregated work environments or by an increase in the number of work environments that are exclusively female' (413).[31]

One female work environment that grew rapidly in Canada between 1941 and 1986 was the service sector. During this forty-five year period, women's participation rates in services rose from 31 per cent to 58 per cent. Along with the major manufacturing employers of women, the service sector absorbed many women entering the labour force in the post-Second World War period. Since this sector, to which the Canadian THI now increasingly caters, is considered a highly feminized domain in Canada and abroad, it is important to consider service sector growth in revising the conventional thesis.

Towards a Revised Definition of the Global Feminization of Employment

A review of recent case studies indicates that four central features that only partially resemble the conventional thesis mark the global feminization of employment. Even more important, these case studies indicate that prevailing global employment trends have a 'feminine' face because of women's historic and continuing role in social reproduction (i.e., the daily and generational maintenance of the labour supply).

The first feature closely mirrors Standing's primary claim that women's formal labour force participation rates are generally rising globally.[32] However, recent case studies further indicate that, for many women, entering into the formal labour force signals the introduction of a third shift rather than a shift from economic inactivity to economic activity. The second feature, related to the increasingly 'feminized' character of a range of job types, is the casualization of employment. Pat Armstrong (1996: 30) characterizes the gendered nature of casualization, or the 'gendering' of jobs, as follows: 'the restructuring that is part of globalization has created more *women's work in the market* [my emphasis] ... This kind of feminization of the labour force does not mean that the position of most women has improved. Instead, it means that the position of some men has deteriorated, becoming more like that of women. While some women and men do have good labour-force jobs, many more women and men have bad jobs.' Armstrong is making two related claims here: first, by referring to the appearance of more 'women's work' in the market, she is highlighting the gendered underpinnings of prevailing employment trends, and therefore justifying why the sum of these trends amounts to the 'gendering' of jobs rather than simply casualization loosely defined. Second, she is suggesting that the type of feminization that is occurring in the labour market is also prompting more men to compete for jobs, particularly 'good jobs' traditionally held by women. This is not to suggest that the gender order in the labour market is changing drastically. Rather, to cite Armstrong (30) once again, it indicates that 'the increasing similarity between women and men can be explained in terms of a *harmonizing down for some men* and *greater economic pressure on many women* [my emphasis]. Most of the good jobs are still dominated by men, but few women have jobs that offer the kind of rewards and opportunities that many men became accustomed to after the Second World War.' While the significance of casualization is underplayed in the conventional thesis, data documenting the rise of highly precarious forms of nonstandard employment in industrialized nations underline the force of this facet of feminization and Armstrong's twin claims (Cohen, 1994; Walby, 1989). Third, contrary to Standing's initial claims, with women's rising labour force participation rates, sex segregation still persists both across occupational groupings and within specific sectors and industries in disparate countries: witness the continued sex segregation within the Canadian service sector and the situation with the Turkish clothing industry (Boyd, Mulvihill, and Myles, 1991; Catagay, 1994). The same is true of the THI, as will be demonstrated in Chapters 4 and 5. Increased income and occupational polarization, both between women and men and among women and men themselves, represents the fourth feature of the revised global feminization of employment thesis. Although few studies formally address the growing income and occupational polarization among women and men themselves, empirical evidence suggests that it is an important trend to highlight, and that it is shaped primarily by variables pertaining to race, immigration status[33] and age (Vosko, 2000).

Global Feminization and Social Reproduction

Few of the recent case studies of feminization offer sufficiently deep explanations of the current shape of global employment trends. Still, empirical work in this area points to women's continuing role in social reproduction as a partial explanation. For example, the fact that women increasingly engage in a 'triple shift' is intricately related to the growing marketization of tasks associated with social reproduction, and, equally significant, the growing inadequacy of state supports in this area (Elson 1995; Ward 1994). Similarly, persisting occupational segregation by sex, and income polarization between men and women, reflects the gendered organization of social reproduction: women tend to be confined to jobs in the labour market that reflect tasks associated with domestic labour, such as paid domestic work and service occupations, and women's assumed access to forms of subsistence outside the labour market (i.e., their presumed dependence on men's wages as daughters, sisters, wives, and mothers), structures their location within it and the types of employment contracts to which they are subject. Indeed, social reproduction is central to the feminization process in its entirety. It therefore operates at a higher level of causality than any of the central manifestations of this phenomenon.

Following Diane Elson (1989, 1995), Antonella Picchio (1981), and Jill Rubery and Collette Fagan (1994), this inquiry defines the system of social reproduction to include the family structure, the structure of waged and non-waged work, the role of the state in the reproduction of the labour force and organizations, social and political, of waged and non-waged labour. As Picchio notes, 'social reproduction is central to labour market analysis; it determines the position of individuals within the labour market, provides the basis for standards of living (and is thus the reference point for wage bargaining), structures inter- and intra-class relationships and the distribution of the product [i.e. labourers]' (Picchio, 1981: 194). It occurs at an intra-state level, involving the daily and generational maintenance of the national population, and at an inter-state level, involving the processes of migration and immigration.

Feminist scholars argue that women's role in social reproduction is of paramount importance to their frequently subordinate location in divisions of labour in the labour market and the domestic sphere. However, there is considerable disagreement over the roots and origins of women's role in social reproduction, leading scholars to stress both material and ideological dimensions. For example, Armstrong and Armstrong (1983: 28) argue that 'the existence of a sexual division of labour, although not its form and extent, is crucial to capitalism' at the highest level of abstraction. Emphasizing the role of biology, while identifying the interpretation of this biological dimension as a historical construct, they suggest:

> That women have the babies, albeit under a variety of conditions, does not necessarily mean that they will rear the children or clean the toilets. Nor does it mean that they must live in nuclear families. However, *because capitalism is premised on the separation of most aspects of workers' reproduction from the commodity production process, and because women have the babies, women will at times be limited in their access to the production process* [my emphasis]. Such limitations permit the elaboration of the sexual division of labour (itself not without contradictions) just as they encourage women's dependence on men for financial support and the dependence of higher wage-earning men on women for domestic services. (38)

Alternatively, Michele Barrett (1988) argues that familial ideology, and hence gender relations rather than sex per se, is most central to women's role in social reproduction; she prefers to adopt a historical approach that de-emphasizes the biological. Patricia Connelly (1983) and Jane Jenson (1986) critique both approaches, concurring that gender relations cannot be reduced to material conditions. Still, they each acknowledge the 'inevitably gendered' character of perhaps the most fundamental aspect of social reproduction, that is, childbirth.

Much of the historic debate among feminist scholars over the roots of women's subordination has centred around these three types of explanations (Jenson, 1986: 24). This work does not set out to evaluate these arguments. It is nevertheless crucial to emphasize, without falling prey to biologist arguments, that gender has an ontological basis (i.e., sex) that institutions like the state, firms, unions, and the family employ as a tool to create and perpetuate labour market segmentation and to reinforce socially constructed gender divisions of labour within the domestic sphere. Even more important, the significance of the supply-side of the labour market, where the daily and generational maintenance of both its core and peripheral workers is assured, cannot be overstated in exposing the gendered nature of prevailing employment trends, as well as labour power's peculiar commodity status at the most fundamental level. Thus, the revised global feminization of employment hypothesis is not only salient in describing the process of employment change but in further accentuating the relationship between women's role in social reproduction and the gendered character of this process.

Global Feminization and Shifting Employment Norms

Flowing from this deeper understanding of the global feminization of employment and its roots, an important question still remains largely unanswered: Does the concept of feminization have resonance in characterizing the decline of the SER as a *normative* model of employment in advanced capitalist welfare states? In this book, I argue that it does. In contradistinction to the SER, which is a masculine employment norm, one of the types of employment relationships that is contributing to displacing it (i.e., the TER) embodies several core features that resemble stereotypically 'women's work' and the feminization of employment more generally.[34] Moreover, the dimension of social reproduction, which is key to making the current process of labour market transformation amount to feminization, is central to understanding the decline of the SER, because, for an expanding group of workers, wages, benefits, and other forms of social protection are not sufficient to maintain a man and his [*sic*] family, as Keynes intended. A growing number of workers, including many workers engaged in TERs, earn wages and benefits and endure terms and conditions of employment resembling those of women presumed to be 'secondary breadwinners' and/or to have alternative sources of subsistence beyond the wage.

The TER is modeled on an employment relationship associated with the historically female-dominated THI. Indeed, with its formal inception in the 1950s, this industry geared itself explicitly to placing white middle-class married women, many of whom had been absent from the labour market for a lengthy period of time or had been displaced from wartime industries with the return of Second World War troops, with client firms requiring temporary clerical support. Backed by state policies and practices that limited women's participation in the labour market, the industry encouraged married women to re-enter the labour force to supplement the incomes of male breadwinners, adjusting the terms and conditions of the TER to accommodate the reproductive demands placed on them. While it has since expanded its marketing strategy to target a broader range of potential workers and client firms, the industry continues to use women's 'necessary' role in social reproduction to sell temporary help work as a viable option for women with dependent family members, offering 'flexible work arrangements' suitable to workers with caregiving responsibilities.

Another central defining feature of the TER is the absence of stability and security with respect to duration and benefits; therefore, the shift away from the SER clearly reflects the casualization of employment, alternatively termed the 'gendering' (i.e., feminization) of jobs. Still, the prime strength of labeling the TER as one among several potential *normative* alternatives to the SER, while fully acknowledging that it is of a different order, lies in its capacity to reflect growing contingency across the economy and persisting dualism, marked by the expansion of the bottom of the labour market, within it (i.e., casualization). An investigation into the decline of the SER also challenges us to deepen prevailing understandings of casualization and to expose its gendered character. The changing shape of the THI offers an interesting view of this core facet of feminization. Although the industry was once highly female dominated, and continues to be marked by a feminized employment relationship and sex segregation, its gender composition is changing to incorporate more men, as well as a more diverse range of occupational groupings and sectors.[35] Thus, its transformation illustrates that casualization is not simply an aspect of the feminization of employment but that shifting gender relations themselves are central to the casualization process (Jenson 1996).

Finally, given that the THI is its sectoral reference point, if the TER is partially to replace the SER, intensified sex segregation and growing income and occupational polarization (both between women and men and among women and men themselves) will likely follow in its path. Recall that the contemporary THI places workers across a range of occupational groupings and sectors mirroring the growing dualism, and, hence, sex segregation, in the labour market documented in recent studies of feminization. While it was a highly female-dominated industry for much of its history due to its original focus on clerical work, women no longer represent a disproportionate percentage of temporary help workers, since the THI now also caters to customers requiring workers at higher ends of the income and occupational spectrum. Nevertheless, internal sex segregation persists within the THI, with women, immigrants, and people of colour frequently occupying the bottom end of the occupational hierarchy and specific groups of men dominating at the higher end.[36] Correspondingly, income and occupational polarization is also increasingly evident across the industry as a whole (see Chapters 4 and 5).

For the four reasons raised above, the accelerated rise in the THI that began in the late 1970s and early 1980s, and the spread of the TER now taking place in the Canadian labour market, reflect the feminization of employment norms. Accordingly, given that it is abstracted from the employment relationship conventionally associated with THI, in *normative* terms, the gender of the TER is female and the erosion of the SER reflects the feminization of employment broadly conceived.

Conclusion

This chapter introduced the three theoretical lenses operating in this book and elaborated its central argument, which relates the spread of the TER to the emergence of a modern labour market intermediary and the shift away from the SER, two developments consistent with our revised conception of the feminization of employment. It also linked historical attempts to limit the spread of precarious employment to the well-known maxim 'labour is not a commodity' and the objectives behind it. What is more important, all three streams of inquiry in the chapter pointed to the tensions in the ILO's founding charter, suggesting that labour power is inevitably a commodity under capitalism and its commodity status is acutely apparent as security and freedom are eliminated from the wage relation. They also delineated an analytic framework for an historical investigation, based on the evolution of the TER in Canada, into the range of means by which the state and employers have differentiated between workers in the twentieth century, how workers have resisted coercive employment practices, and why labour power's peculiar commodity status is relevant to the spread of the TER.

Putting Workers in Their Place: The Early History of Private Employment Agencies

The roots of the Canadian THI lie in the history of labour market intermediaries, specifically private employment agents operating in the labour market in the late nineteenth and early twentieth centuries. In this era TERs did not exist in their present form, nor did temporary help agencies. Nevertheless, several precursors of this type of employment relationship and the 'classic' temporary help agency merit investigation.

This chapter traces the prehistory of the contemporary TER, identifying the various actors involved in its early precursors. Operating in the labour market as early as the 1880s, private employment agents acting abroad to promote immigration, such as padrones[1] and general labour agents, were at the hub of these relationships. As a result of their unethical practices, which organized labour and various immigrant communities publicized and criticized harshly, they were also the initial target of regulation at the national, and provincial levels, and subsequently at the international level. The chapter also describes the activities of private employment agencies operated by typewriter companies in Ontario, the immediate forerunners to the 'classic' temporary help agency, and compares the character of employment relationships common to the private employment agency industry at the turn of the century to those that became prevalent after federal and provincial governments and the ILO began to regulate private employment agencies. Even in the face of growing disapproval of the padrone system and the private employment agency industry as a whole, this small but cohesive new branch of the industry managed to carve out a space for itself in the clerical sector. It escaped regulation because government officials, unchallenged by social reformers or labour leaders, viewed employment agencies run by typewriter companies as legitimate entities; not only did they recruit and place women stenographers and typists in temporary work, they sold typewriter equipment rather than simply the services of their workers.

The ensuing analysis deepens two larger themes introduced in Chapter 1. First, it suggests that many workers engaged by private employment agents at the turn of the century resembled unfree wage labourers, specifically 'contract migrant workers' (Miles, 1987; Satzewich, 1991). A sizeable number of immigrant and migrant workers put to work by padrones, general labour agents, and even agents employed by philanthropic organizations in the late nineteenth and early twentieth centuries not only came to Canada under false pretenses but also were unable to circulate freely in the labour market upon their arrival because of the employment contracts they had entered into outside the country. Moreover, private employment agents used highly racialized nation-building discourses to relegate these workers to the bottom of the labour market. Second, it demonstrates that employment agencies run by typewriter companies in Ontario emerged out of the private employment agency industry, even though they consciously distanced themselves from agents operating at the fringes of the labour market. While their primary workers enjoyed greater freedom of mobility in the labour market, these immediate forerunners to the THI crafted employment relationships very similar to those associated with their more unscrupulous precursors. What gave employment agencies run by typewriter companies legitimacy was their practice of targeting young Canadian-born, well-educated, middle-class women presumed to be dependent upon a male wage; this same strategy also laid the groundwork for the emergence of the THI later in the century, as well as the feminized employment relationship upon which its early success was based.

'Nation-Building' and Private Employment Agents at the Turn of the Century

Beginning in 1880, with the aim of populating the country and providing workers to fill the labour market, the Canadian government drastically altered the immigration campaign that it had initiated to attract permanent settlers upon the formation of the Dominion. As countless scholars demonstrate, Canada's original nation-building goals reflected the ideal of creating an ethnically pure British settler colony (K.J. Anderson, 1991; Bakan and Stasiulis, 1997; Calliste, 1993; Roberts, 1988, 1990; Satzewich, 1991). However, in the forty-year period between 1880 and 1920, employers' labour needs in key areas of expansion, particu-

larly in agriculture, industry, and domestic service, conflicted with the
dominant Eurocentric and gendered nation-building discourses and
policies aimed at establishing a morally and physically 'pure' settler
population loyal to the British Empire. Consequently, the twin demands
for an industrial and agricultural proletariat and a core of female domestic workers altered the shape of Canadian immigration policy, and hence
the influx of immigrants into the country. Developments in this era
reflect Sedef Arat-Koc's (1997: 55) incisive observation that 'Historically,
immigration policies in Canada have been determined by several, at
times conflicting, objectives. These have included the development of a
white British settler society in Canada, establishing settler colonies in
certain regions of the country (with previously sparse European
populations), and meeting the needs of the labour market.' Therefore,
at the end of the nineteenth century, the consequences of the profound
conflict between the Dominion government and the emerging capitalist
class over the 'desirable' immigrant eventually caused the government to
alter its longstanding campaign for a specific group of permanent set-
ters. The new policies aimed to secure a consistent supply of expendable
male and female labourers (Roberts, 1988: 8; Avery, 1995).

Male Agricultural and Industrial Workers

Promoting immigration was essential to fulfilling the late nineteenth-
century Dominion government's expansionary project. In advertising
for immigrants, first largely in Britain and then in other parts of Europe,
the government emphasized the possibility of upward class mobility,
suggesting that male immigrants could easily become land-owning farmers in Canada, even when the reality was that employers wanted farm-
hands and day labourers. As Barbara Roberts (1988: 5) notes, 'The
stated ideal of Canadian Immigration Policy was to attract a permanent
agricultural population. Behind this ideal, thinly concealed and little
denied, lay a more-or-less Wakefieldian system ... Hidden behind that
bitter but still palatable modification of the ideal lay yet another reality: a
massive system of importing industrial workers who could hardly claim
to be farmers even potentially.' Of course, for the many stalwart peasants
willing to risk coming to Canada with the hope of gaining an improved
standard of living, immigration did not result in upward class mobility
(Cunningham, 1991; Avery, 1979, 1995; Harney, 1979). As a consequence, while immigration figures were quite high at the turn of the
century, more people left than entered Canada for five of the eight

decades between the 1860 and 1940 due to poor working conditions and economic crises.

The new corporate capitalist class desired temporary male labourers, contractors, and so-called guest workers (preferably migrating without their families) to engage in day labour, construction, and other forms of industrial work, building railways and physical infrastructure in industrial centres and performing seasonal agricultural work at very low wages (Avery, 1995: 32; Bradwin, 1972: 55–8). They perceived male contract migrants and/or guest workers as ideal sources of labour since the costs of renewing the work force rested almost completely with the sending economy (Roberts, 1988: 7). As well, because they did not pose a threat of labour unrest, many employers also used male migrant contract workers as strike-breakers even though such practices were highly controversial among the public at-large (Avery, 1979: 37; Canada, May 1906; *Labour Gazette*, 1901: 213). Hence, the goals of the capitalist class conflicted with the official policies of the Dominion government for a lengthy period, at least on the surface, and the reality of the conditions of employment endured by immigrants and migrants in Canada contrasted sharply with the images of Canada as a 'civilized' white settler society.

Although the tensions between the Dominion government and the emergent capitalist class remained quite serious until the end of the century, the demands of employers, many of whom viewed Southern and Eastern European male immigrants as highly desirable industrial workers, eventually won over those of the nation-builders. As Donald Avery (1979: 37) asserts, 'Between 1896 and 1914 Canadian immigration policy served, above all else, the dictates of the capitalist labour market. Under the banner of economic growth thousands of immigrant workers were encouraged to enter the country to meet the labour needs of commercial agriculture, railroad construction, lumbering, and other labour intensive industries. Increasingly the long-standing goal of bringing into the country only the settler labour type of immigrants was displaced by a policy of importing an industrial proletariat.' Immigration statistics substantiate Avery's claims. In 1896 only 13.3 per cent of the Canadian population was foreign-born; of this figure, 76 per cent were of British origin. However, while British immigrants still remained the majority of the foreign-born population for the next thirty years, Canada experienced a dramatic increase in the number of immigrants from Eastern and Southern Europe (Avery, 1995: 22). For example, in 1921, 22.2 per cent of the population was foreign-born and 46 per cent was non-British (33).

Urban centres, such as Montreal and Toronto, and rural areas in western Canada attracted the bulk of male Southern and Eastern European immigrants due to pressure from local capitalists. Railway companies were particularly vocal in their demand for a specific type of industrial worker, and they did not visualize the typical white British settler as a desirable day labourer. Canadian Pacific Railway President Shaughnessy noted in 1897: 'Men who seek employment on railway construction are, as a rule, a class accustomed to roughing it. They know when they go to the work that they must put up with the most primitive kind of camp accommodation. I feel very strongly that it would be a huge mistake to send out any more of these men from Wales, Scotland or England ... it is only prejudicial to the cause of immigration to import men who come here expecting to get high wages, a feather bed and a bath tub' (Shaughnessy to James A. Stewart, 1897, as cited in Avery, 1995: 29).

The Grand Truck Pacific, the Canadian National Railway, and the Canadian Pacific Railway all viewed British immigrants, as well as Slavic and Scandinavian immigrants, as undesirable because they sought workers perceived to be willing to commit themselves to menial forms of railway work (Bradwin, 1972). The railway companies repeatedly contravened the *Alien Labour Act* of 1897, which made it illegal to 'pre-pay the transportation of, or in any other way to assist or solicit the importation or immigration of any alien or foreigner into Canada under contract or agreement' by importing Southern and Eastern European men to Canada as de facto guest workers (*RSC* 1897, 60–61, v, C.11:1; Avery, 1995: 38; Bradwin, 1972: 55). As a result, by the turn of the century, a highly racialized division of labour operated in railway construction. In describing the 'ethnic groupings' among the camp men of this period, in *The Bunkhouse Man*, Edwin Bradwin (1972: 92) notes that '[t]here are two distinct groups of workers at once apparent in camps on a piece of railway work, the "whites" and the "foreigners." This semi-racial demarcation is not a pleasant distinction; it may not even be just, but it is always in evidence on any hundred mile piece of new construction.' In this study, Bradwin (1972: 92) illustrates that white male workers either born in Canada or from the British Isles, the United States, or Scandinavia held positions in the camps that 'connote[d] a "stripe" of some kind.' Indeed, they were 'officials in one capacity or another – walking-bosses, accountants, inspectors, the various camp foremen, cache keepers, as well as clerks to perform the more routine works of checks and time keepers,' and they belonged to 'the most remunerated part of railway construction' (92–3). In contrast, the 'foreigners' were said to 'stolidly engage in muckering and heavier tasks' and to be poorly paid (105).

Although the federal government threatened the railway companies with prosecution under the *Alien Labour Act*, partly due to pressure from the Trades and Labour Congress which concerned itself primarily with protecting the interests of core workers, it typically ignored the often coercive practices of the railway companies who were importing labourers in this period.[2] By the second decade of the twentieth century the federal government also ignored similar practices by mining companies operating in western Canada. As works by Avery (1979, 1995), Bradwin (1972), Harney (1979), and Ramirez (1991) show, the federal government tolerated the unethical and unlawful practices of the railway companies and other companies in the resource sector because the bulk of the workers that they recruited either came as guest workers, or, by virtue of their occupation, were not fully protected as citizen-workers in Canada.

Even though the federal government tolerated their questionable employment practices, companies such as the Canadian Pacific Railway, the Canadian National Railway, and industrialists in construction, forestry, mining, and smelting registered their resentment towards its much-publicized drive to encourage permanent agricultural immigrants until the early 1920s. Some industrialists even claimed that they 'did more work on enticing industrial immigrants than the Dominion ever did' (Avery, 1979: 38–9). Ironically, heads of railway and steamship companies were the most vocal spokespeople for so-called open-door immigration policy, although many of them were later implicated in deportations and making false representations to immigrants (Avery, 1979: 30; Roberts, 1988: 8). By no coincidence, agents employed by these companies constitute the earliest group of private employment agents scrutinized in both the popular press and in government circles (Avery, 1995; Harney, 1979: 63–4; *Labour Gazette*, June 1906).

Female Domestic Workers

Alongside the demand for male agricultural and industrial immigrants, the nation-building process also involved the recruitment of female domestic workers: '... from the point of view of labour and immigration policy, domestic labour was to women what agricultural labour was to men" (Pierson and Light, 1990: 258). However, at the turn of the century the recruitment of women domestic workers represented a less controversial terrain than that of the dominant categories of male immigrants, since government officials and social reformers agreed on the type of preferred women immigrants. First cast as 'mothers of the na-

TABLE 4
Background of Female Domestics Coming to Canada, 1904–1930

	Total	British	Western European	Eastern European	Southern European
1904–1914	117,568	90,028	8,094	15,387	1,110
1919–1930	123,983	74,179	14,179	30,814	1,989

Source: M. Barber, Immigrant Domestic Servants in Canada (Ottawa: Canadian Historical Association, 1991), 2.

tion' and later reduced to the status of 'migrant workers,' these women were initially recruited to care for Canada's growing population and to balance out the rapidly expanding immigrant male population that resulted from the influx of single male workers hailing from various parts of Europe (Arat-Koc 1997).

With the passage of the *British North America Act* (1867), the lengthy period between 1867 and 1940 involved the mass immigration of women domestic servants to Canada. The majority of women immigrating to Canada as domestic workers in this period came from Britain. However, from 1900 onwards a substantial proportion of domestic workers also came from Scandinavia, Germany, Austria, Bavaria, Bohemia, Northern Italy, Switzerland, and France, and, between 1914 and the early 1930s, many Finnish women immigrated to Canada as domestic workers (Cunningham, 1991: 54–5; Lindstrom-Best, 1986).

In the early twentieth century, small numbers of women from outside Europe also immigrated to Canada to work as domestics; for example, in 1910–11, the Caribbean Domestic Scheme brought 100 women from Guadeloupe to work in Quebec (Calliste, 1993). However, since their numbers were so limited, official statistics fail to document the presence of non-European immigrant women domestic workers in Canada.

Due to the aggressive overseas recruitment campaign launched by the Dominion government and supported by the social reformers, the 1890s marked a particular high point for domestic service among immigrant women because female domestics became the only independently 'desirable' category of immigrant women workers in Canada during this decade (Cunningham, 1991: 16); the leading occupations among women in 1891 corresponded to this development (Table 5).

Still, studies by Arat-Koc (1990, 1997), Cunningham (1991), and Calliste (1993) indicate that even though the government singled out women domestic workers as so-called 'desirable' immigrants under the regime

TABLE 5
Leading Occupations for Women, 1891

Occupation	Numbers
Servant	77,644
Dressmaker	22,686
Teacher	14,803
Farmer	11,590
Seamstress	10,239
Tailoress	7,834
Saleswoman	4,409
Housekeeper	4,035
Laundress	3,679
Millner	3,277

Source: 1891 Census of Canada as
cited in J. White, Women and Unions.
(Ottawa: Canadian Advisory Council on
the Status of Women, 1980), 4.

of immigration law, domestics were subject to constant state scrutiny since they were charged with the central, yet undervalued, task of social reproduction in the new nation: as Nicola Cunningham (1991: 31) observes, 'immigration law functioned as a means of reproducing a working population in a new locale by importing working classes with an established sexual division of labour.'

Government officials and social reformers took great care in recruiting and placing female domestic workers in Canadian homes. For example, philanthropic organizations sent matrons aboard steamships crossing the Atlantic to ensure that the steamship operators obeyed the protective immigration laws adopted at the turn of the century, to guarantee that the women arrived in Canada in 'pristine' condition, and, most importantly, to segregate domestics from other immigrants so that they would not acquire notions about better employment opportunities (Arat-Koc, 1997; Barber, 1991; Roberts, 1976). Once they were deemed safely placed in Canadian homes, however, neither federal immigration policy nor provincial labour legislation accorded this group of workers an equivalent set of protections to those extended to most other categories of workers in this era (Cunningham, 1991).[3]

Although the Dominion government encouraged immigration among a narrow group of women workers (i.e., domestics), social reformers carried out recruitment and placement. In this sense, mirroring the roles of private employment agents engaging male agricultural and industrial workers, social reformers took on the role of labour market intermediaries at least until domestics were placed in Canadian homes permanently. Hence, female and male immigration remained largely in the hands of the private sector on both sides of the Atlantic until almost a decade after the First World War, at which point Canadian and British laws pertaining to the recruitment and placement of immigrants were introduced.

The private sector employment agents who handled the recruitment and placement of female domestic workers were normally matrons and social workers engaged by private philanthropic organizations. Unlike the profit-driven agents recruiting male agricultural and industrial workers, the female agents recruiting immigrant women domestic workers were largely unpaid volunteers driven by the ideology of domesticity.[4] The Canadian government of course subsidized philanthropic agencies such as the Salvation Army and the British Women's Emigration Association in their involvement in recruiting and placing domestics, just as it gave generous bonuses to profit-making steamship companies and labour agencies recruiting immigrant domestics (Avery, 1995; Barber, 1991; Roberts, 1976).

Focusing at first on Britain, philanthropic organizations targeted a pool of women domestic servants abroad, drawing up employment contracts and providing assisted passage and subsidized housing for the domestic workers upon arrival in Canada. These organizations agitated for stricter and more protective immigration policies for domestic workers and the effective implementation of existing policies. But they did little to support domestic workers once they were placed in Canadian homes. For example, even though provincial master-servant legislation supposedly protected immigrants from exploitative contracts that they may have signed abroad, philanthropic agencies usually failed to monitor the conditions of employment of the women that they recruited for domestic work; consequently, many female immigrant domestic workers became quasi-indentured servants upon arrival to Canada, at least until they paid back the money owed for assisted passage (Arat-Koc, 1997: 66).

For male agricultural migrants and industrial workers, private profit-seeking employment agents and agencies acted as 'middlemen' in the recruitment and placement process. Devoid of a moral imperative comparable to the social reformers, these agents were often engaged by railway, mining, or steamship companies with large contracts with Canada's emerging class of industrial capitalists.[5] Like the social reformers, private employment agents often provided assisted passage and arranged lodging for workers upon their arrival to Canada, and they demanded reimbursement in either the form of a portion of a given worker's wages, direct payment with interest, or work in return for the money owed to them. The numerous philanthropic societies geared to recruiting women domestic workers objected to the activities of private profit-driven employment agents in principle; they particularly disapproved of the 'padrone' system of placing male immigrant workers and the government's bonus system for private profit-driven employment agents recruiting 'desirable' immigrants. Social reformers considered fee-charging private employment agents 'unscrupulous characters who were preoccupied with profit from immigration work and who were not deemed to have the best interests of Canada at heart,' characterizing themselves as having more worthy nation-building aims (Cunningham, 1991: 97).

Despite the protestations of reformers, immigrant women domestic workers recruited by these social reformers and male industrial and agricultural immigrants recruited by private employment agents encountered similar problems. Often faced with large debts to their sponsors, both groups effectively became unfree wage labourers upon arrival to Canada, at least for a limited period. More concretely, government policies such as the *Railway Agreement* of 1925 engaged Canada's two largest railway companies to recruit male immigrants into agricultural and industrial work and women immigrants into domestic service, and to transport both groups of workers to Western Canada, where they were desperately required. These companies embraced this agreement since it increased railway travel, and, more notably, they received a bonus for these newly 'desirable' immigrants, many of whom now emigrated from Western and Eastern Europe.

The Evolution of the Private Employment Agency Industry

For both the male immigrant workers, comprising the growing agricultural labour force and the newly emerging industrial proletariat, and female domestic workers, employment relations were tenuous. Upon arrival in Canada, the jobs they were promised were often nonexistent, inaccurately described, or short-lived. Consequently, their employment histories were characterized by long bouts of unemployment and poor working conditions at low wages, with the low wages made worse by deductions for transportation, placement in employment, and room and board (Bradwin, 1972: 73–6). Private employment agents acting in the labour market exacerbated the uneven pattern of employment, especially among male migrants and immigrants, through their methods of recruitment and placement. Given that employment relationships involving private, profit-driven employment agents represent the early precursors to the contemporary TER, it is instructive to probe the activities of these labour market actors and how they prefigured the evolution of the private employment agency industry.[6]

There were two main types of private fee-charging employment agents operating on the labour market in the early 1900s: the general labour agency, which operated for a fee and confined its business to the exchange of labour, and the padrones, who made their business furnishing gangs of workmen to an employer for a set fee.[7] According to an early North American study of employment agents and agencies, both types of agencies placed contract labourers, general labourers, miners, lumbermen, brick makers, railroad hands, cattlemen, farm-hands, and cattle labourers during this era (Kellor, 1915). However, while some general agencies recruited workers from abroad, the majority recruited workers domestically, catering to businesses in a wide range of sectors in both urban centres and rural areas. In contrast, the padrones drew labourers from a specific country, region, or ethnic background. Normally, they had strong ties with sending agents in local labour markets in countries such as Italy and Greece, transportation companies such as steamship companies operating across the Atlantic, and railway companies operating in Canada; they often used ties based on ethnicity and nationality to cultivate and solidify complex labour-contracting chains.

Although there was considerable evidence of abuse among both types of private employment agents internationally, it was the padrone system that was the initial target of government investigation in both Canada and the United States, even though their practices and those of general labour agencies were often indistinguishable.[8] However, it was the unsavoury image of the padrone, which undoubtedly reflected the racialized characterization of this type of private employment agent as a 'foreigner' involved in recruiting and placing other 'foreigners,' which led to their menacing public image in North America in the early twentieth century. Employing the highly racialized nationalist discourse of the period, Frances Kellor (1915: 184–5) noted,

> The padrone, that most vicious anti-American institution among the foreign workmen to-day, still flourish. Their stronghold is the labour camp, the general contractor is their backer ... The padrone, who used only to deal with countrymen form his home town or province, now has a compre-

hensive system for getting all of his countrymen. He frequently has men on the other side who 'drum up trade' and who consign laborers to him like so many bales of hay. He is frequently the only man that they know in America, their only friend when they arrive, and they are to him so many shares of stock out of which he must squeeze the utmost profit. When the immigrant does not come addressed to his care he has runners and others who keep in touch with his fellow laborers ... He gets copies of the ships' advices so he knows when and where they land and he has many other methods by which he brings these laborers under his influence [sic].

Eventually, general labour agencies also became subject to state scrutiny. But the appearance and spread of the padrone system spurred the earliest reaction from the government due to the outcry in immigrant communities. Growing discontent in the Italian community in the early 1900s led the federal government to establish, in 1905, a *Royal Commission Appointed to Inquire into the Immigration of Italian Labourers to Montreal and the Alleged Fraudulent Practices of Employment Agencies*, which made piercing criticisms of the private employment agency industry as a whole and generated the first coordinated campaign aimed at its regulation in Canada.[9]

In the early twentieth century, the city of Montreal was the hub of the Canadian padrone system, where the 'King of Italian Labour,' Antonio Cordasco, first became famous (and then infamous) for his business practices involving the recruitment of male Italian workers for seasonal labour in the construction trade (Canada, May 1906: 295–6; *Labour Gazette*, November 1907: 212).[10] While press reports indicate that Cordasco was one of the best-known padrones in Canada in this period, he worked in a fiercely competitive local labour market, where his direct competitors (especially his primary competitor, Antonio Dini) spearheaded his downfall. As Robert Harney (1979: 58–9) suggests, 'Cordasco's career and the public assault upon him affords us a rare entry into the world of the *padrone*, the exploitative Italian brokers who were stock – but little understood – villains in the drama of immigration.' To this I would add that it was the burgeoning 'commerce of migration' at the turn of the century that publicized the coercive activities of private employment agents like Cordasco.

In this period there was a convergence between employers' desperate need for labourers (particularly in industries like construction, mining and smelting), xenophobic Canadian immigration policies such as the *Alien Labour Act* of 1897, and rising rates of unemployment internationally. This combination of factors initially led many Canadian firms to circumvent immigration policy and other legislative measures and to enlist the assistance of either private agents engaged by steamship and railway companies or padrones to transport migrants and immigrants in order to furnish them with a consistent supply of workers.

Tracing the rise and fall of padrones like Cordasco and lesser-known general labour agents operating under false pretenses in countries like Britain, exposes the host of abuses perpetuated by labour market intermediaries (Canada, May 1906: 295). Cordasco's well-known case contributed to widespread documentation of the activities of labour market intermediaries and later led to the criminalization of a number of practices. After Cordasco's activities became public, the *Labour Gazette* provided graphic reports of common abuses among labour market intermediaries of all sorts across Canada at the turn of the century (see, for example, *Labour Gazette*, June 1906: 1346–51; November 1907: 212; February 1908: 1024, 1026, March 1908: 1161–2, 1165). These reports indicate that, with rising rates of unemployment, a rapidly expanding group of Canadian-born workers also resorted to labour market intermediaries even though private employment agents primarily targeted recent immigrants. Interestingly, ill-treated workers themselves, whether Canadian-born or immigrant, rarely used the court system to charge the customers of early private employment agencies with committing abuses, thereby blurring the existence of the complex labour contracting relationships. However, the focus on the unfair labour practices of padrones and other disreputable employment agents, driven by the racialized discourses surrounding their image as 'foreigners' apparent in the *Royal Commission appointed to inquire into the Immigration of Italian Labourers to Montreal*, reports in the *Labour Gazette*, and the xenophobic views of labour leaders led federal and provincial governments to shape legislation to target the private employment agent industry as a whole. In turn, workers themselves, as well as representatives of the Crown, began to take private employment agents to court for failure to pay wages, making false representations, and many other abuses.

While abuses also included collusion and extortion, the most widely documented abuses surrounded the issue of misrepresentation, ranging from false promises of work to misleading advertisements that often distorted the position of the agent. Agents advertising abroad often provided inaccurate descriptions of available work, misrepresented the duration (i.e., permanency) of available work, and falsely communicated rates of pay. Many also falsely indicated that 'no fees' to workers, either direct or indirect, were involved in the transaction. With respect to conditions of work, one advertisement by Cordasco in a prominent Italian newspaper in Montreal, which was 'sent in large quantities for distribution in Italy,' read as follows:

A. Cordasco
Sole Italian Agent of the Canadian Pacific Ry. Co. and other Companies
441 St. James St., Montreal

NOTICE

Do you want to be employed in the Railway Works, Water Works and other kinds of work, – last long time and guaranteed – payment sure – at the price of $1.25 to $2.00? Do you want to be respected and protected either on the work or in case of accident or other annoyances, which may be easily met? Apply personally or address letters or telegrams to: Antonio Cordasco, 441 St. James St., Montreal.

Sole agent who will find every security, and guarantee employment for labourers and foremen who know how to do their duty. He is fully trusted by all the greatest companies and contractors who continually request his services. Whoever has claims against any company, Mr Cordasco is the only man who can succeed to have the satisfaction of the said claims made with profit and promptitude. (*Labour Gazette*, June 1906: 1349)

Here, Cordasco appeals to both Italian immigrants in Canada and abroad, claiming to be the 'sole' employment agent of the Canadian Pacific Railway. His advertisement makes a promise of work without specifically indicating the positions available, and it inflates wages.[11] Cordasco used community newspapers to convey the image that he was a man of great power and influence in Canada. He also used celebrations for his workers to legitimize his business,[12] and provided stamped and sealed envelopes, containing literature promoting his services, to his workers, and required them to send these letters to their families and friends abroad (*Labour Gazette*, June 1906: 1349).

In some serious cases of misrepresentation, private employment agents or agencies were found to have inaccurately depicted the nature of the work available. In many of these cases, collusion was very clearly a factor but there were few mechanisms for penalizing customers and private employment agencies together (i.e., for collusion) in either the provincial or federal legislation that regulated private employment agencies.

For example, in November 1906 two newspaper reporters visited the New Method Employment Bureau, a general labour agency in Toronto. First, one went to ask for a position, paid a registration fee of one dollar, and was sent to a firm on Wellington Street to take up a bookkeeper's job, however, upon arrival for work he was told that the position had been filled. One week later, the other reporter went to the Bureau and specifically requested a bookkeeping position. He paid the one-dollar fee and was sent to the same Wellington Street firm, which again did not have an opening (*Labour Gazette*, March 1908: 1162). In this type of case, one of many reported in the *Labour Gazette*, the agent and the employer colluded to collect fees for fictitious jobs. Consequently, in early court cases, several judges deemed that fees were only acceptable if the workers remained in employment for a reasonable duration (*Labour Gazette*, May 1909: 1272).[13] Similarly, when found guilty of abusive practices, early employment agents were often convicted of fraud if they gave positions to the highest bidder, a common practice in the early part of the century (*Labour Gazette*, February 1908: 1026).

Early National Opposition to Private Employment Agencies

Beyond the many individual workers and/or workers' organizations that eventually took private employment agents to court, other interest groups also objected vocally to the underhanded practices of private employment agents, particularly those involved in importing 'foreign' labour. Two groups, with seemingly conflicting goals, took the lead in initiating complaints against padrones and other private employment agents/agencies. One was the Trades and Labour Congress, which first deployed highly racialized nation-building discourses in objecting to the importation of 'alien' workers. In the decade between 1900 and 1910, the congress and its provincial executives lobbied the federal government to enforce the *Alien Labour Act* of 1897 and to prevent the importation of 'alien' labour by railway, steamship, and mining companies. The congress' opposition to private employment agents acting abroad was most fierce under President Ralph Smith (1900–1902). Smith, once leader of the Independent Mineworkers' Union, which vehemently opposed the use of immigrant workers as strike-breakers, later became a Member of Parliament (MP) representing Vancouver (Mouat 1995: 93–6). Under Smith, the congress lobbied for amendments to the act, including the right 'to sue for the infringement of the Act by any person,' and for the Department of Labour to 'assume the deportation of aliens rather than the recovery of a fine' (*Labour Gazette*, 1901: 213; Mouat, 1995: 86–7). In 1901 Smith even went so far as to state that what organized labour wanted was 'an anti-contract law of general application – a law prohibiting as well as voiding the importation under contract, from any country, of labourers of any kind' (*Labour Gazette*, 1901: 213). Alongside its call for the effective enforcement of the 1897's *Alien Labour Act*, the congress opposed the government's increase of the Chinese head tax from $50 to $100. Accordingly, Smith noted in October 1900: 'I do not think that this will accomplish much good, but *will serve only to increase the bonds* of these Chinese whose admission fee is paid by the Chinese Companies, and as this has to be returned out of their wages it only results in *enslaving* them for a longer period' [my emphasis]. (*Labour Gazette*, October 1900: 213). Smith objected to the importation of Chinese labourers and felt that an increase in the Chinese head tax would not serve to limit the influx of 'foreign' workers to Canada. His comments, on the one hand, reflected an anti-foreigner sentiment (specifically an anti-Chinese sentiment) common among leaders of the congress and the congress' more general objective of limiting immigration in the context of high unemployment.[14] On the other hand, he was also objecting to the servile conditions of employment that Chinese workers were being forced to endure in Canada, and the undesirable precedent that it set for Canadian-born workers. Smith thus called on the then Liberal federal government to be accountable to liberal principles and eliminate forms of unfree labour in Canada.

The other group that lobbied actively for regulation was primarily composed of representatives from the Italian immigrant community, who objected to the racialized nation-building discourses and their effect on communities of immigrants (Avery, 1995; *Labour Gazette*, October 1900, 1901, 1904; Ramirez, 1991: 98–109). The Italian community of Montreal did not side with the Trades and Labour Congress on limiting the immigration of workers from abroad. But as Ramirez (1991: 108) notes, after encountering the elaborate mechanisms of exploitation used by padrones, many Italian immigrants 'who in their own native villages had rarely raised their voice against an exploiting *galantuomo*, in the Canadian city drew up civil suits and took *padrones* to court.' Subsequently, many became vocal proponents of a genuinely open-door immigration policy. For example, a number of Italian immigrants sued Antonio Cordasco and the Canadian Pacific Railway for failure to pay wages, collusion, and other illegal practices, spurring the creation of the *Royal Commission appointed to inquire into the Immigration of Italian Labourers to*

Montreal. When the commission undertook its investigation in 1904, many of these same people took the witness-stand, pointing to padrones and other labour agents like Cordasco and calling for their punishment (Avery, 1995: 38–9; Harney, 1979; Ramirez, 1991).[15]

With the growing number of reports documenting abuses by private employment agents and dramatic calls for state intervention from the organized labour movement and immigrant communities, government officials began to raise concerns about the agents' activities. Leading MPs, some of whom had roots in the labour movement, opposed an unregulated private recruitment and placement system. Aiming to hold the Laurier government accountable to its principles, they articulated their concerns on three grounds in House of Commons Debates in 1905 and 1906.[16] First, they expressed concern about how the practices of private employment agents acting abroad contributed to damaging Canada's reputation internationally. MPs were especially disturbed by the private employment agents' attempts to depict themselves as representatives of government, either through using the national coat of arms on their official letterhead, locating their business offices in the same buildings as government offices, or even falsely claiming to be government officials (Canada, May 1906: 2955–6). In the words of Ralph Smith, this false representation led many immigrants to come to Canada 'believing in a way that they were coming under some sort of royal protection' (2956). Second, many MPs feared that these agents were not communicating the official employment needs of the country (i.e., attracting permanent agricultural settlers), and instead were responding to pressure from transportation companies and even attracting 'undesirables' (2958). Third, many MPs and government officials argued that the covert activities of some private employment agencies undermined Canada's 'nation-building' goals. Several also objected to the use of migrant contract workers as strike-breakers (2964).[17] Supporting a motion advanced by Ralph Smith, Minister of Labour A.B. Aylesworth made the following comment: 'We can never expect to build up out of the immigrants from foreign nations a people who will be loyal to our institutions, who will be animated by a proper feeling for their adopted home, or who will be found contented and at peace in the ordinary relations of life if they are settling down in this country under a fixed conviction that they have been brought here under false pretensions and that they have been deceived upon the very vital business considerations which have induced them to come at all' (2964). In the spirit of domestic expansion and improving international channels of communication, Aylesworth went on to propose that ancillary legislation be adopted to regulate the activities of private employment agents acting abroad.

Federal government officials began to reject the quasi-servile status of workers engaged by private employment agencies. Hence, their nation-building concerns and their desire to encourage better labour market practices eventually led them to craft legislation and regulations to curb the employment agents' abuses.

Federal Measures

The federal government used immigration policy as the vehicle for coordinating its initial efforts at regulation. Legislative measures were already in place by the early 1900s in some provinces, such as British Columbia, Manitoba, Ontario, and Quebec, and were useful in crafting immigration regulations at the federal level. From 1905 to 1910 there was intense debate in the House of Commons over the role and function of private employment agencies acting abroad. Debate initially centred on what type of employment agency should have the right to represent Canada overseas. However, as MPs documented the nature of common abuses, the political focus on so-called 'false representations' slowly shifted and expanded. For example, between 1907 and 1909, federal government officials became concerned with specific issues pertaining to fee-charging, licensing, and record-keeping. Consequently, the government enacted basic legislation to protect immigrants against abuses by private employment agents through the *Immigration Act* of 1910 (Sections 55, 56); the provisions in this act included giving the Governor General in Council the power to issue extensive regulations. With the growing consensus that existing legislation was inadequate, the Cabinet of the government issued two important Orders in Council.

On the recommendation of Minister of Labour T.W. Crothers, the Governor General in Council first initiated an Order in Council prescribing regulations for the protection of immigrants seeking employment from companies, firms, persons carrying on the business of intelligence offices, and employment or labour agencies (*RSC*, 1913a). Order in Council No. PC 1028 (April of 1913) was an extremely important measure, since, although it only applied to agents placing immigrants, it set out detailed provisions regulating the conduct of these agents that mirrored and reinforced broader provincial legislation. It required all employment placement businesses dealing with immigrants to obtain non-transferable licenses, keep formal records and limit placement and transportation fees to one dollar. It made written requests from employers detailing wages and the nature of work mandatory. Additionally, it required agencies to post vacancies in several languages and imposed severe fines ($100 or three months imprisonment maximum) for failure to comply with any of the requirements (*RSC*, 1913a). To reinforce the provisions of PC 1028, another Order in Council (PC 1064) extended the provision of fines to *all* persons, firms, companies, intelligence offices, and/or employment agencies not complying with PC 1028 (*RSC*, 1913b).

Despite these new measures for curbing abuses against immigrants, and despite the government's appointment of municipal agents to place agricultural labourers and domestic servants, the press was filled with reports of violations of immigration regulations between 1913 and 1915 (see, for example, *Labour Gazette*, March 1907: 1011–12, May 1914: 1359). The federal government was forced to shift its posture from a largely reactive program designed to quell discontent among organized labour and immigrant communities to a more proactive program aimed at instituting a joint federal-provincial system of public employment offices.

In 1918 the federal government proposed Bill No. 57, the first bill designed to encourage the organization and coordination of employment offices. Although its contents mirrored the *Immigration Act* of 1910 to some extent, they did not duplicate its measures. Still, the House of Commons debates of April 1918 indicate that the impetus for advancing this service came from both the federal and provincial governments' experiences with private employment agents (Canada, 23 April 1918). Since provincial governments were beginning to take responsibility for most labour matters at this time, the federal government opted to address the problem indirectly through initiating a cost- and responsibility-shared public employment service constitutionally. Speaking on behalf of the federal government, T.W. Crothers, who had been responsible for immigration in his previous ministerial post, characterized the general problem of private employment agencies as follows:

> There have been several references to private agencies and to the use that might be made of private labour exchanges. These have not proved themselves satisfactory, generally speaking. One hon. gentleman mentioned some frauds perpetrated upon poor people by some of these agencies which charged them large sums of money. That matter came to our attention four or five years ago when I happened, for the time being, to be in the Department of the Interior. We made regulations then governing all these

private agencies so far as their treatment of immigrants went. *We had no authority to deal with them in any other respect. We cannot abolish them* [my emphasis]. (Canada, 23 April 1918: 1039)

Crothers further indicated that, although Bill No. 57 did not address private employment agents directly, it did attempt to 'facilitate the means of getting the employer and the employee together,' and hence to lessen the power of private employment agents (1039).

After Bill No. 57 passed, the federal government began to institute a public employment service in Canada. Regulations aimed at minimizing abuse among private employment agents acting abroad remained in force, but after 1926, when the federal government reviewed its regulatory role and the Privy Council declared labour a provincial matter, the government relinquished its remaining powers over the conduct of private employment agencies to the provinces.

Provincial and Municipal Measures

As noted above, several provincial governments already had experience regulating private employment agents. There were approximately one hundred agencies in the Dominion by 1903. Of these, twenty-eight belonged to provincial or municipal governments operating free of charge, five were run free of charge either through municipal funds, charitable funds, or labour organizations, and the rest were private employment agencies (*Labour Gazette*, September 1904: 262–4).[18]

Since many private employment agencies had their roots in the period before the formation of the Dominion, municipal by-laws predated provincial legislation. In the case of the Municipality of Toronto, the local government first required private employment agencies to be licensed in 1897, and then, through the *Consolidated Municipal Act*, established the principle of fee-fixing in 1903.[19] It was not until 1914 that the government of Ontario took on the role of regulating employment agencies. Similarly, municipal legislation predated provincial legislation in Quebec, where so-called 'intelligence offices,' a general term which included public, private, and voluntary employment agencies, were first regulated in 1903 under *An Act Respecting Cities and Towns*. This act gave municipal councils the power 'to license and regulate keepers of intelligence offices, and all persons doing the business of seeking employment for or furnishing employees to others and to require such persons to keep registers of their transactions, to make reports thereof' (*RSC*, 1903: 3004).

From 1897 forward, the priority issues of regulation were similar in most provinces. Consequently, while noting key differences between the relevant provinces, it is sufficient to specify the evolution of regulations in the Province of Ontario, since this province has the longest history of coordinated measures in Canada.

The first official version of the Ontario *Employment Agencies Act* of 1914 defined employment agencies as businesses devoted to 'procuring for a fee or reward workmen, artificers, labourers, domestic servants and other persons for the performance of skilled or unskilled labour' and to 'procuring for a fee or reward employment for any class of workmen, artificers, labourers, domestic servants and other persons' (*RSO*, 1914: 231). Thus, the act was designed to regulate two types of private place-ment services, one geared to placing the worker for a fee and the other aimed at satisfying the demands of employers for a fee.[20] This act was precedent-setting on several grounds. It identified those businesses whose activities focused exclusively on securing workers on the basis of em-ployer demand as employment agencies. In addition, it defined 'fees' very broadly to extend beyond monetary forms of remuneration.[21] It also made a crucial distinction between direct and indirect fees, which eventually became the central feature differentiating between temporary and permanent placement, and subsequently the private employment agency business and the THI. In 1917, when the provincial government first revised the *Employment Agencies Act*, both these precedents remained. The only substantive change was that the act now governed the activities of public and voluntary employment services as well as private employ-ment agencies (*RSO*, 1917: 219). This amendment, which seemed rather benign at the time, set the stage for important changes in the next set of revisions.

In 1927 the province introduced legislation that enabled the Lieuten-ant-Governor in Council both to prohibit 'the granting of licenses to any class of employment agency' and to 'limit the class of business which may be carried out by any employment agency' (*RSO*, 1927: 431). Signaling serious concerns on the part of the province about the practices of labour market intermediaries, these measures had a disciplining effect even though the Lieutenant-Governor-in-Council never invoked his power to ban employment agencies.[22]

In this period, most provinces considered the regulation of direct and indirect fees to workers, as well as licensing and detailed recording-keeping, to be the central areas of concern. Modeled on the approach of Ontario, many also addressed the role of both the employment agent/

agency and the customer in the transaction, placing checks on fee-splitting between the agent and the customer and attempting to enforce the employment-related responsibilities of the customer. As well, by classifying business relationships whereby employment agents provided their own labourers for a fee (i.e., labour contracting) as a part of the private employment agency business, provincial employment agency acts also slowly began to recognize and place checks on employment relationships where responsibility did not rest with a single entity. Thus, the provincial legislators involved in crafting these regulations had a comprehensive understanding of the expanding scope of the private employment agency industry.

There is considerable evidence that provincial legislation not only contributed to framing the federal government's rather brief foray into regulation but also affected international debates and developments. At the provincial level, this period culminated with a strong push for prohibition prompted by the widespread documentation of abuses, rising unemployment rates, and organized labour's call for a national public employment service. However, there is little evidence to suggest that the *Employment Agency Act* (1927) of Ontario, or even similar legislation in Quebec, which clearly supported prohibition for a lengthy period, eliminated abuses on a substantial scale. There has always been a high demand for day labourers and other types of temporary workers in Canada and in other advanced capitalist welfare states, one which is often met by intermediaries operating at the fringes of the labour market. To some extent, federal legislation devised in early twentieth-century Canada curbed abuses common among employment agents acting abroad, and/or those targeting recent immigrants to Canada, but many disreputable labour market actors survived this era. Provincial legislation nevertheless contributed to limiting the exploitative activities of the more reputable private employment agencies by undermining their ability to charge exorbitant fees to workers and by forcing them to adapt to a changed regulatory environment.

By the mid-1920s, the regulation of private employment agencies fell almost entirely out of the federal domain, with the provinces taking up virtually all the responsibility for regulation. Still, the federal government took an active role in creating a public employment service in Canada, partly in response to problems generated by private employment agencies.[23] Simultaneously, provincial measures aimed at regulating private employment agencies reflected the direction of international regulation (ILO, 1932).

Regulatory Interventions at the International Level

Approximately a decade after Canada began to devise national measures to protect immigrants engaged by private employment agents, and nearly three decades after the Municipality of Toronto enacted regulations covering private employment agencies, the issue of curbing abuses among private employment agencies became a central focus of international discussion (ILO, 1932, 1933a, 1933b). Chapter 1 notes the history of international debates over the role and function of private employment agencies dates to the Treaty of Versailles and the subsequent formation of the ILO in 1919 (ILO, 1923: 409–11, 1997a: 6).

Part XIII of the Treaty of Versailles entrenched the Workers' Clauses, including freedom of association, the eight-hour workday, weekly rest, the abolition of child labour, equal remuneration for work of equal value, and the maxim that 'labour is not a commodity,' and the ILO was named guardian of these principles upon its inception (ILO, 1994a: 4–5). Thereafter, 'labour is not a commodity' became an important theme internationally after various states, including Canada, began to address problems related to the conduct of private employment agencies. Devised during a period of tremendous economic and social turmoil, this maxim led the ILO to initiate a policy at its first conference that states should 'establish a system of free public employment agencies under the control of a central authority' (ILO, 1923: 471). ILO officials interpreted the maxim 'labour is not a commodity' quite literally to mean that placing workers should not be a commercial activity, even though the general sentiment behind it is that the price of labour power should not be determined solely by market forces. Therefore, the organization promoted the establishment of free public employment services administered and controlled by member states under Unemployment Convention No. 2 and Unemployment Recommendation No. 1. Both Convention No. 2 and Recommendation No.1, which the Canadian government supported, were adopted alongside conventions on the eight-hour workday, the institution of unemployment insurance schemes, and protective legislation for women and children, in October 1919 in Washington (ILO, 1992a: 358–9). These conventions not only made a clear link between the activities of private employment agents and immigration, they also urged member states to take measures towards achieving the prohibition of employment agencies which charge fees or which carry out their business for profit (ILO, 1923: 419–20; 1992a: 358, 420).

Despite early efforts aimed at coordinating regulation internationally, the ILO did not take direct action on the issue of private employment agencies until October 1930, when its governing body successfully proposed to place the question of the abolition of fee-charging employment agencies on the agenda of the Sixteenth International Labour Conference in 1932. Delegates at the conference made a connection between private employment agents and the international economic crisis. Various spokespeople noted that, although private employment agents were not the cause of the crisis, high rates of unemployment were contributing to conditions where abuse thrived amongst labour market intermediaries of various sorts (*Labour Gazette*, May 1932: 562). Therefore, measures designed to encourage the establishment of public employment services had the potential to contribute to alleviating the economic crisis. These delegates' remarks echoed a report by the bureaucratic arm of the ILO, the International Labour Office (ILO 1933b), which argued that public placement should be viewed both as a measure against unemployment and a move to organize the labour market to avoid economic crises in the future.

In the context of these discussions, and what the ILO called 'the march of the depression,' the conference debated how to regulate fee-charging private employment agencies. An important concern was whether the definition of fee-charging employment agencies should exclude commercial employment agencies charging fees to employers. The eventual conclusion supporting their inclusion was a crucial one. The conference also agreed on the need to regulate private agencies carrying on recruitment and placement activities between nations (*Labour Gazette*, May 1932: 572). Indeed, even with the deepening economic crisis and limited financial resources of emerging welfare states, an overwhelming number of member states favoured the creation of a general framework aimed at prohibition with a view to creating free public employment services. Notable exceptions were Britain, Canada, and the United States, which opposed the adoption of a framework aimed at complete prohibition because it contravened existing national legislation. In the case of Canada, some provincial legislation offered prohibition as one among several regulatory options, but the federal government was unwilling to support the creation of an international labour convention requiring provinces to comply with full-scale prohibition (*Labour Gazette*, June 1935). Despite the objections of countries like Canada, the Seventeenth International Labour Conference (ILO, 1933a) adopted a draft convention providing for the abolition of fee-charging employment agencies conducted with a view to profit by a vote of ninety-one to twenty. It also passed a draft recommendation, by a vote of ninety-two to seven, concerning various matters subsidiary to the convention, including 'the adaptation of free public employment agencies to suit the needs of occupations relying on fee-charging agencies' (*Labour Gazette*, August 1933: 787; ILO, 1992a, art. 1.2).

Nine years after the Province of Ontario granted the Lieutenant-Governor in Council the discretionary power to prohibit private employment agencies, the ILO Convention Concerning Fee-Charging Employment Agencies (No. 34) was born, the first international labour convention to deal exclusively with the role and function of private employment agencies. In the end, only eleven nations ratified Convention No. 34, due to its unequivocal call for prohibition. Still, this instrument created a framework for categorizing, monitoring, and regulating the activities of private employment agencies that influenced many countries as well as various provincial and territorial jurisdictions within Canada in developing further regulations. The convention also set the course for future initiatives at an international level by establishing a formal definition of so-called 'fee-charging employment agencies,' identifying criteria for exemptions, setting regulations for all employment agencies not conducted with a view to profit, and, most notably, helping to create an international regulatory environment where prohibition was viewed as the primary long-term objective (ILO, 1992a, arts. 2, 3: 145–6).

Convention No. 34 dictated that fee-charging employment agencies covered a wide range of labour market actors, including '... any person, company, institution, agency or any other organization which acts as an intermediary for the purposes of procuring employment for a worker or supplying a worker for an employer with a view to deriving either directly or indirectly any pecuniary or other material advantage from either the employer or the worker' (ILO, 1992a, art. 1: 145). It thus covered all profit-driven labour market intermediaries involved at every stage of the recruitment and placement process, and, as future debates would demonstrate, it also covered profit-driven intermediaries involved in the employment relationship itself.[24] Many of the exemptions deemed acceptable under the convention consisted of private employment agents representing artists, musicians, and other professionals requiring representation by private agents. Undeniably, however, the most important feature of Convention No. 34 was its goal of gradually achieving prohibition. While it offered member states various options for exemption, the overriding goal of Convention No. 34 was to prevent ratifying states from permitting the establishment of new private employment agencies operating for profit, and to encourage them to replace private employment agencies with public employment services (ILO, 1992a, art. 2: 145).

In this way, efforts to curb abuses by private employment agencies accelerated rapidly at an international level in the 1930s, ushering in a period when the ILO supported prohibition and/or strict regulation, a period that first reflected developments in Canada but subsequently went beyond measures adopted at the federal, provincial, and municipal levels. Few cases of abuse were documented in either the national or international press by the 1930s. Moreover, while charges of misrepresentation against private employment agencies had plagued the period from the turn of the century to the early 1920s, it was only in 1933, with the adoption of Convention No. 34, that the private employment agency industry began to be adversely affected internationally. As a result, the industry began to rebuild its image, based, among other models, on the successes of a small group of private employment agencies catering to the office sector, which managed to escape regulation at the national level in the second and third decades of the century.

Efforts to Escape Regulation in Canada

By the second decade of the century, both federal and provincial legislators in Canada, as well as the popular media, had identified several common criteria for the regulation of private employment agencies, criteria similar to those eventually embraced by the international community. There was a consensus that fees to workers should either be prohibited or strictly regulated, private employment agents should be required to keep extensive records, and that exemptions should only be possible in sectors such as the arts. Simultaneously, the government identified public employment services as the most suitable alternative to the private employment agency industry, a development that was central to the rise of the SER. In this context, the private employment agency industry faced such a formidable set of challenges to its legitimacy that it was forced to rethink what type of customers to target and which groups of workers to recruit and place in employment.

Forerunners of the THI [25]

While there is little evidence of a coordinated industry-wide strategy, a small but cohesive group of private employment agencies run by type-

TABLE 6
Leading Occupations for Women, 1921

Occupation	Numbers
Clerical	78,342
Servant	78,118
Teacher	49,795
Saleswoman	35,474
Housekeeper	23,167
Nurse	21,162
Dressmaker/seamstress	16,612
Farmer	16,315
Textile factory operative	15,193
Clothing factory operative	14,470

Source: L. Kealey (ed.), Women at
Work, 1850–1930, (Toronto: Women's
Educational Press, 1974), 267.

writer companies began to target customers in the burgeoning clerical
sector in Ontario as early as 1914–15, and thrived for decades thereafter.
These agencies surfaced in a period when clerical work vied with domestic service as the leading occupation for women and these agencies
capitalized on such employment trends (Table 6). Thus, in spite of their
limited numbers, these agencies were central precursors to the THI
because of their focus on the clerical sector and the group of workers
they engaged. On the demand side, the success of employment agencies
run by typewriter firms related to employers' desperate need for workers
who could operate new machinery properly. On the supply side, these
agencies had access to a large pool of young women who were largely
Canadian-born [26] and generally well-educated.

The ideology of the domesticity and growing restrictions on women's
employment in both the public and private sector, evidenced by the
movement towards categorizing all married women in the Federal Public Service as 'temporary' late in the second decade of the century
(regardless of the length of their job tenure), contributed to this surplus
(Hodgetts et al., 1972; Morgan, 1988). Indeed, dominant ideologies of
the day made targeting this group of workers acceptable because they
were perceived to have a weak attachment to the labour market. In the
provincial context, employment agencies operated by typewriter companies were most successful in urban centres such as Toronto.

In the century's second decade, Canadian women experienced high
rates of unemployment, particularly in nursing but also in clerical work;

domestic work was the only category of female employment that was virtually unaffected during this difficult economic period. As a consequence of these employment trends, a group of private employment agencies run by typewriter companies intervened to take advantage of the imbalance between supply and demand, with the intention of training women typists and stenographers and helping them find employment. As Graham Lowe (1987: 78) remarks: 'the oversupply of certain kinds of typists and stenographers, at various times during the second and third decades, prompted employment agencies to inject some order into the market. The typewriter firms not only had a vested interest in marketing machines, *but also the women who could effectively operate them*' [my emphasis]. As a result, these firms contributed to creating and standardizing a large female secondary labour force in clerical work (Lowe, 1980, 1987). What is less known, and especially significant for this inquiry, is that they also crafted an employment relationship that served as a template for the THI. Although these firms operated for profit, the provincial government credited them with limiting unemployment among stenographers and typists as well as women in general, a stamp of approval that increased the firms' legitimacy.

At the outset of this period, voluntary employment agencies run by philanthropic women's organizations such as the Toronto Women's Patriotic League Employment Bureau determined that clerical occupations were overcrowded and they called on unemployed women to engage in paid domestic work. However, as stated in the *Report of the Ontario Commission on Unemployment*, private employment agencies run by typewriting companies offered a more nuanced explanation of the employment situation in the clerical sector. In their view, the occupation was replete with 'young, inefficient, poorly trained workers' and thus the logical solution was simply to 'provide training' (Wilgress, 1916: 181). With this rationale, typewriter companies backed by business schools entered into the private employment agency industry in significant numbers arguing that 'three years at a Secondary School is too short a time to fit a girl to become an efficient stenographer ... The standard spoken of as desirable in order to secure the best advantages for the occupation is university matriculation, or three years in a high school, and nine months' or a year's training in a business college' (182). Linking up to local business women's clubs, typewriter companies targeted young, relatively well-educated women seeking opportunities for study, 'outings,' 'social enjoyment,' and 'social improvement.' Thus, the Ontario Commission on Unemployment claimed that employment agencies run by typewriter companies standardized clerical employment as no other women's employment had been standardized, with the exception of nursing.

Catering largely to clients in Toronto, two private employment agencies run by typewriting companies dominated this segment of the labour market in Ontario by 1914. One of these agencies filled approximately 6,000 positions per year, 40 per cent permanent and 60 per cent temporary, and the other filled 1,200 to 1,500 positions per year, 25 per cent permanent and 75 per cent temporary. Moreover, the *Report of the Ontario Commission on Unemployment* noted, '[t]he work of these agencies is so thorough that a stenographer, if she prefers, can keep employed constantly in temporary work' (Wilgress, 1916: 182). Hence, as early as 1916, temporary help work through private employment agencies was defined less by duration and more by shifting sites of employment and employer demands. However, the type of employment relationships that the stenographers of this period engaged in contrasts with the contemporary TER in several respects. While this segment of the private employment agency industry was client-driven, employment agencies run by typewriter companies ostensibly employed stenographers and typists to sell their equipment. They did not extract a direct fee from customers for the services of their workers. Nor did stenographers or typists normally pay fees to register with employment agencies run by typewriter companies. Rather, women stenographers attempted to sell typewriters and/or equipment on behalf of the companies that secured their employment (182). Reporting on the creative marketing and employment tactics of these companies, the Ontario Commission on Unemployment noted that in one employment agency office a large sign read 'Whose bread I eat, His song I sing,' indicating that stenographers were expected to contribute to the success of the company by promoting their products (183).

The typewriter company employment agencies took on the role of placing stenographers and 'office girls' in 'well-thought-of' employment. Consequently, the agencies had significant control over the type of workers who filled the clerical labour market and sold their products (Wilgress, 1916: 182). The primary means through which these agencies attained control was by requiring business school training and testing and providing workers with the opportunity to practice and improve their clerical skills 'free of charge' on their machines. As well, the agencies exercised indirect control over both the behaviour and appearance of stenographers by constructing an image of the successful stenographer. As the Ontario Commission on Unemployment reported, '[t]he appearance of the stenographer is in her favour; she has to dress well, in good taste and neatly if not smartly, and this is not without a good effect on her character and work' (183). These agencies also tended to engage women fresh out of high school, when presumably their skills and physical appearance were at their peak. However, these firms did make some exceptions. For example, 'if a woman retain[ed] elasticity' she would not lose her work in this occupation on account of her age or marital status (184).

Reflecting the ideology of domesticity, the *Report of the Ontario Commission on Unemployment* listed high standards of health and the stenographer's ability to remain at home with her family prior to marriage as the chief benefits of working through employment agencies run by typewriter companies. As well, this form of employment was said to encourage good housekeeping skills and teach women the value of money: 'Like all other girls, it is said of the office girl that she lacks knowledge of what to eat, what to wear and of how to keep herself in health; also that more knowledge of the value of money, how to spend, and how to save would be an advantage to her' (Wilgress, 1916: 183). According to the report, the only noted disadvantages of this kind of work were that offices might be poorly lit or the machines run down. The type of worker perceived to encounter the most difficulty was the untrained stenographer. For this reason, by 1914 employment agencies operated by typewriter companies began to train and place 'girls who have taken typing but are misfit stenographers' in forms of clerical work perceived to require fewer skills for lower wages (184). This move corresponded to growing stratification within the clerical labour market (Lowe, 1987). But it also signaled the potential for extending the type of employment relationships common to women stenographers and typists to other sectors and occupations, especially given the unprecedented degree of legitimacy attained by these private employment agencies in this period.

As illustrated by the remarks of the Ontario Commission on Unemployment, government officials, organized labour, and social reformers did not view employment agencies operated by typewriter companies as either a threat to Canada's nation-building aims or improved labour market practices. Nor were these firms seen as tarnished labour market intermediaries since they did not charge visible fees and since the stenographers and typists were not only female, but young, well-educated, and largely Canadian-born. Their ties with business colleges and philanthropic women's organizations also enhanced the reputation of this segment of the private employment agency industry. As a result these agencies escaped regulation under 1914's *Employment Agencies Act of Ontario* for the bulk of this period.[27] The only recommendations for improvement offered by the Ontario Commission on Unemployment were mandatory licensing for business colleges and uniform testing among employment agencies run by typewriter companies, neither of which were ever implemented by provincial legislators. Thus, because these agencies thrived in Ontario at a time when many private employment agencies faced strict regulation, they offered a model upon which the private employment agency industry could construct the TER and later cement the THI.

Conclusion

Tracing the roots of the contemporary Canadian THI to private employment agents operating in the labour market in the late nineteenth and early twentieth centuries offers several insights into the shape of the early precursors and the immediate forerunners to the contemporary TER. It illustrates that many workers, particularly immigrant and migrant workers, engaged by private employment agents at the turn of the century, resembled unfree wage labourers since they lacked the same kind of civil, legal, and political rights of Canadian-born workers. As well, this historical investigation provides a conceptual link between early private employment agents, such as padrones and general labour agents, and the more reputable employment agencies run by typewriter companies. The latter negotiated a 'new' image for the private employment agency industry, beginning around 1910, bolstered by the approval of entities like the Ontario Commission on Unemployment, and in so doing offered a template for the creation of the THI as well as for the employment relationship upon which it was based.

Many immigrant and migrant workers engaged by private employment agents in the late nineteenth century came to Canada under false pretenses to perform work that was undesirable to the permanent settler population. Some were unable to circulate freely within the labour market, if only for a finite period, upon their arrival. For these workers, including the many male agricultural and industrial workers arriving in Canada in the early decades of the twentieth century but also a considerable group of immigrant women domestic workers, the inability to move about freely in the labour market often came as a result of contracts signed outside of Canada and debts to steamship and/or railway companies incurred from assisted passage and cash advances. If the workers refused to perform the tasks prescribed by private employment agents, they could be subject to state-sanctioned deportation carried out by the very railway and steamship agents that had transported them to Canada (Roberts, 1988).

In response to harsh criticisms from labour leaders and immigrant workers, as well as to scathing government reports, federal and provincial governments began to regulate private employment agents' activities around the turn of the century. Even though their explicit demands amounted to calls for the regulation of these agencies and the establishment of free public employment services, the implicit common goal behind the lobbying efforts of organized labour, immigrant communities, and some social reformers was tied to bringing the SER into being. Subsequently, emulating various regulatory models operating at the national level, including those existing in Canada, the ILO crafted a framework aimed at the gradual prohibition of private employment agencies internationally, one that built on the maxim 'labour is not a commodity.'

In spite of the new national regulatory regime in Canada, a number of employment agencies managed to evade regulation. Agencies, such as those operated by typewriter companies, distanced themselves from the most disreputable segments of the private employment agency industry by adopting a strategy that made them exempt from coverage under provincial legislation, thereby earning approval from various organizations and institutions. They escaped formal regulation and the threat of prohibition at the provincial level by not charging direct fees and by acting as employers. Their strategy was particularly successful due to the well-defined group of women workers that they recruited. While the federal government enacted legislation to protect immigrants engaged by private employment agents as early as 1897, in the *Alien Labour Act*, young, well-educated, middle-class Canadian-born women working for employment agencies owned by typewriting companies were left unprotected due to the dominant ideologies of the day. Moreover, agencies operated by typewriter companies did not come under attack from organized labour, social reformers, or immigrant communities for a similar set of reasons. The incremental rise of the SER, sustained in part by the gradual emergence of a free public employment service also worked in the favour of typewriter firms since employers still demanded a secondary labour force.

The use of immigrant and migrant workers by the private employment agents at the turn of the century, and the use of stenographers and typists by private employment agencies run by typewriter firms a decade or so later, reflect the two distinct means by which the private employment agency industry negotiated two very different regulatory environments. These contrasting pictures are also the product of the nature of the contracts between immigrant workers and early private employment agents, which tended to involve more rigid terms and conditions limiting their mobility in the labour market, versus the nature of the employment relationship between stenographers and typists and employment agencies run by typewriter firms, which did not need to set out to confine workers in a similar manner. Still, there are important connections between the immigrant and migrant workers recruited and placed by private employment agents at the turn of the century and the women workers engaged by employment agencies run by typewriting firms. First, both sets of workers engaged in employment relationships where intermediaries played central and often ongoing roles. Second, the success of the labour market intermediaries that placed these two distinct groups of workers rested largely on the fact that their wages did not provide for their own social reproduction let alone that of their dependents: immigrant and migrant workers' cost of social reproduction was borne largely by the sending economy, and Canadian-born women were presumed to have access to subsistence through a male wage.

At the outset of the period between 1897 and 1933, the transition to a modern labour market was just beginning in Canada; coercive activities were more the norm than the exception, allowing private employment agents to deploy highly racialized and gender-specific nation-building discourses in drawing on quasi-servile migrant and immigrant labourers. By the end of the period, due to the successful struggles of labour leaders, immigrant workers, and some actors within the state itself, government officials and international actors came to espouse modern labour market practices built upon the fragile notion of consent. In many instances, particularly for widows and single women, the new emphasis on consent contributed to improved working conditions for women as well as for men. But instead of extending a range of employment-related benefits associated with the emerging SER to stenographers and typists, the state, unchallenged by organized labour and other social actors, allowed certain branches of the private employment agency industry to thrive in Canada, presumably, in large part, because the workers that they engaged were women. It also simultaneously began to institute a range of exclusionary policies confining women workers to specific segments of the economy and a narrow set of employment relationships, policies that strengthened and legitimized private agencies catering to the clerical sector (Chapter 3). In Ontario, employment agencies run by typewriter firms took advantage of the space created by the absence of provincial regulation and responded by embracing an early precursor of the TER.

'Halfway Houses' for 'Housewives': The Birth of the Temporary Help Industry

As housewives become aware of the labour market value of their former office skills, they cautiously seek possible work opportunities and skill measurements as a preliminary step to work life re-entry. These women are unsure of both their marketability and their real desire to work. They are inhibited in their willingness to seek or accept normal office positions but curious at the possibility. They could best be described as job market 'problems' rather than job seekers. This group of women needs counseling, interviewing, testing and direction which they cannot get on regular job interviews. In many cases, their skills need updating and, in all cases, they need encouragement and assurance that they still have the ability to be productive and will be accepted in the work force. They fear the classic job interview which places a number of applicants into competition for a single job. The THS [temporary help service] offers a suitable 'halfway house' to these job seekers; a modified employment procedure without commitment; a chance to have their skills measured non-competitively; and the opportunity to ask questions about the job market related to their own needs and expectations.

— Mitchell Fromstein, Chief Executive Officer, Manpower Inc., 1978

The period between the mid-1930s and the mid-1940s was relatively uneventful for the private employment agency industry. The postwar boom and the dramatic changes in the labour market that accompanied it contrasted sharply with that inactivity. Indeed, one vital segment of the private employment agency industry contributed to the postwar capital-labour entente. Responding to labour market policies and practices originating as early as the Great Depression, the THI emerged as a formal entity in the Canadian labour market at the end of the Second

World War and it prospered throughout the postwar period. During this era, its success corresponded, on the one hand, to the ascendance of the SER as the normative model of employment, and, on the other hand, to a particular reformulation of the ideology of domesticity.

With the end of the Second World War, the emerging compromise between business, labour, and the state led to two related developments that provide a crucial backdrop for the emergence of the THI: the advent of a male breadwinner norm, which enabled a considerable group of male workers to enjoy full-time, full-year jobs with benefits;[1] and the hegemony of an ideology of domesticity that dictated that the home was the 'proper sphere' for women, especially for the wives of this group of male breadwinners. Despite women's active role in the wartime economy, the return of the troops stimulated a reinvigorated separate spheres ideology as well as the re-introduction of a host of measures designed to curtail women's involvement in the labour market.

Policies and practices aimed at delineating the boundaries of women's labour force participation were debated fiercely in many circles: women themselves were divided over their 'proper' role in society as evidenced by the discourse in the popular women's press of the day (Birt, 1960: 42; Sangster, 1995; Strong-Boag, 1994). As a result, various actors intervened to broker emergent tensions. For example, the federal government attempted to cushion women's expulsion from wartime industries by sponsoring programs such as the Home-Aide Program (Pierson, 1977). To further limit women's labour force participation, it also relied on other direct measures, such as altering the Unemployment Insurance (UI) scheme to constrain married women's access to benefits and creating tax incentives for two-parent families relying on one breadwinner (Porter, 1993). Of course, the state did not mediate all of the wide range of tensions prevailing alongside the postwar compromise, especially the demand among employers to maintain a consistent supply of casual workers.

The 'classic' temporary help agency, which arose partly out of a complex array of supranational and national regulatory developments, played an important mediating role in this regard. Ironically, in the Canadian context it upheld the SER as a norm in the postwar period, targeting white middle-class married women as its chief workers and claiming employer status. Its carefully crafted strategy gave a well-defined group of women the opportunity to engage in paid employment within strict confines, while preserving the sanctity of their role in the domestic sphere. It also enabled the THI to institute a de facto triangular employment relationship, allowing temporary help agencies to pose as employers and thereby evade many regulations that came to govern the rest of the private employment agency industry in Canada. Although the THI first adopted this so-called temporary help formula in North America during the post-Second World War period, its strategy was so successful that it still resonates in contemporary Canada.

Women's Position in the Canadian Labour Market at the Inception of the THI

As illustrated in Chapter 1, the SER surfaced as a *normative* model of employment in advanced capitalist countries in the post-Second World War period. Characterizing it as a product of the reconstruction era, many scholars rightly credit its emergence to the entente, however tenuous, between capital and organized labour (and mediated by the state) that was driven by the growing recognition of the link between mass unemployment and various social and political ills. Scholars also associate its rise with the formation of institutions such as Bretton Woods, the ILO, and the United Nations, each of which contributed to the lengthy period of economic stability experienced by most advanced capitalist states after the Second World War. Hence, there is considerable evidence that the SER originated out of the global political-economic forces driving change in the postwar period. As well, given the wealth of feminist scholarship on the postwar welfare states in Canada and the United States that suggests that many women, immigrants, and people of colour never enjoyed most of the benefits and entitlements associated with the SER, few would deny that it was a white male norm (see, for example, Armstrong and Armstrong, 1989; Fraser and Gordon, 1994; Fudge, 1993; Gordon, 1996; Lewis, 1993; O'Connor 1993). What is less clear is the corresponding set of employment relationships and social relations that reinforced the SER as a norm in the Canadian context, that is, the package comprising the flip side of the postwar bargain. There is a dearth of scholarship that describes and assesses the range of policies, programs, and practices cultivating nonstandard employment relationships common among groups of workers known to be excluded from the SER and the ideological underpinning of such initiatives. To remedy this gap, the ensuing discussion examines the context in which a particular group of women (i.e., largely white middle-class married women) were urged to return to the domestic sphere as the SER was becoming the norm, by, at times, all three parties to the postwar bargain; this group of women constituted the THI's initial pool of principal workers.

TABLE 7
Female Labour Force Participation Rates, Census Years 1931–1961

| Year | Participation Rate | | | |
	Married %	Single %	Other %	Total %
1931	3.5	43.8	21.3	19.3
1941	4.5	47.2	17.3	20.3
1951	11.2	58.3	19.3	24.1
1961	22.0	51.4	22.9	29.5

Source:
B.G. Spencer and Featherstone, *Married Female Labour Force
Participation: A Microstudy* (Canada: Dominion Bureau of *Statistics*,
1970).

Female Labour Force Participation, 1930–1960

With the exception of a few notable dips, women's formal labour force
participation rates rose slowly between the 1930s and the 1960s. Following trends at the beginning of the twentieth century, women continued
to dominate in sectors such as domestic work, began to fill the ranks of
the rapidly expanding clerical sector, and increasingly became engaged
in certain manufacturing industries, such as clothing and textiles. Over
this thirty-year span, women's participation rates varied considerably in
accordance with their marital status, given the rise of the male breadwinner norm and the related notion that married women should, where
possible, take their corresponding place in the domestic sphere. As
Table 7 illustrates, while married women's labour force participation
rates remained relatively low until the Second World War, they increased
dramatically during the war and then fell rapidly in the postwar era.
However, factors such as race, ethnicity, and class were central to shaping
women's labour force participation in this era: they too structured the
nature of women's exclusion from the SER. Even when policies and
practices designed to spur women's exodus from the labour market
reached their height in the postwar period, the state, in conjunction with
employers and various segments of the labour movement, still encouraged certain groups of women to accept casual and intermittent forms of
employment and still preserved several spheres of employment as female
domains. Here again, domestic work is a case in point.

Immigrant Women Domestic Workers

Between the mid-1930s and late 1960s, immigrant women, first hailing from various parts of Europe and subsequently the Caribbean, dominated the ranks of domestic service in Canada. Canadian-born women rarely pursued this form of employment, due to its low wages, live-in requirements, and the common abuses committed by employers. In the 1930s Scandinavian women, especially Finnish women, were a preferred source of domestic workers because they were known to endure extremely harsh conditions of employment (Lindstrom-Best, 1986: 34). Even during turbulent economic times, when, according to Arat-Koc, 'Canadian women lost the few alternative sources of employment open to them [and] ... domestic work became once again the major employer of women as whole,' the Canadian government encouraged Finnish women to come to Canada to work as domestics (Arat-Koc, 1997: 69; Lindstrom-Best, 1986). Given the relatively low status of domestic work in the economy, the federal government was acutely aware that Canadian-born women would abandon domestic service with the arrival of more prosperous economic times.[2]

During the Second World War, when the federal government actively encouraged married women's entry into the labour force, Canada began to experience another shortage of domestic workers, a shortage that peaked in the postwar period. At this point, particularly during the five-year period between 1947 and 1952, women refugees from Europe were recruited by the Canadian government as a primary source of domestic workers (Daenzer, 1997). Finally, in the early 1950s, with the failure of an assisted passage scheme targeting Great Britain and Western Europe, Canada began to focus on Southern European women, especially Italian women as domestic workers (Iacovetta, 1986, 1992). By the late-1950s, the government also actively recruited women from Jamaica and Barbados as domestics even though there was, until 1967, a clause (originating in the Immigration Act of 1910) that allowed it to discriminate on the basis of race (Calliste, 1993; Satzewich, 1989; Silvera, 1983). Thus, as Arat-Koc (1997) argues, the dominant image of the woman domestic worker shifted dramatically over the period under study. Rather than being cast as 'mothers of the nation,' a label familiar to the immigrant domestic workers from Britain in the early part of the century when there were fewer occupations open to women, women domestic workers became known as 'foreign domestic workers,' a label that not only reflected their marginal status in the growing hierarchy of female-dominated vocations, but that also eventually came to entail an absence of citizenship rights as well.

The situation of the white middle-class married women first targeted by the THI stands in stark contrast to the harsh social and economic realities faced by immigrant women domestic workers. As the latter came to be labeled 'foreign domestic workers,' the former shifted roles from 'dutiful housewives' to part-time 'office girls.' The women targeted by the THI, while they were denied entry into certain sectors and occupations and clearly denied access to the SER, benefited indirectly from the location of their immigrant and working-class sisters in less desirable fields of employment such as live-in domestic work. Equally significant, while exclusionary policies adopted by the Canadian government in this period were designed to institute a (white) male breadwinner *norm*, and, hence, to limit some women's access to the labour market, they preserved certain spheres of employment as female domains and encouraged casual and intermittent employment among specific groups of women.

Exclusionary Policies and Practices Directed at Married Women, 1930–1960

Policies and practices designed to curtail women's participation in the Canadian labour market have their roots in the decade after the First World War. But it was in the period from the early 1930s until the mid-1960s that married women endured the most formidable legislative obstacles to labour force participation, and, in the face of these obstacles, received little support from most segments of the organized labour movement. Indeed, various branches of organized labour supported discriminatory policies that were consistent with 'securing a male breadwinner norm' (Finkel, 1995; Guard, 1995). Despite women's participation in labour militancy, many unions' efforts to protect blue-collar workers and skilled craftsworkers, for example, reinforced and complemented the desire of employers and the state to divide the labour force by gender and thereby exclude specific groups of women from key labour and social benefits as well as core segments of the labour market.[3] Thus, the posture of the union movement – particularly, its active pursuit of the 'family wage' in the 1940s and its ambivalence about married women's labour force partcipation after the Second World War – provides an important additional layer of context for understanding the state-sanctioned barriers confronting women in this period.[4]

Perhaps at no point was a woman's marital status more central to her subordinate position in the Canadian labour market than during the Great Depression. In this era, the married woman was not seen as a 'person' in her own right. According to Ruth Roach Pierson (1990: 77–8), 'if she was employed she was seen as a symbol of the cause of unemployment among men and, if she was dependent, as a symbol of the high cost of male employment to society.' The married woman wage-earner even proved to be a contentious figure for women's groups during the Great Depression. Referring to the 'timidity' of the National Council of Women of Canada on the question of whether married women should be permitted to participate in the labour force in difficult economic times, Margaret Hobbs (1993a: 207) notes, 'many women reformers, some of whom were long time supporters of women's rights in other matters, joined in the attacks on employed women who were either married or from well-to-do families.' Thus, women's 'right to work' came under ideological attack from various corners of Canadian society in this period, although some attacks were more predictable that others. But resistance to married women's participation in the labour market extended far beyond the ideological level in the 1930s. There is considerable evidence documenting federal, provincial, and municipal government policies and employer practices designed actively to encourage married women to take up their 'proper' place in the home beginning with the first signs of economic crisis. The nature of women's labour force attachment, therefore, was not only linked to a general climate of animosity but to genuine marriage bars. Their expulsion from employment in certain sectors upon marriage or first pregnancy and the emergence of blatantly discriminatory UI policies underline such measures (Archibald, 1970; Hodgetts et al., 1972; Morgan, 1988; Pierson, 1990).

In the limited range of female-dominated vocations, nowhere were marriage bars more apparent than in the Federal Public Service (Archibald, 1970; Hodgetts et al., 1972; Morgan, 1988; Phillips and Phillips, 1983). Despite the fact that the Federal Public Service was designed for men, in that, according to Morgan, 'it constituted a sort of appendage to political authority, which at that time was, of course, male,' women had made considerable inroads into this sector between 1908 and 1920 for two central reasons (Morgan, 1988: 5). First, clerical work was expanding and women increasingly obtained business school and apprenticeship training as typists and stenographers from about 1910 onwards. Second, and even more critically, salaries were extremely low in the Federal Public Service; thus, in the period leading up to the Great Depression, women were accepting jobs that few men would take. However, the advances made by women, particularly into permanent positions, were not only short-lived but generally limited to the lower grades of the Service because of the belief, on the part of leading bureaucrats, that the higher grades should remain a male preserve. Expressing this sentiment early on, the 1908 *Annual Report of the Civil Service Commission* noted, 'There would be difficulties ... some of them, it is true, the result of prejudice, but nonetheless real, were a woman to be appointed to administer an office or section of a department involving the control and direction of a number of male clerks' (Civil Service Commission, 1908: 17).

By the 1920s, when the federal government was still confronted with the task of reintegrating First World War veterans, fears of the feminization of the Federal Public Service workforce were not only more pronounced but more entrenched. Internal directives allowed deputy ministers to specify the gender of candidates acceptable for certain positions, make women's jobs into temporary positions, and place a formal embargo on married women (Archibald, 1970: 16). From 1921 forward, when a woman working in the Federal Public Service married she had to resign or keep her status a secret, but the latter option usually proved only possible until her first pregnancy (Archibald, 1970: 16; Morgan, 1988: 6). Despite the marriage bar and women's relegation to temporary positions, due to their predominance in clerical work across the Canadian economy, single, widowed, and secretly married women still constituted a large proportion of temporary clerical workers in the Federal Public Service throughout the period of the Great Depression. Certain domains of the Federal Public Service staffed largely by First World War veterans, such as the Post Office department, made entry particularly difficult for women, but this situation was quite different in others, such as the Departments of National Defense and Veterans' Affairs. The most obvious reason that women dominated in the Departments of National Defense and Veterans' Affairs and not the Post Office was that the latter two departments used stenographers of the sort trained and placed by private employment agencies operated by typewriter companies beginning in the 1910s, and the Post Office used mainly clerks and operations personnel (Morgan, 1988, 10). As Morgan (1988: 8) notes: 'Women had become so identified with stenography and typing and the job of a secretary had become a woman's job: to offer it to a man would have been an incongruity bordering on insult. The image of the male secretary was accepted only in the army, and then only for secretaries of generals.' In the interwar years, clerical skills became indispensable to the Federal Public Service and many men were either unwilling or unable to accept jobs as typists and stenographers. Thus, many unmarried women, and married women who successfully kept their marriages a secret, stayed in the Federal Public Service even though harsh restrictions on women's employment remained.

The policies and practices of municipal and provincial school boards were no better than the Federal Public Service. They too required women to relinquish their positions upon marriage, or, alternatively, at first pregnancy (Pierson, 1990; Phillips and Phillips 1983). Other parts of the Provincial Public Service also had somewhat more covert policies prohibiting the simultaneous employment of husbands and wives throughout the 1920s and 1930s. However, as Margaret Hobbs (1993a: 7) argues: 'The intent of regulation was clear. Ontario's Premier Hepburn, for example, after firing six married women who had concealed their marital status, boasted to the public that "We take the position, as have all previous governments, that if a woman marries, her husband should keep her."' As employers, federal and provincial governments were among the worst culprits in that they standardized marriage bars as they normalized the SER.

In the 1920s and 1930s, the federal government not only endorsed exclusionary practices aimed at married women as 'employees,' it also instituted policies designed to discourage women's employment across the economy. Early UI policy is a prime example. Although the subject of the female worker rarely surfaced in the debates surrounding UI policy in the 1930s, its absence was highly significant, as Ruth Pierson (1990: 78–9) notes: '[I]f we understand gender to be a fundamental social category, we are justified in asking where and how concern for women fit into the Depression-era discussion of unemployment insurance. *And if we further understand gender to be relational, to be a category comprising all that which shapes social relations between sexes, then we are justified in examining the gender implications for women of the silences regarding them: that is the measures that made no mention of them, of the concepts into which they were invisibly enfolded and the assumptions through which masculine priority was inscribed*' [my emphasis]. The nature of UI policy in this period substantiates this very crucial insight. Although women were only mentioned once in the *Unemployment Insurance Act* (1935), the legislation had highly discriminatory underpinnings. From 1934 to 1940, UI policy divided women into two categories, female worker and wife/mother, and 'it was, by and large, ideologically anathema for a woman to combine these two categories herself' (Pierson, 1990: 81). Although single mothers and employed married women violated the dichotomy, UI policy did not take their widely perceived anomalous situations into account. For the single mother to receive benefits, she had to be desexed and claim UI as a primary breadwinner like her male counterpart. To be eligible she had to work in a field of employment covered by the scheme, and, not surprisingly, many single mothers were denied access to benefits because domestics, nurses, and teachers, among others, were excluded from coverage (Pierson, 1990: 99). The fate of the employed married woman was even worse than that of many single mothers (and certainly single women) since she was presumed to be looked after by a male breadwinner, and therefore lacked an individual entitlement to UI. Thus, the UI scheme dominant in this period gave married women access to benefits through indirect channels, such as dependents' allowances, except in special cases where it could be demonstrated that married women had worked 'steadily' or had 'less than the prescribed number of contributions paid in respect of them' (Phillips and Phillips, 1983: 28–9; Pierson, 1990: 95). Hence, claiming UI was not only beyond the reach of women in highly female-dominated sectors, such as hospital nursing and domestic work, and women engaged in 'casual' or 'intermittent' employment, but also to most married women (regardless of their occupational location and/ or relationship to the labour market). Many of the harsh restrictions initiated in the inter-war period remained throughout the Second World War and in the postwar era.

With the beginning of Second World War, the mechanisms designed to regulate women's labour force participation changed drastically as significant numbers of married women entered the labour force to replace men who joined the armed forces. The female labour force participation rate rose almost 9 percentage points between 1939 and 1945, even though it quickly dropped back to prewar levels after the war (Armstrong and Armstrong, 1994: 17–18). Sexual boundaries shifted only temporarily during the war, leading feminist scholars to discuss and debate about the validity of the notion of women as a reserve army of labour.[5] In this era, the federal government replaced exclusionary policies, particularly those directed at married women, with policies that encouraged labour force participation among all women, either on a full- or a part-time basis. Hence, married women re-entered the labour market in overwhelming numbers, mainly as a result of economic necessity but also out of their desire to support the war effort.[6] To facilitate their re-entry, the Canadian government created a body known as the National Selection Service (NSS) in 1942, when it recognized that 'the pools of unemployed from the Great Depression had dried up' (Phillips and Phillips, 1983: 29). The NSS had as one of its primary aims the registration and referral of women into wartime employment. Still, the federal government's efforts to induce married women to enter the labour force during the war were not limited to recruitment, referral, and placement. These efforts also included more indirect incentives, often backed by segments of the organized labour movement and employers requiring a larger pool of workers, such as income tax concessions, day nurseries catering to women employed in wartime industries, and even the encouragement of married women's part-time employment in commercial laundries; the incentives were in recognition of the importance of such services to women engaged full time in jobs essential to the war effort (Finkel, 1995; Phillips and Phillips, 1983; Pierson and Light, 1990). However, war's end brought these policies and programs to a halt.

In the postwar era, institutions such as the NSS turned their attention to relocating women dislocated from their wartime vocations either to the home or to traditionally female-dominated sectors, such as domestic work. Simultaneously, the federal government again harnessed various policies and practices to limit women's participation in the labour force. Measures ranged from instituting tax disincentives for married women participating in the labour force to implementing marriage bars in certain sectors of employment to instituting a family allowance.[7]

Alongside these national policy measures and international initiatives, such as the *Philadelphia Declaration* (1944), which encouraged countries to establish comprehensive social security schemes to avert economic and political difficulties akin to those arising during the Great Depression, the notion of an SER began to gain prominence and popularity, particularly among organized labour and the state (ILO, 1944; Lee, 1997). Its counterpart, the 'family wage,' which entailed wages sufficient for a male worker to maintain both himself and his dependent wife and children, also rose to normative pre-eminence in this period (Barrett and McIntosh, 1980; Pierson and Light, 1990: 252); and, to a large extent, leading liberal welfare states (including Canada) wholly endorsed the family wage as a companion to the SER to preserve women's 'proper role' in the domestic sphere and to solidify their commitment to social reproduction. Only a narrow group of male workers ever benefited from the family wage, however, despite its crucial role in upholding the ideology of domesticity. Still, in sharp contrast to the immigrant agricultural and industrial workers recruited, placed, and often exploited by private employment agents in the pre-Second World War period, and even distinct from the young, well-educated, middle-class women stenographers and typists engaged by employment agencies run by typewriting companies, the first group of potential workers targeted by the Canadian THI at its inception were white middle-class married women from households presumed to benefit from a family wage.

For a lengthy period after the war, the federal government viewed domestic work as the most viable option for married women wanting to remain in the labour force. Thus, the NSS launched an initiative known as the Home Aide scheme, a program designed to elevate the status of domestic service as a vocation for women by offering women domestic work on a regular hourly, live-out basis. Introduced in 1945, the notion of the 'Home Aide' represented a new type of domestic servant: 'a diluted hybrid of cook, kitchen maid, parlour maid, babysitter, mother's helper, and housekeeping assistant' (Pierson, 1977: 91). An initiative of the Women's Division of NSS, the home aide was different from the regular domestic servant since she did not do heavy household chores but more routine housework (92). To appeal to a range of women, the scheme was also designed to be a flexible program that could offer the married woman part-time employment, likely a couple of morning or afternoon shifts per week, or the self-supporting single woman full-time employment. Despite its attempts to make domestic service palatable to women expelled from their wartime jobs, however, Home Aide proved to be merely a band-aid measure that temporarily alleviated economic hardship among those women.[8] Even with the growing demand for domestic workers and the fear of unemployment among women after the Second World War, the scheme failed after only two years in operation.

While the government was slow to recognize it, given its overemphasis on domestic work, other growing sectors of the Canadian economy continued to rely on women workers after the war. In the postwar period, the phenomenal growth of clerical work led to a high demand for stenographers and typists, two fields which women came to dominate between 1941 and 1971 (Lowe, 1987). Indeed, although women's labour force participation rates did not again reach their wartime levels until 1966, and although marriage bars lasted in sectors such as the Federal Public Service until 1955, many women held on to their spaces in the labour market specifically because of the feminization of clerical work rooted partly in the accelerating transformation of Canada's industrial economy into a service economy (Boyd, Mulvihill, and Myles, 1991; Morgan, 1988).

As one might expect, many employers' desire to hire women was in tension with the ideology of domesticity underpinning the postwar compromise. However, part-time clerical work emerged as a crucial exception for white middle-class married women in this period, ostensibly because the government (as an employer), along with private sector employers and organized labour, accepted sex segregation in the labour market as a viable alternative to the exclusion of women altogether. Its exceptionalism also rested on the notion of what *Chatelaine* magazine (1953) referred to as the 'White-Collar Wife,' an image that balanced the rise of the SER and coincident rise of the ideology of domesticity with women's growing desire and necessity to remain in, or return to, the labour market on a part-time, casual, or intermittent basis (Katz, 1951). Soon after the notion of the 'White-Collar Wife' became acceptable to Canadians, temporary help agencies entered the labour market capitalizing on this phenomenon.

By the late 1950s, part-time clerical work became a viable alternative for a specific group of married women wanting to participate in the labour force in that it no longer 'conjured up images of gender chaos' (Strong-Boag, 1994: 13). Even more important, although their earnings added more than just 'frills' to the household budget in most instances, married women's participation in clerical work did not undermine the hegemony of the SER because they continued to be ineligible for permanent positions in a range of sectors and had limited individual entitlements to emerging social insurance programs. For example, the UI Commission disqualified women for two years after marriage unless they fulfilled certain conditions that proved their attachment to the labour force. According to Ann Porter (1993: 118, 125), these regulations depicted married women as both 'conniving to defraud the system,' since they were presumably beneficiaries of a family wage, and 'virtuous protectors' of the domestic sphere. They even penalized married women because of pregnancy[9] or if they were forced to relocate (and therefore change jobs) because of their husband's job.

While these discriminatory regulations were revoked in 1957, many employers lobbied to maintain them at the end of the 1950s. Some even supported reinstating them in the early 1960s, with growing rates of unemployment and UI fund depletion (Porter 1993: 141). For example, during the 1961 hearings of the Commission of Inquiry into UI, Office Overload, the first known temporary help agency in Canada, called attention to married women's tendency to abuse the UI system: 'Coming into daily contact as we do with so many temporary workers – as most of these married women are in the labour force for a relatively short period of time ... we are exposed to perhaps more than our share of abuses of the UI Fund' (Gill Commission Records, October 1961: RG 33/48, as cited in Porter 1993).[10] On the surface, Office Overload seemed to support preserving special regulations for married women because it believed that they were prone to defraud the system. However, at a deeper level, it was acutely aware that granting married women individual entitlements to social insurance programs such as UI might contribute to depleting its supply of temporary help workers.[11] Given the nature of its business, Office Overload had a special interest in limiting the spread of the SER to a narrow group of male breadwinners. But it was not alone: employers, organized (male) labour and the state each had a stake in maintaining clear boundaries around the SER. This shared interest not only enabled policies and practices that actively discriminated against married women to endure, it created a highly gendered and racialized space within which the Canadian THI slowly emerged.

The Rise of the Canadian THI in an International Context

As the postwar era progressed, there was growing pressure to incorporate the sizeable group of workers excluded from the SER into the Canadian labour market. Labour shortages, particularly in the expanding clerical sector, and the persistence of exclusionary policies directed at married women had created both an acute demand among employers for additional workers and a captive pool of potential workers ready to fill this vacuum. These corresponding sets of developments opened up a space for the THI. Still, as an outgrowth of the private employment agency industry, the THI faced a twofold challenge at its inception: first, the challenge to distance itself from the questionable historical practices of the private employment agency industry; and second, the challenge to attain legitimacy without undermining the SER as a norm and upsetting the delicate balance between capital, organized labour, and the state which obscured labour power's commodity status. Over the course of approximately two decades, the Canadian THI was able to meet these challenges, following developments in the United States.

History and Origins

As Chapter 2 demonstrated, the Canadian THI has its clearest origins in the early part of the century, when employment agencies run by typewriter companies hired out young women stenographers and typists to sell their typewriters. However, there was a decades-long hiatus between the emergence of employment agencies run by typewriter companies and the birth of the Canadian THI. During this period, the THI first surfaced as a formal entity in the American labour market.

Early American literature and primary industry records on the THI trace the first known North American temporary help agencies to Chicago in the late 1920s and early 1930s (Gannon, 1978; Gonos, 1995; Moore, 1965; Parker, 1994; Seavey and Kazis, 1994). This literature also indicates that the temporary help agency arrived separately in the industrial, clerical, technical, and professional fields. Industrial help, for example, is commonly traced by American experts to D.J. Nugent Co., a stevedoring business in Milwaukee that experimented with hiring out some of its employees to a nearby manufacturing plant in the 1920s (Seavey and Kazis, 1994: III, 3). Then, quite independently, temporary technical workers emerged in the early 1930s when the automotive industry began hiring engineers on short-term assignment to help design models for new cars (Joray and Hulin, 1978). Finally, industry analysts credit Samuel Workman with starting the first temporary clerical firm in the United States (Seavey and Kazis, 1994; Moore, 1975).

Workman was an American entrepreneur whose primary business involved selling calculating machines but who also started a subsidiary operation employing women to do night-time inventory work for his customers in the 1920s. In 1929 he took on this side business full time, supplying temporary help workers first to operate electric adding machines for company clients and then to perform a range of related clerical tasks. His early operation bears a striking resemblance to the private employment agencies run by typewriting companies in Ontario beginning around 1910. However, Workman's business stands out for an additional reason: although he began by using temporary help workers to sell his calculating equipment, he eventually supplied workers to his customers for a fee. In this respect, Workman's business offered a template upon which the North American THI emerged, one that eventually allowed it to distinguish itself from the private employment agency industry as a whole.

There are competing perspectives on which individual temporary help agencies were the first to emerge in North America and what type of business constitutes the earliest 'classic' temporary help agency. However, stories recalling the earliest images of the THI converge from the mid-1940s onwards, when several of the largest temporary clerical firms were first incorporated. Manpower Inc. was the first temporary help firm to incorporate in 1947, Kelly Services quickly followed suit in 1948, and Olsten formed by the end of the decade; each of these firms surfaced first in the United States, initially focusing their businesses on the clerical and industrial sectors (Gannon, 1978; Moore, 1965; Seavey and Kazis, 1994). However, other large firms also incorporated soon after, including Labor Pool Inc., Employer's Overload and Western Girl (Moore, 1965). Some analysts suggest that these firms formed out of a climate of harsh regulation towards the private employment industry (Gonos, 1994; Parker, 1994). But within the industry, officials often tell a version of the following story to account for the industry's origins: 'This is how the story goes. I used to work for Kelly Services and it's my understanding that Kelly Services is the creator of the industry. This happened during the war days ... [Mr Kelly] had a friend who had his own business. He was having difficulty because he had too much work on his desk and he needed a hand in getting the work done. *So, he happened to say to Kelly, "I need help" and Kelly said, "I know somebody, my wife." So he started putting his wife out to work and it bloomed from there, from the wife to the wife's friends and so on* [my emphasis] ... Kelly Services was known as the "Kelly Girls" because it was the war days [*sic*]' (M1).

The Second World War and the labour shortages that accompanied it gave most segments of the emerging THI a boost, one that continued throughout the postwar era. For example, in the United States, temporary help agencies specializing in the clerical sector that started with a couple of 'office girls' during the war had approximately 20,000 employees by 1956 (Moore, 1965). As well, due to the high demand for skilled labourers and general labourers for wartime production, higher-tech firms providing temporary assistance made considerable gains; indeed, four of the five biggest American-based temporary help agencies that provided skilled and general labourers as well as clerical workers were founded between 1946 and 1950 (Joray and Hulin 1978). Clerical work nevertheless became the mainstay of the THI in the postwar period, and the temporary clerical worker, captured famously by the notion of the 'Kelly Girl,' provided the image of the prototypical 1950s temporary help worker. The THI's early focus on clerical work, keenly evident in its early marketing strategy, was also apparent in the Canadian context.

In Canada, the first known temporary help agency arrived on the scene several years after its American counterparts. Formed by William Pollock and James Shore, two young office-equipment salespeople, Office Overload entered the Canadian market in Winnipeg in June 1951.

Shore and Pollack started the business, when like Mr Kelly described above, they noticed that the offices they visited often had too much or too little work for the staff at a given time. As a consequence, they decided to form a registry of former office workers willing to return to part-time work to 'help harassed employers' (Hutton, 1957: 19).[12] Like the above-mentioned anecdote tracing the origins of Kelly Services, Office Overload's history started with part-time stenographer Betty Green. By 1956 the company had opened offices in Toronto, Montreal, Vancouver, and Hamilton. At this juncture, the Toronto office led the business, which by then claimed to have a registry of over 20,000 women who had been clerical workers prior to getting married. Soon after Office Overload emerged, several other companies, such as Kelly Services and Manpower, joined the Canadian market, with the result that estimates of the size of the THI's work force reached 30,000 by 1957. One commentator characterized the mid-1950s explosion in the Canadian THI as follows: 'Several thousand women in addition to Office Overload's twenty thousand have been added to *Canada's feminine working force for periods that vary as widely as a woman's mood* [my emphasis] – all the way from an occasional half day's work to six months of steady employment' (Hutton, 1957). Evidence also suggests that employer demand matched, and perhaps even exceeded, the size of the temporary clerical work force in Canada in this period. In addition, highly successful Canadian temporary help agencies, like Office Overload, quickly took their businesses abroad. For example, many had entered the British, Dutch, and American markets by the mid-1960s (Hutton, 1957; Seavey and Kazis, 1994).

The 'Classic' Temporary Help Agency and the Early TER

The shape of the 'classic' temporary help agency and the nature of the employment relationship that it constructed was key to the international success of the early THI. In the postwar period, temporary help agencies gradually began to characterize themselves as 'temporary help services.' In contradistinction to other private employment agencies that acted exclusively as intermediaries, they embraced a triangular employment relationship: in this relationship, the agency acts as the employer and the customer is said to be engaged in a commercial contract for services with the temporary help agency (Dombois, 1989; Gonos, 1994, 1995; Cordova, 1986; ILO, 1994a). Reflecting on the central difference between the 'temporary help service' first emerging in the post-Second World War period and the typical private employment agency, Mitchell Fromstein, president and chief executive officer of Manpower, made the following remarks in 1978: 'A Temporary Help Service is an independent organization engaged in the business of providing its own employees to perform work, on a time basis, for its customer firms – usually at the customer's place of business and usually of a short term nature. The key element in the above definition that excludes the THS from being a labor market intermediary is "... providing its own employees ..." *This phrase and the actual functioning of a THS makes the firm an employer rather than an intermediary in almost every sense of the word* [my emphasis] (230).

Although the notion of the 'temporary help service' only became common parlance in Canada in the late 1980s, temporary help agencies distinguished themselves from other private employment agencies at the inception of the THI by adopting what scholars now label the 'temporary help formula' (Gonos, 1994; Parker, 1994). The notion of the temporary help formula concerns the set of practices comprising the arrangement that allows customers of the temporary help agency to use its workers without taking on the social, legal, and contractual obligations associated with the SER (Gonos, 1994; Mangum, Mayall, and Nelson, 1985). The underpinnings of this formula are best understood by describing how the TER came to operate in the post-Second World War period.

From recruitment to registration and finally to placement, the process of placing temporary help workers on assignment with customers came to be characterized by a complex array of procedures in the postwar period, a process that endures to date. The first step involved worker registration. After responding to advertisements in newspapers and magazines, or simply hearing of temporary help work through word of mouth, potential temporary help workers registered with the agency. Although this initial step resembled the process common to the private employment agency industry, several facets of the registration process distinguished the temporary help agency from the typical private employment agency. The most notable difference was that upon registering with an agency, and even upon placement, the worker was not asked to pay a direct fee. As well, at the point of registration, the temporary help agency normally administered tests designed to assess the skill of the potential worker in the field of work that s/he desired. For example, if the applicant was seeking clerical work, temporary help agencies routinely administered typing tests, examining accuracy and speed, and filing tests, where the applicant was required to alphabetize entries.

The second major step in the process occurred when the customer approached the temporary help agency for assistance. At this point, the agency attempted to match the client's needs with the workers available, using files on individual applicants to find the best temporary worker for the assignment. When the agency located a suitable applicant, it provided the potential temporary help worker with a description of the work available, including hours, duties, and an estimate of the duration of the assignment. Referring to the flexibility that temporary help work offered to applicants in this era, one early commentator noted: 'One major attraction of the arrangement is that the worker is given a clear understanding that she [sic] can refuse any assignment offered, although the worker who repeatedly refuses assignments will likely cease to receive calls' (Moore, 1965: 621). Formal placement represented the third step of the assignment process carried out by the temporary help agency. In most instances, upon placement, agencies provided clients with a performance guarantee of sorts: principally designed to ensure customer satisfaction, this guarantee usually offered the client the option of replacing a temporary help worker were s/he found to be unsuitable for the assignment, and it also guaranteed the client a replacement if the temporary help worker left the placement prematurely or had a lengthy absence. Upon placement, the temporary help worker was also usually required to sign a restrictive covenant agreeing that for a specified period of time s/he would not accept an offer of permanent employment from the customer to whom s/he was assigned, a practice that continues to date (621).[13] This last feature was designed to ensure that the temporary help worker's primary loyalty rested with the agency, at least for a fixed duration. The customer was also routinely made aware of the covenant between the agency and the temporary help worker, and was informed that buy-outs could be arranged should it discover that it wanted to retain its temporary help permanently (Fromstein, 1978).

Beyond its complex registration, matching and placement processes, what made the early temporary help agency distinct from the typical private employment agency was that the agency itself paid the worker; the agency also withheld income taxes and social security contributions and provided the worker with mandatory social benefits, such as vacation pay and pension pay-outs, either over the course of a given assignment or upon its completion (Fric, 1973; Gannon, 1978, 1984; Moore, 1965; Parker, 1994). Most early agencies also provided liability insurance and a type of fidelity bond for every worker assigned to a customer (Fromstein, 1978: 235). To protect its role as a service provider that carried out selection, testing, placement, and other employment-related responsibilities for a fee, the agency also always billed the customer directly. Overhead costs, including recruitment, registration, and placement costs, legal obligations, and other internal procedures, were subsumed within the amount billed to the customer (Fromstein, 1978: 236; Moore, 1965: 622). At the inception of the THI, fees beyond the payment of wages and benefits that accrued to the worker became known as the 'mark-up'; in contrast to the present situation, early temporary help agencies tended to be open about wage levels as well as about the size of the mark-up.[14]

Early Challenges to the THI

While the 'classic' temporary help agency actively took on employer status in the postwar period, its legal status was a point of controversy in many countries. At its inception in the United States, for example, a few unions and branches of government vehemently opposed the employer status assumed by temporary help agencies. To limit the profitability of the temporary help formula, some unions successfully negotiated clauses to bring temporary help workers under the terms and conditions of existing collective agreements.[15] Some national governments also leveled charges against temporary help agencies acting as strikebreakers, continuing a theme first raised by labour leaders in the early twentieth century. Spurred by several developments at the international level, such as the creation of an International Labour Convention Concerning the Co-ordination of the Public Employment Service (No. 88), to be described below, the feud between public employment services and the private employment agency industry escalated at an international level throughout this period (Ricca, 1982). Although it assumed employer status, and therefore did not threaten the function of public employment services to the same extent as the typical private employment agency, the temporary help agency was not totally unaffected as public employment services and private employment agencies jostled for positions in the labour market.

In the wake of these challenges, the THI, now an international entity, waged numerous court battles over its claim to employer status in both the United States and Europe from the 1950s onwards (Veldkamp and Raesten, 1973; Gonos, 1995).[16] It was successful in some of these cases; for example, in 1956 a Florida court rendered a decision that labeled Manpower Inc. an independent contractor as opposed to an employment agency.[17] However, in other cases, the industry's version of a TER, whereby the agency assumed employer status, was disallowed. In the post-Second World War period, in a range of national jurisdictions, courts denying temporary help agencies employer status used the following reasoning as their central justification. First, the judgments indicated that the customer exercised direct control and supervision over the temporary help worker while s/he was on-site. Second, they found that in most jurisdictions, with the exception of those where the TER was governed by an indeterminate contract of employment, the temporary help worker was not employed by the agency until s/he was on assignment with an outside party. Third, numerous cases indicated that the temporary help agency did not supply its own materials or use its own tools, 'nor does it guarantee or take responsibility for a final product or service, in the usual manner of an independent contractor' (Gonos, 1995: 8). Therefore, the temporary help agency belongs in the category of 'labour-only contractors' (Axelrod, 1987; Epstein and Monat, 1973).[18]

Even though the courts often denied temporary help agencies legal employer status, in many jurisdictions, particularly in countries like Canada where the THI did not pursue employer status through formal legal channels, they attained de facto employer status in the postwar era. From the perspective of the THI, the underside of this otherwise positive development was that temporary help agencies in most North American and European countries were treated as private employment agencies throughout the postwar period. They were therefore required to obtain licenses, keep formal records, and, in many cases, they also had to follow fee-scale limitations.[19] Such measures enabled the THI to survive early challenges to its legitimacy.

Law and regulation were not, however, the primary basis of the THI's claim to legitimacy, which it drew from both its workers and its client base. In North America, in particular, the THI attained legitimacy by recruiting workers from a relatively confined segment of society – workers who were not perceived to be as vulnerable to exploitation as those immigrant and migrant workers who had been targeted by early private employment agents acting abroad – and marketing its services to a well-defined group of customers. This strategy was particularly successful in Canada throughout the postwar period, where the THI targeted white middle-class married women as its core workers and individuals and firms requiring temporary clerical help as its primary clients.

The Shape of the Early Canadian THI

From its inception until the late 1960s, the Canadian THI experienced two distinct stages of evolution, following in the footsteps of its American counterparts. It first emerged with the narrow aim of providing individuals and firms requiring temporary clerical assistance with temporary workers for short-term assignments. In this period, customers used temporary clerical workers as a 'stop-gap' or emergency measure. Thus, in 1951, providing temporary help workers for staffing emergencies was Office Overload's primary marketing strategy. By the late 1950s, however, the Canadian THI began to market itself as providing workers for planned usages, stand-ins for employees on sick leave or vacation, as well as filling gaps in times of peak demand (Hutton, 1957). Therefore, in the 1950s and 1960s, the image of the typical temporary help worker remained rather static, as did the industry's client base.

A Profile of the Typical Temporary Help Worker

The early Canadian THI catered largely to firms in the clerical sector or to customers requiring clerical assistance, and it recruited primarily white middle-class married women as its core workers. Therefore, the image of the typical temporary help worker came to be marked by several core features from the 1950s onwards. She was a housewife just married, possibly expecting a baby or with school-aged children, and normally a former office worker. She was in need (or in want) of some 'extra' money to add frills to the household budget, and she often desired greater economic independence from her husband.

Profiled in a 1957 *Maclean's* magazine, 'Mrs.' Betty Downing was presented as the prototypical temporary help worker. Downing was one of Office Overload's first temporary help workers. She joined the organization in the summer of 1957 and she had been employed 'a little more than half of full-time, in stints ranging from one day to a two day arrangement' (Hutton, 1957: 89). The *Maclean's* article focused on her first assignment, which involved acting as Bob Hope's private secretary while he was performing at the Canadian National Exhibition. However, Office Overload depicted Downing as a model for several other reasons, intricately related to the image of the THI that they aimed to project. Before marrying and having two children, Downing had worked as a stenographer; hence, Downing's skills surpassed Office Overload's minimum standards of 100 words per minute for shorthand and 50 words per minute for typing, with 90 per cent accuracy. She first took up an offer of a temporary assignment because her husband was in the midst of changing careers, they had just bought a new house, and her son needed an operation. However, after all these bills were paid, Downing continued to work with Office Overload, financing a new dining room set and a nice garden.

According to *Maclean's*, like most other temporary help workers in the 1950s, Downing adjusted to her double day rather adeptly: 'With less time in which to do her housework, Betty has devised methods of combining chores with recreation – like setting up her ironing board in the living room and watching television while she irons' (Hutton, 1957: 90). It further indicated that the combination of housewifely duties and temporary help work was ideal for women like Downing, since they doubtlessly did not desire permanent employment, as well as for employers in need of clerical workers, who presumably did not view married women with children as good risks for permanent employment: 'The inconvenience of being both a housewife and a free-lance secretary are just enough to make her immune to the occasional permanent offers she gets from her part-time employers ... *Office Overload seldom has a girl "stolen" by a customer. The very reasons why they work for Office Overload – because they want to work when, where and for as long as they decide – make them poor risks for permanent employment'* [my emphasis] (Hutton 1957, 90–91). Indeed, the *Maclean's* profile also suggested that, although Downing represented the type of temporary help worker that agencies liked to send to outside clients, companies like Office Overload also employed an internal pool of temporaries for clients wanting specific jobs, such as payroll and other more unconventional tasks, performed outside the office. The *Maclean's* article cited the following example:

> The production departments of Office Overload's branches have learned not to be surprised at customers' demands. Donna Lambert, the petite nonstop red-head who manages Toronto production, recently had to find half a dozen girls who had husky, exciting telephone voices. The client was a businessman who was running for president of his service club. The girls were provided with the names of all the club members, including first names and nicknames, and on the day of the election meeting they called the client's colleagues and cooed into the phone: 'Hellooo, Steve – I'll be seeing you tonight ... Where? Why, at the club meeting. And don't forget, vote for good old Bill.' (Hutton, 1957: 93)

Ironically, despite their 'husky' voices, the author of the article described the women staffing this internal pool of temporaries as 'an expectant mothers' club,' since, at that time, Office Overload did not assign women workers to outside clients after they were four months pregnant.

Policies excluding married and pregnant women from participating in the labour market made temporary help work a viable option for women like Betty Downing, trained as secretaries before marriage. Correspondingly, they also made married women an ideal pool of potential workers for the THI. These women had neither lost their skills nor their desire to use them, but, for a lengthy period, they could not put them to 'permanent' use in institutions such as the Federal Public Service (Archibald, 1970; Morgan, 1988). Other federal measures restricting married women's individual entitlements to social insurance, such as the UI regulation concerning married women that existed until the late 1950s, only reinforced the already marginal position of these women in the labour market (Pierson, 1990; Porter, 1993). Thus, the THI relied extensively on labour market conditions and exclusionary public policies to sell temporary help work to married women.

In much of its promotional literature, the THI exploited the potential insecurities of married women absent from the labour market for a lengthy period as a means of capturing this group of workers as its primary labour force. To governments, employers, and the public-at-large, it constructed married women labour force re-entrants as 'job market problems' in need of assistance and counselling to get them accustomed to the postwar labour market. The industry positioned itself as facilitating not only women's entry into temporary help work but their smooth re-entry into the labour market as marriage bars were lifted. Typical of the THI's general approach to treating this important source of labour supply, Mitchell Fromstein (1978: 242–3) of Manpower Inc. characterized married women as requiring a 'halfway house' designed to facilitate their return to the labour force gradually, and to treat them in a noncompetitive manner. Fromstein's image of the halfway house creates a picture quite different from the one of the confident Betty Downing portrayed in *Maclean's*. From his perspective, not only were these married women 'job market problems' because they had not kept up with changing skills requirements, they were also timid and reluctant workers. However distinct, these images were both consistent with the THI's marketing strategy. They effectively tapped into the logic of the ideology of domesticity, which suggested that women's primary place was in the home, while still encouraging a particular type of labour force re-entry among married women.

Since it viewed itself as providing a vital 'service' to client firms, the THI's strategy also involved convincing its customers that they needed temporary help workers. Even after the marriage bars were lifted and the new UI regulations targeting married women were removed, the THI educated its customers on how they would benefit from drawing on temporary help workers. As well, the kinds of remarks made by Fromstein, and the profile of Office Overload in *Maclean's* and other popular magazines, implied that married women were poor risks for permanent employment. By the late 1960s and early 1970s, industry leaders began to argue that using the THI had other key advantages. Customers could avoid the costs of employment-related benefits and the costs accrued from hiring and dismissal, assuring customers that these types of advantages were morally justifiable due to the shape of the labour supply (Fromstein, 1978; Gannon, 1978; Ginzberg, 1978). After all, married women were perceived to enjoy the variety offered by temporary help work without having to commit themselves to full-time permanent employment.

Exclusionary policies that encouraged many Canadian married middle-class women to engage in temporary help work, and the high degree of demand among employers for clerical workers, were not the only factors contributing to the success of the early Canadian THI. There were other forces – ideological forces – at work during this period. Building on sentiments characteristic of the depression era, the married woman wage-earner, especially if she had children, was a contentious figure in the postwar period. If she remained in the labour market after the return of the troops then she was defying her proper place in the domestic sphere (Sangster, 1995; Strong-Boag, 1994). However, in the later half of the post-war period, families increasingly needed more income to sustain themselves. Equally important, many married women had enjoyed their time as wartime workers and they resented being prohibited from participating in the labour market. Still, the 'double day' posed its own problems. The THI, with the assistance of commentators in the popular press (Katz, 1951; Macpherson, 1945), sold temporary help work to women as the best remedy for this set of problems. In response to an article in *Chatelaine* (1960), where a married woman (Anita Birt) reflected bitterly on her short stint in the labour market – she argued against combining motherhood and employment, because both working as a full-time stenographer and being a full-time mother was too taxing – an executive from Office Overload responded as follows: 'It's easy to see that [Anita Birt] bit off more than she could chew. The modern compromise for the married woman is part-time temporary work: working hours tailored to suit her particular responsibilities, the bonus interest of varied offices and industries to work in, and that extra kick, a few more dollars in the family purse! What more could a woman want? Wilbur can have the measles without the whole fragile structure of the mother's working life toppling around her ... This compromise satisfies some forty-thousand women across Canada who work on such a basis for the company I represent' (Keith, 1960:148). This solution was praised in debates about women's role in the labour market in the popular press: temporary help work was perceived to achieve the ideal balance for married women, providing them with a modicum of liberation without undermining the harmony of the conventional nuclear family. Hence, for approximately a decade, the type of worker that the THI targeted and that its primary customers desired remained relatively consistent, as did the sex composition of the THI.

In Canada and in North America more broadly, the THI was a product of its time. Industry leaders were keenly aware of the tensions created by the persistence of exclusionary policies directed at married women and the growing economic necessity for more than one breadwinner per household, as well as the acute need for workers to staff the growing clerical sector. Hence, leaders crafted a temporary help formula that allowed temporary help agencies to claim de facto employer status, target a narrow group of workers, and rid themselves of the images associated with the early private employment agency industry. Beyond creating an important niche for the THI, this formula also upheld the underside of the postwar compromise, allowing the THI to incorporate a crucial group of so-called secondary workers into the labour market without bringing them into the fold of the SER and granting them access to its associated package of benefits and entitlements.

International and National Regulatory Developments, 1933–1966

While the success of the 'temporary help formula' underpinned the legitimacy earned by the Canadian THI in the postwar era, the THI did not gain complete legitimacy in Canada or elsewhere after the Second World War. Nor did it completely avoid regulation since many of its practices fundamentally challenged central tenets of the postwar entente, leading various countries to impose relatively rigid regulations and/or restrictions on temporary help agencies. For example, the THI's attempt to distance itself from the private employment agency industry by claiming legal employer status heightened tensions in both North America and Europe in this period. Still, as Gonos (1995: 24) notes: 'It is well to remember that legality and social legitimacy are two very different things. Legitimacy refers to a condition in which a given social practice finds widespread acceptance in a society, because it lies within the general framework of accepted social norms and widely-held beliefs ... Legality, of course, is also anything but a fixed state of affairs.' The evolution of international and national approaches to regulating the THI in the postwar period reinforces Gonos's claim. Although the THI gained conditional legitimacy in various countries and regions in this era, the legal status of temporary help agencies was anything but fixed at either the national or the supranational level from the inception of the THI until the late 1960s. Ironically, however, the lack of legal certainty surrounding the role of the THI in the international labour market, in combination with the well-crafted temporary help formula, facilitated its early success in the Canadian context.

International Developments

In the arena of international regulation, the period after the original 'Convention Concerning Fee-Charging Employment Agencies' (No. 34) came into force was very quiet. Between 1933 and 1944, only eleven member countries ratified Convention No. 34, primarily because of its unequivocal stand on prohibition and technical obstacles to ratification (ILO, 1997a: 52). But the Second World War had also created a standstill with respect to the promotion of international labour standards since member states were preoccupied with restoring peace. In the aftermath of the war, however, ILO member states expressed a desire to define the ILO's future policy program to suit the principles of social justice emerging in the reconstruction era (ILO 1944: i). Consequently, at the International Labour Conference in 1944, they endorsed the *Philadelphia Declaration*, a covenant that committed the ILO to expand its mandate to emphasize the 'role of economic and *social policies* [my emphasis], as opposed to only labour legislation for attaining social objectives' (ILO 1944, i). The *Philadelphia Declaration* explicitly committed the ILO to attaining the following objectives, which were collectively designed to cement the SER along with other central aspects of the postwar compromise:

- full employment and rising standards of living;
- the extension of social security measures to provide a basic income to all in need of such protection and comprehensive medical care;
- the provision of adequate nutrition, housing and facilities for recreation and culture;

– the assurance of equality of educational and vocational opportunity
  and provision for child welfare and maternity protection. (Lee, 1997:
  470–41)

It also renewed the constitution of the ILO, reaffirming the guiding
principle that 'labour is not a commodity,' while enlarging the ILO's
mandate to include a range of issues related to social security.

In the ensuing years, the ILO constructed a framework for the creation of national public employment services out of these measures. More
specifically, member states adopted two new instruments that offered a
framework for the creation and coordination of national public employment services: the Convention Concerning the Organization of the
Employment Service (No. 88) and the Recommendation Concerning
the Organization of the Employment Service (No. 83), which still exist.
Although neither instrument covered fee-charging employment agencies, both extended the mandate of Convention No. 34 and the general
belief that workers should be entitled to free public assistance in obtaining employment. Recommendation No. 83 asserted that 'systematic efforts should be made to develop the efficiency of the employment service
in such a manner as to obviate the need for private employment agencies
in all occupations except those in which the competent authority consid-
ers that for special reasons the existence of private employment agencies
is desirable or essential' (ILO 1992a: 446). Together with the *Philadelphia
Declaration*, these instruments spurred the ILO to re-examine the role of
fee-charging employment agencies in the labour market at the end of
the 1940s and eventually led it to revise Convention No. 34.

Convention No. 96 (Revised)

In 1949, just as the THI was emerging in the Canadian labour market,
the ILO revised Convention No. 34, which led to the adoption of the
Convention Concerning Fee-Charging Employment Agencies, Revised
(No. 96). Since the ILO took the position of *following* rather than *leading*
international regulatory developments pertaining to private employment agencies, Convention No. 96 (Revised) did not explicitly address
the status of temporary help agencies. Still, the convention's substance
clearly informed the THI's strategy of distancing itself from the private
employment agency industry: it had the effect of encouraging the THI
to deepen the temporary help formula and to use it as a means of
attaining greater legitimacy.

Convention No. 96 (Revised) was indeed built on Convention No. 34, and thus the general maxim that 'labour is not a commodity.' As a result, it preserved the basic features of the original international labour standard governing fee-charging employment agencies. For example, Convention No. 96 (Revised) retained the definition of fee-charging employment agencies first set out in Convention No. 34, defining them as 'any person, company, institution, agency or other organization which acts as an intermediary for the purpose of procuring employment for a worker or supplying a worker for an employer with a view to deriving either directly or indirectly any pecuniary or other material advantages from either employer or worker' (ILO, 1992a: 145).

However, to encourage a higher level of ratification, Convention No. 96 (Revised) departed from the substance of the Convention No. 34 in several areas. It offered ratifying states two options for eliminating common abuses among fee-charging employment agencies: progressive abolition or regulation (ILO 1997a: 52).[20] Part 2 of the convention set out a framework for abolition that remained virtually unchanged from Convention No. 34, with the exception of eliminating the three-year timetable for achieving prohibition and reversing the prior restriction on opening new private employment agencies (ILO, 1992a: 420). Quite distinctly, Part 3 of the convention outlined a framework for regulation. It assumed that both public and private employment agencies could contribute to the smooth functioning of the labour market, although private employment agencies should do so only under strict limitations (ILO, 1994a: 8). The regulatory framework that it set out for fee-charging employment agencies included provisions mandating yearly licensing, supervision, fixed-fee scales, and special rules for recruitment and placement.

Sweden's Request for Clarification

Since it offered member states a fair degree of flexibility, Convention No. 96 (Revised) removed many of the technical obstacles to ratification posed by Convention No. 34. As a result, the level of ratification of Convention No. 96 (Revised) far exceeded that of its predecessor, and just under half of the member states ratifying this convention opted to abide by Part 3 of the instrument.[21] However, by the time it came into full force in 1950, the labour market was in transition. New types of private employment agencies were entering the labour market. Emerging in the 1950s, temporary help agencies represented the largest category of new private employment agencies.

Due to the growing international prominence of temporary help agencies in the early 1960s, Sweden requested clarification from the director general of the ILO as to whether 'ambulatory typing agencies,' whose activities conformed with those of temporary help agencies placing clerical workers in the North American context, were covered under Convention No. 96 (Revised) (ILO, 1966: 391). Under Swedish labour law of the day, these agencies were perceived to be involved in the 'hiring out of labour'; their main purpose was to supply labour, and, in practice, they only employed (largely women) temporary help workers so long as they were assigned to an outside party (396). Consequently, Sweden expected that they would be excluded from coverage since they did not engage in permanent placement. However, the director general found that ambulatory typing agencies did indeed fall within the scope of Convention No. 96 (Revised). Referring to its definition of fee-charging employment agencies, the director general indicated that it included 'indirect employment operations' carried out for profit, and he stressed that the instrument intended to cover 'the variety in forms and methods of placing for profit' (394). He also classified them as intermediaries, a factor that was to shape national and international debates and discussions for decades. However, the director general still indicated that exclusions could be made for these categories of private employment agencies under the terms of the prevailing instrument. For example, he suggested that part-time and casual clerical workers might not be best recruited and placed in employment by public employment services for the following reason: 'Although public services do to a certain extent cater both for vacancies of this kind and for persons seeking employment of this kind, it is possible that the arrangements do not adequately meet the needs of the persons concerned and that the public services might hesitate to undertake additional work – testing, taking up references, assuming responsibility for handling questions of remuneration, taxation, social security, employment permits for foreign applicants – which may make private employment agencies more attractive to both the employers and the applicants for employment' (ILO 1966: 395–6).

In making these remarks, the director general openly recognized the wide range of new activities, extending beyond recruitment and placement, that private employment agencies were involved in and increasingly the very group of workers that they placed, including the many women workers perceived to be dependent upon a male wage. His remarks also provided some leverage for temporary help agencies, which were already often successfully claiming that their recruitment, testing, matching, and placement procedures distinguished them from the private employment industry at the national level.[22] Thus, despite the substance of his legal pronouncement, the director general offered ratifying States both an option and a viable justification for excluding temporary help agencies from coverage under the terms of the instrument.

Still, several member states expressed concern over the director general's characterization of ambulatory typing agencies as 'intermediaries' in the ensuing years, disregarding his crucial qualifier that temporary help agencies could be excluded from coverage from Convention No. 96 (Revised) (ILO, 1994b: 1, 8). Some renounced Convention No. 96 (Revised) on these grounds. Others ignored the director general's interpretation altogether, placing temporary help agencies outside the scope of national regulations directed at private employment agencies due to the type of workers they targeted and pressing employer demand. Still others took direction from Sweden's request for clarification. By the late 1960s, the legitimacy of Convention No. 96 (Revised) came under attack by both national governments desiring clarity, employers' groups demanding exclusions for temporary help agencies and workers' groups demanding a new international labour standard explicitly designed to cover temporary help agencies (ILO 1994a). The conflicting demands of these three core sets of actors in the ILO's organizational structure produced a decades-long stalemate on the issue of regulating private employment agencies at the supranational level. The demands also led member states to adopt three divergent approaches to regulating temporary help agencies in particular and the TER more generally.

Regulating Temporary Help Agencies

In the context of developments at the supranational level, the three approaches to regulating temporary help agencies that emerged in the late 1960s and early 1970s were prohibition, regulation, and nonregulation. A country's approach to regulating temporary help agencies in the postwar period usually reflected the type of stand it had originally taken in 1933, with the ILO's introduction of the convention prohibiting fee-charging employment agencies.

Based on the principles contained in Convention No. 34, a common approach to regulation dominant in the early part of the postwar era was prohibition. A significant group of member countries prohibited temporary help agencies for a lengthy period in the postwar era. Measures designed to achieve complete prohibition endured longest in Italy, Spain, and Greece; in all three cases, the reasons behind adopting this approach reflected the need to control the labour supply in labour markets with a history of high unemployment and a record of significant abuses on the part of labour market intermediaries (Koniaris, 1993; Rodriguez-Sanudo, 1993; Treu, 1993). Still, over the decades in question, many temporary help agencies penetrated each of these national labour markets due largely to the lack of enforcement mechanisms in existing legislation. While measures designed to achieve prohibition remained on the books in all three countries for decades, legislators began to ignore them in practice by the late 1970s, allowing temporary help agencies a considerable degree of autonomy in local labour markets (Rodriguez-Sanudo, 1993: 258; Treu, 1993: 202).

In the later part of the postwar period, a number of European countries that were unsuccessful at enforcing either Convention No. 34 or Convention No. 96 (Revised) (Part 2) or chose to endorse Convention No. 96 (Revised) (Part 3) opted to regulate the activities of temporary help agencies. For example, in the late 1960s France showed signs of lifting its decades-long ban on these labour market actors and began to create a framework for the regulation of temporary help agencies and the TER more broadly, as a means of confronting the spread of non-standard forms of employment (Rojot, 1993; Veldkamp and Raesten, 1973: 126). At this juncture, the French government faced a dilemma: it felt obliged to regulate the TER, yet it did not want to undermine the primacy of the SER in principle or in practice. Consequently, its initial regulatory interventions reflected two goals aimed at limiting abuses on the part of the temporary help agencies and their customers. First, they aimed to restrict the substitution of contracts of fixed-term and temporary help work for permanent jobs. Second, they aimed to provide guarantees to temporary help workers that preserved some protections associated with the SER (France, 1972). Given these goals, more than any other country in Europe, France adopted a coherent strategy of 'regulating precariousness' (Vosko, 1998a) that had its origins in the early 1970s, but, as will be discussed in Chapter 6, reached its height in the late 1980s. It was the first ILO member state to institute a model of regulation that went beyond regulating the recruitment and placement activities of temporary help agencies as private employment agencies to regulate the TER itself.

While its approach to regulation differed sharply from France, Germany also opted to regulate the temporary help worker's conditions of employment after the ILO's important pronouncement in 1966. In the

German context, where the government actively committed itself to the SER and its comprehensive package of protections in the postwar period, the state took a unique approach to regulating what it labeled 'employee-leasing firms' and protecting temporary help workers. Although its approach led to outcomes similar to the French case, Germany came to govern the TER by a *normal* unlimited contractual relationship between the temporary help agency and the temporary help worker (Weiss and Schmidt, 1993: 114). Originating in the 1970s, German legislation characterized the employee-leasing firm (i.e., temporary help agency) as the employer of record and the temporary help worker was to receive benefits customarily associated with the SER (Weiss and Schmidt 1993: 129). Thus, temporary help work was considered *temporary* only insofar as workers were only permitted to work for a limited duration on the customer's site. In legal terms, the employment relationship between the agency and the worker was defined as long-lasting. Hence, beginning in the later part of the postwar period, the German government allowed businesses to 'borrow' workers from employee-leasing firms as long as these workers retained their entitlements to the minimal set of protections guaranteed to workers engaged in the SER. In this respect, the social priorities of France and Germany were similar but they used different means to regulate temporary help agencies and the TER more broadly. As Chapter 6 illustrates, the French model became a template for the European Community during the late 1980s and early 1990s since it accommodated the decline of the SER. The German model fell apart precisely because it rested on the stability of the SER as a normative entity.

In contrast to the Continental European approach to regulation, many countries, such as the United States, Canada, Denmark, Ireland, and Great Britain, took a more lenient approach to monitoring the activities of temporary help agencies in the postwar era (Gonos, 1994; Hepple, 1993: 452; Jacobsen, 1993: 77). Some, such as Canada, the United States, and Great Britain, regulated their activities in accordance with legislation pertaining to private employment agencies. However, distinct from many of their European counterparts, who shifted their efforts away from regulating temporary help agencies as labour market entities towards regulating the TER in the postwar period, countries opting for nonregulation failed to establish by definition any firm regulatory parameters surrounding the TER. Canada is a case in point since it chose only to regulate private employment agencies as labour market entities.

In the Canadian context, temporary help agencies were normally regulated under provincially based employment agency acts from the mid-1930s onwards. No proactive legislation governing the TER itself emerged at either the federal or the provincial level during the postwar era.[23] Provincial employment agency acts, many of which had their origins in the prewar period, generally required temporary help agencies to obtain licenses and keep detailed records. The majority also prohibited direct fees to workers or established fixed fee-scales by classifying them as private employment agencies garnering indirect fees from the client firm (see, for example: RSA, 1942, 1948; RSBC, 1919; RSM, 1950; RSO, 1950). Some even granted the appropriate authorities the power to prohibit specific types of private employment agencies, thereby extending provincial measures first set out in the late 1920s (RSQ, 1941; RSO, 1950). For example, the *Employment Agency Act* (1950) of Ontario continued to give the Lieutenant-Governor-in-Council the authority to prohibit specific types of private employment agencies and/or individual private employment agencies of undesirable character until 1960, although this measure was never invoked in either the pre- or postwar period. Still, beginning in the postwar period and continuing over the course of the decades-long stalemate at the ILO, temporary help agencies gained de facto employer status in most provincial jurisdictions, even in Quebec, which crafted the most rigid provincially based regulatory regime pertaining to private employment agencies in post-war Canada.[24] Simultaneously, the THI gained considerable legitimacy in the Canadian labour market by offering to provide both a 'crucial extra service for its business clients' (i.e., taking the role of the legal 'employer') and 'employment opportunities' to a relatively narrow group of workers excluded from the SER (Gonos, 1994: 241).

Ironically, mirroring the practices of countries opting for more active forms of regulation in the postwar period, Canada did not codify the employer status of the temporary help agency into law. In this respect, Canada's passive approach to regulating temporary help agencies differed from its American counterpart where numerous branches of the THI actively engaged in legal battles for employer status from its inception until the mid-1980s, battles that only intensified after the ILO's pronouncement in 1966 (Gonos, 1995). Still, like their American counterparts, Canadian provinces were relatively silent on the issue of regulating temporary help agencies throughout the postwar era. Most provinces accepted temporary help agencies' claims to employer status in practice (since they did not undermine the SER), thereby preserving their mediating role in the labour market. However, they were reluctant to grant them unconditional legitimacy as employers, perhaps partly due to the configuration of debates at the international level. In the meantime, the THI continued to carve out a space for itself in the Canadian labour market, maintaining its focus on both a narrow pool of workers and well-defined client base. Still, its changing role would concern Canadian policy-makers as well as policy-makers in countries opting for prohibition and regulation for decades to come.

Conclusion

This chapter traced the emergence of the Canadian THI, detailing its dramatic rise in the clerical sector and the complex set of national and supranational developments that contributed to its early success. It illustrated, first, that the THI played a pivotal mediating role in the postwar era and therefore contributed to upholding the entente between capital and organized labour (mediated by the state) from the late 1940s until the early 1970s. It then demonstrated how the THI contributed to negotiating the tension between sustaining the SER as a norm and preserving dualism in the labour market, by catering to individuals and firms requiring temporary clerical assistance as its primary customers, targeting white middle-class married women as its chief workers, and claiming employer status. The chapter developed this argument by charting the nature of women's participation in the Canadian labour market at the inception of the THI, the strategy adopted by early temporary help agencies and the changing shape of national and supranational regulatory regimes governing private employment agencies in the postwar era.

By focusing on the shape of women's labour force participation from the early 1930s to the late 1960s, it becomes clear just how crucial policies and practices that curtailed married women's employment were to the formation of the Canadian THI. Evidence suggests that these measures created a captive pool of potential workers for the THI to draw on. Still, policies beyond explicit marriage bars, which facilitated labour market segmentation based on race, ethnicity, and immigration status, as well as gender, also contributed to positioning white middle-class married women as an ideal workforce for the THI. As the SER gained ascendancy, immigration policies relegated a substantial number of women to specific occupations such as domestic service, where, for example, minimum wage legislation did not apply.

In the postwar period, measures limiting married women's entitlements to social insurance and marriage bars in various fields of employment had the effect of curtailing their labour market participation to the extent that temporary help work was among their few viable employment options. Correspondingly, immigration policies that led the government to recruit specific groups of women into occupations that were undesirable to Canadian-born women, particularly live-in domestic work, also set rigid boundaries around their labour market participation. Excluded from the SER, each group's mobility in the labour market was constrained, limiting their entry into vocations of their own choosing. The relative force of the ideology of domesticity only aggravated persisting tensions. It heightened racialized gender divisions of labour in the waged sphere, trapping many immigrant women wage-earners in a few narrow segments of the labour market, and it fueled attacks on married women wage-earners' 'right to work.' Of critical importance to the foregoing argument, it also contributed to generating a highly gendered and racialized space in the labour market, which the Canadian THI further shaped to its advantage.

Upon its inception, the THI constructed largely white middle-class married women as 'ideal' temporary help workers. From the vantage point of the THI, this narrow group of women represented a suitable pool of workers due to their assumed dependence upon male breadwinners – a presumption fostered by the ideology of domesticity – and their supposedly 'natural' role in social reproduction. The THI then transformed the idealized image of the temporary help worker into a reality by adeptly building on pre-existing racialized gender divisions in the Canadian labour market. By distancing itself from the early private employment agency industry and targeting a group of workers that lacked a range of benefits and entitlements associated with the SER and were barred from certain fields of employment, the THI avoided challenges akin to those directed at private employment agents in the pre-Second World War era. This complex strategy allowed temporary help agencies, like their earliest precursors, to capitalize on the legal disentitlements of married women and to avoid the full costs of reproducing these workers.

The early Canadian THI used the temporary help formula, a coherent strategy that complemented pre-existing exclusionary policies and highly racialized ideologies of domesticity, to solidify its client base and capture its ideal workforce. In the early 1950s, temporary help agencies such as Office Overload seized on the labour shortage in the clerical sector by catering to individuals and firms in need of clerical assistance. Simultaneously, they offered flexible work arrangements to a group of married women, who, although they were excluded from the SER, still needed part-time and temporary employment to sustain themselves and their families. Both these facets of the temporary help formula enabled the Canadian THI to bolster its legitimacy, and, even more important, to introduce the TER as a viable alternative for attaining a means of subsistence for certain marginalized segments of the working population. Indeed, the TER surfaced as a de facto triangular employment relationship at the inception of the Canadian THI. In the postwar era, temporary help workers were normally assigned to several worksites off the employer's premises, were rarely party to indeterminate employment contracts, and they could be dismissed with limited notice (Cordova, 1986: 641). Although the core features of the TER violated all of the central tenets of the SER, it gained conditional legitimacy alongside the THI due largely to the characteristics of the typical temporary help worker and the emergence of a more reputable type of private employment agency. Given that the THI narrowly targeted white middle-class married women as its chief workers and simultaneously distanced itself from the private employment agency industry by claiming legal employer status, the TER did not pose an immediate threat to the SER, nor to any of the parties central to the postwar entente. Although temporary help agencies began to treat workers as their primary 'commodities' in this period, the central actors that granted the THI legitimacy at the national and the international levels overlooked this development.

In the Canadian context, the THI became a success very shortly after its birth. However, the role of the temporary help agency did not go unquestioned in the supranational regulatory arena in the postwar era. The configuration of developments that occurred at the both national and the international levels did indeed open up a space for the THI. Still, for a lengthy period, prominent members of the international community viewed the THI as an outgrowth of the private employment agency industry and carefully scrutinized its activities. Even though international labour conventions governing private employment agencies predated the emergence of temporary help agencies, and thus did not cover these labour market entities definitively, the ILO still ruled that they fell under the scope of Convention No. 96 (Revised) in 1966. This controversial ruling spurred some member states to prohibit temporary help agencies and thus symbolically preserve the maxim 'labour is not commodity,' others to develop measures to monitor and regulate them, and still others to renounce the convention and call for the repeal of such supranational measures. In the interim, the Canadian THI earned a special status that set it apart from the early private employment agency industry, thereby relieving it of focused state scrutiny. Combined with the cleverly crafted temporary help formula, this special status only strengthened the THI's mediating role in the postwar era.

From Stop-Gap Workers to Staffing Services: The Expansion of the Temporary Help Industry

'Staffing' is a broader [term] than 'temporary.' It seems to capture all the types of work arrangements and services that we are providing. In the public's mind, temping seems to have a slightly negative connotation ... The image that comes to mind is still one of the 'Kelly Girl.' It's not too glamorous. It's not a great way to work. But, there is a way to counteract that. By using 'employment' and 'staffing,' we want to communicate to the public that the industry has changed. It's no longer necessarily just providing temps *per se*. It's doing so many other things. (I1)

In the postwar era, the THI was quite successful in balancing the concerns of capital, organized labour, and the state and upholding the SER as the norm by targeting a narrow group of workers and a well-defined set of customers. But it brokered a somewhat different range of interests in the period spanning from the early 1970s to the late 1990s. By the 1970s, the industry had gained sufficient legitimacy in Canada and other nations pursuing a strategy of nonregulation that it no longer needed to rely on the SER as a counterweight to preserve its place in the labour market. As a result, it gradually abandoned its prior mediating role and began to situate the TER as an alternative to the SER, building on dramatic changes in the labour market, the exceptionally stable regulatory regime surrounding private agencies (reinforced by the stalemate at the ILO and the absence of a proactive stance against against the THI on the part of the Canadian labour movement), the removal of marriage bars, and the diminishing force of the ideology of domesticity.

In the post-1970 period, the THI turned its attention to growth and expansion, targeting new customers, shifting its marketing strategy from supplying 'stop-gap' workers to providing 'staffing services' and appealing to a larger cross-section of workers. To capture a wider range of customers, temporary help agencies focused on broadening the occupational spread in the industry by expanding into new sectors, especially in high-technology fields. They also tapped into the growing desire among employers for so-called labour flexibility (especially 'numerical' flexibility) by extending their services beyond supplying temporary help workers to assuming responsibilities related to hiring, dismissal, health and safety, and the provision of benefits, thereby absorbing more of the costs and risks normally associated with employing workers.[1] Simultaneously, temporary help agencies employed a range of new tactics to appeal to workers. Using the state-sanctioned decline of the SER to their advantage, they now cast temporary help work as a suitable option not only for women with family responsibilities but for people with a diverse range of skills and occupational backgrounds. Still, the legacy of the 'Kelly Girl' – the gendered imagery that the THI first used to carve out a space in the labour market – and the fact that the THI initially distanced itself from the private employment agency industry by basing its reputation on providing temporary help, had lasting effects on the shape of the TER as well as on the regulatory regime that surrounded it.

This chapter traces the rapid expansion of the Canadian THI from the mid-1970s to the early 1990s, focusing on the strategy that it crafted to adapt to changes in the labour market and the new relationship that it cultivated between temporary help agencies and their customers. By examining the changing strategy of the THI from the end of the post Second World War era to the late 1990s, it establishes the TER as one of several emerging alternatives to the SER. It also lays the foundation for developing another core claim of this book: the argument that it is both possible and necessary to extend the concept of feminization beyond the biologically based category of sex to explore the gendered character of prevailing employment trends in contemporary Canada. The chapter begins to advance this claim by revealing that the THI took heed of women's mass entry into the labour force in transforming itself from a female-dominated industry, one that situated the TER as a supplement to the SER to cater to a specific regulatory environment and a particular set of employment norms, to an industry where sex parity is emerging, one that is now positioning the TER as one among several alternatives to the SER.[2]

Destabilizing the SER

In the Canadian context, the SER reached its peak as a *normative* model of employment in the mid-1960s, a period when white middle-class married women constituted the THI's primary pool of workers. At this juncture, the stability of the SER depended upon a tight constellation of forces; it relied on the ideology of domesticity and the corresponding notion of a 'family wage,' whereby the wage secured by a male breadwinner was enough to satisfy the needs of a 'man' and his family, and a system of free collective bargaining. Significant cracks first began to appear in the SER in the early 1970s, corresponding with a host of international and national developments such as the end of the gold standard and the oil shocks, and unprecedented new policy measures such as wage and price controls and UI reforms. Still, the SER only became visibly unstable in the 1980s when Canadians began to experience the feminization of the labour force and to confront the rise and spread of nonstandard forms of employment.

International Developments

At an international level, the late 1960s and the early 1970s were a period of tremendous political and economic turmoil. The most profound changes in the international system began to occur around the mid-1960s when the United States was no longer the dominant economic power that it had been for almost two decades. By 1970 several Western European countries and Japan were narrowing the gap between themselves and the United States; there was increasing dissatisfaction with the American dominance of the international monetary system, and, in particular, the privileged role of the American dollar as the international currency (Gill and Law, 1988; Spero, 1990).

August 15, 1971 marked an important breaking point. On this day, American President Richard Nixon announced a new economic policy: the American dollar would no longer be convertible into gold, a move that denoted the end of the Bretton Woods system. In response to Nixon's announcement, other national leaders attempted to repair the system of international monetary management. Through what was known as the Smithsonian Agreement, they negotiated with the United States to provide a 10 per cent devaluation of the dollar in relation to gold, realign other exchange rates, and allow for greater flexibility in exchange rates. However, their efforts were made in vain. Less than two years after this agreement was reached, fixed exchange rates were replaced by floating rates, inflation erupted globally, and there were worldwide commodity shortages (Gill and Law, 1988: 173–4; Gilpin, 1987: 140–1; Spero, 1990: 45). At the same time as international leaders were attempting to stabilize the monetary system, there was a dramatic rise in the price of petroleum, creating many new problems including a recession and accelerating inflation.[3]

In this context, the major monetary powers known as the Group of Seven (G7), met in France to craft a new monetary regime in November 1975. This meeting, which was the first of what would become annual summits of the seven major industrial powers, formally established a system of floating exchange rates and thereby symbolized the return of the multilateral management of the monetary system (Gill, 1993: 99). It was also extremely significant because it prompted leading countries to call for greater surveillance of the exchange rate system and closer management of national economic policies by the International Monetary Fund (IMF); one outcome of the meeting was the implementation of IMF-driven austerity measures in many countries. Related to its new commitment to the tighter management of national economic policy by the IMF, the G7 endorsed a platform to fight inflation that mandated the following set of measures at its two successive annual meetings: the coordination of national economic policies, expansion among countries with balance of payments surpluses, and the imposition of anti-inflationary programs in countries with balance of payments deficits (Gill and Law, 1988; Spero, 1990). Although this platform failed almost immediately, prompting accelerating inflation in Germany and other countries with balance of payments surpluses, Canada continued to follow the wisdom of the IMF and the World Bank, and attempted to curb inflation.

National Developments

In the national context, inflation became a central policy issue for the federal government in 1968 when it first confronted stagflation – stagnant growth and rising inflation. At this juncture, the government posed its new goals of reducing inflation and curbing unemployment as creating a dilemma at the policy level, implying that Canada's postwar full-employment objective (and the social policy program that it generated) had contributed to rising inflation and therefore must be modified. In his study of the full-employment objective in Canada, Robert Campbell (1991: 10) characterizes the tenor of the federal government's gradual adoption of anti-inflation measures as follows: 'Fiscal and monetary policy in the late 1960s was directed to easing inflationary pressures. *While there was no "formal" abandonment of the full employment goal, it was clear that the latter had to be "sacrificed" or traded-off for the goal of price stability'* [my emphasis]. The rising level of 'natural' unemployment in this period further substantiates Campbell's claims.

The shift from the so-called Old World order to a New World order surely played an important role in prompting Canada to prioritize anti-inflation over its full-employment objective in the 1970s. However, it is crucial to emphasize that Canada led the call for a coordinated international strategy targeting inflation at both the G7 summit in Puerto Rico (1977) and in Bonn (1978) (Gill, 1993: 99). Indeed, Canada's central role in both summits may be explained by the fact that by the time the most profound shifts had begun to occur at the international level the federal Liberal government was already beginning to advance an anti-inflation program, and therefore to abandon the postwar full-employment objective that brought the SER to dominance.

For a short period in the early 1970s, the Liberal government was reluctant to initiate controls on inflation since it was acutely aware of the political consequences of rising unemployment. Thus, in its budgets, it targeted unemployment, aiming to decrease it modestly, and attempted to reduce inflation through indirect measures. However, after the resignation of Liberal Finance Minister John Turner, who resisted the introduction of wage and price controls, and with the supply shocks of the early 1970s, the government began to reduce public spending and explicitly target inflation. For example, the 1976 budget made significant changes to UI, which included raising the number of weeks that workers had to work to qualify for UI by 50 per cent, and tying benefits more closely to the number of weeks worked, and it also initiated a standstill on government spending to last until the early 1980s.[4] Curbing inflation became the central policy objective of the federal government, and the full-employment objective, key to establishing the SER as a norm at a policy level, quickly faded away.

The federal government initiated the first sustained attack on inflation in the Anti-Inflation Program (AIP) of September 1975.[5] This program introduced wage restraints in a range of settings in an attempt, in the words of one advocate, to 'facilitate an orderly winding down of inflation' without inducing unemployment (Weiler 1980, as cited by

Panitch 1976; Panitch and Swartz, 1988: 254). After its inception, inflation declined quite sharply but unemployment climbed to a new peak of
8.4 per cent in 1980. As a result, it looked as if the government might
lessen its attack on inflation for a brief period in the late 1970s, as it
removed the measures initiated under the AIP (Maslove and Swimmer,
1980: 32–9). However, it merely changed course by introducing the
Public Sector Compensation Restraint Act (Bill C-124). Also known as the '6
and 5' program, this legislation enacted measures aimed at restraining
public sector wages and prices in most provinces similar to (but even
harsher than) the AIP (Canada, 1985: 308–9). As Panitch and Swartz
(1988: 35) note, '*The Public Sector Compensation Restraint Act* (Bill C-124),
introduced in June 1982, was not as comprehensive as the *Anti-Inflation
Act* of 1975–78, which covered both public and private sector workers.
*However, what it lacked in comprehensiveness, it made up in the severity of the
treatment of workers'* [my emphasis], and '6 and 5' did more than roll back
the wages of public sector workers in signed agreements with increases
above 6 and 5 per cent: it temporarily removed their right to strike and
bargain collectively by arbitrarily extending existing collective agreements for two years. Although most of its measures were phased out by
1985, '6 and 5' symbolized a growing willingness on the part of the
federal government to limit the hard-won free collective bargaining
rights of public sector workers. It also corresponded with the increasing
resort to ad-hoc back-to-work legislation on the parts of federal and
provincial governments so that there were forty-three cases between
1980 and 1987 (Panitch and Swartz, 1988: 30).

   If the AIP and '6 and 5' did not undermine the foundations of the SER
sufficiently by issuing wage restraints and infringing on the right to free
collective bargaining in Canada, then proposals for reform contained in
the *Royal Commission on the Economic Union and Development Prospects for
Canada* (Canada 1985) certainly made it clear that the state no longer
viewed the SER as an ideal. A template for future policy development in
a wide range of areas, the Macdonald Commission, which applauded the
Canadian government for its anti-inflation programs of the 1970s, recommended a wide range of UI reforms. Chief among them were proposals to reduce UI benefits to 50 per cent of a worker's previous earnings,
raise entrance requirements, tighten the link between maximum benefits and the minimum employment period, and eliminate regional
differences in the program (Canada, 1985: 611). The much publicized
rationale for these recommendations was that UI should not be treated
as a means to 'deliver redistributive goals,' but as a pure social insurance

program funded exclusively by workers and employers (602). The subtext of the commission's rationale was not only that national unemployment rates of over 8 per cent were acceptable but also that the nature of employment itself was changing, so that fewer workers could expect to engage in SERs and therefore receive full UI coverage. As a result of these developments, the recommendation of the Macdonald Commission was to maintain UI as a program that delivered the most comprehensive benefits to standard workers and offered only limited benefits to the increasing number of workers falling outside this mold.

Many of the Macdonald Commission's recommendations were formally integrated into the proposals of the *Commission of Inquiry on Unemployment Insurance* (Canada, 1986) chaired by Claude Forget. Set in place to restructure UI, the Forget Commission made a range of policy recommendations. First, it recommended that self-employed fishermen's [*sic*] eligibility for UI be phased out over a five-year period, attempting to reduce the number of workers covered by the package of benefits and entitlements that came to be associated with the SER in the postwar period (Canada, 1986: 72). Second, reminiscent of the Economic Council of Canada's study *People and Jobs* (1976), it recommended that the UI Act should better recognize and interpret the concepts of so-called 'voluntary' and 'involuntary' unemployment and strengthen entitlements for the involuntarily unemployed (Canada, 1986: 75). Third, it proposed that the financing of the UI system be based solely on premiums from employers and workers (77). This last proposal followed directly from the Macdonald Commission, and it built upon pre-existing federal government initiatives such as the AIP and '6 and 5' since it signaled the state's complete repudiation of the postwar full-employment objective and its related commitment to devising a comprehensive framework of social protections for Canadian workers.

The shift towards an international order characterized by a multilateral system of monetary management and the adoption of national policy measures aimed at reducing inflation made the late 1960s and early 1970s a turbulent period. International developments suggest that the postwar compromise began to fall apart in this era, as evidenced by declining American hegemony, commodity shortages, and rising inflation. Similarly, at the national level, the federal government's new emphasis on implementing anti-inflation policies and programs, and its subsequent abandonment of the full-employment objective illustrate that the SER was highly unstable in this era. In the Canadian context, we see more evidence of the erosion of the SER by examining the gendered employment trends and the rise of nonstandard forms of employment that accompanied these developments.

Labour Market Trends

Coinciding with developments at the national and international level that contributed to destabilizing the SER, dramatic shifts also began to take place on the Canadian labour market in the mid- to late-1970s. These changes involved an unprecedented rise in women's labour force participation rates (in part because formal marriage bars to paid employment were absent and the ideology of domesticity was no longer hegemonic), profound shifts in men's labour force participation which dropped from 78.4 per cent in 1975 to 73.3 per cent in 1993), and the rise of nonstandard forms of employment (Lindsay, 1995: 10).

Numerous scholars locate the roots of the feminization of employment in the late 1970s and early 1980s in both Canada and abroad, associating it with the rise of a supply-side politico-economic agenda (Armstrong, 1996; Bakker, 1989; Cohen, 1994; Rubery, 1994; Standing, 1989). To recall, the most uncontested facet of the feminization of employment is women's mass entry into the formal labour force; this dimension of feminization is increasingly characterized as a 'third shift' to denote that women's rising labour force participation rates often reflect a movement from the informal economy to the formal economy rather than a shift from economic inactivity to economic activity (Tiano, 1994; Ward, 1994). A second common dimension is persisting (and possibly even intensified) sex segregation in the labour market. The casualization of employment, which is linked to the increasingly 'feminized' character of a range of job types, represents a third feature. Finally, a fourth common aspect is increased income and occupational polarization, both between women and men and among women themselves, frequently attributable to variables pertaining to age, immigration status, and race.

There is clearly a relationship between the feminization of employment as a whole and the extraordinary growth and expansion of the THI, particularly its shift from a highly female-dominated industry to one where sex parity is emerging. More specifically, there is a definitive relationship between the growing casualization of employment in Canada, or the 'gendering of jobs,' and the precarious nature of the TER; Chapter 5 addresses these relationships in detail. However, more than any other facet of the feminization of employment, the feminization of the labour force (i.e., rising and/or consistently high rates of labour force participation among women) was pivotal in allowing the THI to recreate itself in the 1970s and 1980s.

Between the early 1970s and the early 1990s, women's labour force participation rates rose dramatically – by 1993 they comprised 45.2 per cent of the labour force in Canada (Lindsay 1995). In contrast, men's labour force participation rates stagnated between 1975 and 1981, when they began to decline at an accelerated rate, a development that left more women without male economic support. Consequently, even though labour force participation rates declined for both women and men between 1990 and 1993, women's share of the labour force still increased in these years. Moreover, even though the unemployment rate rose significantly for both sexes between 1990 and 1993, with men between the ages of fifteen and twenty-four experiencing the largest increase,[6] rising female unemployment rates had little impact on women's growing share of the labour force. They may, however, have contributed to the rather unchanged terms and conditions of women's employment (Chapter 5).

The only other trend of a similar magnitude to the feminization of the labour force in this period was the proliferation of nonstandard forms of employment. From the mid-1970s to the early 1990s, there was a considerable increase in nonstandard forms of employment, including part-time work, contract work, temporary work, home-based work, self-employment, and on-call work, in both Canada and abroad.

At the international level, this phenomenon affected every country belonging to the OECD, most of whom experienced substantial increases in at least one form of nonstandard employment from the mid-1970s to the early 1990s. For example, in some countries, including the United Kingdom, Portugal, New Zealand, Canada, and Australia, self-employment grew considerably between 1973 and 1993. In others, such as France, the Netherlands, and Spain, temporary employment expanded extremely rapidly between 1983 and 1993. Notably, part-time employment grew sharply throughout OECD countries in this period (ILO, 1997; OECD, 1993, 1995).

In the Canadian context, the Economic Council of Canada first addressed the rapid growth of nonstandard forms of employment in detail in its widely cited study *Good Jobs, Bad Jobs*, defining them as 'those which differ from the traditional model of a full-time, full-year job' (Economic Council of Canada, 1990, 12). After this study was released, the federal government also began to produce numerous reports acknowledging their unprecedented growth (Advisory Group on Working Time and the Distribution of Work, 1994: 27; Human Resources and Development Canada 1994: 49). For example, in 1996 Human Resources and Development Canada reported that the growth of nonstandard forms of employment was so extensive that in 1995 only 33 per cent of Canadian workers were said to hold so-called 'normal' jobs – that is, full-time, full-year jobs with benefits (Lipsett and Reesor, 1997). There was particularly rapid growth in some forms of nonstandard employment, such as temporary help work and self-employment, and more steady growth in others, such as part-time employment. From 1976 to 1994 the proportion of workers employed part-time climbed from 11 percent to 17 per cent, with fifteen to twenty-four-year-olds experiencing the brunt of this trend (Krahn, 1995: 35–6). Corresponding with the growth in part-time work, multiple job-holding also increased in Canada over the same period. Between 1989 and 1994 increases were particularly sharp for women aged fifteen to twenty-four, suggesting that the disproportionate number of young people engaged in part-time work would prefer full-time work, or at least more hours. Self-employment also grew quite rapidly in Canada beginning in the 1970s, although it continued to be the preserve of older workers in the early 1990s (Crompton, 1993; Krahn, 1995). In contrast, temporary employment, which grew in the later part of this period (i.e., 9 percent of workers identified themselves as temporary in 1994 versus 8 percent in 1989), was especially common among young people, who represented 32 percent of all temporary workers in 1995 (Krahn, 1995: 38; Statistics Canada, 1996: cat. 71M003GPE).

Obviously, nonstandard forms of work are by no means mutually exclusive; for example, temporary workers often work part-time as do many of the self-employed. Nor are they necessarily synonymous with precarious employment. If the period from the mid-1970s to the late 1990s is any indication, however, there is a relationship between growing precariousness in the Canadian labour market, a core facet of the feminization of employment to be addressed in Chapter 5, and the spread of nonstandard forms of employment, particularly those characterized by divided employment relationships such as temporary help work.

Industry Profile: More than Simply Supplements

With the profound changes in the Canadian labour market from the mid-1970s to the early 1990s, the THI altered its marketing strategy. It no longer targeted a narrow group of women workers or a well-defined set of customers. Instead, it built upon one of the most central aspects of the feminization of employment, namely, the feminization of the labour force. In this period, rising female labour force participation rates and the unprecedented decline in male participation rates allowed the THI to expand and deepen its pool of workers, and, for the first time since its inception, target male workers previously in SERs. These trends enabled it to retain its niche in the clerical sector, since, for the most part, the feminization of the labour force meant 'more of the same for women,' while simultaneously enticing a wider diversity of workers. The THI recast its image with an acute awareness of the rise of nonstandard forms of employment and the growing desire among companies for 'labour flexibility.' The decline of the SER opened up a space for the THI to shift from casting the TER as a supplement to the SER to promoting it as an alternative.

Evidence suggests that the growth of the Canadian THI accelerated in the 1980s, and peaked in 1989 alongside its American counterpart, but it is impossible to chart its performance statistically before the early 1990s. This is because Statistics Canada first began collecting statistics on the THI in 1984 and only recently began to publish this data due to imperfections in the survey instruments first used to collect data in the mid-1980s.[7] Still, it is instructive to describe the growth of the American THI from the mid-1970s to the late 1980s, since, as many studies show, the Canadian THI has followed a similar trajectory (Abraham, 1990; Akyeampong, 1989; Carré, 1994; Golden and Applebaum, 1992; Hamdani, 1996; Mangum, Mayall, and Nelson, 1985; OECD, 1993).

In the American context, personnel supply services[8] grew at an annual average of 11.5 per cent between 1972 and 1986 and the THI grew almost 20 per cent per year between 1982 and 1986 (Abraham, 1990: 87). While the industry employed approximately 20,000 workers at its inception in the mid-1950s, by the mid-1980s estimates ranged from one million to two to three million (Abraham, 1990: 87; Gannon, 1984: 26). Beyond the unprecedented growth of employment in the American THI in this period, what is striking is that nonclerical temporary help work grew much more rapidly than office temporary help work in the late 1970s and early 1980s. According to Katherine Abraham (1990: 87) 'Agencies specializing in non-office temporaries accounted for only a third of total temporary-help service employment in 1972 but for more than 45 percent of the total by 1982.' As Abraham (90) observes, this shift in the composition of the THI is consistent with the 'anecdotal evidence that businesses broadened the scope of their reliance on temporary workers' in the 1980s. It also supports the hypothesis that, with the rise of nonstandard forms of employment and the feminization of the labour force, the American THI shifted away from catering primarily to customers in the clerical sector to targeting a more diverse set of customers beginning in the 1970s.

The pattern of growth in the American THI mirrored what Statistics Canada officials began to report in the late 1980s. For example, a study entitled 'The Changing Face of Temporary Help' released in 1989 reported: 'According to industry sources, the focus in those days [i.e., the 1950s] was the supply of clerical secretarial and manual labour to fill in for permanent employees who were sick, on maternity leave or on vacation. Most of the jobs were of short duration. However, over the years, the industry has evolved to meet the diversified and changing needs of Canadian business. *Today, many workers contracted out have specialized professional and technical skills. And these persons are often hired as supplementary labour rather than as temporary replacements for permanent staff absent from work*' [my emphasis] (Akyeampong, 1989: 43). Although analysts only recently began to acknowledge the magnitude of change in the Canadian THI, where it exists, data on its size and shape and the demographics of its workforce in the late 1980s suggests that it began to shift course in this decade.

A Snapshot of the Canadian THI

After peaking in the late 1980s, the size of the THI (as well as its revenues) remained relatively constant. Data on the shape of the industry illustrate that in the early 1990s temporary help agencies were successful both at expanding into new markets, such as the health-care sector and the public sector as a whole, and broadening and deepening their pool of workers. In the Canadian context, the THI's strategic move towards providing 'staffing services' translated into unprecedented diversification.

Size

Relative to its American counterpart, the Canadian THI has always been quite small, as have its profits. However, by Canadian standards, revenues in this industry were quite high in the early 1990s, and its size remained relatively constant. Revenues hovered between $1.3 and $1.5 billion between 1990 and 1993 and there were approximately 1,300 temporary help agencies operating in Canada in this period. The majority of temporary help agencies operated out of Ontario, Quebec, and Alberta (Statistics Canada, 1993: cat. 63–232).

Temporary help agencies with revenues below $2 million dominated the THI on a national basis in the early 1990s and the majority of agencies had revenues of less than $250,000. On a provincial basis, Ontario had the largest percentage of agencies with revenues over $5 million in this period, followed by Quebec and Alberta (Statistics Canada 1993: cat. 63–232).[9]

What is notable about revenues in the THI is the proportion of revenues derived from placing workers. Between 1991 and 1993, for temporary help agencies with revenues above $250,000, this figure remained constant at approximately 98.5 per cent (Table 8a). That is, virtually all expenses incurred by the THI came from paying wages, salaries, and basic benefits (Table 8b). Since the payment of wages represented over 80 per cent of the THI's expenses in the early 1990s, it was easy for firms to establish new branches. Overhead costs were predictably low because temporary help workers are dispatched to different work sites. Moreover, even though a number of large transnational temporary help agencies operated in Canada, small agencies maintained a sizeable niche in the labour market.[10] As well, since temporary help agencies normally do not require a license to operate, start-up costs were (and continue to be) mainly confined to capital for rent, office-staff wages, computer equipment, and advertising.

Diversification and Specialization

While the overall size of the Canadian THI, as well as its revenues, remained constant in the early 1990s, what is most striking about the current period is the growing diversification in the industry, highlighted in particular by the proportion of temporary help agencies that place professional workers.[11] The Canadian THI continues to place workers in clerical and administrative work, general labour, and construction work, but the number of agencies specializing in placing professionals, particularly in the health-care sector and in management, grew in the early 1990s (Hamdani, 1996). Together, professional workers and health care-givers accounted for the third largest source of revenue for the THI in 1993 (Table 9).

The growth of temporary placements in the health-related professions

TABLE 8a*
Revenue Sources for Personnel Suppliers (SIC 7712) Canada, 1993

	1991 Total ($)	% of Total	1992 Total ($)	% of Total	1993 Total ($)	% of Total
Total Service Revenue	1,260,516,399	98.67	1,187,864,421	98.91	1,267,335,480	98.51
Other commissions	1,753,567	0.14	1,392,781	0.12	4,599,596	0.36
Training/education	12,706	0.00	13,745	0.00	3,325,289	0.26
Other operating revenue	6,278,322	0.49	4,502,017	0.37	5,133,920	0.40
Total operating revenue	1,268,561,004	99.30	1,193,772,964	99.40	1,280,394,285	99.52
Non-operating revenue	8,971,793	0.70	7,184,974	0.60	6,151,361	0.48
Total Revenue	1,277,532,797	100.0	1,200,957,938	100.0	1,286,545,646	100.0

Source: Statistics Canada, *Survey of Employment Agencies and Personnel Suppliers* (Ottawa, 1993), cat. no. 63–232.
*Revenue Sources are not imputed for firms with revenues below 250,000.

TABLE 8b*
Source of Expenses for Personnel Suppliers (SIC 7712) Canada, 1993

	1991 Total ($)	% of Total	1992 Total ($)	% of Total	1993 Total ($)	% of Total
Cost of goods sold	914,280	0.07	24,492	0.00	6,456	0.00
Wages, salaries and benefits	1,034,498,798	80.98	976,460,745	81.31	1,047,647,805	81.43
Rent or lease of:						
land or buildings	28,224,336	2.21	25,130,032	2.09	24,645,256	1.92
vehicles	6,698,010	0.52	6,237,868	0.52	5,545,110	0.43
computer equip.	1,588,510	0.12	2,128,581	0.18	3,044,796	0.24
other equip.	1,872,689	0.15	1,503,265	0.13	1,995,845	0.16
Repair and main.	2,411,958	0.19	2,289,444	0.19	1,583,120	0.12
Legal, etc.	20,455,570	1.60	20,355,279	1.69	22,693,071	1.76
Advertising	17,022,276	1.33	14,860,367	1.24	14,951,747	1.16
Insurance	3,590,991	0.28	2,954,913	0.25	2,865,683	0.22
Taxes, permits, and licenses	4,949,073	0.39	4,580,369	0.38	9,028,736	0.70
Heat, light, and power	1,665,222	0.13	1,179,422	0.10	1,591,538	0.12
Telephone	12,064,485	0.94	11,256,053	1.16	12,048,396	0.94
Travel and entertainment	13,698,739	1.07	13,895,609	1.16	13,534,797	1.05
Royalties	4,515,199	0.35	3,110,715	0.26	4,937,963	0.38
Depreciation	6,917,617	0.54	6,974,757	0.58	6,692,221	0.52
Interest	11,996,469	0.94	10,376,548	0.86	8,422,602	0.65
Other supplies	21,198,695	1.66	18,994,747	1.58	16,209,276	1.26
Other expenses	48,986,492	3.83	55,514,890	4.62	57,637,045	4.48
Total expenses	1,243,279,409	97.32	1,177,828,096	98.07	1,255,081,463	97.55
Profit margin	2.6		1.93		2.45	

Source: Statistics Canada, *Survey of Employment Agencies and Personnel Suppliers* (Ottawa, 1993), cat. no. 63–232.
*Sources of expenses are not calculated for firms with revenue below $250,000.

TABLE 9
Temporary Help Service Industry, Revenue by Product (Type of Labour), 1993

	Number of Firms	Revenue ($ millions)	Revenue (%)
Administrative and clerical	179	382.8	37.9
General labour	119	187.4	18.6
Drivers and equipment operators	67	136.1	13.5
Professionals (excl. health)	67	108.6	10.8
Health Caregivers	27	55.8	5.5
Construction	47	47.1	4.7
Informatics and EDP	50	33.1	3.3
Other (incl. executives)	90	58.9	5.8
Total		1,009.8	100.00

Source: D. Hamdani, 'The Temporary Help Service Industry: Its Role, Structure and Growth,' Service Indicators, 2nd Quarter (Ottawa: Statistics Canada, 1996), cat. no. 63–016XPB.
Note: This table is based on data from a panel of 283 survey firms, and only service revenue is included. The number of firms cannot be added because of multiple responses.

and other highly skilled fields corresponds with the high degree of specialization in the contemporary THI (Table 10). Specialization is particularly common for agencies placing professional workers. However, temporary help agencies still find workers willing to engage in general labour easiest to attract, and consequently a large proportion of agencies still place general labourers. Agencies concentrating on placing unskilled workers also tend to have higher volumes of business than those specializing in placing professionals since the degree of profit per worker is lower (Hamdani, 1996).[12]

Growing diversification makes the THI's services more accessible to businesses in sectors of the economy that the industry has not traditionally targeted. As well, increasing specialization amongst agencies boosts the image of the THI, making customers more confident about the calibre of temporary help workers, a development that underpins its growing legitimacy.

Worker Demographics

Alongside broader occupational diversity in the THI, both the characteristics of its workforce and the shape of the TER shifted dramatically in

TABLE 10

Specialization and Diversification in the Temporary Help Service Industry (firms deriving 50% or more of their revenue from their main activity), 1993*

Service	Total Revenue ($000)	Admin/ Clerical (%)	General Labour (%)	Constr. (%)	Informatics and EDP (%)	Health Care (%)	Prof. (%)	Drivers and Equip. Operators (%)	Other (%)
Admin/clerical	412,766	79.81	8.54	1.28	2.42	5.76	0.57	0.43	1.118
General Labour	168,395	18.07	72.52	1.44	1.33	0.27	0.53	0.43	1.18
Construction	32,530	0.69	1.17	95.38	0.16	0.00	0.00	0.00	2.05
Informatics and EDP	28,584	18.22	2.43	0.00	78.51	0.38	0.12	0.00	0.34
Heath Caregivers	34,195	3.48	0.00	0.00	0.00	90.13	0.00	0.00	6.39
Profs. (excl. health)	108,045	3.43	0.67	0.00	0.47	0.00	91.72	0.00	3.71
Drivers and Equip. Operators	135,500	3.77	5.07	0.28	0.00	0.48	0.00	90.21	0.21
Other (incl. executives)	42,565	2.53	2.69	0.06	0.02	0.00	0.00	3.19	91.52

Source: D. Hamdani, 'Temporary Help Service Industry.'
* This table is based on data from a panel of 283 survey firms. Non-operating revenue is excluded.

the early 1990s. While the Canadian THI remained highly female-dominated throughout the 1980s, its sex-composition began to change in the
1990s. In 1990, as Table 11 shows, women constituted 79.6 per cent of
those employed by personnel suppliers and employment agencies. However, by 1995 women represented only 61.5 per cent[13] of those employed
by personnel suppliers and employment agencies.[14] If employment trends
in the United States are any indication of the direction of change,
women's concentration in the THI likely will continue to fall (Table 11).

Despite the prevalent assumption that temporary help workers are
employed for short periods of time, data from Statistics Canada's *Survey
of Work Arrangements, 1995* (1996) indicate that a high proportion of
temporary help workers now report having job tenures of more than a
year. As Table 12 illustrates, in 1995 approximately 18.4 per cent of all
temporary help workers reported that they had worked for an agency for
between one and five years, and, even more striking, 12.4 per cent
reported that they had worked for an agency for over six years.[15] These
are interesting figures for an industry built on supplying *temporary* help
workers. They too reflect the recent move towards providing 'staffing
services' in the THI, where the duration of the assignment becomes less
crucial to the customer than the nature of its relationship with the
worker, so long as the agency preserves 'labour flexibility' for the customer by playing the role of 'employer' when it comes to hiring, dismissal, workers' compensation, and the administration of benefits.
Conceived in this way, 'staffing services' are the product of the THI's
efforts to repackage 'numerical flexibility.'

Figures on job tenure also correspond with the rising number of
average weekly hours worked by nonsupervisory workers in the THI
from the mid-1980s to the mid-1990s. In 1985 nonsupervisory workers
engaged by personnel suppliers and employment agencies worked an
average of 20.8 hours per week. By 1995 their average weekly hours
reached 28.3 (Statistics Canada, 1995: cat. 72–002).[16] Still, even with the
consistent rise in weekly hours worked, average wages for temporary
help workers declined between 1991 and 1994 (Statistics Canada, 1995:
cat. 72–002).[17]

Customers

In conjunction with the growing occupational spread among temporary
help workers, the THI is diversifying its customer base. With cutbacks to
the public sector and restructuring in the health care system, it now

TABLE 11

Percentage of Women Employed in Personnel Suppliers and Employment Agencies (SIC 771), Canada vs. Personnel Suppliers, United States (SIC 7363), 1985–1995

	1985	1986	1987	1988	1989	1990	1991	1992	1993	1994	1995
Canada	72.7	76.2	73.6	73.4	70.4	79.6	77.7	67.9	60.9	64.2	61.5
USA	60.8	60.8	59.5	59.6	59.4	59.1	57.5	57.9	57.1	55.5	54.2

Sources: United States Department of Labor (1996). LABSTAT Series Report, Series EEU80736302; Labour Force Survey, 1996.

TABLE 12
Job Tenure by All Temporary Workers, Agency
Temporaries, and Other Temporaries, 1995

Tenure	Agency Temporaries
1–6 Months	61.7
7–12 Months	7.6
1–5 Years	18.4
6 Years +	12.4

Source: Statistics Canada, *Survey of Work
Arrangements, 1995* (Ottawa: Statistics
Canada, 1996), cat. no. 71M0013GPE.

caters to a larger proportion of health institutions, federal, provincial, and local governments, and other publicly funded services, such as public utilities and public transportation (Krahn, 1995: 39). One manager noted accordingly: 'In Ottawa, they lost 45,000 [public sector] jobs last year. That's 45,000 jobs for our industry' (M5). Despite the THI's growing recognition of the potential for increasing its presence in the public sector, the private sector, dominated by manufacturing, transportation, and construction, remained the THI's largest class of customer in the early 1990s, comprising 76 per cent of the customer base in 1993 (Table 13). Some industry analysts argue that businesses, particularly in the manufacturing sector, tend to use temporary help workers to create a 'just-in-time workforce' to accommodate the move towards just-in-time production (Carré, 1992; Hamdani, 1996).

Others suggest that, from the perspective of the customer, the central advantages of using temporary help workers are not solely related to their need for a 'just-in-time workforce.' Rather, they argue that the draw of the contemporary THI relates to employers' desire to shift their employment-related responsibilities, such as recruitment, hiring, dismissal, payroll, benefits, and even training to the temporary help agency, and their increasing willingness to use nonstandard forms of employment to capitalize on 'labour flexibility' to lower costs (Abraham, 1990: 97). Customers' desires for just-in-time workers and the appeal of staffing services represent two sides of the same coin; they both reflect employers' desire to minimize their involvement in the 'management of labour' and capitalize on the growth of nonstandard forms of employment. Still, since there is a dearth of scholarly analysis probing the shape and content of staffing services, the latter claim deserves greater scrutiny.

TABLE 13
Class of Customers as Percentage of Industry, SIC 7712,
Canada,* 1991–1993

	1991	1992	1993
Individuals	3	4	3
Business			
Retail trade	16	9	7
Travel and accommodation	1	1	1
Wholesale trade	3	3	2
Agriculture	3	2	2
Manufacturing	12	13	15
Construction	8	9	9
Transportation	16	17	17
Communications and utilities	2	3	2
Financial and real estate	4	4	4
Other business	16	21	17
Total business	81	82	76
Institutions			
Education	1	1	1
Health	3	2	4
Other institutions	1	2	8
Total institutions	5	5	13
Governments	10	10	9
Foreign customers	0	0	0

Source: *Survey of Employment Agencies and Personnel
Suppliers* (Ottawa: Statistics Canada, 1993), cat. no. 63–232.
*Because of the nature of the formula used, the available
data do not add up to exactly 100 per cent.

The Emergence of 'Staffing Services':
Towards a New Industry Strategy[18]

In the late 1980s and early 1990s, the Canadian THI began promoting itself as providing 'employment and staffing services' rather than simply supplying 'stop-gap workers' to take advantage of the 'changing nature of employment.' Although it continued to adhere to several central tenets of its post-Second World War strategy and follow many of the practices that initially earned it legitimacy, the THI expanded its scope of legitimacy and packaged its services in a different way to preserve its niche in the labour market. It began to establish the TER as a genuine alternative to the SER rather than simply a supplement.

Temporary Help

Although current features and conventions in the THI, such as the enduring triangularity of the TER based on the notion of a 'temporary help formula,' are remarkably similar to its previous form and function, there are important differences in the role that the industry played in the Canadian labour market in the postwar era and the one that it assumes in the late 1990s. From the early 1950s until the mid-1970s, businesses tended to use the services of temporary help agencies in a limited way. They called on the THI in urgent situations, usually when they needed temporary clerical assistance, and they occasionally used temporary help workers for maternity leaves, sick leaves, or preplanned vacations (Akyeampong, 1989; Carré, 1994; Gannon, 1978; Mangum, Mayall, and Nelson, 1985). Even by the late-1960s, when the THI began to deliver the message that temporary help workers could serve as buffers in the case of fluctuations in demand, companies were reluctant to incorporate temporary help workers as a regular part of their workforces; this practice only became prevalent in the late 1970s and early 1980s, coinciding with what Carré (1994: 49) labels large-scale structural changes in the employment practices of firms that use temporary help workers.

Given its prior role (and marketing strategy) of providing 'stop-gap' workers, and employers' initial reluctance to embrace the notion of 'staffing services,' one might expect that the THI would have partly lost its basis for legitimacy in the 1970s as the SER began to show signs of decay and married women began to take more advantage of the right to full participation in the Canadian labour market. Ironically, however, from a regulatory standpoint, the 'special status' of temporary help agencies stabilized by the 1970s as a consequence of the stalemate at the ILO and the regulatory inertia at the national level, a change from the interwar and early post-Second World War periods.[19] Thus, the THI needed to renew itself primarily to affirm its legitimacy. This combination of forces led the industry, following its American counterpart, to alter its practices, keeping the form and function of temporary help agencies in sync with the existing regulatory regime while advancing to a new stage of legitimacy.

Employment and Staffing Services

The strategy first adopted by the Canadian THI in the late 1970s and early 1980s updates many features of the old. The THI still relies upon the temporary help formula, as well as the triangular employment relationship that it generates, and it still caters to employers' demand for 'numerical flexibility.' The shape of the TER has not changed substantively since the postwar era. It still involves at least three parties, and the division of responsibility in the employment relationship, although it is now defined more rigidly, is consistent with old patterns. But in cultivating a new strategy in the 1980s, the THI modified the legal apparatus surrounding the TER, updated its recruitment and selection procedures, and also began to perform a range of new functions. In order to take up a new space in the labour market, it began to market itself to customers as providing 'employment and staffing services' in an attempt to distance itself from the mediating role that it played in the postwar era.

The THI's concept of 'employment and staffing services' refers to its entire package of services from recruitment to dismissal. For the average temporary help agency, one that places workers in a mixture of settings and sectors, five sets of services comprise the package, and these services are delineated through a service contract between the agency and the customer.[20]

The Service Contract

In sharp contrast to the postwar era, where the formal legal apparatus surrounding the TER was limited, the THI operates within a more complex legal framework in the late 1990s. The service contract, which aims to assuage customers' anxieties about the absence of legal certainty surrounding the TER and provide them with an array of guarantees where staffing services are concerned, lies at the centre of this apparatus. Since it governs the procurement of workers, this contract is somewhat atypical where service contracts are concerned. Its role is to set out the employment-related responsibilities that the agency shall assume, as well as those that remain with the customer. To this end, service contracts always indicate that the hourly rates charged to the customer include allowances for the provision of mandatory benefits, vacation pay, workers' compensation, severance pay (if applicable), and statutory holiday pay. In return for the administrative services of the agency, service contracts normally require customers to sign time cards confirming the number of hours that the temporary help worker worked during a given pay period. Many also contain clauses requiring customers to give the agency sufficient notice prior to termination, particularly in cases where severance pay provisions apply. Additionally, they tend to include a clause that requires customers to pay a standard permanent placement fee should they decide to hire a temporary help worker on a permanent basis within the first six months of the assignment.[21] Under all service contracts, the customer is required to provide worksite-specific health and safety training, although the agency commits itself to contributing to Workers' Compensation; this attests to the fact that the agency and the customer share liability where health and safety are concerned. Finally, service contracts usually contain a general clause affirming that temporary help workers are 'under the care and supervision of the customer' when they are on assignment. This last clause reveals an important tension in the relationship between the agency and the customer. It indicates that, although the agency is assuming a range of employment-related responsibilities, given the prevailing legal context, it can only go so far in acting as the employer, thereby revealing the central paradox of the triangular employment relationship.

The service contract between the agency and the customer has attained sufficient legitimacy for customers to accept the potential risks, such as liabilities pertaining to health and safety, as well as secondary responsibility in instances where the agency fails to pay wages and/or contribute to mandatory social security schemes or workers' compensation. Indeed, the growing legitimacy of the THI seems to override the fact that the triangular employment relationship still rests on shaky legal ground. But, beyond the growth of temporary help work, the decline of the SER and the diminishing force of the ideology of domesticity, what accounts for the increasing appeal of the THI? For employers, the THI's move towards providing staffing services, ranging from advertising and recruitment to payrolling, lies at the core of its appeal.

Advertising and Recruitment

In addition to the advertising that agencies do on a regular basis to maintain a consistent supply of workers, which routinely involves advertising in the newspaper, on radio, and on local television, as well as small-scale recruitment campaigns at postsecondary institutions, agencies offer specialized advertising and recruitment to the customer. They usually place ads in the classified section of newspapers, including a brief job description, the number of workers required, the rate of pay, the hours of work, and the location of the job. Since they rarely mention the issue of duration, these advertisements resemble typical help-wanted ads with one notable exception: they name the temporary help agency as the employer.

Advertisements placed by agencies often create confusion among job seekers. For example, when a worker engaged in administrative work for a large transportation company first saw an ad, it referred to the company requiring assistance but listed the temporary help agency as the employer. A woman applied for the job on the basis of the company involved, and it was only after being interviewed twice and offered the job that she realized she would actually be working for a temporary help agency. She learned that it would take care of her paychecks, benefits, and evaluation, and that the duration of the job was indefinite (fieldnotes, 4 December 1996).

The set of advertising services offered by the temporary help agencies allows customers to reduce their human resource management costs and shift the burden of employment to the agency at the outset. As one temporary help agency manager put it: 'Eventually, we're just going to become one extension of one's human resource department, and then we're going to have one person working in there and then [we'll do] their whole hiring for them' (M3). By offering a wide variety of recruitment and advertising services, the THI sets its larger, long-term objectives into motion early in its relationship with the customer.

Interviewing, Screening, and Testing

Interviewing, screening, and testing services build upon the processes set in place by the THI in the postwar period. However, to promote further its expertise in the human resource management business and distance itself from the disreputable actors in the private employment agency business, the THI expanded its screening and testing procedures significantly in the 1980s. Since then it has become common to book pre-interviews with workers to which all applicants are asked to bring a resumé and two letters of reference. The interviewing and testing normally takes two to three hours (fieldnotes, 2 December 1996). A manager, who had worked in the THI since its inception, emphasized the advantages of a rigorous screening and interview process:

> I've seen so many people that have been put to work with no kind of application process, no initiation process, no background checks. I know of a customer of mine, this is going back a few years now, that was actually

closed down by the RCMP one day [because he used a disreputable agency].
He used seventy or eighty temporaries a day and 70 per cent of them were
illegal immigrants. Somebody put a word out to the RCMP and the RCMP
went and closed them down for a day while they checked everybody in the
parking lot. Can you imagine what kind of ramifications that had for that
customer? We're talking about a large manufacturing company at that
time. There are still agencies like that around, unfortunately – and I say
unfortunately because it is unfortunate – that deal with transient type of
workers. They're on the road at 6:00 in the morning and at 6:05 they'll be
forty people in the room waiting to go to work. Their dispatcher will get a
phone call from A.B.C. Company, saying, 'I need ten people doing the
trucks.' There's no selection process. There's no interview process. There's
no nothing. [pointing his finger] It's you, you, you, you, and you. That's the
end of that, and off you go. I like setting this example up for companies
that use those types of agencies because it becomes a very easy sell as to why
we do a better job. (M2)

Despite the shifting demographic profile of the THI, most temporary
help agencies still tend to have two streams of interviewing, one for
industrial work and another for clerical work. Although interviews with
applicants seeking industrial work tend to be shorter than those with
applicants seeking clerical work, they share a common framework involving an oral interview, the screening of a video about temporary help
work, skills testing, and psychological testing.

A typical clerical interview begins with a typing test that measures
accuracy and speed and is followed by standardized computer tests
designed to measure the applicant's proficiency in a range of computer
programs, including Windows, Word, Word-Perfect, Exel, and Lotus.
Many temporary help workers find this process quite onerous and stressful. One commented, 'It's kind of tense. It felt kind of like a little
laboratory. You are put into a little booth and there's a little clock there,
or a little timer, and a bing goes off and you are supposed to stop typing
... You just feel under pressure doing the tests' (T1). After the skills
testing is complete, the applicant is directed to a video room and shown
a short orientation video about temporary help work. This is the only
time that the nature of TER is described to the applicant in any detail.
Applicants are told that the agency is their legal employer, and they are
instructed to report any problems – which may relate to health and
safety, illness, or supervisory issues – directly to the agency (fieldnotes, 3
December 1996). The video also explains the purpose of the time cards

and describes how temporary help workers should fill them in when they are on assignment. The same orientation video is shown to applicants for clerical and industrial work.

The orientation video is normally followed by a video on health and safety. However, the content of the health and safety video differs for clerical and industrial workers. In the case of clerical workers, the video describes hazardous office materials and appropriate office attire, and instructs workers to avoid heavy lifting and to use proper equipment (i.e., step stools rather than chairs) for accessing high shelves. In accordance with provincial standards, the health and safety video shown to all applicants for industrial work describes a range of hazardous industrial materials and the labelling associated with these materials. Immediately after applicants view this video, they are required to take a test that asks them to identify hazardous materials. If they do not pass the test, they are ineligible to proceed (fieldnotes, 5 December 1996).

Once both the skills testing and informational component of the interview are over, applicants are asked to complete a computerized application form with their name, address, social insurance number, and other relevant personal details. Applicants are also asked whether they have ever worked through a temporary help agency, and if so, to name the agencies. Agencies use this question to determine whether a temporary help worker is really available for work, as well as to gauge the degree of competition they are up against (fieldnotes, 4 December 1996). At this stage of the interview, if the agency personnel deem the applicant to be a suitable candidate for temporary help work, then s/he is asked to take a computer-administered psychological test.

Developed in the mid-1980s, psychological tests are designed to determine whether a given applicant has the 'right personality' to do temporary help work. A branch manager described their role: 'The purpose of the [psychological] evaluation is to give me an understanding as to how they really think, what their personality is all about. The questions that it asks are strictly for the temporary worker. The evaluation does not work if they are a permanent worker. [For example,] it asks, "If you are out on an assignment and another service calls and tells you that they can get you a dollar more an hour working for another company, do you think that it is okay to go? Do you think it is not okay not to go?"' (M1). This manager acknowledged that the role of the psychological test was to provide insight into whether the applicant is honest and trustworthy, and most of all to determine the level of his or her commitment to temporary help work in general and to the agency in particular. How-

ever, given the types of questions, the psychological test plays a disciplining role as well – that is, it prepares the applicant for the often
underremunerated nature of temporary help work. For example, one
question in a psychological test that I took was, 'If you knew that someone else doing the same job as you was making more money, how likely
would it be to affect how hard you work?' (fieldnotes, 6 December 1996).
This question is not only constructed to establish what motivates the
temporary help worker, but the degree to which s/he is willing to accept
the low status, low pay, and insecurity associated with many forms of
temporary help work. It is designed to help provide the customer with
workers who are compliant and obedient.

In some instances, an applicant's performance on a psychological test
is used to assess whether s/he could tolerate a potentially stressful working environment. In one case that I observed, office staff examined the
outcomes of the psychological testing scores to find a suitable replacement for an executive secretary in a work environment known to be very
hostile to women. In attempting to fill the request for this position, the
conversation between two staff people went as follows:

> Staff person 1: What 'type' are you looking for?
> Staff person 2: The person has to work for a VP who screams a lot and is
> very demanding. Ninety per cent of the workload is for the guy – the VP.
> The pay is $32,000–34,000, but the job's worth $36,000 to $38,000 and
> they're totally inflexible.
> Staff person 1: Anything else?
> Staff person 2: This is an HR [human resource] assignment that we're
> taking over. I've spoken to the payroll lady in charge. She is petrified of
> everyone there but she is very effective. They need a stable woman who is
> comfortable being subservient. This is old school.
> Staff person 1: Do they have to make coffee?
> Staff person 2: It's a very old school environment and the job is advertised
> as nine to five, but it's really nine to six-thirty. They have to be comfort-
> able working in an all male environment. (fieldnotes, 5 December 1996)

In an attempt to make light of the situation and acknowledge the dis-
turbing character of the customer's demand, after this exchange took
place one of the staff people turned to me and asked: 'Do you know
anyone who likes to be yelled at?' (fieldnotes, 5 December 1996).

Applicants are never told how they perform on the psychological tests, even though agency personnel inform them of their scores in the skills-testing component of the screening process.[22]

Training

While a few large temporary help agencies pride themselves on training, most agencies provide a rather limited set of training options. Many firms offer their regular temporary help workers computer time to improve their skills, and some offer specialized courses to workers at cost. One long-time temporary help worker, who had been with the same firm for over two years, noted enthusiastically: 'They have in-house training. They have a room set aside with about thirty terminals, and you can do your own tutorial with the computer or you can attend seminars in class. I think you pay $5. or something. You can get twenty or thirty people together to learn Excel in a day' (T1). In contrast, other temporary help workers expressed considerable cynicism about the training provided by temporary help agencies. One worker who was a science teacher by profession but had no job prospects, made reference to the training required for her light industrial job as follows: 'I don't even need language. When I learned this work, my eyes learned it' (T4). Thus, although managers promote worker-centred training, workers give it mixed reviews.

Many customers, on the contrary, commend the customer-centred training provided by some temporary help agencies, especially training that involves site- or customer-specific training. My research revealed two examples of client-centred training, one that catered to a client in sales and another in industrial work. In the first case, the agency and the customer had an agreement that the agency would train the temporary help workers for direct sales in a department store. It hosted sessions about the product for sale and trained workers as sales representatives for a specific product, in this case long-distance telephone services (fieldnotes, 5 December 1996). In the second case, the agency was bidding for a multimillion-dollar contract with a waste management company and was proposing to train workers to sort recycling materials. The agency proposed to do seminars for temporary help workers to orient them with the different types of recyclable products and then to provide on-site training (fieldnotes, 4 December 1996). In both cases, the customers were quite happy with the arrangement, especially in the case of the sales training, which required the agency to host weekly sessions for new workers because there was a high rate of worker turn-over. From the customer's perspective, the agency assumed all of its staffing responsibilities, leaving it to prioritize product development.

Selection and Follow-up

As well as interviewing, testing, and screening workers, temporary help agencies are also closely involved in worker selection. In some cases, the agency carries out selection entirely. For example, agencies often make quick judgment calls in the case of industrial workers, particularly if the customer requires a temporary help worker immediately. Sometimes the agency even transports the worker to the worksite to 'fill an order' (fieldnotes, 5 December 1996). As other studies have reported, however, in many cases customers simply require 'warm bodies' (Gonos, 1994; Henson, 1993; Parker, 1994; Rogers, 1995). This makes the selection process extremely straightforward. As one manager noted, 'Some positions require somebody who's just happy to do the same thing over and over and over again. So you don't want to place somebody who's really ambitious, really high energy. You want a steady worker. For example, picture a manufacturing environment where they do the same thing all day long, they're putting cassette cases together. All day long, that's all they do. Seven-and-a-half hour or eight-hour shift and all they do is take two pieces of a cassette case or a CD case and assemble it together' (M3).

When the skills and the personality of the temporary help worker are important, the agency and the customer tend to work together. More reputable agencies send the customer the resumes of the top three applicants and the customer chooses the best candidate, knowing that s/he still has other options if the first applicant does not work out. I observed one selection process where the agency worked for three days trying to find the best long-term, part-time receptionist for a local doctor who had used the agency in the past; in these interviews, applicants were told that the right person could hold on to this assignment in the long term, possibly even for years if they played their cards right (fieldnotes, 4 December 1996).

Once the workers are placed, the agency still provides some central services. Managers tend to highlight the role of the agency after placement to distance the THI from the private employment agency industry and promote the concept of 'staffing services' (fieldnotes, 3 December 1996). On the first day of a placement, the agency telephones the customer twice unless they are asked not to call: once, at the beginning of the day, to ensure that the worker has arrived on time, and a second time, at the end of the day, to inquire into the worker's performance (fieldnotes, 2–5 December 1996). If the length of the placement is indefinite, the staff of temporary help agencies make spot visits. If more than one worker is on-site, as is quite common with industrial work, then agencies usually arrange a routine visit with the customer. Agency personnel often distribute paychecks at these visits.

After a set period of time, usually sixty to ninety days, some customers request what is known as a 'buy-out,' an arrangement where the customer takes on the temporary help worker permanently for a one-time fee. If the agency has a good relationship with the customer, or if the worker's wage is relatively low, the agency may waive the fee normally charged for a buy-out. However, if the worker is highly skilled and/or if s/he has only been on assignment for a short period, the agency and the customer often negotiate a fee for the buy-out. Customers report a range of experiences with the buy-out process: 'Your terms are in the contract ... I hired one engineer through the agency, and, if we maintain him through them for the required number of weeks, then we won't have to pay an agency fee to put him on full-time ... The difference would be working a person for sixteen weeks. The agency was giving me a deal on him. They were making $6. an hour on him versus [me] paying out between $15,000 or $20,000 [up front]' (C1). The same customer indicated that, in her experience, there is an industry standard that 'after twelve weeks, the person is yours. You can take them on your payroll without penalties' (C1). Other customers rejected the notion of a buy-out. Instead, they characterized the advantage of working through a temporary help agency as a means of extending the typical probationary period indefinitely, to test a potential employee. One client noted: 'Most agencies usually have a ninety-day replacement guarantee. It's a rarity, but some will even go as far as six months. If you're not happy with that person's performance, they'll start the search over again' (C4).

Although these customers each had different experiences of the buy-out process, the type of selection and follow-up services and the provision for buy-outs provided by the agency normally relate to two variables: the level of the markup that the agency is charging on the worker and the degree of customer loyalty. Customers reported paying a 15 to 35 per cent surcharge on top of the temporary help workers' wages to cover the cost of benefits and to pay for the administrative services of the agency (C1, C2, C4). Thus, for highly skilled workers it is usually in the interest of the agency to avoid an early buy-out. On the other hand, if the agency is dealing with a long-term, high-volume customer and the markup on the workers is rather minimal, they often waive the buy-out fee (fieldnotes, 4 December 1996).

Payrolling

For many customers, payroll services are the most important service that the THI provides. Payroll services include paying the worker, providing mandatory benefits, keeping track of hours, contributing to workers' compensation, and a host of other employment-related services. They reduce the human resource manager's paperwork and eliminate a host of employment-related responsibilities. Some customers use temporary help agencies solely because they take care of the payroll. One manager described his relationship with a particular company as follows: 'We have a company, a very large client, who uses a number of temporaries because they have a frozen head count. They're not allowed to hire any more permanent people, and that's directed from their head office in Europe. But they call us and tell us who's starting. "We have somebody starting on Monday and can you fax me over an application so he can fill it out, so you can put him on your payroll for us?" They dictate his work, they give him his job description, they tell me how much to pay him. They find him ... They call me and say, "He's going to be finishing next Friday." They call me and say, "He's taken a week off"' (M3). One customer reported: 'They hire the people. It's much easier for us to keep an arm's-length relationship with the representatives [temporary help workers] that way' (C2).

The fact that temporary help agencies assume all the responsibilities related to the administration of benefits, from severance pay to workers' compensation, is also a key source of their appeal. As one customer noted, 'They [the agencies] pay if there's an injury ... In this industry, we have a lot of pinch points. You know, we get a lot of repetitive strain or clothing caught and stuff. It's nice to know that if that happens, its on their WCB [Workers' Compensation Board Insurance], not ours. We don't take a loss. Our premiums don't go up and our stats look better too' (C4).

In some cases, the primary attraction of using a temporary help agency is that they are responsible for firing the worker, as well as for the range of costs the dismissal generates. One customer put it simply: 'If somebody needs to be released, then I just call [the agency] and say, "we don't need this person any longer"' (C2). Another stated: 'In the back of your mind, it's nice to know that if it doesn't work out, it's easy to let them go. It's easy to phone the agency and say, "Bill isn't working out. Thank you very much, but I don't want him back tomorrow"' (C4). Managers are aware of how much customers appreciate their services related to dismissal. One affirmed: 'When it comes to them having to lay people off, they have all of that paper work to deal with and the government enumeration and so on and so forth. It's much easier for them to pick up the phone and call up a temporary service' (M2). In return for these services, there is an expectation that the customer will inform the agency if it sees an assignment ending, especially if the thirteen-week mark is approaching, when severance pay requirements begin to apply (fieldnotes, 5 December 1996). Indeed, this type of clause is written into many service contracts (M3). Many agencies make it part of their routine to call the customer at the beginning of the thirteenth week to ensure that the customer intends to keep the worker for the long term (fieldnotes, 3 December 1996).

Some customers emphasize that using temporary help workers is not only cost-effective in the long run, due to lower workers' compensation premiums and UI claims, but also in the short run because of the relatively low average hourly wages of temporary help workers in contrast to permanent workers and to other temporary workers hired directly by firms in the manufacturing, service, and clerical sectors. One customer noted: 'Sometimes it's cheaper to go through an agency ... For example, for us to get a packaging operator is $2. less an hour than bringing them on our payroll. It doesn't often happen, but sometimes there are those considerations as well' (C4). This rule, however, only holds in nonunionized workplaces, where the THI has its strongest hold. In plants where there is a union, customers report paying union wages to temporary help workers because contracting-out clauses in their collective agreements normally require equal remuneration (but not benefits) for temporary and permanent workers: these firm- or workplace-specific contracting-out clauses are the primary check that individual unions use to curb the spread of the TER. As a result, many customers limit their use of temporary help workers to nonunionized segments of their workforces. One noted accordingly: 'Quite frankly, I don't use the temp industry at all for the factory because it's a unionized environment. I only use it in the office [where there is no union]' (C1).

From the perspective of the customer, there are also some disadvantages to 'staffing services.' Potential disadvantages include a lack of consistency in a given workforce, problems associated with protecting trade secrets, and the costs associated with training and retraining work-ers. Customers and workers also consistently report that loyalty is the most significant trade-off. One worker expressed this sentiment bluntly: 'I think that there are instances where companies will discover, even if they're contemplating it, that it's [using temporary help workers] simply not strategic because one of the things that you give away when you give away permanent staff is anything that even approximates loyalty. For a permanent employer, if I'm in the middle of something and the clock strikes five and it's fifteen minutes more to finish it, I will finish it. In temp-land, the clock strikes five, I've got my coat on and I'm out the door, forget it. I think that employers will discover that your employees treat you the way you treat them' (T7). While some customers acknowl-edge the importance of worker loyalty, most still claim that the benefits of the payrolling services offered by the THI far outweigh the disadvan-tages, particularly if they retain only a limited number of full-time per-manent workers and primarily rely on contract, temporary, and on-call workers, an increasingly common practice (C5).

New Services

Some temporary help agencies provide other specialized services aimed at securing the agency's role as the 'employer of record.' Chief among these is the provision of on-site managers. On-site managers are hired, usually on contract, by the temporary help agency to supervise tempo-rary help workers at the customer's work site. They are common in high volume industrial work sites as well as in sales and services.[23] For exam-ple, in the proposal for the waste management company described above, the agency offered to provide an on-site manager to supervise the workers. It is also common for agencies to hire a supervisor for direct sales placements who coaches workers and monitors their perform-ances; the supervisor usually works just as closely with the customer as s/he does with the agency (fieldnotes, 5–6 December 1996). One cus-tomer in the service sector described the role of an on-site manager: 'He's the motivational guy. He's a great salesmen, so he looks after the on-the-floor training. I do the training session in the classroom setting. He does the floor. He coaches them. If they're having a problem, he goes in and shows them how to do it. He'll go in if somebody's having a bad day. He'll try and pump them up' (C2). From the perspective of the customer, the advantages of having an on-site manager go well beyond the direct supervision that s/he provides. The manager reinforces the arm's-length relationship between the worker and the customer, which is particularly important in cases where workers are on assignment with the customer indefinitely, as is increasingly common in call centres, mail-rooms, and direct sales (Wymer 1993).

Another 'new' service provided by the THI is transportation to the work site.[24] With the growing volume of business, particularly in manufacturing and industrial work, agencies are routinely confronted with requests from customers to provide transportation. Even the most reputable agencies – those that were reluctant to provide transportation to workers in the 1950s and 1960s due to their desire to maintain a healthy distance from private employment agencies that provided day labourers, and to minimize the liabilities involved – are beginning to provide drivers. For example, a staff person described the pros and cons of having a driver: 'We are considering renting a van [and hiring a driver] because we're looking at taking on a client where we're going to have to accommodate our people getting to work on time. We will only be able to guarantee that by driving them there. That is something that this service doesn't normally offer, but there are other services out there that do. The disadvantage is the day the van breaks down. You have several people that are stranded, and, not only does one person not get to work, but everybody that's sitting in that van doesn't get there either. Of course, there are other safety liabilities as well ... So there's pros and cons to it' (fieldnotes, 4 December 1996). This staff person felt pressure to keep up with the trends in the THI to remain competitive.

Sometimes the on-site manager also serves as the driver. In one instance that I observed, an agency was interviewing for an on-site managerial position. Responsibilities were to include transporting workers to and from the work site, supervising at the work site, taking disciplinary actions, handling dismissals, and above all ensuring that the agency maintained the volume of workers requested by the customer on a daily basis. In this case, the on-site manager was to be in constant contact with the office by cellular phone, arranging to dispatch workers to the work site as they were needed (fieldnotes, 4 December 1996).

Twenty-four hour staffing is another service that agencies increasingly provide. When asked about growing trends in the industry, several managers named around-the-clock staffing as the way of the future. One reflected, 'We pay somebody to be on call until midnight every night for our clients who forget to place orders, who have problems, who have no-shows. We call them on the weekends. Clients have some of our home phone numbers and we're all on cellphones so that we can be reached whenever because clients operate seven days a week, three shifts. They operate all the time and it's great if they have a problem at 8 a.m. on their Monday shift but what if they have a problem at 10 p.m. on their Friday night shift ... They need to be able to reach the agencies' (M3).

An additional service, known as 'temp to perm,' is also becoming prevalent in the THI. Temp to perm involves providing a worker to the customer with a clear understanding at the outset that the customer may opt to hire her or him directly after an extended period, normally three to six months. Temp to perm also reflects a renewed affiliation between the THI and the private employment agency industry since it is prompting agencies to have permanent specialists on site. Temp to perm involves certain obvious costs and risks (i.e., agencies must obtain a license because of provincial legislation). Yet, industry officials argue that building this service is a wise long-term investment because it appeals to customers who rarely use the services of the THI, and it is an excellent way to showcase the THI's services to customers who require professionals, such as engineers, lawyers, teachers, and nurses. Predictably, temp to perm is most common at the high end of THI, where customers generally use it to screen potential employees and to avoid the penalties associated with hiring and dismissal (C2, C5).

Some branch managers have mixed feelings about promoting this service. One manager remarked, 'Obviously, when they go perm it's great for the client and our associate [i.e., the temporary help worker] – that's what we like to see for them – but it's lost revenue for us. On the business management side of it, I'd like to see it at a very minimum. On the other side of the coin, I'd like to see it a lot more because it tells us one thing, that we're finding the right people for the job ... I'd say that our temp to perm is maybe 20 per cent' (M2). Another indicated, 'We lose a lot of our really good people to permanent positions ... If the agency is doing their job right, it should be common because you get a lot of orders where there are open positions. If you really understand the clients requirements, and the environment – you've been out there and you've seen it and you know who fits – then you should be able to actually place somebody who they would consider on a permanent basis. When that happens, we have mixed emotions' (M3). Managers view temp to perm as crucial to the expansion of the contemporary THI. However, they are reticent to market this service too aggressively since it has the potential to deplete their supply of high-calibre workers in the short run, and since they clearly have an interest in preserving the role of the agency as the longstanding employer of record.

Ranging from advertising and recruitment to payrolling, the services described above constitute what the contemporary Canadian THI now calls 'employment and staffing services.' By packaging its pre-existing services in a different way, developing new services, and crafting a unique type of contract between the customer and the agency (one that pushes the boundaries of legality), the THI changed course in the 1980s. It effectively began to market the ability of temporary help agencies to act as employers and/or as managers of labour, paying significantly less attention to the issue of employment duration and more attention to the division of responsibility between the agency and the customer, while still upholding their well-established image as suppliers of temporary help. The THI was keenly aware of the uncharacteristically stable regulatory regime surrounding the TER in this period, and thus was careful not to upset it. In fact, its cognizance of the delicate balance that temporary help agencies had reached at the regulatory level led the THI to introduce the concept of 'staffing services' gradually, retaining practices that initially earned it credibility while establishing new practices to extend the bounds of its postwar legitimacy. The result is that the contemporary Canadian THI still bases its new strategy on the pre-existing regulatory regime; it continues to retain and call attention to its 'special status,' based on its reputation of supplying short-term temporary help workers. However, at the same time, the logic of the THI's marketing strategy is changing alongside the decline of the SER.

Establishing the TER as an Alternative to the SER

Against the backdrop of profound changes in the labour market from the early 1970s to the mid-1990s, the THI's new strategy of providing employment and staffing services clearly contributed to its expansion and diversification in Canada in this period. Even more important, the shape of the Canadian THI changed dramatically with the adoption of this new strategy. Its client base expanded to include more public and quasi-public sector institutions and a wider group of clients from the business sector. Simultaneously, the occupational spread in the industry broadened to include more professional workers, health caregivers, and construction workers. Revenues also rose sharply in the industry, reaching over $1.5 billion in 1990. As its profile grew, so did its legitimacy; consequently, from the mid-1960s to the mid-1990s, temporary help agencies enjoyed a relatively stable regulatory environment at both the national and the international level. In this way, the THI's new emphasis on marketing staffing services has helped it advance the spread of temporary help work into new areas. But, most centrally, the new strategy has contributed to shifting the 'burden' of employment off the customer and on to the agency. In promoting itself as providing employment and staffing services, the contemporary Canadian THI is selling far more than the services of temporary help workers; it is selling a new type of employment relationship to its customers, one that allows both the agency and the customer to adopt a range of distancing strategies. In so doing, it is advancing the TER as a genuine alternative to the SER.

Given the new division of responsibility between the customer and the agency, and the arm's-length relationship that the THI is cultivating between the customer and the worker, the emerging TER contravenes the SER in almost all of its central aspects. It is characterized by a triangular employment relationship that may or may not be full time, where the worker may be assigned to several work sites off the employer's premises, and where employment-related responsibilities are shared between two or more parties. Moreover, it involves a commercial contract for services between a temporary help agency and a customer and an 'employment agreement'[25] between the agency and the worker. Thus, it violates all three core features of the SER: the worker establishes occupational connections with several employers rather than one, is not party to an indeterminate contract of employment, and may be dismissed with little notice from the agency and no notice from the customer (Cordova, 1986).

The fact that the shape of the TER differs sharply from the SER is not new either. What is new is the means by which the THI is attaining legitimacy for the TER in contradistinction to the SER. At its inception, the THI crafted the TER to minimize relations between customer and worker, and this continues to be the case. However, in the post-Second World War era, the fact that agencies provided a rather narrow group of temporary help workers, chiefly white middle-class married women, to a rather narrow set of customers, primarily firms requiring temporary clerical assistance, was the means by which the THI cast it as a legitimate supplement to the SER. At present, the marketing of 'employment and staffing services' is the primary means by which the THI is securing legitimacy in the labour market.

Shifting employment norms have contributed to the recent change in course on the part of the THI. By adopting a new strategy in the late 1980s and early 1990s, the THI began to position the TER as an alternative to the SER. At this juncture, the SER was clearly unstable as a normative model of employment, women's labour force participation rates were rising, and nonstandard forms of employment were proliferating. Since then, although their participation rates stagnated in the early 1990s, women's share of the labour force remains relatively constant, and nonstandard forms of employment have continued to spread (Krahn, 1995; Lindsay, 1995; Lipsett and Reesor, 1997).

These employment trends suggest that neither the feminine face of the THI nor its role of supplementing the SER is fixed. Even though the THI first staked its place in the labour market based on image of the 'Kelly Girl' and on supplying 'stop-gap' workers, these variables are not crucial to its continued legitimacy in and of themselves. Rather, they were key pillars of its post-Second World War strategy. Although the variable of gender still remains central to how the THI operates in the labour market, and the provision of temporary help still represents a core service provided by the THI, the terrain has shifted dramatically. With the decline of the SER, there is a now a growing vacuum where a *normative* model of employment is concerned. This gap is creating a space where employers are not only aware of 'new' employment options, but are increasingly willing to accept the risks involved in embracing a host of so-called distancing strategies.

Conclusion

Given the absence of a single alternative to the SER as a *normative* model of employment and the highly stable regulatory environment, the Canadian THI is likely to continue along its present course. Although some are more tentative than others, customers, managers, and industry officials generally predict the THI's increased emphasis on servicing more and more facets of the employment relationship. One human resource manager employed by a large manufacturing firm suggests that the THI could potentially undermine the role of her entire department: 'There has been a trend in human resources. I don't know if it has materialized. I heard this a couple of years ago – that they are outsourcing human resources, and don't have [human resource] departments anymore, and have people that come in and do recruiting' (C3). These remarks reflect the current direction of change in the THI. When asked to discuss the future of the THI, an agency manager noted: '[w]hat I see happening in the future is agencies such as ours staffed twenty-four hours a day ... It's going to get to the point that eventually we're just going to become one extension of their human resource departments' (M2). According to another official, the most innovative segments of the contemporary THI, particularly in the United States and France, are already providing what is known as 'facilities management,' and the Canadian THI is following suit. This official noted: '[The customer], for example, they have a mailroom. Every company has a mailroom. But [the customer's] business is retail of its merchandise. [The customer's] management really don't want to concern themselves with running the mailroom because that's not their core business. So that part of their business is outsourced to a company that is in the business of facilities management, that knows the kind of skill sets needed to run a mailroom ... It might be mailrooms. It might also be – let's think of another example – call centres' (I1).

These remarks all suggest that, given the growing movement towards contracting out among large companies, the industry is likely to continue to situate the TER as an alternative to the SER. Indeed, customers and managers repeatedly acknowledge that minimizing the customers' employment-related responsibilities is the chief objective of the THI. When asked about new directions in the industry, they take this notion even further by suggesting that contracting out the 'management of labour' in its entirety is the way of the future.[26]

Of course, the insights of customers and managers only take·us so far in exposing the implications of the apparent shift in THI from simply supplying 'stop-gap' workers to selling 'staffing services.' They help reveal the dimensions of the THI's new strategy but leave many pressing questions unanswered. With respect to the current period, several sets of questions still require scrutiny: first, given the feminization of the labour force and the rise of nonstandard forms of employment, to what extent does the TER amount to a precarious employment relationship? More specifically, does the shape of the contemporary TER (and its rise and spread) reveal the erosion of the SER as a gendered, or, more accurately, feminized process? Chapter 5 addresses these questions by putting temporary help workers' experiences at the centre of analysis and examining them against the shape of the contemporary TER and the conditions of employment surrounding it. Second, given that the TER is spreading, given that the prevailing regulatory regime in Canada and other nations opting for nonregulation after the Second World War still takes the SER as its central reference point, and given that organized labour became more vocal in expressing its concerns about the TER in the late 1990s (especially at an international level), what are the prospects for regulating temporary help work at the national, international, and supranational levels? In examining the options for regulation, Chapter 6 addresses this most pressing question.

Promising 'Flexibility' and Delivering Precariousness: The Shape of the Contemporary Temporary Employment Relationship

> We perform a function. We're not actually human beings. We're tools that perform functions. I think that many of us are tremendously underutilized. God knows I am, but I don't think that's unique to me as I talk to my colleagues [at the call centre]. We are all, in fact, capable of all kinds of stuff. But the system isn't designed to use that. The agency doesn't want it because [the customer] is given your name only so that you can perform a particular task. They have no idea that you could do other things ... That's the nature of temping. (T7)

The Canadian THI gradually adopted a new marketing strategy from the early 1970s to the mid-1980s, one that complemented the decline of the SER and the feminization of the labour force and took advantage of the 'special status' that temporary help agencies first attained at the regulatory level in the post-Second World War era. In offering to provide 'staffing services,' temporary help agencies shifted their emphasis away from supplying temporary help workers to assuming a range of responsibilities typically accorded to the employer in a bilateral employment relationship. The THI's new strategy was highly attractive from the perspective of its customers since it gave them considerable 'flexibility' by cultivating arms-length relationships between clients and workers.

From the vantage point of workers, however, the radical shift in the THI's strategy only entrenched the shape of the TER. Consequently, temporary help work increasingly amounted to precarious employment in the late 1990s. To capitalize on shifting employment norms and minimize uncertainty at the regulatory level, the THI became preoccupied with delineating the responsibilities of the customer and the agency in the 1980s and 1990s. But the drive for greater clarity among temporary help agencies in their relationships with customers created few positive qualitative changes for workers. Rather, the legal apparatus that the THI crafted to surround the TER and the firm-based practices that it perpetuates curtail temporary help workers' ability to resist their substandard conditions of employment.

The success of the THI still rests on casting temporary help workers as commodities – bought, sold, and traded in the labour market. However, conditions in the contemporary Canadian labour market are different from those confronted by workers employed by the earliest precursors of the modern temporary help agency, as well as by the 'classic' temporary help agency. Although it builds on developments in the early part of the twentieth century and in the post-Second World War era, a new configuration of factors contributes to the tenuous nature of the TER. At the macro-level, there appears to be a growing relationship between the feminization of employment and the rise and spread of the TER; the regulatory stalemate at both the national and the international levels, which enables the Canadian THI to self-regulate through a complex legal apparatus, only reinforces this relationship. What is equally crucial to the persistently precarious nature of the TER, however, is the host of policies and practices operating at the micro-level that are designed not only to create an arm's-length relationship between customers and workers but also to minimize the agency's employment-related responsibilities.

By examining both the conditions of employment to which temporary help workers are normally subject and the relationship between temporary help workers and their two 'bosses' (i.e., the agency and the customer), this chapter probes the impact of the contemporary TER on the worker. It suggests first that if the spread of temporary help work and the terms of employment surrounding the TER are indicative of the direction of change in the Canadian labour market, then the decline of the SER is bringing about qualitative changes in the conditions of employment endured by many workers. Second, taking the TER as a case in point, it shows that growing instability in the SER has gendered underpinnings. Prevailing employment trends indicate more than simply consistently high labour force participation rates among women and the spread of nonstandard forms of employment, two pillars upon which the contemporary THI rests: these trends add up to the feminization of employment. Indeed, they signal the extension of 'new' feminized employment relationships in the labour market and the feminization of employment norms more broadly.[1] Third, by examining micro-level processes that heighten the precarious character of temporary help work, the chapter highlights the weight of the regulatory challenges posed by the spread of the TER, since it is at the level of intra- and inter-firm relations that temporary help workers experience a profound degree of commodification and that the THI's ability to prevent large-scale worker resistance is most apparent.

The Erosion of the SER: A Gendered Process

The economic uncertainty characteristic of the period between the early 1970s and the mid-1990s generated dramatic changes in the labour market, shifts that contributed to destabilizing the SER in both Canada and abroad. At the international level, growing instability in the SER coincided with significant changes in the structural and institutional arrangements dominant in the post-Second World War period, as evidenced by the crumbling international monetary regime and commodity shortages. At the national level, these developments corresponded with the federal government's abandonment of its postwar full-employment objective in favour of anti-inflationary policies and programs that contributed to women's rising labour force participation rates and the growth of nonstandard forms of employment in Canada.

Chapter 4 focused attention on the dramatic rise in women's labour force participation rates. Yet this trend is by no means the only facet of the feminization of employment. If feminization is to be useful as a descriptive concept, applicable to a range of settings cross-nationally, it must encompass trends such as persisting sex segregation; increased income and occupational polarization between men and women as well as among women and men based on variables pertaining to race, immigration status and age; and, finally, the casualization of employment, or, more precisely, the 'gendering' (ie., feminization) of jobs. Given that we have explored the relationship of women's rising labour force participation to the THI's strategy of situating the TER as an alternative to the SER in the late 1980s, it is instructive to examine the degree to which employment trends in Canada reflect these other facets of feminization.

The Canadian Case

Consistent with an expanded conception of the feminization of employment, sex segregation and income and occupational polarization persisted, and in some respects even intensified, in the Canadian labour market in the 1970s and 1980s. Thus, growing labour force participation rates have meant 'more of the same' for women – typically, relegation to the bottom tiers of the labour force, isolation to specific job categories, relatively low average hourly wages, and consistently low rates of unionization (Armstrong and Armstrong, 1994). As numerous scholars have emphasized, feminization has also entailed downward harmonization in wages and conditions of employment for some men, particularly in light of de-industrialization (Armstrong, 1996; Brodie, 1994; Cohen, 1994). Contrary to the predictions of early proponents of the conventional thesis, who implied that feminization might entail the substitution of women for men in 'men's jobs,' sex segregation has persisted in the Canadian labour market, and, in some limited areas, men are taking jobs traditionally held by women (Armstrong, 1996; Gunderson, Muszynski, and Keck, 1990: 77–8). In describing women's position in the labour market in the late-1980s and early 1990s, Pat Armstrong (1995: 396) argues that '[a]lthough the labour force participation of women has risen dramatically and women have made some important gains, *most remain segregated in the lowest paid, least attractive, and most precarious forms of work*' [my emphasis]. To this we should add the qualifier that Armstrong (1997) and others make: even though inequalities between women remain smaller than those between men, immigrant women, women of colour and Aboriginal women experience the brunt of sex segregation, and therefore income and occupational polarization by sex, making their average annual earnings disproportionately low and intensifying the effects of sex segregation (Cameron, 1995: 193; Leach, 1993: 66; Ocran, 1997: 148, 152–3).

Even with more men entering female-dominated sectors, such as the service sector, women's concentration in certain fields remained quite high into the 1990s: for example, women's share of service sector jobs was 57.6 per cent in 1971 and 52.0 per cent in 1991(Armstrong and Armstong, 1993). More important, in the 1970s and 1980s women, immigrants, and people of colour were concentrated in traditional segments of the service sector, which are normally labour-intensive, characterized by non-standard forms of work, low wages, and dominated by small firms (J. White, 1993: 166).[2] In contrast, men tended to dominate in more dynamic services, such as in finance and transportation.

Indeed, the expansion of the tertiary sector, particularly from the early 1960s to the mid-1980s, brought more women into the labour market, and therefore contributed to the shift in the THI's strategy away from targeting a narrow group of white middle-class married women as its chief workers towards cultivating a more diverse workforce. It also brought more so-called 'women's work' (i.e., jobs with low status, limited stability, and low pay) into the labour market. However, it had a negligible effect on sex segregation in the labour market. The decline of public sector employment, where women made limited gains in the 1960s and 1970s despite initiatives such as '6 and 5' and the AIP, only reinforced such outcomes (Archibald, 1970; Gunderson, Muszynski, and Keck, 1990; Morgan, 1988). Moreover, massive job losses in goods-producing sectors can hardly be said to have alleviated sex segregation significantly in the Canadian labour market from the mid-1980s to the early 1990s, although they led to declining male wages and participation rates and also contributed to intensified income and occupational polarization between men based on race, if the THI is a case in point (Rashid, 1993).

Trends in the THI are consistent with the persistence of sex segregation and income and occupational polarization in the Canadian labour market in the period under study. While gender parity is emerging in the THI, the evidence suggests that the THI remained internally sex segregated in the mid-1990s, with women (especially immigrant women and women of colour) dominating in job categories at the bottom of the industry, such as clerical work, nursing and related fields, and service work, and men dominating in general labour, but also in high technology and in administrative and managerial job categories. Interestingly, the rise in male employment in the THI mirrors growing occupational diversification in the industry, particularly its expansion into sectors related to science and technology and other professional fields. Given the outcomes of Statistics Canada's *Survey of Work Arrangements, 1995* (1996), which found that temporary help workers engaged in managerial and administrative, medical, transportation, and materials-handling occupations, had the highest average hourly wages of all temporary help workers, and those that engaged in clerical occupations had nearly the lowest – it is reasonable to surmise that income and occupational polarization, largely based on variables related to sex, race, ethnicity and age, continue to characterize the THI (Statistics Canada, 1996: cat. 71M0013GPE). Thus, sex segregation and the related trend of income and occupational polarization not only persist in the contemporary Canadian labour market, but both these dimensions of the feminization of employment also remain integral to the shape of the THI itself.

Another central dimension of feminization that this study has yet to examine in the Canadian context is the casualization of employment or the 'gendering (i.e., feminization) of jobs.' Casualization represented a significant employment trend in Canada from the 1970s onwards, one that intensified in the late-1980s and the early 1990s, leading to greater uncertainty in employment relationships. The result is that a growing proportion of workers lack benefits commonly associated with the SER; are forced to engage in fixed-duration contracts, short-term, intermittent, or nonpermanent employment; must confront downward pressure on wages; and may have more than one employer (or no employer at all). Casualization usually occurs alongside the growth of nonstandard forms of work, although the two trends are not necessarily intertwined. It is also often accompanied by the growth of small firms and declining rates of unionization. Bluntly put, growing casualization means that more forms of employment resemble 'women's work,' not only the types of employment relationships that women are normally confined to and/ or the type of employment contracts to which they are often subject (Fudge, 1991; Jenson, 1996), but also the inferior conditions of employment that women frequently face related to both their presumed role in social reproduction and their 'presumed' status as 'secondary' bread-winners.

In the Canadian context, four recent developments provide evidence of the casualization of employment. First, downward pressure on wages occurred during the 1980s, so that men's average wages declined between 1980 and 1990 for the first time in seven decades (Rashid, 1993: 18). This decline in male wages led many single-breadwinner families to rely on more than one income-earner, not only forcing more Canadians into the labour force but into precarious forms of employment (Fudge, 1995). Second, Canadians experienced a growth of irregular work schedules, including on-call and shift work, a development that indicates that employment relationships became more unreliable in this period (Statistics Canada (1996): cat. 71M0013GPE). Third, in the wake of the *Macdonald Commission* (1985) and the *Royal Commission on UI* (1986), as well as the federal government's more recent forays into social policy reform, unemployed workers endured declining UI coverage rates and other cutbacks to occupationally based social programs, even in the face of rising unemployment rates. For example, while 87 per cent of the unemployed were receiving UI in 1990, only 58 per cent were receiving it in 1994 (Canadian Labour Congress, 1995: 2). Fourth, rates of unionization stagnated in Canada in this period, and the contraction of public sector employment promises to continue this trend since a majority of unionized workers are concentrated in this sector (Akyeampong, 1997: 47; Galarneau, 1996).

Clearly, the preceding developments attest to the erosion of the SER and its associated package of benefits and entitlements described in Chapter 4. However, the fact that growing casualization, intensified income and occupational polarization, and persisting sex segregation accompanied rising labour force participation rates among women and the growth of nonstandard forms of employment warrants special emphasis. The coincidence of these trends from the mid-1970s to the early 1990s might seem to suggest, at least at first glance, that sex matters less in the contemporary Canadian labour market than it did in the post–Second World War period when there were definitive male and female employment norms; the logic behind this interpretation is that the casualization of employment is making everybody (i.e., all men and all women) worse off, since it entails downward harmonization in the labour market. But the persistence of sex segregation and income and occupational polarization based on sex in the labour market, and the fact that when men vie for jobs traditionally held by women they frequently compete for women's 'good' jobs (i.e., those characterized by decent wages and considerable security) belies this interpretation. A more accurate and nuanced way to interpret these trends is *not* to suggest that sex matters less in shaping the contemporary labour market, but that gender, as relational and ideological concept, requires greater attention in labour market analysis. Indeed, the erosion of the SER is a gendered process. Sex and gender remain crucial variables in shaping employment trends even with downward harmonization in the Canadian labour market as a whole. Women are not simply entering the labour market in greater numbers on a global scale and therefore 'taking men's jobs.' Rather, feminized employment relationships and employment norms are becoming acceptable alternatives to the SER, possibly even templates for employment change.

It may seem counter-intuitive to view the changes in the THI, which are leading more men to engage in temporary help work, as indicative of the feminization of employment. However, the THI affords us a rare entry point in probing the 'gendering of jobs' precisely because sex parity increasingly characterizes the industry, but the shape of the TER remains virtually unchanged from the post–Second World War period when the THI cast it as a supplement to the SER and organized it on the presumption that its chief workers were married women dependent upon a male wage. The TER is still a highly precarious model of employment, indicative of the casualization of employment, or more accurately the 'gendering (i.e., feminization) of jobs,' even despite the rising occupational diversity in the THI.

The Shape of the Contemporary TER

A range of factors and indices operating at the meso- and micro-levels contribute to shaping the TER. However, the legal agreement, known as the 'employment agreement,' between the temporary help worker and the agency underpins the insecure character of temporary help work. This is particularly evident when its terms are examined against the conditions of employment normally associated with the TER. Together, these dimensions of the TER illustrate that the THI is crafting an employment relationship that not only differs from the SER in all its central aspects, but, as an ideal-typical model, is also considerably more precarious.

The Employment Agreement

Complementing the service contract, which is atypical for a commercial contract because it governs the supply of workers, the employment agreement is the legal instrument through which agencies formally engage temporary help workers. Even though managers and industry officials argue that the agency is the employer of temporary help workers, they refuse to characterize the employment agreement as an employment contract (fieldnotes, 4 December 1996). They justify their reticence on a range of factors, such as the intermittent nature of temporary help work, the fact that most temporary help workers register with more than one agency, and the fact that customers are entitled to terminate employment virtually at will. Yet the primary rationale for characterizing the arrangement as an 'agreement' rather than a 'contract' is to limit the agency's employment-related obligations. The employment agreement is a distancing tool, and as such it differs from a standard employment contract in many respects.

Unlike a standard employment contract, the status of the employment agreement changes depending upon whether the worker is on assignment. Most agencies require workers to sign the agreement after completing mandatory testing and interviewing, but the bulk of its provisions only take effect when the worker is placed with a customer. Unlike standard employment contracts, which detail the rights and responsibilities of the worker and the employer, employment agreements require the worker to agree to a range of terms while minimizing the agency's reciprocal commitments. In signing these agreements, temporary help workers effectively relinquish their rights to a number of standard labour protections accorded by provincial law, such as notice of termination, and agree to accept constraints on their mobility rights in the labour market.

Employment agreements are normally short, even in comparison to the service contract, and contain five to ten clauses. Most begin with a clause asserting that the temporary help worker is an employee of the agency, and therefore the worker's loyalties rest with the agency rather than with the customer. This clause typically requires temporary help workers to promise not to invite or accept an offer of employment made by the customer without prior consent of the agency, and to acknowledge that accepting an offer of employment may result in a placement fee being charged to the customer. For the agency, the aim of the clause is to prolong the service contract, maintaining the temporary help worker on the payroll of the agency as long as possible (M1, M2, M4). The corresponding effect for the worker, however, is that his or her freedom of movement in the labour market is curtailed so long as s/he is on assignment through the agency. Combined with a parallel clause in the service contract, which dictates that customers may be charged a placement fee if they hire the worker directly, this clause creates a disincentive for hiring the worker on a permanent basis and therefore underscores the instability inherent in the TER.

Another standard clause requires the worker to acknowledge that s/he understands that the agency will not provide notice of termination (or payment in lieu of notice) as required by law because of both the temporary nature of the employment and the fact that s/he may accept or reject assignments without penalty.[3] This is an important clause intended to obtain the temporary help worker's consent to opt out of standard labour protections, making temporary help work a legitimate form of employment at will, and heightening the precarious nature of the TER. The clause has virtually no legal force, since, as employers, agencies are obligated to pay severance and/or give adequate notice of termination. The parallel clause in the service contract requires customers to inform the agency in advance when an assignment is ending, in the event that the agency is required to cover severance pay and/or give sufficient termination notice. The coexistence of these two clauses gives the agency various options to minimize its costs.

Finally, as a matter of course, employment agreements contain a clause stating that the worker understands that the agency provides no guarantees regarding the duration of their employment relationship with the agency or the length of any given assignment. This clause highlights the lack of permanency in the TER, although it in no way suggests that assignments with the agency are of short duration. There is no parallel clause in the service contract.

Both the structure of the employment agreement and its substantive provisions require temporary help workers to relinquish a number of rights and protections commonly accorded to standard workers. However, the absence of certain provisions in generic employment agreements is equally crucial to establishing the TER as a precarious model of employment. Although service contracts routinely dictate that the agency's administrative fee covers statutory charges, such as mandatory pension and UI benefits, most employment agreements lack clauses denoting that the agency shall make contributions to these schemes. The attempt is to reinforce the one-way nature of the employment agreement. Similarly, except in the case of specialized employment agreements, such as those that involve a so-called co-employment relationship or those where the agency is placing a highly skilled temporary help worker in what promises to be a long-term assignment, few employment agreements provide workers with extended benefits normally accorded to workers engaged in SERs – benefits such as extended health coverage, dental coverage, maternity benefits, and paid sick leave. The most these agreements offer to workers with respect to extended benefits is the opportunity to join group benefit plans if they fulfill certain eligibility requirements. Where such opportunities exist, however, eligibility requirements are often onerous and the cost of purchasing extended benefits is prohibitive; managers report that few temporary help workers make use of the extended benefit plans offered by some agencies for these reasons (fieldnotes, 3 December 1996). The most generous group benefit plan surveyed required temporary help workers to work 100 hours with a single agency over a one-month period in order to become eligible to purchase group-based benefits, and to work seventy-five hours per month to retain eligibility. Since temporary help workers tend to work through more than one agency, even these minimal eligibility requirements may place extended benefits out of their reach. Given the absence of such employment-related benefits, it is not surprising that few temporary help workers report having extended benefits.

In sum, the employment agreement is effectively a one-way agreement between the temporary help worker and the agency, where the worker agrees to accept a minimal level of social protections and waives certain fundamental rights accorded by Canadian law in exchange for the prospect of obtaining temporary help work. Still, the employee's existence preserves the agency's central role in the TER. On a practical level, the form of the employment agreement, along with the service contract, allows the agency to retain its status as an employment agent or intermediary in the true sense of the term, even though it poses as the employer to its customers. It is only in the service contract that the agency agrees to administer statutory benefits to the temporary help worker. 'Administer' is the key word here, because neither the employment agreement nor the service contract clearly defines who is the employer of record.

Through the combination of the employment agreement and the service contract, the agency attempts to negotiate a delicate balance. It requires unqualified loyalty from temporary help workers, to ensure that they view the agency as their principal employer, and it takes on sufficient employment-related responsibilities so that customers are relieved of responsibilities related to hiring, dismissal, and other administrative tasks. Yet it still affirms that the customer is responsible for the control and supervision of temporary help workers while they are on assignment. The apparatus that surrounds the TER is open to several legal interpretations, ranging from the view that agency and customer are co-employers – an increasingly common legal rendering – to the interpretation that the agency is the employer, to the finding that the customer is the employer (Axelrod, 1987; ILO, 1994a). From the worker's perspective, the impact of this apparatus is clear: the employment agreement is considerably weaker than a standard employment contract, and the service contract and the employment agreement both minimize the employment-related responsibilities of the customer and the agency, cultivating a casualized employment relationship. It has the effect of establishing the TER as a much more precarious model of employment than the SER and clearly prefigures the poor conditions of employment and levels of benefits that temporary help workers face.

Conditions of Employment

While both the employment agreement and the service contract are relatively recent innovations in the THI, managers, customers, and industry officials contend that these 'new' agreements simply represent the industry's attempt to standardize its age-old practices and secure its place in the labour market. Thus, the conditions of employment associated with the contemporary TER, which are formalized by the cumbersome legal apparatus that surrounds it, conform with many pre-existing conditions in the THI. As Chapter 4 demonstrated, women still predominate in the THI, particularly in the field of clerical work, but the gender composition of the industry's workforce is changing, the industry's customer base is much more diverse, and the average length of job tenure is getting longer. Thus, one might expect the conditions of employment surrounding the TER to have changed to accommodate shifting employment norms and to entice a more diverse group of workers. One might also anticipate the THI to be adopting a new rationale for the nature of the TER that accounts for the greater diversity in the industry. But, even though the industry's practices are subject to greater scrutiny than in the post-Second World War era, and even though industry leaders are actively seeking legitimacy for its practices at the national and supranational level, this type of rationale is surprisingly absent. In the Canadian context, increased legitimacy for the THI is by no means amounting to greater legal certainty, security, or higher levels of social protection for temporary help workers.

The range of entitlements and the package of benefits normally surrounding the TER are very limited. Like many other workers in nonstandard employment relationships, temporary help workers are subject to the inferior set of labour protections provided by minimum standards legislation rather than having full access to the occupational welfare system like most standard workers.[4] And, unlike standard workers, temporary help workers do not generally have the option of joining or forming unions because the worksite-based model of unionization dominant in Canada cannot accommodate the type of employment relationships to which they are subject, and because occupational forms of unionism are not sufficiently widespread (Chapter 8); consequently, the best (and most viable) way for temporary help workers to benefit from the wage guarantees and social protections attained by unionized workers is through coverage under a collective agreement negotiated by a union representing workers in a host firm. When combined with the legal arrangements surrounding the TER and the limited options available to temporary help workers regarding unionization, the asymmetrical model of labour market regulation operating in Canada has negative effects on temporary help workers' conditions of employment. Until the early 1990s it was virtually impossible to demonstrate the precarious character of the TER statistically. However, data derived from the *Survey of Work Arrangements, 1995* provide a clear picture of the wages and other forms of remuneration surrounding temporary help work.

TABLE 14

Hourly Wages (in $) by Occupation for Permanent and Temporary
Subdivided by Agency Temporaries and Other Temporaries, 1995

| | Permanent | Temporary | | |
		Agency	Other	All
Management, Admin.	19.57	19.69	15.92	16.04
Science, etc.	18.94	9.22	15.95	15.91
Teaching	21.24	6.00	17.99	17.95
Medicine	18.14	12.18	17.04	16.66
Clerical	12.92	7.06	10.64	10.55
Sales	10.49	n/a	8.10	8.10
Service	10.26	8.94	8.23	8.23
Resource	13.56	n/a	11.22	11.22
Processing	15.25	7.61	11.59	11.36
Construction	17.89	n/a	15.53	15.60
Transportation &				
Materials Handling	13.92	9.90	10.37	10.35

Source: Statistics Canada, Survey of Work Arrangements, 1995 (Ottawa:
Statistics Canada, 1996), cat. no. 71M0013GPE.
Note: The following occupational groups were excluded from the calcu-
lations: never worked before; last worked more than one year ago; and
permanently unable to work.

Wages and Benefits

Data reveal that temporary help workers receive even lower levels of
remuneration than other temporary workers engaged in similar types of
work. For example, average hourly wages for temporary help workers
engaged by agencies were $10.33 in 1995 while average hourly wages for
other temporary workers were $12.38 in the same year (Statistics Canada,
1996: cat. 71M0013GPE).[5] Permanent workers enjoyed higher average
hourly wages than temporary help workers in every occupational grouping surveyed (Table 14). In large part, the difference between the average hourly wages of all temporary workers and temporary help workers
may be accounted for by the 'mark-up,' that is, the portion of the service
fee that goes to the agency. When asked about the mark-up, some
temporary help workers were acutely aware of it and objected to it, as
well as the secrecy surrounding it: 'You get paid for something and you
have a right to know what you're actually worth. I'm working for an
assignment right now and they're paying me $9.50, but I have a right to

TABLE 15
Extended Health Coverage for Permanent and Temporary
Workers Subdivided by Agency Temporaries, 1995

Permanent Workers	Temporary Help Workers	All Temporary Workers
64.3	8.2	19.3

Source: Statistics Canada, Survey of Work Arrangements, 1995.

know because I work in front of the computer for eight long hours a day and I have to finish the assignment no matter what. If it's something like doing inventory and I have to finish every single inventory even if I have to stay until 6:30 in the evening – I have to finish and they won't let me come out of the office – I have a right to know how much I'm worth. Probably they're [the agency] taking in more than $17.00 an hour for me' (T6). Still, rather than naming the mark-up as the root of the problem, most workers simply emphasize the inadequacy of their wages. One woman noted, 'It's difficult. I work to pay for myself and I have kids. It's very difficult. Very, very difficult ... I have three kids ... I pay $875. a month for this apartment. If I work full time [temporary] for a whole month, I get $900. How do I pay my rent? How do I pay for my food?' (T4). Like many of her counterparts, this worker felt powerless in acting against the agency to improve her conditions of employment even though it was impossible for her to subsist on the wages provided by the agency.

Benefits

Data derived from the *Survey of Work Arrangements, 1995* also indicate that temporary help workers have limited access to extended benefits, in comparison to their counterparts engaged in permanent employment and to other temporary workers. As Table 15 illustrates, only 8.2 per cent of temporary help workers, versus 64.3 per cent of permanent workers and 19.3 per cent of all temporary workers, reported having extended health coverage in 1995. What is even more striking is that only 2.2 per cent of temporary help workers, as opposed to 60 per cent of all permanent workers and 16.5 per cent of all temporary workers, had dental coverage in the same year (Table 16). Many temporary workers, particularly those in long-term assignments, resent the absence of benefits. A temporary help worker, who was approaching retirement age, had worked

TABLE 16
Dental Coverage for Permanent and Temporary Workers
Subdivided by Agency Temporaries, 1995

Permanent Workers	Temporary Help Workers	All Temporary Workers
60.0	2.2	16.5

Source: Statistics Canada, *Survey of Work Arrangements, 1995.*

for a large company on a permanent and full-time basis for twenty-five years before she was laid off. She had been on one assignment through a temporary help agency since, and noted, 'Every normal company gives you benefits when you become permanent. After working for three months, you automatically get the benefits and all those things. Through the agency, I have not got any benefits like every other company I used to work for and I work more ... I've been there [with the agency] for more than three months. I should get all the benefits from them. Even medical, dental, and all those things. Nothing, they don't give me any' (T9). Many workers recognize that customers use temporary help workers to escape paying into benefits schemes, which is of particular value to them in cases of long-term employment. For example, at the same time as she reflected on the poor conditions of employment attached to the TER and how permanent workers normally have superior benefits, one worker noted that her work resembled permanent work in many respects: 'The system in this company is that if they don't tell you, you have to come in the next day. So we go in every day as if permanent. We work as if permanent from 7:00 a.m. to 3:30 p.m., and sometimes overtime. The same [as permanent]' (T4). Another worker asserted: '[My job] is considered temporary, but it's permanent because it's not said, "Well, your job is going to be over in six months." As far as I know this is going to be for an indefinite time. Unless they decide they don't like me' (T8). Both these workers were cognizant that the customer was using the THI to abdicate employment-related responsibilities even though they needed workers on a permanent basis.

With respect to paid sick leave, 62.1 per cent of all permanent workers and 19.3 per cent of all temporary workers reported having some access to sick days in 1995. However only 4.6 per cent of temporary help workers had access to paid sick leave in the same year. When the statistics are disaggregated by gender, the picture is even bleaker: only 2.1 per

TABLE 17
Paid Sick Leave for Permanent and Temporary Workers Subdivided by Agency Temporaries and Gender, 1995

	Permanent Workers			Temporary Help Workers			All Temporary Workers		
	M	F	All	M	F	All	M	F	All
Yes	63.2	61.0	62.1	7	2.1	4.6	17.7	20.8	19.3
No	36.8	39.0	37.9	93	97.9	95.4	82.3	79.2	80.7

Source: Statistics Canada, Survey of Work Arrangements, 1995.

cent of all female temporary help workers, versus 7 per cent of male temporary help workers, were guaranteed some form of paid sick leave. After describing how costly it is to pay for prescription drugs for her children because she is ineligible for extended medical coverage as a temporary help worker, one worker noted, 'We have no benefits. It's terrible. If I get something now, if I'm sick, who pays for me? Nobody. If you are sick, you stay home, no problem. No problem, but no money. That's it' (T4). These figures demonstrate that the package of benefits associated with the TER is inferior to that associated with the SER, and that women temporary help workers are even more disadvantaged than their male counterparts despite their frequent responsibility for dependent children and seniors (Table 17).

Multiple Job-Holding

Another indication that temporary help work is a form of precarious employment is the sizeable percentage of temporary help workers who hold more than one job. In 1995, 10.6 per cent of all temporary help workers, versus 4.7 per cent of all permanent workers held multiple jobs (Table 18). The reason that many temporary help workers resort to multiple job-holding is because they simply require more hours of work and not because they are seeking more variety in their working lives, as industry officials suggest. The following figures, pertaining to temporary help workers' desire to increase their hours of work, attest to this assertion. Over 50 per cent of temporary help workers had an interest in increasing their hours of work in 1995. The equivalent figure for permanent workers was only 25 per cent (Table 19). Not only do these figures reflect the polarization in hours of work that Canadians are currently experiencing, with a sizeable percentage of workers working excessive

TABLE 18
Multiple Job-Holding among Permanent and Tempo-
rary Subdivided by Agency Temporaries and Other
Temporaries, 1995

	Temporary Workers		
Permanent Workers	Agency	Other	All
4.7	10.6	7.5	7.6

Source: Statistics Canada, Survey of Work Arrangements, 1995.

TABLE 19
Interest in Increasing or Decreasing Hours of Work at the Same
Wage Rate, Permanent and Temporary Subdivided by Agency
Temporaries and Other Temporaries, 1995

		Temporary Workers		
	Permanent Workers	Agency	Other	All
Fewer hours	6.3	3.6	3.9	3.9
More hours	25.0	51.1	47.4	47.5
Same hours	68.7	45.3	48.7	48.6

Source: Statistics Canada, Survey of Work Arrangements, 1995.

overtime and a growing proportion of workers working fewer than twenty-
five hours a week, they indicate that temporary help workers are disproportionately affected by this trend.

Unionization

Under the workplace-based system of collective bargaining in Canada,
the fact that temporary help workers are dispatched to different and
multiple worksites makes it nearly impossible for them to organize collectively. Some temporary help workers are covered under collective
agreements when they are placed on assignment in a unionized workplace;
these workers tend to have higher wages than their counterparts who are
not covered by collective agreements, and some have access to extended
benefits. However, the majority of temporary help workers in Canada,
and temporary workers more broadly, are not unionized or covered by a
collective agreement, and, as Chapter 8 illustrates, the obstacles to creating new modes of representation are quite significant.[6]
The generally poor conditions of employment surrounding the TER,

particularly in contrast to the SER, mirror the terms and conditions set out in the employment contract and the service contract. In Canada, in the late 1990s, temporary help work is a form of precarious employment: workers' low wages, the intermittent nature of employment, and the limited set of benefits normally attached to the TER are evidence. Moreover, its precarious nature is particularly notable given that the THI is transforming from a female-dominated industry to one where sex parity is emerging. Still, despite the growing body of statistical data confirming the substandard conditions of employment common to temporary help work, the policies and practices permeating the day-to-day operations of the THI provide perhaps the most compelling evidence of the precarious character of the TER. As the ensuing section shall demonstrate, the often coercive practices operating at the firm level are largely responsible for the commodification process that is so integral to the TER.

Qualitative Dimensions of the TER

A range of informal processes operating within the THI at the micro-level are central to the precarious character of the contemporary TER. Thus, it is crucial to describe qualitative dimensions of the TER that heighten insecurity among temporary help workers and limit their capacity to resist their generally poor conditions of employment, and in turn to explore how managers and customers justify and perpetuate the often coercive firm-based customs, policies, and practices. This type of examination makes it possible to highlight more fully the role of feminization (and sexism) and racialization (and racism) in institutionalizing uncertainty within the TER.

Flexibility or Insecurity

Although the insecurity inherent within the TER was a primary complaint among all the workers interviewed, several workers remarked on the flexibility and variety that temporary help work has the potential to offer. Workers were more tentative about flexibility than managers and officials, however, who saw temporary help work as desirable for 'moms who are at home, who don't want to be working on a permanent basis' but 'want a schedule that accommodates their kids,' and for 'people taking care of the elderly at home,' who 'just want something that gets them out of the house for a couple of days a week' (M1).

An actor who did administrative and clerical work through a temporary help agency reported that temporary help work allowed her enough flexibility to attend night-time rehearsals and miss the odd day of work for a performance (T1). Still, the same worker emphasized the high degree of uncertainty associated with temporary help work and the stress generated by the absence of security and stability in the employment relationship: 'A lot of times, you get half a day's notice. I've been called in the morning to come in at noon and take over for somebody who is sick, so you have to be adaptable ... I get sick of waiting by the phone. Temp work also moves fast. One day you're working and then for a whole week, you're not. I don't recommend it, if you're not adaptable or if you're not spontaneous' (T1). She believed she paid a premium for the limited amount of flexibility that she gained by engaging in temporary help work, noting that her low wages and on-call status reflected the costs of working through an agency: 'I always felt that I should be compensated somehow for being so on call, you know, ready to jump up and fill in anywhere. I mean, I think that's a special skill and it deserves more than $10 an hour. It's like you're a performer, in a way, when you do it. You really are' (T1). Her intuition that the ability to be 'on call' is a valuable asset – an asset that the customer pays the premium for – reflects the findings of Chapter 4. She added that temporary help work was not in her long-term interest: 'I don't want to just get by. I mean, if I'm going to keep learning new skills, I think that should equal something even though I'm not permanent' (T1).

While this temporary help worker was confident in her ability to refuse the odd assignment for a performance or take a sick day without the threat of reprisals, other temporary help workers reported that even though the employment agreement explicitly acknowledged their right to refuse work, turning down assignments is not an acceptable practice in the THI. This was confirmed by managers, one of whom reflected: 'We look for somebody that's flexible, that we can count on whenever we need to. We get a lot of people who come in begging ... I've got to get work. I've got to do this. We'll make four or five contacts with them. It's all noted on their files. Then, they say "No, I can't go out today, I've got a doctor's appointment," Or, "No, I can't go tomorrow, I've hurt my left toe."' (M2). Another remarked quite candidly: 'If you need a temp, then you need them there yesterday. Temporaries are not allowed to be sick, you know. A permanent employee can be sick but if you book a temporary employee out on assignment, they have to be there ... So it makes it difficult sometimes, because they do get sick, and often we're forced to apologize for things we have no control over' (M3). Some managers even openly inform prospective temporary help workers that refusing work is highly problematic. One told a group of social assistance recipients who had never worked through the THI before: 'Temporary positions can be from one day to a week and more. If you have positive feedback from your temporary placement, you can expect more work. But if you refuse work, or are not flexible, then you will probably receive less work' (fieldnotes, 3 February 1997).

For some workers, variety in work assignments represents another key attraction of temporary help work. One worker left a long-term permanent job with a publishing company because his responsibilities had grown substantially when the company laid off a number of his co-workers. He highlighted the benefits of short-term assignments, indicating that 'just knowing that you will not be there for very long' makes temporary help work enticing (fieldnotes, 3 February 1997). This worker is not alone in his sentiments. Indeed, many temporary help workers, particularly those who once worked in sectors or industries affected by economic downturns and public sector cutbacks, such as health caregivers and industrial workers in major manufacturing industries, appreciated the potential for independence offered by temporary help work. Still, many of these workers report that there is a trade-off between opting for variety over security. For example, after working through an agency intermittently for several months and being forced to resort to social assistance, the worker who left his job at a publishing company reported that he deeply regretted his decision to leave his permanent job (T10).

Who's the Boss?

A host of qualitative dimensions of temporary help work, ranging from the extraordinary demands placed on workers to work quickly and the monotonous tasks often associated with temporary help work, adds to its uncertainty. At the micro-level, workers' confusion over the role of the agency lies at the centre of their experience of temporary help work as precarious employment. When asked to name their employer(s), many temporary help workers express considerable uncertainty. Some believe that the agency is their employer, by indicating that their paychecks come from the agency or that they have only signed a contract with the agency, while others are reluctant to label the agency the employer without some qualification. Many temporaries report that the agency and the customer share employment-related responsibilities, although they are not necessarily aware of how the division of responsibility operates in practice. As one worker noted, 'People who work for temporary agencies – *they have two bosses* [my emphasis]: the agency and whoever they work for when they get sent out. I'm sure when agencies are dealing with certain companies all the time and there's a flow of people, the agencies and the employer must speak to each other?' (T9). Another worker said, 'That's tricky. I never really knew [who my employer was]. I still don't know, because it's partly the temp agency but it's partly your supervisor ... If I was there for a day, it was just the temp agency – I felt that the temp agency was my boss. If it was two or three days or even a week, I would lean towards the supervisor, whoever was in charge of me, to be my boss. But I always felt split on that, and I remember asking my temp agency. They said, "Well, you really work for us, first of all, but you're also working for them"' (T1).

For many workers, the length of the assignment is key to establishing 'who is the boss?' The longer they work on assignment, the more likely they are to view the customer and/or their immediate supervisor as their genuine employer. Partly for this reason, when a customer indicates that s/he plans to use temporary help workers for an extended period, it is common for the agency to hire an on-site supervisor. This is an attempt to preserve their status as the employer of record, by retaining control over the workers, and to remind workers that their primary loyalty lies with the agency. Customers recognize the importance of having agency personnel on-site. For example, one customer affirmed, 'We are going to have a full-time [agency] person in our office, right next to my boss. He's going to have an office at our office. The [agency] promised us somebody that was going to be dedicated to us so that we don't get into any co-employment problems' (C2). At a practical level, however, agencies and customers both gain from the confusion over who is the employer. This confusion heightens tensions for workers, leading them to work faster, put up with poor working conditions, and accept monotonous work from whomever they work for, since they are unsure of who is responsible for retaining them. While its effects on workers are primarily visible through the informal processes operating at the firm level, the confusion over roles and the tensions that it generates at the worksite intensifies the uncertainty inherent within the TER.

Pace and Intensity of Work

Another dimension of temporary help work that contributes to its precarious character, one that partly stems from the confusion over roles, is that temporary help workers often feel pressure to work more quickly than other workers at the worksite. Many acquiesce to unreasonable demands precisely because of the insecure nature of their jobs, even if they feel that their workload is already too heavy. One temporary help worker engaged in office work reflected on the intensity of her workload on an average day: 'Fifty per cent of the time, I feel like it [the work] is too much ... Usually, I just go right at it and do not take a break until 12:00 noon or 1:00 p.m. or I just work right through' (T1). Another said: 'The intensity, the amount of work is a maximum ... The agencies do charge them [the customer] so it's their right to get the work done ... In this particular job, I don't get time to actually go and get myself a cup of tea or something even with the half-hour [instead of an hour] of lunch that I take. I have seen other [permanent] people walking around taking teatime and going out for tea ... but I don't know how they have the time' (T6). Not only are customers aware that temporary help workers tend to work harder than temporary workers hired directly by the company, they take advantage of the insecure nature of the TER by expecting more from temporary help workers than from their permanent staff. One customer asserted: 'I think hard work is something that is really expected and appreciated here [from temps]. You get those slackers [i.e. permanent workers] that, in all fairness, should probably be terminated but we're not going to terminate them because their mother used to work here or there's some tragedy in the family. So sometimes there is that added pressure on temps ... "Look, you know, our full-time isn't coming through for us so you've really got to"' (C3).

Temporary help workers are well aware of their role in supplementing the work of permanent workers. One noted, '[w]e have to help them. We have to finish their work ... We work harder than the permanents ... We work hard so that the company will keep us at work' (T4). Still, rather than acknowledging the high expectations placed on temporary help workers by their 'two bosses,' some customers also refer to what is known as the 'halo effect' to explain why temporary help workers are so efficient. A long-time human resource manager of a plant put it this way: 'The managers often say, "you know, oh gosh, he works better than my full-time people." *I think that there tends to be what they call a "halo-effect"* [my emphasis]. First off, this person is working for an agency so I think that they're probably trying a little harder to show themselves [in order] to be brought on payroll and to get the higher benefits ... I don't know if it's conscious to not work as hard. But, when they become permanent, there is a difference. [They think] I'm here now and I'm making another

$2.50 an hour or sometimes even higher – if you went from an agency as a packaging operator to our payroll, your take-home would be $5.00 more an hour – and they say let's relax now' (C4). This human resource manager, who occasionally uses the THI as a screening device for perspective permanent workers, justified the often unreasonable demands placed on temporary help workers by indicating that the best ones often get rewarded with offers of permanent employment or contract work with her firm (C4).

Common Assignments and Typical Tasks

One consequence of the spread of the TER is the underuse or misuse of workers' skills. While they accelerate the pace of temporary help workers, customers rarely take advantage of the workers' high skill levels. They report using overqualified workers to perform monotonous work simply because these are the workers that the agencies send to them. As one sales representative, who was looking for people to do direct sales in a department store, indicated: 'I had a guy that went through for the priesthood. I don't know how many seminaries he'd been to. He had a full string of degrees. I interviewed him and I just said: "Don't you think you're a little over-qualified for this? He really wanted it. He said he could do it. So, I hired him ... I've had people with PhDs. I've got one person now with a PhD. It's kind of scary"' (C2). Similarly, a temporary help worker who was working at a clothing manufacturer and packaging women's clothes for shipping indicated that her supervisor had no idea that she had been a science teacher and a pharmacy assistant before she immigrated to Canada from Egypt (T4).

Most temporary help workers find the assignments they obtain through the agency uninteresting, suggesting that customers routinely fail to take advantage of their skills. In the words of the worker cited at the outset of this chapter: 'I think that many of us are tremendously underutilized ... We are all, in fact, capable of all kinds of stuff. But the system isn't designed to use that' (T7).[7] Reminiscent of the classic image of the 'Kelly Girl,' making coffee and running errands is still quite common for women's clerical temporary help work: 'You do everything. You have to run across the street and do all of these errands. Pick up dry cleaning, make coffee, clean up messes, call people' (T1). Other tasks that require manual labourers, such as packaging clothing or stuffing envelopes, are also prevalent, and, depending upon the workplace, they are performed by both male and female temporary help workers. Thus, even though many temporary help workers are efficient, highly skilled, and educated, customers still position them in work situated at the bottom of the labour market (M2, C2). As one customer noted, 'I give everybody that I interview this scenario: *I tell them that it's not a very nice job* [my emphasis]. I tell them the very worst of it and then I ask them if they can do the job' (C2).

Customers tend to demand highly efficient workers that accept low wages and monotonous work, so the agency benefits when their workers are known for productivity as well as their willingness to stick with repetitive work. Indeed, providing efficient workers or 'high-quality staffing services' in industry parlance, is the agency's prime means of driving away its competitors. The benefits that agencies accrue from their workers' level of efficiency, however, generate significant losses for workers, particularly with respect to the quality of their work environment and the security of the employment relationship. When workers come from a top agency, customers and even co-workers put tremendous pressure on them to perform exceptionally. They also make them keenly aware that there is always another worker in the wings if they fail to perform adequately. Thus, the accelerated pace of work, the monotonous nature of much of temporary help work, and the fact that many workers are overqualified for the work they do underscore and perpetuate its menial character.

Provision of Equipment and Uniforms

Beyond the fact that the uncertainty surrounding the TER prompts workers to work harder and faster and take fewer breaks, customers and agencies also get the most out of temporary help workers in other respects. Other conventions common at the firm level – blatantly coercive practices that sometimes contravene the terms of the service contract – also contribute to lower costs for customers. For example, customers often play on temporary help workers' confusion over 'who is the boss' to avoid paying for equipment such as safety boots, hard hats, and uniforms. In some instances, they shift the burden of these costs directly to the worker, eliminating any investment on their part beyond the payment of wages and the service fee. One temporary help worker said that one of her friends spent $76. on a pair of safety boots only to find that she would be placed on assignment at a manufacturing plant for six hours (T9). Her take-home pay was not enough to cover the cost of the boots. In other cases, customers pay for safety equipment but they expect loyalty in return, highlighting the contradictions inherent in the triangular employment relationship: 'We actually buy them safety shoes. Probably, what the alternative would be is that they buy them themselves. Again, we're quite generous in this respect. We'll pay up to $70 for safety shoes. We will buy them. We have said, and this has proven to be quite effective ... We tell them: "If you keep those safety shoes clean, and if ever we need help again, you'll be the first that we call back because you've already got shoes." But we tell them, "We don't want you shovelling manure or anything." We don't even like cross-contamination between plants.' (C4). This customer went on to say that she liked to retain a loyal group of temporary help workers for the sake of consistency.

Barriers to Attaining Permanent Work

In return for quickening their pace, performing monotonous tasks, and, in many instances, paying for their own equipment and uniforms, temporary help workers often hope to obtain permanent work. When asked to explain why they are doing temporary help work, the answer is usually quite simple: they cannot find suitable permanent work. Managers generally suggest that workers seek temporary help work because 'They need to top-up an income that they're receiving through another source. They want temporary work because they can't give that commitment to a full-time job. Maybe somebody in their family is ill. They're seeking temporary work because they have to work and they are hoping to expose themselves to many different companies that aren't hiring through the papers, that aren't taking resumes through the front door. They're coming through a service like ours. They're getting the exposure that they want in order to get that full-time job' (M1).

However, some workers put it more bluntly: 'It gets frustrating. You know that this isn't what you want to do with your life. It's something that you have to do to pay the bills' (T1). Agencies play on workers' aspirations for permanent employment to increase their efficiency and situate temporary help work as a suitable 'labour force re-entry vehicle,' as was common in the post–Second World War era. They also describe people who have used temporary help work as a stepping-stone for obtaining permanent work to encourage discouraged workers to stick with temporary help work. 'Ultimately what we want to do is help people find jobs,' one manager said. She continued,

One fellow that we helped, he was on welfare when he applied to us. We had trouble with his references. They were kind of iffy, but he kept calling us every day for work. He seemed so eager and he was really pleasant so I called him in, and we talked about his references, and I asked him to give me some detail about why another agency would not employ him again. It turned out that the one agency that he had let down, they had placed him with [a company] that does garbage pickup. They told him that he would be working inside the recycling plant for the day, but when he got there they put him on the back of a garbage truck. This was in February and he wasn't properly dressed for it. He got home that night, his toes were frozen and his hands were cold. He stuck the job out for the day but he refused to go back the next day. Well, that's kind of extenuating circumstances, I think ... So he seemed like a good risk and we placed him out to work. He worked for two companies, short-term – he did such a great job that we got more business from them because of him and the work he did. And then, the third company that he went to, they kept him on our payroll for about six or seven months and then they hired him. He's making about $5. an hour more now than he was when he was on our payroll. He works about sixty hours a week and he gets all the overtime he wants and they love him. They think he's just wonderful. And he was on welfare when he came to us and couldn't find employment. So, that's my success story. (M3)

This manager used stories like these to motivate discouraged temporary help workers and inform critics of the THI's important successes.

According to workers, however, agency personnel often use the promise of permanent work to more manipulative ends. For example, several workers revealed that managers often try to convince workers to stay with 'bad bosses' or remain in difficult work environments by claiming that there is something in it for them in the long run. One temporary help worker reported that a manager convinced her to stay on assignment at a bank, with the elusive promise of permanent work and steady assignments:

There was one assignment that I definitely could not handle. I never got a desk. I always had to work on a counter. I was working for a bank and they would never give me a desk to work on. I worked on the floor. I was doing all of this like really in-depth filing, collating all of these reports, and photocopying stuff. I thought this is it. I'm giving them one more day. By tomorrow, when I come in here I better have a desk. I didn't have a desk when I came in and I lost it. I phoned the agency, and said, 'I'm leaving right now.' They said: 'Don't leave now. We'll get you a desk.' I still waited for almost a week for a desk ... That's when I turned thirty. I said, 'That's it, I'm thirty, I deserve to be working at a desk.' (T1)

This worker went on to suggest that the reason she held out for so long was that they told her this might turn into a permanent position. Other practices central to the daily operations of the THI compound the false promise of permanent employment. Although workers must provide two references before reputable firms will place them on assignment, agencies usually refuse to provide workers with references when they are applying for jobs outside the confines of the THI (fieldnotes, 2 December 1996). According to workers, the excuse provided by managers is that the agency is not in a position to provide a reference because they did not oversee the worker when s/he was on assignment with a customer. Customers also refuse to give references because they are unwilling to provide any evidence that could be used to cast them as the employer. In seeking to move beyond temporary help work and into the wider labour market, therefore, workers face a double bind cultivated by the complex legal arrangements surrounding the TER. One worker argued that the practice of refusing to provide references created the following situation: 'It perpetuates and increases the development of a workforce of sheep. You are profoundly disempowered by doing this. Precisely because you're disposable, there aren't any avenues to complain, to appeal, to do anything. I've found that tough. Not that I have necessarily felt the need to do it [i.e., complain or appeal], but I have felt keenly the impossibility of doing it if I wanted to.' (T7). These sentiments highlight the feeling of powerlessness experienced by many temporary help workers unable to find work and frustrated by the legal manipulation in the THI.

Alienation

Temporary help workers often speak of 'just putting in time' and 'feeling like guests everyday.' Some also self-identify as 'disposable workers' or 'second class.' In discussing the quality of their working lives, many temporary help workers reveal that their relationships with other workers at the worksite, particularly those hired directly by the customer, intensify their sense of marginalization. Antagonisms between temporary help workers and other workers at the worksite are commonplace in the THI, and customers and agencies often build on these tensions in order to maximize their returns.

It is common for temporary help workers to work alongside other temporary workers hired directly by the company, on-call workers, and workers with fixed-duration contracts, as well as permanent workers.

This situation creates tensions not only between temporary help workers and permanent workers, a common theme reported in other studies of the THI (Henson, 1993; Rogers, 1995), but also between temporary help workers and other nonstandard workers. Paradoxically, it often leads to jealousy and competitiveness among workers rather than generating a climate of collective resistance against customers and agencies.

One temporary help worker recalled an instance where several permanent workers demanded that she slow down because she was showing up the permanent workers. She initially responded to their demands by politely indicating that she had to continue to work at this pace to keep her job. The permanent workers responded to her refusal to slow down with a range of reprisals. This was an assembly line situation where workers were folding, packaging, and boxing clothes for shipping, so they sabotaged her work, forcing her to re-package clothes, thereby reducing her productivity and slowing down production altogether. However, their retaliation went even further. At lunchtime, the permanent workers refused to eat with the temporary help worker, forcing her to take a table at the far end of the cafeteria, and they discouraged other temporary help workers from associating with her by threatening them with similar treatment. They also taunted her for not having a permanent job but still having to work faster than her co-workers to keep her assignment. When the supervisor at the plant confronted the temporary help worker because her productivity had dropped, the worker faced a dilemma: either she could report that the other workers were sabotaging her work, and risk the accusation of lying and/or revealing her co-workers' misconduct, or apologize for slowing down and try to work faster. She chose the latter option, leading her to harbour tremendous resentment towards the permanent workers. Rather than blaming the customer, this worker characterized her situation as follows: 'The permanent workers ... they think they are the owner of this company and that we work temporary as slaves' (T4).

While this worker's story is a rather extreme example of the antagonisms between temporary help workers and other workers, numerous temporary help workers report that the permanent workers treat them poorly at the worksite. Many recognize the roots of their hostility, suggesting that it is reasonable for permanent workers to reject the friendship of temporary help workers. As one noted, 'Why should they [permanent workers] get to know you? Why should they invest time in getting to know you when you are just there for a day?' (T1). This worker indicated that the best assignments are those where there are other temporary help workers, ideally from the same firm, on-site: 'If it's a really big firm, like for the banks, I am with other temps. Most of the time, we share a room. That's cool' (T1). Temporary help workers report being most comfortable with workers from the same agency because the intensely competitive nature of the THI has the potential to create antagonisms between temporary help workers from different agencies. It is not un-common for temporary help workers from different agencies to earn different hourly wages, since, particularly in high-volume industrial work, agencies constantly try to undercut their competitors (fieldnotes, 5 De-cember 1996). A temporary help worker who had been working at a large call centre made the following observations: 'By the time I got there, there were five permanent full-time staff and then everybody else was temps. There were two kinds of temps. There were the temps that were hired through the agencies and there were the temps that were hired directly by [the customer], and we all earned different salaries. The ones who were best paid in terms of our hourly rate were those of us who were hired directly' (T7).

On the whole, temporary help workers enjoy contact with other tem-porary help workers, even if they earn different salaries. Contact mini-mizes their sense of marginalization: 'You need to have another person in your life that is doing or has done the same thing ... [Temporary help work requires] a 12-step program, you need that support because it can be rough, especially if that's not what you want to do with your life ... We shouldn't have to put up with this bullshit but we do because we're temps. We have to make the best of it until the big break comes' (T1). As this worker suggests, connections between workers in similar situations have the potential to empower them to resist their poor working condi-tions. However, temporary help work 'occupies an institutional space that spans multiple locations' and consequently temporary help workers are not only inhibited from organizing but they rarely come in contact with one another (Gottfried, 1992: 447). Customers often mix tempo-rary and permanent workers at the same worksite and pit them against one another by paying them different wages. Even so, some workers hint at the prospect of resistance. But many others are 'profoundly disempowered' by doing temporary help work (T7). Thus, through intensifying the pace of work, fuelling the illusion that temporary help work will eventually lead to permanent work, and requiring highly skilled workers to perform monotonous tasks, the micro-level practices – those that are an essential part of the commodification process – contribute to inhibiting resistance among workers and increasing their alienation.

Justifying the Shape of the TER

Industry officials, branch managers, and customers are conscious of the conditions of work surrounding the TER, and the informal customs and conventions operating at the micro-level that heighten its precariousness. They are also aware of how these informal processes, when combined with macro-level developments such as the decline of the SER and the complex legal framework surrounding the TER, compound workers' sense of alienation and marginalization. Still, all three sets of actors have an interest in the continued spread of temporary help work. To this end, they use several justifications to demonstrate how the THI benefits workers and why the TER is a viable alternative to the SER – and is often even preferable to it. Managers and customers justify the THI's place in the labour market by citing the flexibility it provides and the opportunities it offers to recent immigrants seeking to gain experience and exposure in the Canadian labour market. These justifications perpetuate sex segregation, a racialized division of labour and income and occupational polarization within the THI given the coercive customs, policies, and practices operating at the micro-level that are associated with them.

Flexibility

Despite the clear tension between flexibility and insecurity, the promise of flexibility continues to be central to the marketing strategy that the THI directs at both workers and customers. At its inception, the THI sold temporary help work to white middle-class married women by promising them some extra money in the household budget without having to sacrifice family responsibilities. This strategy is still prominent today, especially among agencies that provide clerical workers. However, to attract a broader group of workers, the THI increasingly promotes temporary help work as an attractive item on the expanding menu of employment options, a good way to test out a job or attain a flexible work schedule. One manager suggests that it offers workers with different types of aspirations and limitations, different types of flexibility: 'Without committing yourself and getting that bad mark attached to you – that well, "this person moves around an awful lot" – you can come in here and you can go spend two months at company A to decide whether it's a type of environment you want to work in. And then you can move on to company B, and then move on to company C, or whatever it may be. A lot of people use them [agencies] for that reason. A lot of people also use them, like homemakers – that's not a good word – that have schedules that dictate they can only work certain hours' (M2). These remarks indicate that greater 'choice' in employment arrangements is a primary selling feature for the THI. On the flip side, managers simultaneously market the services of the THI to customers on the basis of providing 'flexible staffing.'

For most workers, the elusive promise of flexibility generates neither 'new' nor improved conditions of employment. Despite the emphasis on expanding the menu of employment options for workers, the internal organization of the THI remains largely unchanged. Although sex parity increasingly characterizes the THI, the prevalent means by which managers promote flexibility still enable it to maintain internal segmentation by sex. As one woman worker reported, 'Companies treat men as being more capable, especially with software programs ... The women traditionally are assigned as reception or executive assistant, secretary or other secretarial positions. If you are a young woman, you are guaranteed reception ... As women [temporary help workers] people think that you are there to serve. You are there to be a secretary. You are there to be a receptionist, a file clerk, whatever. Women get a lot of the desk jobs ... *women get locked into that*' [my emphasis] (T1).[8] Customers' demands also reflect this, but they appreciate the internal segmentation in the THI because they prefer to hire temporary help workers with characteristics similar to their permanent workforce:

> I would say that the majority of them [temporary help workers] are female. Like here, clerical is especially female-dominated ... I like that. (C2)

> [In the THI,] manufacturing tends to be more male-dominated, but packaging is unbelievably female-dominated like with us ... The agencies do a lot of manual dexterity tests ... That's one thing that I like about them. They truly choose the best candidates ... women have smaller hands. They're better at dealing with little things than men. The men get in the way. They're too clunky. They can't deal with the little things. Sometimes you'll have a tray of pills come along and there's a capsule missing and you'll have to pop a pill in. Women tend to have smaller hands and they can do that without popping all the rest of the pills out of the tray. We also have blister packs, and you have to fan them with your hands to get them flat. You can break things if you aren't gentle enough. (C4)

When asked about whether gender matters in the THI, managers emphasized that the flexibility the THI offers has historically benefitted women with family responsibilities most, but that the THI does not discriminate and agencies simply try to meet the needs of their customers (M1). Some managers candidly observed that there is always tension between upholding a policy of nondiscrimination and satisfying their customers' demands. One justified the internal segmentation characteristic of the THI as follows:

> There are times when you're forced to do so [hire a woman] because the job being done does not tolerate a man doing it. I'm going to use the example of dexterity. A man's hands are much bigger than a woman's. So, when they're in a position using tiny little parts, a woman is usually quicker. They're usually more accurate the first time, than a man trying to do the same job. So, we get into situations where a company will only put a woman in that position because a woman is more successful at the job. We also have positions where a company will require a man ... I have one client who has told me that they want a man on their line. That's because, if the equipment stops, for whatever reason, they need somebody to climb a ladder. They wouldn't want to put somebody who was pregnant on this ladder. They don't want to risk anybody's safety but they feel a man is more stable in that position ... Although we're not allowed to discriminate, if you don't service with what the needs are, you don't have the business. So, what you have to do is make a judgment call on this. You decide, is it a discrimination issue? Yes or no. No. It's not because this company will still hire women, but they get different positions in the company. So, really, they're not discriminating. (M1)

While this manager believes that choosing a man for a specific job based purely on the demands of the customer is morally wrong, and recognizes that it is illegal, she suggests that for some jobs, particularly where one sex dominates at the worksite, it is justifiable to fulfill a customer's request for a worker of a specific sex. This manager is effectively arguing that, in such cases, sex is a bona fide occupational requirement.

Most managers and industry officials do not go as far in defending their customers' requests for workers of a specific sex. However, to avoid addressing the gender issue, they emphasize that the testing done through the THI makes it one of the most nondiscriminatory industries around. As one industry official noted, 'We do not discriminate in any way. Quite frankly, we don't discriminate because we're interested in skills. We're interested in abilities, and that's what makes a temporary help company attractive to its customers. Whereas someone doing their own hiring with their own set of biases might discriminate' (I1). For this official, the process of interviewing, testing, and placement is a neutral process that guards against discrimination. However, workers' experiences of temporary help work undermine these claims.

Many discriminatory practices considered acceptable in the post-Second World War period, given the hegemony of the ideology of domesticity, have become increasingly unacceptable in the contemporary Canadian labour market, but they persist in the THI. In the 1950s and 1960s, agencies did not place women who were noticeably pregnant, normally offering them in-house work from the four-month mark until they gave birth. While discrimination against pregnant women is illegal in the 1990s, temporary help workers still report that being pregnant is a real disadvantage. For example, a long-term temporary help worker, who had been working through one agency steadily for over a year, was not only dismissed from an assignment because she was pregnant, but believed that she was no longer considered for new assignments by the agency for this reason. She described her experience as follows:

Before I was pregnant I was temping. I was probably two to three months pregnant and I was still temping, but they [the agency and the customer] didn't know ... I was actually in a job where they were looking to hire someone full time. And, I just mentioned it, well I thought that it would be fair to say, 'I'm pregnant.' I thought they should know that they'd only have me for five months and then I'd be off. Well, I guess that was a boo boo for me because when I mentioned it they just didn't want me at all, even temping. It was a Wednesday or Thursday that I mentioned it and they must have phoned the temp agency and said, 'We only want her until Friday now.' They must have decided, 'we'll let her finish the week.' They told me on the Thursday, 'Tomorrow is your last day' ... I was teed-off and I decided to go to the temp agency and tell her [the office supervisor] about what happened, and that I thought that they were discriminating. Then I ended up telling the agency that I was pregnant, and then they stopped finding me jobs because I was pregnant. I was only three months. I wasn't even showing. I mean I still had another five more months but I guess for them to send off somebody that was pregnant, they didn't want to do that. That shouldn't be the case, of course. I mean you're pregnant, you're still willing to work – but after I told her, she didn't even bother to look for a job for me doing temp work ... After about a month of phoning and calling to see what was available, and not getting anything, I just said forget it. I gave up. (T3)

Stories like these are not uncommon in the THI. Not only do they reinforce the precarious nature of the TER in practice, given that workers may be dismissed with limited notice, they add to the evidence that the promise of flexibility that the THI promotes primarily benefits its customers. Managers, industry officials, and even some customers use the language of flexibility to argue that temporary help work is contributing to an expanding menu of options for workers, offering women with family obligations the chance to have a work schedule 'that accommodates their kids getting on and off the bus,' and promoting occupational diversity in the industry. Yet informal practices such as failing to place pregnant women on assignment indicate that this is not so. Indeed, the internal gender division of labour in the Canadian THI has remained relatively static over the course of the last fifty years, and discriminatory practices are still prevalent at the micro-level.

Canadian Job Experience

Customers and managers also justify the THI's place in the labour market by claiming that it provides recent immigrants with Canadian job experience. Just as officials argued that the industry represented an ideal labour force re-entry vehicle for women absent from the labour force while raising children in the late 1960s and early 1970s, they now argue that temporary help work is a suitable means for immigrants to gain experience and exposure in the Canadian labour market. One official put it this way: 'New Canadians find that it [doing temporary help work] is a great way for them to get experience. Often they're told, "I'm sorry, you don't have any Canadian experience," when they apply for work. But in our industry, when they apply, [we look at] their skills. If they have referrals, we research them. It doesn't matter if that person has worked in India previously, we do the reference checking and make sure that they've got the skills and then they get work' (I1).

Several temporary help workers who recently immigrated to Canada also reported that when they first arrived and applied for jobs, employers told them they needed Canadian experience. This creates a vicious cycle for immigrant workers, forcing them to seek social assistance and/or assistance from Canada Employment and Immigration Centres (CEIC). The THI positions itself as providing a solution to these workers' common problem. Agencies promote their general services to social assistance and CEIC officials, and advertise in community newspapers that they place people without Canadian job experience. Consequently, workers report being directed to the THI by the social assistance department. One worker indicated that she felt lucky to obtain work through the THI only three months after her arrival in Canada. She noted, 'You hear so many things about unemployment, but you never know. When I got work, I said, "These people are liars' because they said there's no work. I got work after three months. I didn't get permanent [employment] but I did get work"' (T4). However, this worker also added that she hoped to move beyond her light industrial job and return to her profession as a science teacher, given the poor conditions of employment in the THI.

Corresponding with the THI's apparent openness to place immigrant workers, customers also commonly report preferences for immigrant workers, suggesting that they have a stronger work ethic than 'Canadians,' especially white Canadian men. A high-volume customer that placed temporary help workers in direct sales positions asserted boldly: 'White Canadian men don't cut it today. I hired a guy a couple of weeks ago ... When he walked in, as soon as I saw him come through the door, I said to [the on-site supervisor], "I want him." He came in and I hired him. When he went out, [the on-site supervisor] said, "He's not going to last" ... He never even came back after training. He never even made it to the store. He'd just graduated with a degree from some university or something. You know, these guys come out of university and they want to make $40,000 in their first year. They want to be president of the company the second year. They think they know it all' (C2). Attitudes like these, which seemingly praise immigrants' skills and work ethic, actually reinforce a racialized division of labour in the THI. They also contribute to agencies' tendency to place immigrant workers and workers of colour in jobs at the bottom of the wage and occupational hierarchy.

Managers, industry officials, and customers are surprisingly open about the racialized division of labour within the THI. They are careful to assert, however, that it has nothing to do with discrimination since the testing procedures are neutral and agencies are bound by codes of ethics that prohibit race and sex-based discrimination (M2, I1). One manager made a clear statement acknowledging the racialized division of labour common to the THI, but claimed that it occurred naturally: '[W]e have a lot of new immigrants that apply, and that unfortunately can sometimes become a segregated area. Unfortunately, you see it happen. It's uncontrollable. If we're recruiting for LID [light industrial], we have a lot of new immigrants good for that area that come in' (M2). Another manager was embarrassed when asked about the apparent racialized division of labour with the THI. He said:

There was this one particular instance of this individual and this person, I can't remember where he was from. He was from a Third World country that just slips my mind now. This guy had more degrees and doctorates than I've ever seen. This is one of the most highly educated people that I've ever seen and he was stacking shelves for us at $7 an hour. He'd been in Canada about two or three years ... I remember the client calling me. I guess they'd just had the opportunity to have a coffee one day at a break or something like that, and this person started to wheel off what his educational background was. The client was just amazed. He couldn't believe it. He actually felt bad that he had somebody of this level and this intelligence out in his warehouse stacking shelves for $7 an hour. (M2)

On the other hand, some customers indicated that it was not only justifiable to use over-qualified immigrant workers to do light industrial work, and acceptable to pay them low wages, but that the conditions of work in the THI were acceptable to the workers themselves. The same customer who dismissed young white men as lazy said: 'If you've grown up in Canada, you're spoiled rotten. You can complain and carry on all you want but we have it made here. The majority of people have never been outside of North America. They have no idea how the other half of the world lives. If somebody has come here from Africa, most of these people up and down this street have absolutely no idea whatsoever what an African goes through every day. They have no earthly idea. So you bring them [new Canadians] here and pay them $8 an hour. They think that's wonderful. Or somebody from India, they're just happy to have a job. They'll do everything they can to please you, to try and make sure that they have that job tomorrow' (C2). Customers like this one, who prefer immigrants to Canadian-born workers or who indicate a preference for workers of a particular nationality or ethnic group, are not new to the THI. Indeed, the THI and its customers have a poor, but well-documented record of human rights abuses against immigrants and visible minorities. This is especially true in Ontario, where the Canadian Civil Liberties Organization has made formal complaints to the Ontario Human Rights Commission after repeatedly finding temporary help agencies willing to accept discriminatory job orders (Canadian Civil Liberties Organization 1983, 1991, 1992, 1993).

Workers are aware of the racism endemic in the Canadian labour market and capitalized on by the THI. They speak frankly and forcefully about the poor conditions surrounding temporary help work. One worker noted: 'What does a landed immigrant mean? They take everything from you. Whatever you have over there. They say there is no bias but there is ... They should set up some standards for this particular kind of job ... At least they [the government] should help immigrants set up before they have to do this dog work ... When you land over here you bring this money over here and you don't get a job, you only get temporary work. You get dog work and sometimes you even have to pay for it. You're caught' (T3). This worker predicted that in the future temporary help agencies would charge immigrant workers fees and the government would permit it.

Like this worker, many workers report being trapped in the THI. Their experiences indicate that the racialized division of labour in the THI is a product of two overtly racist practices that reveal the ideological nature of the industry's promise of 'Canadian experience': namely, placing workers of the same background together intentionally, and thereby perpetuating segmentation, and refusing to provide references to recent immigrants.

Mirroring the racialized division of labour in the Canadian labour market as a whole, workers speak of being placed in workplaces with no prospect for permanent work where immigrant workers dominate. Managers even confirm that they consciously place workers of similar ethnic origins together: 'We look at what their culture is all about and try, to the best of our ability, to put the same type of people together ... It's easier to be successful [in this industry] if you have that right kind of mix' (M2). Although the THI does not sanction these behaviours, the practice of placing workers of similar ethnic backgrounds together and paying highly qualified workers low wages are strikingly reminiscent of the practices of private employment agents operating in the Canadian labour market at the turn of the century, when railway and steamship agents placed Chinese immigrants in railway work and Italian immigrants in construction (Avery, 1995).

Still, the practice that stands out most, and that most resembles the charge of misrepresentation common to the padrone system in the early twentieth century, is the THI's refusal to provide references to workers. This practice, described in detail above, debunks the THI's claim that temporary help work provides immigrants with the job experience they require to gain entry into the Canadian labour market. One worker reflected on the experiences of her immigrant co-workers at the call centre where she worked:

Some people think it is a viable and good option to acquire Canadian job experience. But, it's an impossible way to get it ... They will not give you references. It's a very interesting problem. One of my colleagues, for example, left [the customer] after five years there as a temp. That was her only Canadian job experience. She requested a letter of reference from her supervisor. Now, bear in mind that this is a man who's been monitoring her, at the very least monthly, for five years. He's quite able to say how good an employee she is. The most that he could do was write a letter saying that she had worked at [the customer]. He couldn't actually give her a reference. Now, what use is a letter saying that you've worked there? In fact it's probably to your disadvantage ... Still, I think that there are people probably going in there [into temporary help work] thinking that, in fact, they can get a letter of reference out of it at the end. That's not a whole lot to expect, but they can't. (T7)

Beyond the clear examples of racism revealed by the Canadian Civil Liberties Organization, the notion that the THI provides immigrant workers with so-called Canadian experience not only enables the THI to entrench a racialized division of labour but perpetuates racist practices in the industry.

Together, the promise of flexibility and the industry's claim that it plays a crucial role in providing workers' with 'Canadian' job experience contribute to the growing income and occupational polarization within the THI and intensify its gendered and racialized character. The call centre where the customer refused to provide workers with letters of reference, even after five years of steady employment, is a good example. According to one worker:

The bosses of our unit were four young men. All probably in their early thirties. Four young white able-bodied guys, and, in the entire time I was in my unit there were maybe three able-bodied white straight guys ever. I mean the place was women and immigrants and people of colour. Period. With these four white boys telling us what to do. I used to laugh at that actually. I thought it was pretty funny, and a number of the temps, when I would point this out, would see some humour in it, but what were they going to do? Their boss [the three supervisors' boss] was a white woman. So we would console ourselves with thinking that was [the customer's] attempt at equity. But it was actually kind of neat because they were very similar to one another. And, well, I think I have actually probably referred to them as 'the boys' because that's literally how we thought of them. And they all had their little cubicles along the window. But they were very nice guys. They were just like boy cheerleaders. (T7)

The occupational hierarchy in this call centre was composed of four distinct strata. The human resource manager was located at the top of the hierarchy. She was employed directly by the customer to manage the call centre. The temporary help workers' bosses, or 'the boys,' as the temporary help workers call them, occupied the second strata. These young men were on-site managers employed by temporary help agencies on contract; their jobs were to supervise the temporary help workers and relieve the customer of any employment-related responsibilities. Temporary workers of various sorts resided at the bottom two rungs of the occupational hierarchy. Those that were employed directly by the customer were multilingual. They earned more money than the temporary help workers and had a higher status in the workplace, and therefore occupied the third level. Those that were engaged by the THI resided in the bottom tier, although their wages and conditions of employment differed because they were employed by different agencies.

Given that the human resource manager was a white woman, that the on-site supervisors were young white men, and that the majority of the temporary help workers were women, immigrants, and people of colour, the call centre was characterized by a racialized and gendered division of labour. In the context of this workplace, 'the boys' had the greatest potential for mobility. Since they were on contract with the THI, rather than working as temporary help workers in the conventional sense, they were using the THI as a stepping stone in a tight labour market. Thus, they represent part of the expanding group of managerial and professional temps that are attracted to the THI because of the flexibility that it offers; they resemble high-end independent contractors much more than their counterparts engaged in light industrial or clerical temporary help work. Conversely, although many of the temporary help workers answering the phones at the call centre were educated people working in the THI to gain 'Canadian job experience,' their mobility was highly constrained both in the THI itself, due to the tendency among agency managers to place immigrants with other immigrants, and in the Canadian labour market as a whole, due to the policy of refusing to provide references. Although they both represent part of the expanding THI, these two sets of workers could not be more different. Nor could their wages and conditions of employment.[9]

The experiences of these workers and their co-existence within one workplace exhibits the increasingly polarized nature of the THI, and, if the changing shape of the THI is indicative of larger trends, the Canadian labour market more broadly.

The Feminization of Employment Norms

The micro-level practices endorsed by industry officials, branch managers, and customers illustrate that the TER differs from the SER not only in form, as Chapter 4 demonstrated, but in substance. It is a precarious model of employment. Measured against nonstandard forms of employment, such as temporary help work, the SER is a relatively solid standard. Although it was 'not the best of all worlds,' the post-Second World War labour market in which the SER functioned most effectively was also 'the best among the historically existing systems for commanding labour and distributing the means of subsistence,' particularly when compared with the contemporary labour market (Picchio 1992:6). However, the SER is eroding as a *normative* model of employment, along with the institutional bases for labour market regulation that it brought to dominance; the rise and spread of the TER is a testament to this development. Although it is premature to attempt to identify 'successors,' if the growth of temporary help work and the conditions of employment surrounding it reflect prevailing employment trends, then the erosion of the SER is changing the terms and conditions of employment for an expanding group of workers.

Recent developments in the THI reflect the feminization of employment in all its central aspects. Although women no longer represent a disproportionate percentage of the THI's workforce, partly due to their consistently high labour force participation rates, sex segregation still characterizes the industry, with women predominating in clerical and service-related occupations and men predominating in industrial, managerial, and professional occupations. Moreover, workers in segments of the industry dominated by women and immigrants generally earn lower hourly wages than their counterparts in segments of the industry dominated by (white) men. Income and occupational polarization is particularly evident in high-volume worksites, such as the call centre described in the third section of this chapter (pp. 194–5), where women, immigrants, and people of colour were largely confined to the lower tiers of the occupational hierarchy while young white men occupied the top layers. Indicative of growing casualization, the Canadian THI self-regulates to great effect for its own benefit. Consequently, temporary help workers are subject to one-way employment agreements rather than standard employment contracts: these agreements mandate that workers accept minimal levels of social protection and waive certain fundamental mobility rights accorded by law in exchange for the prospect of obtaining temporary help work. Questionable customs and conventions operating within the THI only reinforce the weak legal infrastructure surrounding the TER. These processes create considerable alienation among workers by contributing to confusion over 'who's the boss?' and prompting workers to work harder and faster at what are often monotonous tasks. Combined with the common means that industry officials, branch managers, and customers use to justify the existence of the THI and to promote the TER to workers, they also uphold a racialized gender division of labour within the industry.

The case of the THI illustrates that, contrary to the arguments of proponents of the conventional thesis, the feminization of employment means much more than women's mass entry into the labour market and even the creation of more 'women's work' in the labour market. It amounts to the rise and spread of feminized employment relationships. Even though women's shifting position in the labour market and the decline of the SER have led more men to enter the THI, and have, therefore, contributed to increased occupational diversity in the industry, the notion of feminization resonates in the context of the THI. It has salience at both a descriptive and an explanatory level because of the continuing subordination of women as well as immigrants and people of colour in the industry, and because of the continuing overriding assumption amongst industry officials and customers that many temporary help workers (particularly those in the industry's bottom tiers) are secondary breadwinners, and therefore their wages need not be sufficient to cover their full costs of subsistence. In the post-Second World War era, the THI managed to carve out a space for itself because it targeted white middle-class married women excluded from core segments of the labour force due to marriage bars as well as other marginalized groups who were devoid of certain basic labour rights. In this period, the TER was a feminized employment relationship since it contravened the male standard and was dominated by women. Yet the state, as well as various segments of organized labour (albeit implicitly), treated it as a legitimate exception to the norm because it was designed to be a supplement and because of the THI's female-dominated work force. At present, the THI is indeed composed of more men than previously, and therefore it is more stratified, but the TER remains a feminized employment relation-

ship. Moreover, despite its relatively unchanged character, industry officials, branch managers, and customers are beginning to cast the TER as
an alternative to the SER with surprisingly little negative attention from
the state and limited resistance from organized labour. In this way, the
growth of the THI and the rise and spread of the TER not only signals
the extension of 'new' feminized employment relationships but the
feminization of employment *norms*.

Conclusion

If the spread of temporary help work and the conditions of employment
surrounding the TER are indicative of 'employment change,' the significance of these twin developments (i.e., the extension of 'new' feminized
employment relationships and the feminization of employment norms
more broadly) is far-reaching.

Unlike the SER, which was a male norm, the TER reflects the experiences of women. Given that women, particularly immigrant women,
Aboriginal women, and women of colour, have historically been confined to subordinate positions in the Canadian labour market and white
middle-class married women predominated in the THI from its inception in the mid-1940s until the late 1970s, the extension of feminized
employment relationships like the TER threaten to downgrade the existing standard. Workers can no longer expect (although this expectation
has always been exaggerated) that they will engage in permanent, bilateral employment relationships and enjoy comprehensive social benefits
such as UI, sick pay, and maternity and parental leave, as well as
employer-provided extended benefits. As well, if recent developments in
the THI are indicative of what is to come in the labour market as a whole,
the feminization of employment norms will perpetuate and perhaps
even cultivate income and occupational polarization based on gender,
immigration status, and race. If the TER is a template for the future, the
extension of feminized employment relationships promises to maintain
dualism in the labour market. Regrettably, given its potentially negative
impact on many workers in Canada, the TER is one among an expanding number of possible alternatives to the SER. Chapter 1 argued that
the notion of a TER has the unique capacity to capture growing dualism
in the Canadian labour market, evidenced by the expanding diversity in
nonstandard forms of employment, but at the same time convey the
expansion of precarious employment at the bottom of the labour market. Thus, the power of the TER conceptually relates to its all-encompass-

ing character, that is, its potential to become an employment norm for a wider segment of the population. The fact that 'new' feminized employment relationships like the TER cover an increasingly broad spectrum of workers inhabiting opposite ends of the income and occupational hierarchy, ranging from full-time 'consultants' in fields such as law and computer programming to part-time or casual workers engaged in clerical work or general labour, makes it particularly critical to examine the status of current regulations surrounding the TER, and how state actors, organized labour, and employers view the status quo, in Canada and elsewhere. Chapter 6 directs itself to this task.

Chapter 6

'Flexible Workers,'
Intractable Regulatory Regime:
Regulating the Contemporary
Temporary Employment Relationship

All over the world, people who are the employees of the firm are being made redundant and then workers are supplied by private employment agencies usually at a lower wage and with no benefits. Effectively, employers are ratcheting down the conditions and pay of workers, undercutting what were once decent stable jobs for people and replacing them with precarious jobs that don't carry a lot of basic protections, protections that the trade union movement feels should go with any job.

Governments need to respond to this problem. If you are one of these workers all your life, it means that you don't accumulate any benefits. If you are sick, or when you reach retirement, you have no coverage, no security ... So, why not change the system? ... Let's 'flexiblize' all of the systems around the employment relationship so that they protect the 'flexible worker.' What we have now is a push for the 'flexible worker,' but we have static systems of protection.

– Workers' representative, Convention No. 181
International Labour Conference, 17 June 1997

Temporary help work poses a fundamental challenge to the regulatory framework that grew up around the SER in Canada and other welfare states in the post-Second World War period: the challenge to preserve protections, benefits, and security for workers engaged in employment relationships where responsibility does not rest squarely with one entity.

A central objective of the contemporary THI's marketing strategy is to displace the SER – specifically, the bilateral employment relationship that lies at its foundation – and replace it with a TER. To promote the TER as an acceptable alternative to the SER, the THI is selling the idea of 'staffing services,' a concept designed to entice customers to use temporary help workers to avoid responsibility, and to situate temporary help agencies as 'human resource' experts. This strategy, which rests on a complex legal apparatus, is not only cultivating arm's-length relationships between temporary help workers and customers, but is also minimizing the obligations of the agency itself. In the contemporary THI, contracts of employment are not contracts between workers and agencies that presume workers' economic dependence and allot protections accordingly; rather, they are employment agreements that require workers to relinquish a number of basic rights and protections in exchange for the prospect of attaining temporary help work. Similarly, contracts between agencies and their customers look like typical service contracts even though it is the provision of workers that they govern. Thus, the THI's move towards providing 'staffing services' amounts to continued precariousness for workers: combined with the qualitative dimensions of temporary help work, the conditions of employment associated with the contemporary TER make workers look and feel more and more like commodities. Although these findings are troubling, they are not surprising given that the Canadian THI has effectively been in a position to self-regulate over the last several decades due to a lack of state intervention and limited direct resistance to the TER on the part of organized labour.

There are numerous deficiencies in the weak and limited regulatory framework surrounding the TER, relating principally to the division of responsibility, security, wage levels, and levels of social protection. Many of these gaps are not new per se. Nor are the informal practices that they generate at the micro-level. However, the need for a solid regulatory framework, one that extends a comprehensive package of benefits and protections to temporary help workers, is especially pressing at present since the TER is poised, now more than ever, to become a new employment norm.

Probing recent developments at provincial, national, and supranational levels, this chapter explores the prospects for devising an effective regulatory framework surrounding the TER. To this end, it deepens micro- and macro-level explanations of why the feminization of employment is occurring with such force in Canada by describing the weak set of regulations surrounding the TER, only one among a growing number of employment relationships where responsibility does not rest squarely with one entity. The chapter also revisits several core claims advanced at the outset of the book. Most centrally, it suggests that, although some actors within the ILO are attempting to uphold the maxim 'labour is not a commodity' at a symbolic level, the sentiments behind it are breaking down at the supranational level, with private employment agencies gaining an unprecedented degree of legitimacy through a new Convention Concerning Private Employment Agencies (No. 181). Adopted in June 1997, and based on an agreement between Workers' and Employers' Groups, this convention recognizes temporary help agencies as employers and sets out a limited framework for regulating the TER, reversing the ILO's historic stance against labour market intermediaries and its skeptical view of nonstandard forms of employment. Completing a century's long sketch of the THI's history and prehistory, the chapter confirms that the high level of insecurity faced by workers engaged in TERs has persisted since the turn of the century – only the character of the THI's workforce and the social and institutional bases of labour market regulation have changed.

At the supranational level, and to some extent at the national level, organized labour is vocalizing its concerns about the precarious character of the TER and calling for regulation more than in the recent past. The emergence of national legislation (especially in Europe) aimed at regulating the TER – legislation that is generally superior to the regulatory framework set out in Convention No. 181 – is evidence of its success. However, as Chapter 8 confirms, raising the level of social protections surrounding the TER in Canada requires dramatic changes in the shape of the prevailing collective bargaining regime, as well as a shift in union strategy. Thus, the regulatory options that this chapter advances represent only one prong of a larger program of necessary reforms.

Legislation Governing Private Employment Agencies in Canada

The issue of regulating private employment agencies (including temporary help agencies) fell off the policy agenda in the late 1960s. With the THI's move towards providing 'staffing services,' and with its growing legitimacy in North America as a whole, most provinces began to abandon and/or fail to enforce regulations governing temporary help agencies. By the mid-1970s, the void created by deregulation was so great that the THI began to self-regulate, constructing a complex web of legal agreements surrounding the TER and advancing more general industry-wide codes of ethics. About a decade later, under the auspices of the Employment and Staffing Services Association of Canada (ESSAC), the industry association that formed in the early 1970s, the THI began to lobby for minimizing the provincial regulations that still existed. By the mid-1990s, it was rewarded for its efforts as some provinces, such as Ontario and Alberta, began to actively deregulate private employment agencies, and others, such as British Columbia and Manitoba, opted for passive deregulation (i.e., unchanged regulatory mechanisms). Only in Quebec, which has historically applied the strictest regulations to private employment agencies, did the government entertain the possibility of a more rigorous framework for regulating the TER.

The Status Quo: British Columbia and Manitoba

British Columbia and Manitoba are two examples of provinces where regulations governing private employment agencies remained static between the late 1960s and the mid-1990s. In the case of British Columbia, where private employment agencies have been regulated under the province's *Employment Standards Act* since 1961 (alongside agencies placing farm labourers and contract labourers), the provincial government simply consolidated existing regulations in 1981, 1984, and 1995. In 1995, in the most recent round of revisions to British Columbia's *Employment Standards Act*, the government affirmed that all private employment agencies, including temporary help agencies, must be licensed, and it continued to prohibit direct fees to workers (RSBC, Bill 29, 1995: s.12, 13). Similarly, in Manitoba, while the provincial government continued its prohibition of fees to workers and updated its regulations with respect to licensing in 1980 and 1987 respectively, regulations governing private employment agencies have remained virtually unchanged since 1954, when the provincial government ended its thirty-five year prohibition of private employment agencies (RSM, 1954; RSM, 1980; Reg. 98/87). Thus, these two provinces merely upheld pre-existing (and outmoded) frameworks for regulating private employment agencies in labour markets where new types of private employment agencies were proliferating, the TER was spreading and the shape of the THI was changing.

Deregulation: Alberta and Ontario

In other provinces, regulations governing private employment agencies changed significantly from the mid-1960s to the mid-1990s. Most notably, the province of Alberta, which prohibited fee-charging employment agencies between 1919 and 1927 and strictly regulated private employment agencies from the 1930s until the late 1980s, repealed its *Employment Agencies Act* in 1988. Its failure to replace this act with either an equivalent or updated instrument is precipitating the deregulation of the private employment industry in the province (RSA, 1919b, 1927, 1988).

Developments in Ontario, the province embracing the most regulatory changes in the last two decades, were much more complex, and even more dramatic than in Alberta. Although Ontario adopted some progressive regulatory changes in 1980 and 1990, some regressive changes have emerged since 1980. In 1980, for the first time, the province inserted formal procedures for the suspension of licenses and it made adjustments in the fee scales prescribed by the Act (RSO, 1980). In 1990 it also enacted a new *Employment Agency Act* that introduced a requirement for separate licences for different branches of the same agency – a very important change which meant that a number of franchises that formerly escaped licensing had to be licensed individually. The act also retained a prohibition against 'Class A' agencies, which may be interpreted to include temporary help agencies, from charging direct fees to workers (RRO, 1990, s.11). However, the government of Ontario is currently rethinking these regulations.

Beginning in the mid-1990s, Ontario undertook a review of the *Private Employment Agency Act* (1990), a process that is ongoing. Represented by its lobbying body, ESSAC, the THI is intimately involved in this process, and, as a consequence of the hostile climate faced by unions since the early 1990s, the voice of organized labour is visibly and regrettably absent at the table. Unlike the case of Alberta, the government of Ontario is not intent on repealing the act – nor is the THI for that matter. Instead, the THI's aim is to reshape it. If ESSAC achieves its objectives, the revision of this act could easily amount to self-regulation such that codes of conduct and other extra-state modes of self-regulation play a greater role in the supervision and monitoring of temporary help agencies. A recent submission to the Ontario government, prepared jointly by ESSAC and the Association of Professional Placement Agencies (APPA),[1] substantiates this claim (APPA and ESSAC, 1996).

In a brief to the Ontario government entitled 'An Analysis of the Employment Agencies Act' and presented to the Ministry of Labour on 9 December 1996, ESSAC and APPA analyse the role of the province's *Employment Agency Act* (1990) and propose some key amendments. The bulk of their proposed amendments centre on which bodies should retain 'administrative authority' over the act. The central argument of the brief is that together, APPA and ESSAC 'have the maturity, resources, and expertise to create an industry regulated body that would administer many provisions of the Employment Agency Act' (APPA and ESSAC, 1996: 3). It calls on the government of Ontario to create an administrative authority, to fall under the auspices of the Ministry of Consumer and Commercial Relations and the Ministry of Labour, which would 'work in partnership with government to establish a responsible self-reliant body' to administer the Act (3). Rather than recommending substantive changes to the act, APPA and ESSAC affirm its purpose and support continued licensing (and existing criteria for licensing) and retention of the government's role in setting regulations. However, they propose that the supervisor of the act be an administrative authority composed of Ministry of Labour and industry officials rather than simply the government. A space for organized labour is also absent in this proposed body. Moreover, they recommend that the administrative authority be responsible for hearing appeals to potential licensing disputes through an alternative dispute resolution mechanism rather than through the court system (7).

What is most striking about this latest intervention on the part of the private employment industry in Ontario is their wish to preserve the act but to shift the onus of administration to a body dominated by industry. The industry's desire to retain the act reveals that it is in the interest of the THI to preserve, but legitimize, the intermediary status of private employment agencies by law so that agencies can avoid assuming all the responsibilities typically accorded to employers. This intervention is especially interesting given that temporary help agencies are selling 'staffing services' (i.e., their services as employers) to their customers; it also speaks to the weakness of the act.[2] However, the proposal for creating an administrative authority suggests that the THI wants to have greater control over the act. While APPA and ESSAC are currently seeking only a monitoring and supervisory role, there is nothing preventing them from calling for (and administering) further deregulation in the act if they assume this role. Indeed, at the outset of their submission, they argue that the private employment agency industry is quite capable of self-regulation, that it already has in place an extensive code of conduct which all private employment agencies belonging to APPA and ESSAC must follow (3).[3]

If the government of Ontario accepts the proposals of APPA and ESSAC, or devises regulations based on their recommendations, the THI will increase its credibility while assuming greater control over the regulations that exist. Even more importantly, a model of the sort that APPA and ESSAC are proposing would allow the THI to maintain the focus of regulation on private employment agencies (including temporary agencies) and prevent the emergence of strong regulations governing the employment relationships that they generate, protective legislation that could place the conditions of employment surrounding the TER at the centre of regulation. To recall, provincial employment agency acts, like the one in the province of Ontario, only address placement and recruitment. They do not regulate the employment relationship (i.e., the TER) that the THI generates, and therefore do not address levels of social protection and the division of responsibility between agency and customer. Ultimately, this is the type of regulation that the THI wants to avoid, but is one that labour standards should be vigorously promoting for the welfare of workers. Thus, in Ontario, APPA's and ESSAC's coordinated strategy for shifting the onus of the administration of the *Employment Agency Act* to industry (i.e., self-regulation), while still maintaining the substance of the act for the sake of legitimacy, is the ideal solution from the vantage point of the THI but very troubling from the perspective of workers.

Prospects for Strengthening Regulation: Quebec

Like Ontario, the Province of Quebec is revisiting the question of how to regulate private employment agencies. However, unlike Ontario, it abandoned efforts to modify existing legislation designed to regulate private employment agencies in 1982, turning its attention instead to the growing role of temporary help agencies in the labour market and its impact on workers (Laflamme and Carrier, 1997; Trudeau, 1998). Spurred by a decision first issued by the Quebec Court of Appeal and subsequently upheld by the Supreme Court of Canada in *Pointe-Claire (ville) and S.E.P.B., Local 57*, which highlights the discrepancy between current labour law and 'new' types of employment relationships, Quebec is considering new regulations that focus explicitly on protecting workers engaged in TERs (personal communication, Luc Desmarais, Conseiller en development de politiques, 22 May 1997; Trudeau, 1998: 373). Although the Quebec Ministry of Labour has not yet proposed new legislation, it recently released a discussion paper entitled 'Agences De Placement Temporaire' (1993) prepared by R.J. Tapin, which argues that temporary help work is frequently precarious in nature, and therefore its spread mandates new legislation aimed at protecting temporary help workers.

Quebec is unique among the provinces in that its *Labour Code* contains a clause similar to the *Canada Labour Code*, which states that 'an employer who enters into a contract with a subcontractor, directly or indirectly through an intermediary, is responsible jointly and severally with that subcontractor and that intermediary for the pecuniary obligations fixed by this Act' (s. 95). As an official with the Ministry of Labour indicates, this clause makes it possible for an employee to have more than one employer; therefore, it opens the door for creating specific protections for workers engaged in TERs and establishing a clearer division of responsibility between temporary help agencies and their customers (personal communication, Luc Desmarais, Conseiller en development de politiques, 22 May 1997). Building on this clause, and responding to pressure from organized labour and the recent Supreme Court decision, the government of Quebec is considering three sets of options for devising a framework of social protection surrounding the TER.

First, it is entertaining the option of extending the same set of protections guaranteed to part-time workers under the *Labour Code* to temporary help workers (personal communication, Luc Desmarais, Conseiller en development de politiques 22 May 1997). Unlike most provinces, the Quebec *Labour Code* makes it illegal for an employer to discriminate against part-time workers with respect to remuneration or annual leave (i.e., vacation, etc.). For example, it is illegal for an employer to pay an employee at a lower wage rate than that granted to other employees performing the same tasks in the same establishment for 'the sole reason that the employee usually works less hours each week' (s.41.1). The intended effect of these clauses is twofold: on a practical level, they are designed to ensure that part-time and full-time workers are treated equally with respect to vacation and leaves, and, more generally, they are designed to discourage employers from resorting to part-time workers with the exclusive aim of lowering labour costs. If Quebec were to adopt identical provisions for temporary help workers, the effect would be quite similar.

A second mode of legislative intervention that the province is considering involves facilitating sectoral negotiations for the employees of temporary help agencies through the *Collective Agreement Decrees Act* (1934), a highly unique piece of legislation that allows for industry- and/or sector-wide collective bargaining under certain circumstances. This type of measure could provide a means for employees in the same sector to attain the same levels of protection, wages, and union representation regardless of whether they are engaged in a bilateral or a triangular employment relationship. As Trudeau (1998: 375) has noted, sectoral agreements could also 'provide an interesting way of protecting employees in fragmented and competitive sectors with low union density,' sectors that are prone to the encroachment of the THI. Facilitating sectoral negotiations could complement the recent addition of equal treatment provisions in the *Quebec Labour Code*. Thus, the first two options are by no means mutually exclusive.

The third, and most radical, option that the Province of Quebec is considering involves crafting a range of legislative measures to be incorporated in the *Labour Code* that aim to regulate the hiring of temporary personnel through an agency. This is a highly controversial option, even among proponents of stricter regulations surrounding the TER, since it would certainly have the effect of further legitimizing temporary help agencies in the act. Although the Ministry of Labour is recommending a number of new measures for potential inclusion in the *Labour Code* (or elsewhere), five are particularly noteworthy. First, it is recommending mandating an equal level of social protections for workers engaged in TERs and SERs (Tapin, 1993: 71). Second, it is proposing to allow temporary help workers who have experienced short interruptions in assignments but have effectively worked continually through the THI access to benefits beyond job tenure, such as severance pay, which normally require continuous employment on the part of the worker (71). A third proposal involves establishing a minimum daily payment for workers placed on assignment even if they do not work a full day (72). Fourth, the discussion paper proposes devising a provision that would create a *prime de precarite*, a tax that the agency would pay the worker that would amount to 10 per cent of the earnings from a given assignment (72). This proposal is similar to measures existing in countries such as France, to be discussed in the third section of this chapter (p. 226). Fifth, and finally, to prevent workers from being trapped for long periods in temporary help work, the government is recommending that buy-outs, which require the customer to pay a fee to take the worker on as a permanent employee (thereby discouraging the customer to hire the worker) be made illegal (73).

Together, the three sets of legislative options under consideration in Quebec make it the only provincial or territorial jurisdiction in Canada where there is currently any prospect for strengthening regulations surrounding the TER, and the only jurisdiction where unions have taken the issue of regulating the TER to the highest provincial court for greater clarification. Quebec stands out as an anomaly in the contemporary Canadian context, although it may be following trends in continental Europe. However, even though discussions are underway in the province, the degree of deregulation that is occurring in other provinces, such as Alberta and Ontario, and pressures from the THI to allow it to self-regulate, have the potential to contribute to stalling present deliberations in Quebec (personal communication, Luc Desmarais, 22 May 1997). It is thus an open question as to whether the province will embrace further measures designed to regulate the TER or be forced to follow developments at the supranational level, where greater legitimacy is on the horizon for the THI and the framework for regulating the TER is relatively weak.

Supranational Developments

Just as Canada, with the notable exception of Quebec, embarked on a path of deregulation, a dramatic turn of events occurred at the supranational level. After three decades, the stalemate over the interpretation of the Convention Concerning Private Employment Agencies, 1949 (No. 96, Revised) – a convention that offered governments the option of either progressive abolition or regulation – ended as a result of a bargain between Workers' and Employers' Groups in 1994. At this time, Workers' Groups reluctantly agreed to construct a new convention on private employment agencies (i.e., with an acute awareness of the risk of deregulation) on the condition that Employers' Groups commit themselves to negotiating a new instrument on contract labour to address the growing insecurity experienced by workers involved in triangular employment relationships and other contracting and subcontracting arrangements (IL1, IL2). As a result, Workers' and Employers' Groups, along with member states, entered into talks in 1995 and 1996, setting the parameters for the creation and adoption of the new Convention on Private Employment Agencies (No. 181), which took place in June of 1997.[4] Simultaneously, the three groups agreed to hold a general discussion on contract labour in June 1997, with a view to creating an international labour convention on this issue. Although this general discussion continued in the ensuing year, it failed dismally. Not only did Workers' and Employers' Groups and member states fail in their objective to create a new international labour standard on contract labour, they failed to come to a mutually acceptable definition of contract labour. In the end, therefore, Workers' Groups were forced to concede too much. Along with Employers' Groups and member states, they adopted a convention on private employment agencies that now recognizes temporary help agencies as employers, providing even further validation for their activities and greater coordination between public employment services and the private employment agency industry. Even though it continues the prohibition on fee-charging, Convention No. 181 gives powerful legitimacy to a triangular employment relationship, and, all the more surprising considering the ILO's long prohibition of private employment agencies and its skeptical view of nonstandard employment relationships, fails to provide a comprehensive framework of social protections for temporary help workers.

At the outset of deliberations over revising Convention No. 96 (Revised), Workers' Groups and several member states had hoped that a far superior convention would replace Convention No. 96, which had cast private employment agencies (including temporary help agencies) as labour market intermediaries, but failed to deal with the TER altogether. After the ILO Director General's controversial pronouncement in 1966, numerous countries had renounced Convention No. 96 (Revised), while some countries had backed Workers' Groups' calls for a new instrument aimed at regulating temporary help agencies explicitly and only a few, such as Sweden, Cyprus, Spain, and Portugal, took direction from the pronouncement and prohibited temporary help agencies alongside other private employment agencies.[5] According to the ILO (1994a), during the stalemate between 1966 and 1994, eighteen different types of private employment came to operate in the labour market, and most of these agencies took on de facto employer status. Still, in the 1980s and 1990s, Workers' Groups continued to charge private employment agencies with significant abuses, particularly those acting abroad or placing immigrants (fieldnotes, 6 June 1997; ILO, 1994a; personal communication, Helen Moussa, World Council of Churches, 7 July 1997). Moreover, with the rise of nonstandard forms of employment, governments expressed growing interest in placing checks against 'new' forms of employment, such as temporary help work and contract labour (ILO, 1997; OECD, 1993). Thus, a new convention, ideally supplemented by a strong recommendation, was necessary.[6]

Unfortunately, however, the new convention, Convention No. 181, closes the important chapter of ILO history that began with the maxim 'labour is not a commodity,' and supranational measures designed to advance the important sentiments behind it. For the first time, it formally extends coverage to 'service providers,' such as temporary work agencies, staff-leasing firms, and job shops, and it addresses an expanded range of activities related to recruitment, placement, and employment. The four central dimensions of the convention include the end of the

ILO's support for a public monopoly on placement in employment, the extension of coverage to 'service providers,' the inclusion of a clause prohibiting direct fees to workers, and measures aimed at establishing a framework for regulating the TER. Although these features preserve several crucial aspects of Convention No. 96 (Revised), they shift the balance in favour of the THI without the necessary protections for workers.

Ending Public Control over Placement

In sharp contrast to Convention No. 96 (Revised), Convention No. 181 legitimizes private employment agencies. Indeed, the preamble of the convention acknowledges 'the role which private employment agencies play in a well-functioning labour market' and juxtaposes this recognition with the growing need for 'flexibility' in the labour market (ILO, 1997c). This affirmation represents the end of the ILO's support for a public monopoly on employment placement, a policy that lasted nearly fifty years, and certainly one of the organization's most significant achievements.[7] In a report that it prepared after the general discussion in 1994, the International Labour Office announced that 'a monopoly of placement and even the spirit of Convention No. 96 (Revised), seem to be a remnant of the past ... The monopoly ended, in fact, a long time ago' (ILO, 1994a: 60–61). It then noted that the public employment service fills no more than 25 per cent of vacancies in most countries, concluding that private employment agencies are often in a stronger position, especially in areas such as temporary help work, to fill the remaining vacancies (60). The report also examined the utility of the three prevailing means for continuing the ban on private employment agencies: a limited ban on private enterprises engaged in placement; a total ban on all private employment agencies regardless of their activities; and a partial ban on private employment agencies. In its report, the ILO demonstrated that the first option was easy to circumvent because of its narrow mandate, the second option created a tremendous obligation on an already overstretched public employment service, and the third option had the potential to create endless lawsuits for the public authorities (61). Consequently, it endorsed a 'shared management model' based on a framework for cooperation between public employment services and the private employment agencies (61–2). Thus, instead of endeavouring to strengthen public services, Convention No. 181 extends legitimacy to a variety of enterprises and allows private employment agencies to operate in the labour market, with few regulations governing their conduct.

The convention still allows member states to prohibit private employment agencies 'from operating in respect of certain categories of workers or branches of economic activity,' making specific references to abuses against migrant workers. However, it gives legitimacy to three types of private employment agencies (ILO, 1997c): placement services, service providers, and other services related to job-seeking. Therefore, countries insistent on retaining a complete ban on any of these types of agencies are ironically not in a position to ratify Convention No. 181 because it gives legal recognition to private employment agencies (ILO, 1997c: art. 8).[8]

Extending Coverage to 'Service Providers'

Another significant change in Convention No. 181 is the formal inclusion of 'services consisting of employing workers with a view to making them available to a third party' (i.e., service providers), a clause that elicited surprisingly little debate at the International Labour Conference in 1997, especially given the lengthy stalemate over the status of temporary help agencies (ILO, 1997c: art. 1.1(b)). As part of the bargain struck in 1994, a backroom consensus on including temporary help agencies was reached prior to reopening the discussion. Consequently, at the outset of the 1997 talks, both the spokesperson for the Employers' Group and the spokesperson for the Workers' Group remarked favourably on the rapid growth of new forms of private employment agencies, naming temporary help agencies specifically, and then proceeded to support the inclusion of service providers in the new instrument. The Employers' Group representative supported their inclusion for the sake of legitimacy: his remarks indicated that including service providers, such as temporary help agencies, under Convention No. 181 would bring the issue of coverage to a close and eliminate the possibility of prohibition. In contrast, the Workers' Group representative supported including service providers for the sake of establishing a comprehensive set of protections for workers *employed* by private employment agencies (fieldnotes, 4 June 1997). Thus, Convention No. 181 ignores the 'noncommodity' thrust of Convention No. 96 (Revised), although it does seek to extend crucial protections to workers by adding several important new clauses specifically related to 'service providers.' Articles addressing nondiscrimination,[9] appropriate treatment for migrant workers,[10] and fee-charging represent the clearest attempts to update the fundamental principles contained in Convention No. 96 (Revised), while those detailing the duties and responsibilities of service providers further define the terms of the new standard.

Fee-Charging

Perhaps the most important provision of Convention No. 181 concerns fees. Article 7 reads: 'private employment agencies shall not charge directly or indirectly, in whole or in part, any fees or costs to workers' (ILO, 1997c: 6). However, it allows states to make exceptions to this rule. In a dramatic speech at the opening of the International Labour Conference, the Workers' Group representative stressed the importance of 'abiding by the fundamental principle, which guided the first instruments specifically concerning the operations of private agencies adopted in 1933, that "labour is not a commodity"' (ILO, 1997b: 4). She then asserted forcefully: 'Workers should not have to pay to work. Labour standards should be governed by standards different from those that govern commodity markets' (4). Neither governments nor the Employers' Group representative took exception to these remarks because they had already achieved their chief objectives. The Employers' Group was satisfied with the substance of Article 7, particularly its provision for granting exclusions, and member states approved that exclusions could apply to 'specified types of services' and categories of workers such as musicians and artists.

Ensuring Adequate Protection and Allocating Responsibility

The fourth dimension of Convention No. 181 is its movement towards regulating the triangular employment relationship between the 'service provider,' the customer, and the worker. While Convention No.181 looks promising on this front, it is less impressive upon close scrutiny. The critical tone of the provisions directing governments to ensure adequate protections for workers engaged in triangular employment relationships is appropriate, given the precarious nature of 'new' forms of employment such as temporary help work. Still, the convention does not establish how responsibility should be allocated or provide binding guidelines for the division of responsibility. Rather, it leaves it up to national law and practice; in essence, this means that countries that ratify Convention 181 may do as they please. As well, the most extensive provisions on the allocation of responsibility, which name areas where protections are necessary, are contained in the body of the Recommendation, and therefore are nonbinding. Convention No. 181 is thus useful primarily as a framework for regulating the TER.

Convention No. 181 directs member states to ensure adequate protection for workers employed by private employment agencies (i.e., service providers),[11] allocate responsibilities to both user enterprises and service providers, and extend collective bargaining rights to workers employed by private employment agencies (ILO, 1997c: arts. 4, 11, 12). The associated Recommendation also encourages member states to ensure that workers employed by private employment agencies are informed of the conditions of employment (preferably through a written contract), to prevent the use of workers engaged by private employment agencies as replacement workers, and to limit restrictions on the mobility of these workers (ILO, 1997d: Paras. 5, 6, 8(a), 15).

Each of the preceding provisions was subject to debate during the course of the 1997 discussion because of the controversial nature of the triangular employment relationship as a new area of intervention for the ILO. The Workers' Group wanted a well-defined set of protections for workers employed by private employment agencies, specifically temporary help agencies, and highlighted other important conceptual issues regarding the nature of the relationship between these 'service providers' and workers. The Workers' Group indicated that it was only concerned with clarifying the roles and responsibilities of one category of private employment agencies (i.e., service providers) and customers. Nevertheless, the parties differed over these amendments, knowing that they would expand the mandate of the instrument into uncharted areas. Article 11, which lays out criteria where adequate protections are necessary, was adopted after a limited debate over the areas of protection that it was to govern, and, most importantly, after the Workers' Group representative conceded that the article 'would indicate that the workers covered under this provision were "employed by" the service provider' (ILO, 1997b: 39–41). In making this demand, the Employers' Group was attempting to establish 'service providers,' specifically temporary help agencies, as genuine employers, and in this way it was expressing its discomfort with the possibility of a divided or co-employment relationship. Thus, the addition of Article 12, which dictates that governments shall allocate responsibilities to service providers and customers, was even more contentious for the Employers' Group, and represented a mild victory for the Workers' Group.[12]

While the parties reached a consensus in the end, the deliberations over both Articles 11 and 12 are extremely significant since they reveal tensions surrounding shifts in the *normative* model of employment and provide insight into the direction of employment change. In particular, they confirm the ILO's intention to acknowledge the existence not only of a triangular contractual relationship, but also of a triangular employment relationship. In its preparatory report of 1994, the International Labour Office characterized certain private employment agencies (i.e., temporary work agencies, contract labour agencies, and staff leasing firms) as engaged in a triangular contractual relationship: 'with workers in the form of a standard employment contract and with client enterprises in the form of an enterprise contract or a contract for services' (ILO, 1994b: 41). However, it did not discuss the potential employment-related responsibilities of the user enterprise. Thus, supplemented by guidelines contained in the Recommendation (which are obviously non-binding), the inclusion of Articles 11 and 12 represent a notable and desirable, but still symbolic, change for workers in the substance of the new instrument.

Protections for workers employed by private employment agencies outlined in the Recommendation further define the appropriate terms of the triangular employment relationship. For example, the Recommendation suggests that workers employed by private employment agencies (i.e., temporary help workers) should, ideally, be informed of their conditions of employment through a written contract (ILO, 1997d: 4). This clause was only accepted after a lengthy discussion about the potential relationship between the use of temporary workers and the desire to undermine the SER. The Workers' Group and several governments supported this provision because they wanted to 'avoid the development of a second-class workforce which had second-class wages and benefits and might be used to undermine the terms and conditions provided for under collective agreement. More and more workers found themselves under triangular work arrangements and there was no rationale for excluding them from normal wages and benefits' (ILO, 1997b: 53).[13]

Additionally, with respect to paragraph 15, the Recommendation dictates that 'service providers' should not: '(a) prevent the user enterprise from hiring an employee of the agency assigned to it; (b) restrict the occupational mobility of an employee; (c) impose penalties on an employee accepting employment in another enterprise' (ILO, 1997d: 4). The Employers' Group was willing to accept these paragraphs so long as their employees could be prevented from accepting employment contracts until the end of an assignment. However, the Workers' Group disagreed with this proviso, because in many instances there is no written contract between the service provider and the worker, and therefore no definitive end to a given assignment. In the end, the parties agreed to make this provision subject to national law covering the termination of contracts of employment. Another potential stalemate was averted, but the force of the provision was considerably reduced (ILO, 1997b: 60–62).

In the end, therefore, Convention No. 181 embraces a new *normative* model of employment, and it does so without advancing a comprehensive framework of protections for workers engaged in triangular employment relationships. The convention does not establish how responsibility should be allocated between 'service providers' such as temporary help agencies, and their customers. Nor does it provide guidelines for the division of responsibility or a means (i.e., a test) for determining responsibility. Furthermore, by calling for an end to the public monopoly on placement, and extending coverage to 'service providers,' Convention No. 181 grants private employment agencies legitimacy, yet it does not establish strong guidelines for regulating the TER. Thus, it facilitates a shift away from the package of benefits and protections associated with the SER, which will almost certainly mean lower levels of social protection for workers engaged in TERs than those associated with the SER.

National Laws Governing the TER

Recent developments at the provincial level in Canada, and even at the supranational level to a large extent, convey the unfortunate message that countries have few alternatives where the regulation of the TER is concerned. There is a common perception that temporary help workers cannot enjoy an equivalent level of social protection to standard workers since the TER contravenes the regulatory regime brought to dominance alongside the SER. However, a survey of national laws designed to regulate the TER (and other triangular employment relationships) in eleven jurisdictions disproves this presumption.[14] Indeed, most countries that are legitimizing triangular employment relationships establish special protections for temporary workers and allocate responsibility between temporary help agencies and their customers such that workers employed by temporary help agencies enjoy levels of social protection mirroring those accompanying the SER. Despite the tenor of Convention No. 181 and the direction of regulatory change at the provincial level in Canada, there is no necessary correlation between legitimizing the triangular employment relationship and promulgating lower levels of formal social protection for workers. Where regulating the TER is concerned, there are solid models (i.e., models that are both more developed and more comprehensive than Convention No. 181) for Canada and the provinces to follow.

Legitimization

At the national level, there is a growing trend to recognize triangular employment relationships within legislation specifically designed to regulate temporary help work. Most national legislation governing the TER begins with a clear articulation of the legal status of the temporary employee and the type of business enterprises involved in the employment relationship. For example, the Belgian *Temporary Employment Act* (Belgium, 1987: art. 7.3) sets out the following definition: 'The temporary employee is an employee who enters into a contract of employment with a temporary work firm to perform, for remuneration, work as permitted by the Act to the benefit of one or more users.' This relatively standard conception clearly defines the temporary help worker as an employee of the temporary help agency.[15] However, it does not specify the nature of the employment contract (i.e., contract of indefinite duration or fixed-term contract), a specification that differs from country to country. Still, the conception indicates that temporary help workers may perform work for a range of customers. Thus, the temporary help agency[16] comes to be defined as an enterprise whose primary activity consists of hiring out[17] its workers to customers on a temporary basis.[18]

National legislation normally requires two formal contracts: (1) a commercial contract between the temporary help agency and the customer; and (2) a contract of employment between the worker and the agency. Labeled as a hiring-out contract in many jurisdictions, the commercial contract is the legal vehicle through which the customer obtains the right to direct and supervise the 'borrowed worker.' The fee associated with this contract reflects the recruitment, placement, and administration costs that the temporary help agency incurs in maintaining the employee. Despite its status as a service contract, in most of the jurisdictions under study the commercial contract has the effect of conferring employment-related responsibilities on the customer rather than cultivating an arm's-length relationship between the worker and the customer. For example, Spanish law dictates that labour legislation and social legislation applies to the relationship between the agency and the worker, and the relationship between the customer and the worker (Spain, 1994: 77). By entering into a contract for service, it dictates that the customer take on some employment-related responsibilities. In the cases of Sweden and Norway, where legislation on the roles and responsibilities of the customer is not as highly developed, the responsibilities that the contract for service confers upon the customer are highly contested (Eklund, 1997: 242–4). By convention, the Nordic countries generally view the contract for service as the means by which the temporary help agency delegates its authority to direct and allot work to the customer. At the other extreme, in the case of Japan, the contract for service acts as protection against employer-related responsibilities for the customer: Japanese legislation is distinguished by its narrow focus on the commercial side of the contract.

In contrast to the contract for service, the contract of employment is the legal vehicle dictating the terms and conditions of work for the temporary worker; normal conditions, such as wages, benefits, and vacation pay; and special conditions, such as the clause whereby the worker is informed that s/he may be sent to a range of workplaces. With the exception of the EC, every jurisdiction that has legislation governing the TER requires a written contract of employment dictating such terms, with the form differing from country to country. For example, in Belgium workers must enter into a general contract at the commencement of employment. This contract mirrors the employment agreement common in Canada but is much more reciprocal. Belgium additionally requires contracts pertaining to specific assignments two weeks before each new assignment begins (Belgium, 1987: art. 8). Many countries also place restrictions on the duration of fixed-term contracts in the area of temporary help work; for example, Japanese legislation officially sets a one-year maximum for each contract, renewable for up to three years, and German legislation sets a nine-month maximum for each contract, which may be extended for persons considered 'difficult to place' (Goka, 1997: 15; Halbach, et al. 1994: 212).

In mandating two types of contracts, national legislation governing the TER legitimizes a triangular employment relationship operating between the agency, the worker, and the customer, mirroring Convention No. 181. This recognition is made explicit in the legal definition of the TER normally presented in the preambles of national legislation. However, unlike national legislation, ILO Convention No. 181 neither mandates the two types of contracts normally involved in this triangular employment relationship nor does it acknowledge their potential utility in determining and establishing employment-related responsibilities: this represents a serious defect in Convention No. 181. Canadian legislation is similarly defective, because, while the legal apparatus surrounding the TER in Canada includes a service contract and an employment agreement, the very role of these legal instruments is to distance workers from both the customer and the agency and thereby lower levels of social protections for workers.

Worker Protection

Where national legislation exists, governments attempt to ensure adequate protections for workers in three common areas: occupational health and safety; social security; and salaries and benefits. In all of the countries surveyed, the customer is responsible for the health and safety of the worker while s/he is at the worksite, as well as for adhering to normal labour standards such as those pertaining to night work, child labour, maximum hours of work, and days of rest. However, in several countries, such as Japan, Norway, and Sweden, as well as the EC, the temporary help agency has the duty to inform its workers of the normal conditions of work and conditions pertaining to occupational health and safety on-site. Additionally, in France, the user enterprise must provide special medical supervision for temporary workers, and in Spain, the user enterprise is responsible for covering increases in social security contributions 'in the event of an accident at work or an occupational illness occurring in its workplace during the validity of the hiring-out contract and attributable to a lack of safety measures' (France, 1996: art. 124–4–6; Spain 1994: 3, art. 16.3). As the principal employer of workers, the agency is responsible for the payment of wages and social security contributions in all jurisdictions where legislation exists. However, there are significant national variations regarding the role of the customer if a temporary work agency defaults on the payment of wages. For example, in Spain and France, the customer is responsible for contractual obligations, pertaining to wages and social security, in a secondary capacity (France, 1996: art. 124–4–6; Spain 1994, 3: art. 15.3). More general clauses also exist in other national legislation that refer to the joint obligations of both the temporary help agency and the customer to the worker. For example, Belgian legislation suggests that the temporary help agency is responsible '*together with the user* [my emphasis], for the payment of wages, and indemnifications to which the temporary employee is entitled, as well as the payment for social security contributions' (Blanpain, 1993: 61). And, in an attempt to set a minimum level of protection for temporary help workers, the European Parliament also recently drafted a directive that, when it is finally formally adopted, will effectively make the temporary help agency primarily responsible for social security (European Community Commission, 1990b).

Most of the countries under study not only consistently view setting criteria for occupational health and safety, social security, and the payment of wages as essential aspects of national legislation, they also allocate responsibility in a range of other areas. In France, which has the most comprehensive legislation on the TER, employees are entitled to precarity pay of the sort under consideration in Quebec, whereby they receive a lump sum of money from the temporary help agency at the end of an assignment,[19] equal treatment with respect to wages and conditions of work, the provision of safety equipment, and collective bargaining rights; many of these entitlements are the joint responsibility of the temporary help agency and the customer (France, 1996: art. 124–4–6; France, 1972). As well, Japanese and German legislation also deem that the agency is responsible for providing access to training for workers (Halbach et al. 1994: 213; Japan, 1987: art. 30). Additional areas where countries allocate responsibility include complaints, disciplinary and dismissal procedures, and special medical supervision. There is also a growing recognition of the importance of secondary responsibility and issues surrounding the conversion of temporary help contracts into employment contracts of indefinite duration. Although the allocation of responsibility is not identical across these areas, national legislation provides a range of examples that delineate where it is necessary and/or feasible.

In its enumeration of areas where states must ensure that workers have adequate protection, Convention No. 181 and its associated Recommendation excludes several criteria frequently named within national legislation on TERs. These criteria include the provision of protective equipment, special medical supervision for temporary help workers engaged in dangerous work, and precarity pay in recognition of the insecure nature of the triangular employment relationship and its frequently short duration.[20] Thus, where there is an absence of national legislation, countries require a more concrete set of guidelines as to where social protections are necessary than Convention No. 181 is providing.

Allocation of Responsibility

Where national regulations governing the TER exist, countries normally assign employment-related responsibilities on the basis of legal criteria such as control, direct supervision, and the payment of wages. They also tend to use equivalent criteria in determining secondary responsibility. Along with defining common areas where adequate protection is necessary, they adopt similar approaches in allocating employment-related responsibilities. Convention No. 181, on the other hand, includes occupational health and safety, social security, and the payment of wages within its list of criteria for adequate worker protections, but does not provide guidelines for determining how to allocate responsibilities related to ensuring adequate worker protections.[21] Nor does the convention acknowledge the importance of secondary responsibility, where either party fails to fulfill its employment-related obligations. Undeniably, national laws prioritize and allocate employer-related obligations differently, but that factor should make more imperative a common approach to allocating responsibility, one that complements existing laws and assists countries in devising new legislation, without prescribing rigid rules. Countries with legislation governing the TER currently allocate responsibility on the basis of objective criteria related to control, direct supervision, and payment, criteria derived using the SER as a model. For this reason, for example, existing national laws assign the primary responsibility for occupational health and safety to the user enterprise. Hence, given the standard-setting role of international labour conventions, a core function of Convention No. 181 should have been to devise guidelines for approaching the allocation of responsibility. This serious defect means that Convention No.181 cannot fulfill a central component of its expanded mandate, that is, to assist states (like Canada) opting to legitimize the TER in devising appropriate measures for regulating it. By not doing so, Convention No. 181 effectively condones the behaviour of countries that provide lower levels of social protection for workers employed by private employment agencies than those tied to the SER.

The adoption of Convention No. 181 in June 1997 was quite timely since it followed growing acceptance of the TER in many national jurisdictions. But in legitimizing the TER, establishing criteria for worker protection and allocating responsibility, this instrument does not meet its full potential. Where it exists, national legislation regulating the TER tends to be both more comprehensive and more innovative. Indeed, the substance of national laws in this area demonstrates that there is no inherent correlation between legitimizing the TER and adopting a new *normative* model of employment that embodies lower levels of social protection for workers than the SER. It indicates that triangular employment relationships, specifically the TER, may require regulatory measures, such as those devoted to the allocation of responsibility in divided employment relationships, that substantially deviate from those associated with the SER. However, different forms of regulation need not amount to inferior standards of protection.

Towards a Framework for Regulating the TER in Canada

Regulatory developments at the provincial level in Canada and at the supranational level within the ILO indicate that temporary help agencies are attaining unprecedented legitimacy in the late 1990s. In the case of the ILO, which historically viewed all types of private employment agencies with skepticism, flowing from its foundational principle 'labour is not a commodity,' and which played a central role in establishing the SER as a *normative* model of employment in the post-Second World War period, events that took place at the International Labour Conference in June 1997 signaled a dramatic and unfortunate shift in course. In its newest Convention on Private Employment Agencies (No. 181), the ILO not only sanctions the activities of private employment agencies engaging in recruitment and placement, but by extending coverage to so-called service providers (i.e., temporary help agencies, staff leasing firms, and job shops), it also legitimizes triangular employment relationships that contravene the SER without crafting an adequate framework of social protections for the growing number of workers engaged in TERs. To compound matters, the ILO's decision to abandon its long-standing mandate instead of strengthening it, is occurring at a time when the SER is declining, nonstandard forms of employment are proliferating, and the feminization of employment is taking place on a global scale. Even more striking, there is every indication that the direction of change in Canada from the 1970s to the 1990s mirrored, and perhaps even prefigured, developments at the supranational level.

In the Canadian context, most provinces have not acknowledged that there is a need for extending critical social protections for workers engaged in TERs, and for devising a framework for allocating responsibility between temporary help agencies and their customers. This is not surprising given that the THI intensified lobbying efforts from the early 1970s onwards. Nor is it surprising given that organized labour has been virtually silent on the question of private employment agencies since the post-Second World War era, due largely to both the difficulties associated with organizing temporary help workers collectively and the relative stability of the SER until rather recently. Where it still exists, legislation only deals with private employment agencies as labour market entities and fails to address the TER in any measure. Thus, as a whole Canadian regulations are even less forceful than measures recently adopted at the ILO. In this way, recent developments in Canada and at the supranational level highlight the real and troubling prospect of establishing the TER as a viable alternative to the SER without creating a floor of social protections for workers.

Alternative Models

As the TER gradually becomes a new employment norm, the need for a sound regulatory framework surrounding it becomes particularly pressing. Convention No. 181 represents only one among several competing regulatory models for states to follow. This chapter has shown that there are other more extensive models that countries moving towards regulating the TER could opt to follow. These models offer more promise in reducing the precariousness inherent in the TER than does Convention No. 181 and its associated Recommendation.

Countries with legislation on the TER have obviously opted to legitimize the THI. However, whether countries should make this move is still open to debate; indeed, the debate between prohibition and regulation has permeated discussions at the international level since the inception of the ILO. In the post-Second World War period, this debate led to the emergence of three areas of regulation internationally: prohibition, regulation, and nonregulation. However, prohibition is no longer considered a viable option in most countries. Indeed, the vast majority of countries continuing to ban private employment agencies either fail to enforce regulations or have simply forced the private employment agency industry underground. Still, it is important to recognize several potential dangers posed by legitimizing the THI and the TER. Countries such as Sweden, which prohibited temporary help agencies for over three decades following the ILO director general's 1966 ruling on 'ambulatory typewriting agencies' but legitimized them in the 1990s, repeatedly stressed this at the International Labour Conference in 1997. Most importantly, extending legitimacy to these labour market actors would contribute to deteriorating conditions of employment for workers, especially if states take primarily defensive measures in regulating the TER (fieldnotes, 9 June 1997). In other words, without implementing sound safeguards, regulating the TER could potentially amount to 'regulating precariousness' (Vosko, 1998a), that is, preventing the hypercommodification of labour power but still settling for establishing a lower level of social protection for workers engaged in TERs than the package of benefits and entitlements typically surrounding the SER.

Options for Canada

In Canada, the federal and provincial governments face a formidable set of challenges in the early 2000s with the growing evidence that the THI is expanding and diversifying, and the TER, along with other triangular employment relationships, is spreading. Governments need to recognize the precariousness of the TER, given the conditions of employment normally attached to temporary help work, the legal apparatus surrounding the TER that minimizes social protections and entitlements for workers, and the qualitative dimensions of temporary help work. As well, the spread of the TER promises to continue in the future precisely because it is a precarious employment relationship, precisely because it allows employers to abdicate responsibility. If recent initiatives at the level of social policy in Ontario are indicative of its position on the spread of the TER, then the Canadian state itself is not only likely to pose the TER as a viable alternative to the SER but to hold it up as a model in conditioning workers, particularly those already at the bottom of the labour market or on social assistance, to accept more precarious forms of employment as the reality of the modern labour market (see Chapter 7). In the face of these trends, one of the only prospects for improving the conditions of employment among temporary help workers is to extend a range of social protections typically associated with the SER to workers engaged in TERs.

Should Canada and the provinces be pressured by unions and other entities to take up the issue of enhancing protections, benefits, and security for workers engaged in TERs, there are a number of obstacles and challenges to overcome, including how to design legislation, where to incorporate new measures (i.e., within existing laws, such as Employment Standards Acts and Labour Codes and/or within new legislation), and what types of measures to endorse. Still, given the status of regulation in Canada and the templates existing in other jurisdictions, a set of six initial measures would contribute to ameliorating the precarious conditions surrounding the TER. They include altering the form of the legal contracts surrounding the TER, ensuring adequate protections, guaranteeing equal treatment for temporary and permanent workers, instituting precarity pay,[22] improving antidiscrimination legislation, and eliminating the buy-out.

Service Contracts and Employment Agreements

To begin with the most basic measure, a prime means of attaining greater certainty in the TER involves crafting legislation that prohibits agencies from using service contracts and employment agreements as a means of distancing themselves and their customers from the temporary help worker, and thereby lowering the levels of workers' social protections. This type of legislation would ensure that the express purpose of the service contract would be to delineate the employment-related responsibilities of each party to the TER. Mirroring legislation in France, Spain, and Luxembourg, provinces could also require that service contracts contain clauses establishing secondary responsibility in the event of an unjustified break in the employment relationship, or where one party defaults on its contractual or statutory obligations.

Worker Protections

Another necessary requirement of legislation designed to create a comprehensive set of social protections surrounding the TER is that it guarantee worker protections in areas where there is wide documentation of problems such as occupational health and safety, social security, and special medical supervision. As well, given that it is common for employers to use temporary help workers in workplaces known to be dangerous, Canada and the provinces should take direction from the EC and ban the use of temporary help workers at dangerous worksites where their inexperience might put them at risk.

Equal Treatment

It is also widely accepted that employers frequently resort to temporary help workers to lower labour costs, which not only results in inequities within workforces and workplaces but also places downward pressure on working conditions and wages as a whole. Thus, equal treatment for workers engaged in substantially similar work is essential with respect to wages, conditions of employment, the provision of safety equipment, and collective bargaining rights.

On the issue of ensuring that temporary help workers can genuinely take advantage of freedom of association and collective bargaining rights, the creation of sectoral agreements would certainly reinforce equal treatment laws, particularly in sectors with low rates of unionization and where the THI engages a considerable share of the workforce. These types of measures are already feasible in Quebec under the *Collective Agreement Decrees Act*, but may also be possible in other provinces with minor changes to legislation designed to embrace a solidaristic model of labour market policy (Cameron, 1995: 200–8). In France, where the THI is quite a large and dominant force in the economy, temporary help workers belong to occupationally based unions and therefore benefit both from sectoral agreements and from a federation of temporary help workers. Even though temporary help work continues to be more precarious than standard work in France, this model places more checks on the TER. Thus, in theory it should improve conditions of employment for temporary help workers.[23]

Precarity Pay

A measure to introduce some form of precarity pay, to take into account the insecure nature of temporary help work, could also contribute to improving wages and conditions of employment for workers engaged in TERs. The Ministry of Labour of Quebec has already raised the possibility of introducing such a measure. However, it has yet to define its terms – although it is proposing end-of-assignment pay of 10 per cent. Nor has it proposed a means of introducing this measure. A potentially effective means of implementing precarity pay would be to make it a statutory social security requirement.

Improved Antidiscrimination Legislation

Temporary help agencies and private employment agents acting abroad and within nations have a bleak history of making false representations to immigrant and migrant workers, one that continues to the present. At the supranational level, this poor record was documented most recently at the meeting of the Expert Committee on Migration held at the ILO in the winter of 1997. In Canada, there is also continued evidence of a racialized division of labour in the THI as well as racism more generally: witness the false promises that temporary help agencies make to workers with respect to acquiring the 'Canadian experience' necessary to circulate freely in the labour market, the practice of placing workers from the same ethnic backgrounds together at one worksite or in one industry, and the study conducted by the Canadian Civil Liberties Organization which found agencies in the Metropolitan Toronto Area willing to consider requests for workers of specific sexes and/or races (see Chapter 5). Thus, improved antidiscrimination measures are essential now for many of the same reasons that they were required at the turn of the century. Quebec is currently considering implementing some type of monitoring system to minimize such problems. However, it has yet to implement any formal measures.

Buy-outs

A final proposal under consideration in Quebec, which is unique and certainly complements all five other proposals mentioned previously, involves making illegal the 'buy-out' (i.e., the practice whereby the agency charges the customer a fee to hire workers permanently) (Tapin, 1993). If adopted, this type of measure would remove a disincentive for customers to hire temporary help workers into permanent jobs within their enterprises. Ideally, other measures which allow customers to use the THI primarily for the purpose of denying rights or avoiding obligations under labour and social legislation would be eliminated at the same time. A case in point is where a worker is on long-term assignment with the customer but is dismissed and rehired every thirteen weeks so that the agency can avoid paying severance.[24] Temporary help workers report this to be a common practice in the THI in Ontario (fieldnotes, 4 December 1996; T7). Instituting a mandatory conversion clause in employment agreements would be the most suitable means of encouraging assimilation in such cases. Conversion clauses are already mandatory in Belgium and Luxembourg; in both cases, conversion automatically takes place when the customer continues to employ the worker after severing its ties with the agency, fails to live up to the terms and conditions of the service contract, and/or when temporary help workers are used for the sole purpose of escaping obligations under social and labour legislation (Blanpain, 1993: 68–9; Luxembourg, 1994: arts. 4, 5). Conversion clauses were also subject to considerable discussion in the ILO's 1997 failed talks on drafting a new international labour standard on contract labour (ILO, 1997d: para. 20; Vosko, 1997).

There are various options for designing legislation applicable to workers engaged in TERs. Following the proposals that the government of Quebec is entertaining, as well as those in France and Germany, employment standards acts and/or provincial and federal labour codes offer the most suitable arena primarily because they represent 'living' legislation. Separate legislation could also be developed, as is common in Spain and Belgium. However, given the history of inactivity at the provincial level where updating and enforcing legislation governing private employment agencies is concerned, adding new measures to employment standards legislation is preferable so as to place the TER at the centre of labour legislation rather than treating it in a subsidiary manner.

Conclusion

Devising a solid regulatory framework surrounding the TER, one whose mandate is to extend a comprehensive set of labour and social protections to temporary help workers, is not only unlikely given the current regulatory climate in Canada, it also would be insufficient on its own. As evidenced by the nature and consequences of legislative interventions in the EC, where strong directives are in place but are nonbinding to its members, the need for sound enforcement mechanisms is also key to minimizing the precarious character of the TER. Even more important, given that the SER is the central unit of analysis used in crafting contemporary social and labour legislation and the central model around which it is gauged, regulating the TER requires greater openness to 'new' paradigms of regulation among law and policy-makers. Equally important, it demands a change in attitude among all the parties to the TER as well as other actors in civil society, especially among various segments of organized labour, where the struggle necessary to stimulate change is most likely to develop. In other words, changes in customs, habits, and practices that upheld the SER as the *normative* model of employment are crucial if the rise of nonstandard forms of employment, such as temporary help work, continue. Otherwise, the type of benefits package tied to the SER will cover fewer and fewer people.

The need to adapt the system of collective bargaining in Canada to accommodate the growing pluralism in employment relationships in the late 1990s is particularly pressing if we are truly to protect freedom of association and collective bargaining rights for all workers in Canada, including the growing number of workers engaged in TERs and other triangular employment relationships. From the perspective of policy-makers and labour board officials, making the regime of collective bargaining more hospitable to non-standard workers will require adapting formal and informal policies, principles, and procedures governing such issues as bargaining unit determination. From the perspective of organized labour, meeting this challenge will inevitably require recovering and updating modes of organizing workers that predate the post-Second World War period, practices that differ from those associated with the worksite-based Fordist regime of collective bargaining, and strengthening existing systems of organizing that serve marginalized groups of workers.

There is a tremendous tension within the prevailing regulatory regime associated with the SER in Canada: this tension centres on extending protection, benefits, and security to workers engaged in employment relationships where responsibility rests with more than one entity, while preserving crucial elements of the existing regime. The magnitude of this tension is overwhelming. Moreover, if changes at the level of the labour market continue along their present trajectory, the need for a paradigm shift is quite compelling, since workers, such as temporary help workers, who were formally at the margins of the labour market, are moving towards the centre. Transforming the prevailing regime does not necessitate abandoning existing models. However, it does require developing new modes of protecting workers.

Chapter 7

'No Jobs, Lots of Work':
The Rise of the Temporary
Employment Relationship and the
Emergence of Workfare-Driven Social Policy[1]

People have this concept of what a job is. A job is something where you go in and you are now secure. You have tenure. You are there for life, until retirement. Jobs no longer exist. Everything nowadays is temporary. It may be for an hour, a day, a week, a month, five years, but it is still temporary. We need to get away from the concept of 'job' in the way that it used to be considered – you know, among the parents and the grandparents – and start thinking in terms of work. Work is effort for pay ... Work may turn into a job. However, there are very few jobs out there. But, there is a lot of work available. (M4)

An official involved in a new welfare-to-work program in the province of Ontario made the preceding remarks to describe the changing nature of employment and justify the shape of this initiative. The program, known as Workfirst, seeks to match 'employable' social assistance recipients with temporary help agencies with the objective of reducing the welfare rolls. Thus, it reflects what some analysts label 'workfarism,' a labour market reorganization strategy that involves privatizing the design, administration, and delivery of employment training and placement, and marketizing welfare policy. In contrast to welfarism, which involved a sustained commitment to maintaining the SER as the *normative* model of employment (Brodie, 1994; McFarland and Mullaly, 1996; White, 1995), workfarism seeks to transform the institutional and social bases of labour market regulation (Jessop, 1993; Peck, 1996).[2] Examining Workfirst is an appropriate means of concluding the empirical dimension of this book, since the shape of this program provides a glimpse of the future and an opportunity to probe the nature of the Canadian state's role in legitimizing the spread of the TER. Indeed, the implicit aim of Workfirst is to condition marginalized workers for a volatile labour market, where wage relations offer even less security and freedom than in the past, so they will be more willing to accept work outside the boundaries of the SER.[3]

The preceding chapters documented the rise and spread of the TER by probing the host of forces contributing to its ascendancy. In examining what is driving prevailing employment trends, they have drawn special attention to the changing employment practices and marketing strategies that the THI first embraced in the late 1970s and early 1980s, shifting employment norms and the unprecedented openings at the regulatory level beginning in 1966. They have also shown that, even though the TER amounts to a precarious model of employment, this triangular employment relationship had considerable formal legitimacy at the international level in the late 1990s; the de-regulation of private employment agencies that is currently occurring at both the federal and provincial levels in Canada and the provinces, and the absence of measures designed to regulate the TER only reinforce this conclusion. Shifting our focus to the level of social policy, however, has the potential to deepen these findings.

This chapter probes the nature of the Canadian state's response to the TER by describing the origins, design, and delivery of Workfirst. It illustrates that, in the case of Workfirst the state is not only sanctioning the rise of the TER but situating this employment relationship as a new employment norm. In so doing, the chapter addresses the growing convergence between shifting employment norms and new directions in social policy, a development that not only provides further evidence of the contraction of the SER and growing dualism in the labour market but also reminds us of the ever-present danger in capitalist labour markets of heightening the commodification of labour power.

Origins

Workfirst is one of several municipally operated programs that falls under the Ontario Works scheme. Ontario Works was first legally established under Regulation No. 537, a general regulation to the *General Welfare Assistance Act* (1958) of Ontario. Since the scheme was introduced, however, there have been significant legislative changes to the provision of social assistance in Ontario, changes that are dramatically re-shaping the design and delivery of social assistance in the province. As of 1 May 1998, the *Ontario Works Act* (1997) replaced the *Family Benefits Act* (1967) and the *General Welfare Assistance Act*, the two pre-existing welfare laws in the province, and formally created Canada's first workfare program (Bezanson and Valentine, 1997; Ministry of Community and Social Services, 12 June 1997; National Council on Welfare, 1997: 69).[4]

With respect to the arguments advanced in this chapter, specifically the contention that the emergence of programs like Workfirst signal growing coercion in the labour market, the introduction of the *Ontario Works Act* is significant for three key reasons. First, and most centrally, the act formally introduces a harsher and more punitive welfare regime, which confers a more onerous set of obligations on social assistance recipients and institutes a more imposing application procedure. For example, the act allows municipalities to establish a system of finger-printing applicants for welfare (although it does *not* require that such measures be implemented); it also allows them to require all adult dependents of welfare applicants (e.g., spouses and children residing in the same household) to sign application forms and consent forms before processing applications (Ontario Social Safety Network, 1998: 5; Ministry of Community and Social Services, 12 June 1997: 4). Second, it undermines the rights of social assistance recipients by, for example, replacing the Welfare Appeal Board with a small tribunal with reduced scope and forcing sole support parents to participate in workfare unless publicly funded education is unavailable to their children (National Council on Welfare, 1997: 69; Ministry of Community and Social Services, 12 June 1997: 4).[5] Third, the act establishes an explicit legal framework for the privatization of welfare services to an extent that was not legally possible previously, a component of the act that the provincial government claims will assist in streamlining delivery at the municipal level.[6] The introduction of this last measure was particularly crucial to establishing Workfirst at the municipal level, given its requirement for a private sector broker to deliver core components of the program.

Building on these and other related legislative changes, the Ontario Works scheme is composed of several streams that form a continuum of workfare-type programs that range from 'pure' workfare programs to 'new style' workfare programs. Although workfare is conventionally defined as mandatory work in exchange for welfare payments (i.e., 'pure' workfare),[7] in contemporary Ontario the term is also increasingly used to refer to a broader set of work-related obligations such as training, job-seeking, schooling, and community work (i.e., 'new style' workfare), where the social assistance recipient receives either direct or indirect income transfers from the state.[8] Thus, in the case of the Ontario Works scheme, the notion of a workfare continuum is useful as a conceptual tool since it has the potential to encompass the wide range of programs linked to the coercive and/or restrictive work incentive strategy currently emerging in Ontario (Lightman, 1995).

The three streams incorporated into Ontario Works are community participation, employment support, and employment placement. The set of programs most closely resembling 'pure' workfare fall under the community participation stream (McCrossin, 1997). This stream involves the direct exchange of unpaid work for welfare benefits from the state; under the current provincial guidelines, social assistance recipients must work up to seventy hours per month in either a project created by the municipality or a private nonprofit organization (Ministry of Community and Social Services, August 1996: 9–11). In contrast, the employment support stream entails structured job search assistance activities, which include basic education or job-skills training programs in exchange for welfare benefits and basic assistance with job search as well as provision for expenses (i.e., child care and travel) required to engage in a job search (2). These support programs target those social assistance recipients who face formidable barriers to entry into the labour market. Finally, employment placement programs, the focus of this chapter, deal with 'employable' social assistance recipients who are first prepared for private sector unsubsidized jobs in exchange for welfare benefits and then are forcefully directed into these jobs (16). This third stream of Ontario Works encourages municipal social assistance departments to enlist the services of private employment agencies to help place social assistance recipients in paid employment.[9] The selected agencies are compensated 'on a performance basis using a *share* [my emphasis] of the funds that would otherwise be paid out in social assistance to the participant' (2). In effect, they are rewarded a percentage of the savings incurred from matching social assistance recipients with employers.[10]

Regardless of the stream to which they are assigned, under the Ontario Works guidelines, eligible social assistance recipients are obligated to participate in some form of workfare and they are strongly encouraged to sign a participation agreement, in order to continue to receive their social assistance benefits. This 'voluntary' agreement outlines the new conditions for receiving social assistance in Ontario and serves as a tool for monitoring the progress of social assistance recipients involved in any municipally operated program that falls under Ontario Works. While there is a standard participation agreement, case workers have a significant degree of discretion in tailoring agreements to individual social assistance recipients. Municipal officials may also design participation agreements to suit the parameters of specific projects or programs under any of the three streams (Ministry of Community and Social Services, August 1996: 23).[11]

Design

Initiated in the Regional Municipality of Peel, in the Greater Toronto Area on 25 October 1995, Workfirst falls under the employment placement stream of Ontario Works. Besides the participation agreement that normally exists between the social assistance recipient and the social assistance department, the program involves a service agreement between the municipal welfare department and a private sector broker who is 'experienced in the provision of labour to private sector employers' (Brief to the Human Services Committee, 30 January 1996: 2). Together with the participation agreement, this partnership confers responsibilities (and obligations) on three parties: the municipal social assistance department, the broker, and the program 'participants.'

As the public administrator of Workfirst, the municipal social assistance department was initially charged with designing and implementing a program to reflect Regulation No. 537 to the *General Welfare Assistance Act*, which permitted Ontario Works to emerge. As interpreted at the municipal level, Regulation No. 537 first required people receiving social assistance, except people with disabilities, seniors, and sole-support parents, to accept offers of community placement, training, and/or employment support or placement as an ongoing condition of eligibility (Ministry of Community and Social Services, August 1996: 1–2). However, with the passage of the *Ontario Works Act*, the obligation to participate in the Ontario Works programs, such as Workfirst, expanded to include a larger group of single parents formerly eligible for Family Benefits, and people who are sixty to sixty-four years of age (Ontario Social Safety Network, 1998: 6). Since the mandate of Workfirst is to match 'employable' social assistance recipients with temporary help agencies, for the social assistance department, adapting first to Regulation No. 537 and then to the *Ontario Works Act* itself, has meant making it mandatory for a specified group of 'employable' social assistance recipients to register with temporary employment agencies in their job search process (Brief to the Human Services Committee, 30 January 1996: 1). The work of the social assistance department initially involved selecting a private sector broker to administer the program and then oversee the program as it was phased in. However, as the program becomes self-sustaining, the municipal government predicts that the role of the social assistance department will diminish. If it is correct, ongoing responsibilities of the department will fall mainly on case workers who will assign social assistance recipients to the program, monitor their participation, and advise the broker when 'participants' are no longer receiving social assistance. In the long run, municipal authorities expect that the administrative branch of the department will be involved only in paying the broker and undertaking periodic reviews of the Workfirst program (Legal Agreement, 31 July 1996: s.4).

Unlike the role of the municipal social assistance department, which aims to limit its involvement in administering Workfirst, the responsibilities of the broker are far-reaching. At the time the research for this chapter was conducted, the broker was responsible for providing regular orientation sessions on temporary help work to 'participants,' registering them with at least three local temporary help agencies, tracking their success at being placed in temporary help work, and reporting to the social assistance department on the success of placement (Brief to the Human Services Committee, 30 January 1996, 5–6). Its services included providing three pre-approved training facilities to host the orientation sessions, appropriate staffing and materials for half-day orientation sessions, confidential computerized referral and tracking to temporary help agencies, computerized reporting to the region, and training and certification in basic health and safety procedures for selected 'participants' (Legal Agreement, 31 July 1996: s.3).[12]

The obligations conferred upon social assistance recipients selected for Workfirst are far more extensive than under pre-existing municipal welfare guidelines. Reflecting provincial regulations first introduced under Regulation No. 537 and later entrenched in the *Ontario Works Act*, as well as policy guidelines established at the municipal level, all social assistance recipients selected for Workfirst were initially required to attend a half-day orientation session, register with at least three temporary help agencies recommended by the broker within five working days of the session and be 'willing to accept any work which the agency recommends is suitable' to remain eligible for social assistance (Brief to the Human Services Committee, 30 January 1996: 3).[13] Since the inception of Workfirst, the obligations of the 'participants' have changed slightly because the contents of the half-day orientation sessions are now incorporated into two briefing sessions, one from case workers and another from the broker itself. However, the tenor of the obligations conferred upon 'participants' remains the same: they must register with the temporary help agency and accept the work that they are offered or face punitive sanctions.

It is the penalties for noncompliance established at the provincial level and implemented at the municipal level that make the requirements binding to 'participants.' Under all three streams of Ontario Works, the refusal to accept work, referral to a placement, or an offer of a placement are grounds for a loss of entitlement for up to three months for a single social assistance recipient or a reduction in entitlement for social assistance recipients with dependents (RRO, 1996: reg. 537, s.4.3 (7) & (9)). Under Workfirst, social assistance recipients are also subject to sanctions if they quit temporary help work or are fired without an acceptable reason. For the single social assistance recipient, the penalty for quitting without a justifiable reason or being fired for an unaccept-able reason is ineligibility for three months. For the social assistance recipient with dependents, the penalty is a reduction in their entitle-ment for three months. Furthermore, if 'participants' refuse to accept employment, referral to a placement or an offer of a placement more than once, they become ineligible for social assistance for six months (General Welfare Assistance Policy Directive, 1 August 1996:.3).

Given the penalties for not complying with Workfirst rules, it is hardly surprising that the municipality expected to reduce its social assistance expenditures drastically through Workfirst. Initially, the municipality outlined three potential sources for expenditure reduction. The first source was indirect as it was to come from the income that 'participants' receive from placement in employment, and since it would have the effect of reducing the sum total of social assistance payments. The sec-ond source was to result from 'participants' who fail to make reasonable efforts to find employment; in the context of the initial policy guidelines, failing to make 'reasonable efforts' included refusing to attend a Workfirst orientation session and/or register with a designated temporary agency. The third source was to come from participants who are found ineligible for *General Welfare Assistance* because they refuse work (Ministry of Com-munity and Social Services, August 1996: 41). During the first eight months of the program (August 1996 to April 1997), the broker placed 296 'participants' in temporary help work and reduced social assistance payments by $200,000.[14] According to the municipality, these reductions were obtained both through employment placement and by temporarily disqualifying 'participants' from social assistance due to their failure to make what the Region referred to as 'reasonable efforts' in seeking employment or their refusal to accept offers of work (Human Services Committee, 16 April 1997).[15]

The potential for expenditure reduction for the municipal social assistance department makes taking part in the delivery of Workfirst a lucrative venture for the broker. As the provider of the service, the broker receives a percentage of the value of the reduction in social assistance credited to Workfirst; this percentage is calculated based on savings resulting from increased earnings only. The terms and conditions of Workfirst currently entitle the broker to 10 per cent of the first $1,894,150 saved in increased earnings and 12.5 per cent thereafter (Brief to the Human Services Committee, 30 January 1996: 6). Furthermore, general program guidelines for Ontario Works permit brokers participating in the employment placement stream of the provincial scheme to charge supplementary fees 'if the Ontario Works participant is retained by an employer other than the employment placement agency and is retained as a direct result of the actions of that agency' (Ministry of Community and Social Services, August 1996: 41). In other words, these guidelines do not prevent buy-outs between the broker/agency and its prospective customers, nor do they require the broker/agency to alter its typical fee structure.

The Design of Workfirst, the Rise of Workfare-Driven Social Policy, and the Contraction of the SER

While Workfirst is not 'pure' workfare, the design of this 'new style' welfare-to-work program is consistent with the movement towards workfare-driven social policy in Canada. The provincial legislation formally establishing workfare in Ontario, the Ontario Works guidelines, municipally devised policies and practices, and the legal documentation surrounding Workfirst reflect the harmonization of training policy and welfare policy and the marketization of welfare; together, they are contributing to reconfiguring the institutional forms and forces that are imminent in the labour market (Peck, 1996: 188). Central to the larger argument of this book, the design of Workfirst also reflects shifting employment norms; it reinforces the erosion of the SER and introduces a highly precarious employment relationship as one among several alternatives. This is not to suggest that Workfirst guidelines aim to completely replace the SER with a TER, but to indicate that the TER is emerging parallel to the SER as the core of standard workers in the Canadian labour market is shrinking.

The design of Workfirst makes participation in training,[16] registration with temporary help agencies, and accepting temporary help work compulsory for 'employable' social assistance recipients. It therefore denies social assistance recipients the right to refuse work and/or training for welfare. Consequently, the design of the program builds on the recent cancellation of the federally based *Canada Assistance Plan*. As Scott McCrossin (1997: 177) aptly notes, '[t]here is an inherent lack of voluntariness in this arrangement.'

It also signals an attempt by provincial and municipal governments to alter what is perceived to be not only acceptable but ideal employment for social assistance recipients in Ontario. Under the *General Welfare Assistance Act* regulations, social assistance recipients in Ontario have *always* been legally obligated to seek and accept any full-time, part-time, or casual employment which they are physically capable of undertaking. However, actively placing social assistance recipients into temporary help work has never before been a structural component of social assistance design in Ontario. In this way, Workfirst signals a dramatic shift in emphasis on the part of the state, one that has significant implications for unemployed workers drawing on various sources of state support ranging from training subsidies and employment insurance to social assistance. Prior to the design of Workfirst, social assistance administrators normally viewed attaining a permanent job as the ultimate goal of the welfare-to-work transition. However, the design of Workfirst turns the assumption that a permanent job (ideally, one with benefits) is the *most* suitable alternative to welfare (or unemployment) on its head by making temporary help work the *object* of the program. In making participation in Workfirst compulsory for 'employable' social assistance recipients, the program guidelines convey the message that recipients who have not actively sought temporary help work in their job-search process are missing out on suitable opportunities for employment (Brief to the Human Services Committee, 30 January 1996: 2).[17]

In addition to casting temporary help work as a more viable alternative to welfare than in the past, Workfirst also privatizes social assistance in a number of crucial respects. Most centrally, it opens the delivery of social assistance to private sector actors and engages a broker to provide training and placement to social assistance recipients. Ironically, there is an implicit assumption within the Workfirst guidelines that private employment agencies operate along the same principles as their counterparts in the public sector; however, unlike the public employment service, these agencies obviously operate for profit. As an industry official involved in Workfirst noted, '[w]e want to be successful in doing this because we want the program to work. Obviously we want to be able to take the program to other regions and we want to guide those programs because it's business for us' (M4). Moreover, while the legal agreements between the social assistance department and the broker recognize that they have distinct roles to play, standard-setting is essentially devolved to the private sector in the design of Workfirst. The broker orients participants to the domain of temporary help work, determines where (i.e., in which types of employment) 'participants' are best placed and matches them with its customers.

Finally, by simultaneously reducing the role of the state in the provision of social assistance and elevating the TER as a desirable alternative to welfare, the design of Workfirst also contributes to lowering the level of social protection accorded to many workers during the post-Second World War era. As demonstrated in preceding chapters, temporary help workers rarely have access to the full range of social security benefits, such as employment insurance coverage, maternity benefits, and extended health benefits attached to the SER. As well, the relatively low wages, the degree of insecurity, and the legal arrangements conventionally associated with temporary help work (which minimizes employment-related responsibilities for both the agency and the customer) make the TER a highly precarious model of employment. Given its explicit objective of selecting a large group of 'employable' social assistance recipients for the program, Workfirst not only aims to provide an expanded pool of workers for the THI to draw upon, it also poses temporary help work as a suitable alternative to social assistance. Faced with the potential loss of entitlement for refusing temporary help work, this pool of workers may be forced to accept lower wages and presumably even worse working conditions than the existing pool of temporary help workers currently enjoy, not only lowering the bottom of the labour market as a whole but also the bottom of the THI itself. One agency manager characterized the advantage of Workfirst as follows: '[Y]ou now have this larger pool of workers that you can call upon. Some people see it virtually as a limitless pool of new workers' (M4).

Delivery

Since the *design* of Workfirst only partly reveals the tenor of the Ontario government's response to the rise of TER, it is instructive to examine the *delivery* of the program, especially the model initially used in the orientation session. In particular, it is crucial to consider the following three related questions: does the delivery of the program take the precarious nature of the TER as given? If so, what methods does the broker use to socialize the participants into this 'new world of work'? If Workfirst manages to achieve its stated objectives, how and to what extent could it contribute to undermining the SER as a *normative* model of employment?[18] To address these questions, this section describes and interprets the model used in the orientation session for the first two and a half years of the program and the response of 'participants' to Workfirst.

When Workfirst was first introduced, the broker held half-day orientations to acclimatize participants to temporary help work.[19] Prior to attending the orientation, selected social assistance recipients were assigned to a specific session and told that they must attend the orientation and register with three temporary help agencies in order to continue to receive social assistance.[20] At this stage, they were offered only limited information on the design of the program and how it reflected larger changes in the provision of social assistance in Ontario. As one 'participant' noted, 'They don't tell you anything. You just get this little thing in the mail telling you that you have to report on such and such a day to such and such a place and that's it ... I mean it's really threatening. It tells you that you either do it or you don't get any money ... If you don't go, you're cut off for three months apparently' (T10). Thus, the broker was left to explain the purpose and the guidelines of the program at the orientation session.

The three-hour orientation session was divided into three distinct parts: Introduction and Check In; The Pre-interview Process; and the Employment Agency Interview. While 'participants' were encouraged to ask questions, the bulk of the session was reserved for a presentation from the instructor.

Introduction and Check In

The substantive portion of the orientation session to Workfirst started after the instructor took attendance. The instructor began by describing the state of the economy and how things have changed over the last twenty-five years. In this part of the session, emphasis was on dispelling the myth of the 'lifelong job.' One instructor noted, 'We are out of work not because of a stupid government or a stupid employer but because of a global phenomenon. You can parallel it to the industrial revolution. Lifetime jobs used to be the norm but now they aren't' (fieldnotes, 3

February 1997). Another noted, 'You guys are going to have to hustle. Be prepared to look for work over and over again over the years' (fieldnotes, 7 February 1997). In this part of the session, 'participants' were not blamed for their unemployed status, yet they were encouraged to adopt a particular view of the labour market, one that required them to take a new approach to the job-search process. This view involved understanding that there are at least three types of employment today: core jobs, which are the closest thing to the lifelong job, full-time and part-time contract work, and full-time temporary help work. The 'participants' were told 'the core is a synonym for the part of the operation that gets benefits, eye plans, health plans, and pension plans' (fieldnotes, 7 February 1997). They were also told that the next best thing to being part of the core is being on contract and then there are 'the people that are rented out from agencies' (fieldnotes, 7 February 1997).

While getting into the core was touted as a possible outcome of participating in Workfirst, instructors asserted that attaining this outcome involved a great deal of commitment and investment and a lot of luck. They also indicated that the best way to get into the core is by recognizing that there is a hidden job market. They stated repeatedly that very few employers advertise for personnel in the newspaper and even fewer accept hand-delivered résumés. Rather, most employers deal with private employment agencies to fill their vacancies or they search for the suitable candidate inside their own operations. Consequently, one of the best ways to get access to the core is by working through a temporary help agency. One instructor noted accordingly: 'There is always a way to get into the core. The core is always a living, breathing thing. It's always evolving. People die, get sick, get promotions, or move. That's your chance. This is your opportunity when you are working for an agency. This is your chance to impress someone. Usually, she [the human resource manager] can't advertise. It's more likely that she'll hire internally ... Only one per cent of people who work at agencies get to work in the core, but it's still a chance. It's still better than buying a [Lottery] 649. It's one in a hundred not one in a million – now this is my estimate. I know one guy who got one. Core jobs are out there. They do happen' (fieldnotes, 7 February 1997). Thus, 'participants' were urged to monitor company job boards for permanent positions when placed in a temporary assignment because internal advertisements have the potential to give them access to the core. In this way, instructors still posed the SER as an elusive goal while simultaneously casting the TER as an emerging employment norm.

Once the instructors established the similarities and differences between core jobs and temporary help work, they described the role of temporary help agencies and attempted to dispel myths about these agencies. For example, they assured 'participants' that employment agency personnel are honest business people. While the client pays the agency a fee, the worker is not directly penalized. One instructor noted, 'There is this idea that employment agencies skim things off the top. Not true. There is a fee – agencies don't work for charity – but the clients pay. You won't be paid less than if you were hired directly by the company' (fieldnotes, 3 February 1997). Despite efforts to make 'participants' comfortable with registering with temporary help agencies, instructors also repeatedly reinforced the differences between private employment agencies and public employment services. Private employment agencies were depicted as businesses geared to their customers not to the workers that they place. Distinguishing between temporary help agencies and public employment services, one agency manager and occasional Workfirst instructor reported that he routinely warned workers: '[D]on't go in there [to a temporary help agency] expecting that these people are now devoted to finding you work. A lot of people assume that employment services – their function is to find you a job. It's not. Their function is to find clients and to find workers for their clients. Okay? So they're working on behalf of their clients. They are not working on your behalf. All right? So what that means is that the effort is still on the part of the candidate. The candidate can't just simply walk in, hand in their résumé, and then sit back and wait for the phone call' (M4).

Instructors also encouraged 'participants' to unlearn many of the outdated job-search methods prescribed by the social assistance department, indicating that Workfirst was contracted out to a private employment agency because agencies are more efficient at direct placement than the public employment service. Throughout the orientation sessions, 'participants' were told that the social assistance department is in the payment business, to provide financial support for people who are either experiencing short bouts of unemployment, or people with long-term disabilities, not in the placement or skills-matching business.

Pre-interview Process

After introducing Workfirst, instructors devoted a significant amount of time to positioning the TER as an alternative to social assistance. The pre-interview process was where the conditioning process was most apparent. During this component of the orientation session, instructors raised 'common sense' issues such as dressing appropriately, arriving on time, and making eye contact; several 'participants' reported that these discussions were degrading (T9, T10).

At the outset of the pre-interview component of the orientation session, 'participants' were given a checklist to use in preparation for the interview; this checklist was intended to remind the participant to bring a résumé, a Workfirst registration form, a social insurance card, photo identification, the location of the employment agencies, and a pen to fill out an application for the agency interview. Once the instructor went over the checklist, s/he identified three issues to consider when preparing for the interview with the agency. Instructors stressed the importance of making a good first impression. Second, they described 'appropriate dressing and grooming habits' and provided a handout for future reference. 'Participants' were told to 'wear clean clothes' and to 'shower and use deodorant,' and women were told to 'avoid excessive jewelry' (fieldnotes, 3, 7 February 1997). These instructions were reinforced with a handout given to all 'participants' entitled, 'Dressing and Grooming.' Instructors asserted that dressing appropriately is particularly important for women in the THI since they are likely to be placed in clerical positions and they may have to deal with the general public. For example, one instructor noted. 'In the summer, ladies could wear open-toed shoes so long as they match their dress' (fieldnotes, 7 February 1997). Later in the same session, the same instructor joked about fancy attire stating that employers 'have a problem with people who are richer than they are.' As well, 'participants' were told to wear the clothes that they would wear on the job because they 'could be Johnny-on-the-spot' and be required to take up a position immediately following the assessment, a practice which is acceptable under the program guidelines (fieldnotes, 3 February 1997). As a general rule, men were encouraged to dress in casual work clothes since they would most likely be placed in light industrial work, and women were to 'dress for the office,' exemplifying the internal sex segregation in the THI. The overt gender bias in the dress instructions prescribed by orientation leaders is particularly significant given that more women, especially single mothers, are being introduced into the Ontario Works caseload. Not only do these instructions have the potential to reinforce sex segregation in the THI, whereby women comprise the majority of clerical workers and men the bulk of general labourers, they highlight the real danger of positioning women social assistance recipients in highly segmented areas of the labour market where there are few prospects for job advancement. Finally, instructors told anecdotes that stressed the importance of arriving at the interview on time.

The Employment Agency Interview

The conditioning process continued when instructors discussed the employment agency interview.[21] In this segment of the session, instructors talked about 'the art of interviewing,' which involved preparing 'participants' for commonly asked questions, providing strategies for discussing one's strengths and weaknesses in the interview setting and coaching 'participants' on how to express their willingness to learn new skills. In this segment of the session, instructors stressed the importance of differentiating between 'skills' and 'experience.' They had 'participants' identify so-called hidden skills, important skills that are often omitted from résumés. In an interview, the agency manager who doubled as an instructor suggested that female participants would be wise to tap into skills associated with 'women's work' and emphasize all of their household duties:

> A lot of the people that come through Workfirst have no résumé at all. Part of the reason for that is because they don't recognize their own skills. Part of what we do during this process [the orientation session] is try to help people realize that there's a difference between skills and experience ... What employers are looking for now is what you can do based on the skills that you have. *So somebody for example, who did nothing over the past ten years other than stay at home – I'm talking, you, know single mothers, single fathers, anybody, actually – has a significant number of marketable skills. They can balance budgets. They can manage a household. So there's some organizational skills in there. The very fact that they can talk on a telephone, those are telephone skills* [my emphasis]. These are skills that, if they're presented appropriately inside a résumé, can be marketed. (M4)

Standard to every orientation session, the discussion of 'hidden skills' was riddled with stereotypical assumptions about social assistance recipients. Combined with a discussion of 'appropriate dressing and grooming' and 'arriving on time,' discussing hidden skills served to remind 'participants' of their 'place' in the labour market. While it is important to valorize so-called hidden skills, such as those associated with domestic labour and 'women's work' more broadly, the emphasis here was to prepare social assistance recipients for highly precarious forms of temporary help work.

Once instructors concluded the orientation to the employment agency interview, they placed a list of potential jobs in front of 'participants.' The list only included jobs that fell under the categories of so-called light industrial work (i.e., general labour) and clerical work.[22] There was no space on the agency application form for Workfirst 'participants' to register for jobs outside these two narrow categories, which reflect the most precarious form of the TER. In one session, the following exchange took place between an instructor and a participant. It is a clear example of how Workfirst socializes 'participants' into accepting employment in specific segments of the labour market, even if they have extensive skills, qualifications, and experience. And it also highlights the racialized division of labour, frequently legitimized by the claim that most employers require 'Canadian experience,' common to the THI as a whole.

> Participant: I am an engineer. I was an engineer in India.
>
> Instructor: I have a lot of people like you. Through the agencies, they don't help you a lot in this kind of work. You might have to go through other professional agencies. Use the *Yellow Pages* to find them.
>
> Participant: They always ask for Canadian experience. How can I resolve these problems?
>
> Instructor: Right now, you're going to have to accept this [the possibility of obtaining a light industrial placement] and continue to look for other ones. You have to try. That's all that I can tell you ... Also, sometimes it pays to have two résumés – because sometimes companies will say that you are over qualified – one with simple qualifications and another with all your qualifications. (fieldnotes, 3 February 1997)

After this exchange, the instructor proceeded to describe a situation where a former Workfirst 'participant' worked free for two weeks in order to prove that he was the best person available for a temporary light industrial job. By telling this anecdote, the instructor was sympathizing with the 'participant's' situation, while at the same time reminding him that he must accept any type of work in order to maintain his entitlement to social assistance. When the same 'participant' asked whether he was eligible for skills assessment, the instructor responded that Workfirst is strictly an employment placement program. Under Workfirst, the only option for 'participants' is to apply for either light industrial or clerical positions, and the orientation leaders were careful to make 'participants' aware of this rule. This focus on placement, to the exclusion of training and assessment, illustrates that the privatization of the delivery process has the potential to contribute to narrowing and deepening the 'skills deficit' among social assistance recipients: unless they are deemed unemployable by the temporary help agencies where they are assigned, Workfirst 'participants' are not offered genuine skills assessment, training, and/or upgrading opportunities.

Throughout the entire Workfirst orientation session, instructors reminded 'participants' to think positively. With the moral consensus about the desirability of forcing social assistance recipients into the labour force behind them, they acted as cheerleaders whose roles were to encourage 'participants' to find temporary help work and to remind them of the penalties involved in refusing any work on offer. Although instructors provided 'participants' with a sense of optimism on the surface, this optimism was tempered with another message about the changing nature of employment. Every orientation session began and ended with the following quotation from Charles Handy's popular book, *The Age of Unreason* (1991): 'It has been said, that by the end of the decade, less than half of the work force in the industrialized world will have full-time jobs, the rest will be part-time, temporary workers or unemployed' (fieldnotes, 3, 7 February 1997). As with the rest of the session, this quotation aimed to socialize participants into accepting the increasingly precarious nature of employment, to encourage them to use private employment agencies and to begin to accept the TER as an emerging employment norm.

The Delivery of Workfirst, the Rise of Workfare-Driven Social Policy, and the Rise of the TER

During the various components of the orientation session, instructors delivered all the mandated content set out in the design of Workfirst. However, they delivered several other messages as well. Reinforcing the decline of the SER, one message is that social assistance recipients must recognize and accept the increasingly volatile nature of the labour market. Another equally important message is that they have no choice but to accept their location at the bottom of the labour market: low-waged, casual industrial work and de-skilled clerical work are the most viable alternatives to social assistance. Thus, Workfirst, as it is delivered by the broker, matches and elaborates upon its design. Although Workfirst is not 'pure' workfare, it is consistent with the move towards workfare-driven social policy in Canada. While the design of Workfirst creates a state-sanctioned space for the TER in the labour market, the delivery of Workfirst – both the orientation session upon which it was first based and the streamlined orientation process which is now in place – is a means of introducing unfamiliar forms of compulsion into the eligibility criteria for social assistance. Through its delivery, Workfirst reconstitutes welfare as workfare to social assistance recipients themselves by turning what was once the de facto status quo (i.e., encouraging social assistance recipients to accept whatever type of work is on offer) into a structural component of the regulation of marginalized workers. It introduces 'participants' to the 'new world of work,' where the SER is presented as an anomaly and wage relations are characterized by growing insecurity. As a new-style welfare-to-work program, Workfirst is not only forcing 'employable' social assistance recipients to exchange their benefits for precarious forms of work, it is situating the TER as a companion to the contracting SER. Despite the substandard conditions of employment normally attached to temporary help work, the program openly positions the TER as a parallel *normative* model of employment of the future. In so doing, it is contributing to altering the institutional bases of labour market regulation by abandoning the conventional bilateral employment relationship as the ideal model and introducing the triangular employment relationship associated with the THI as an acceptable alternative. By situating the TER as a prototype, Workfirst also sanctions at-will employment as a viable alternative to social assistance and virtually eliminates possibilities for unionization. For example, in 1997 the government of Ontario drafted and subsequently enacted (December 1998) a bill entitled 'An Act to Prevent Unionization with Respect to Community Participation under the *Ontario Works Act*' (Bill 22), despite vehement opposition from organized labour. This Bill is designed to deny Ontario Works 'participants' assigned to the community placement stream the right to join a union and to be covered by collective agreement under Ontario's *Labour Relations Act*. Although it does not apply to participants in the employment placement stream, this legislation underscores the coercive nature of the Ontario Works scheme, and the reactions of organized labour signal its growing concern with regulating the TER (Ontario Federation of Labour, 1998).

Conclusion

Workfirst represents one among many new welfare-to-work initiatives arising from the movement away from welfare-oriented social policy at the federal level in Canada, marked by the erosion of the right to refuse work for welfare formerly accorded to social assistance recipients in the now defunct *Canada Assistance Plan* (for other examples, see Low, 1996; McFarland and Mullalay, 1996). However, the significance of the program goes well beyond the unconventional approach that it takes to the provision of social assistance by linking benefits more closely to narrow work-related obligations. In the context of this inquiry into the history and evolution of the TER, what is particularly notable about Workfirst is that it ties social assistance recipients' eligibility for benefits to their willingness to compete for and accept temporary help work. It therefore signifies the Ontario government's affirmation of the TER as a model employment relationship for workers at the margins of the labour market. The fact that the provincial government is endorsing such a precarious model of employment without first devising a coherent set of protections to surround it is also striking, especially because many temporary help workers generally face substandard conditions of employment and earn lower wages than workers engaged in SERs.

Although Ontario, or, more accurately, the Regional Municipality of Peel, is only promoting this type of employment relationship for a well-defined group of social assistance recipients, Workfirst offers a glimpse into the future, one that is highly instructive in light of this study, but also very troubling. The design and delivery of the program provide evidence of the erosion of the SER as a norm, adding to the documentation presented in Chapters 4 through 6. They also signal the decline of the profound, though highly gendered and racialized, mediation of an inherent tension in capitalist labour markets – the tension between encouraging the market circulation of labour power while maintaining sufficient constraints on capital so as to enable workers to reproduce themselves – that arose out of the capital-labour entente in Canada in the post-Second World War period. But even more than the evidence of the precarious character of the TER presented in Chapter 5, an examination of Workfirst demonstrates clearly that pressure to intensify the commodification of labour power is building in the contemporary Canadian labour market. It also contributes to deepening two core arguments in this study: first, the claim that temporary help workers, whose ranks are growing, are particularly vulnerable to being treated like commodities given the shape of the TER; and, second, the related theoretical contention that the decline of security and freedom in the wage relation heightens the commodity status of labour power. Indeed, Workfirst 'participants,' who now face an unprecedented number of limitations on their politico-legal freedoms as a consequence of the *Ontario Works Act*, have even less freedom to circulate in the labour market than workers occupying the bottom tiers of the THI. And, they confront greater obstacles to unionization than their counterparts in temporary help work not subject to the added state-driven compulsion to engage in TERs.

Workfirst harnesses a welfare-to-work initiative to the TER, thereby revealing the mutually reinforcing relationship between shifting employment norms and workfare-driven social policy, and in so doing it further undermines the capacity of social assistance recipients to move freely in the labour market. Participation in the program is mandatory for 'employable' social assistance recipients, and the penalties for noncompliance are either reductions in social assistance benefits or ineligibility for a finite period. Additionally, once they are engaged in the Workfirst program, the ability of the 'participants' to move within the THI itself is even more constrained: the only types of work on offer are clerical and light industrial work. Thus, the provincial government of Ontario is not only delimiting the terms of unfreedom amongst Workfirst 'participants' (Miles, 1987: 182–3; Satzewich, 1991: 41), it is exercising a coercive role by conditioning social assistance recipients to accept the TER as a norm. Given the two narrow types of work that social assistance recipients are placed into, the composition of the group of workers participating in the program, which, according to program officials, customers, and 'participants' comprises mostly women and recent immigrants, and the substandard conditions of work common in the bottom tiers of the THI, there are some striking similarities between Workfirst 'participants' of the present and workers engaged by private employment agents at the turn of the century. Both groups of workers are situated in the margins of the labour market, and the TER (and its precursors) is the common denominator for their subordinate location. However, if developments in Ontario are indicative of larger trends, then the Canadian state is beginning to treat the present manifestation of the TER (and the agencies positioned at the helm of this triangular employment relationship) quite differently from its precursors. The government virtually ignored the question of regulating private employment agencies in the late nineteenth and early twentieth centuries until organized labour and immigrant communities took political action. However, at present the provincial government of Ontario is taking an active role in legitimizing the activities of private employment agencies (including temporary help agencies) and the TER against the vehement opposition of unions and other social movement groups to all three streams of Ontario Works (Ontario Federation of Labour 1998) and workfare in general. In the case of Workfirst, it is limiting options for social assistance recipients: coercion is replacing consent as a means to secure their participation in the labour market.

Workfirst is only one example of the government's response to the rise of the TER. Nevertheless the design and delivery of this program underscores the need for a comprehensive package of benefits and entitlements surrounding the TER, even though most provincial governments (except Quebec) are not only reticent to take such measures but are moving in the opposite direction. Even more crucially, it highlights the importance of organizing temporary workers collectively. After all, temporary help workers are more vulnerable to downward pressure on wages and working conditions than most groups of workers, especially standard workers, by virtue of the fact that they are rarely unionized and that there are few avenues available for collective representation under the prevailing regime of collective bargaining. This makes them less able to resist the introduction of welfare-to-work initiatives in their industry than, for example, public sector workers, who have demonstrated the capacity to organize against the introduction of such policies because they are backed by strong, vocal unions.

To recall, the comprehensive package of protections surrounding the SER and the measures that curtailed the activities of private employment agencies came about through struggle on the part of individual workers, organized labour, and other segments of civil society, not simply through the Canadian government's tepid endorsement of the sentiments behind the maxim 'labour is not a commodity' (Chapters 1 and 2). There is evidence of this in the Canadian context, where immigrant workers' complaints led to the 1905 *Royal Commission appointed to inquire into the Immigration of Italian Labourers to Montreal* (their testimonies of abuse sparked widespread public criticism of the private employment agency industry), and where representatives of organized labour successfully lobbied for stricter regulations governing the activities of these actors. Indeed, there is a historical basis for this type of employment relationship, and history may also provide some lessons in how to minimize the coercive dimensions of its newest manifestation.

Chapter 8

The Challenge of Limiting
Labour Market Fragmentation

In certain historical moments it becomes clear that (a) not all those who want to work for a wage can be employed; (b) not all those who work for a wage receive a wage sufficient to satisfy their historically given habits and tastes; and (c) not all work provides autonomous access to the means of subsistence ... These problems which become politically prominent in particular historical moments are in fact general and persistent because they are part of the system's basic structure. (Picchio, 1992: 119)

This book began with the dual observation that the norm of the full-time permanent job – along with its typical package of benefits – is giving way to the spread of nonstandard employment relationships and that temporary help workers, whose precarious employment relationships reveal the character of this development, have the appearance of commodities that are listed, bought, sold, and traded in the labour market. Its central objective was to probe the commodity status of labour power under capitalism and the gendered ways that states have dealt with it historically through a case study of the TER. Chapters 2 through 7 examined the various manifestations of the TER in Canada from the turn of the century until the late 1990s, finding important points of intersection between the evolution of this employment relationship and the forces compelling countries like Canada to neutralize labour power's commodity status by following the maxim 'labour is not a commodity,' contained in the ILO's founding charter. In turn, the powerful sentiments behind this maxim served as the basis for national and supranational initiatives designed to curtail the activities of private employment agencies and to encourage the establishment of a system of free public employment services beginning in the post-First World War era. As the century progressed, these measures also contributed to the rise of the SER in advanced welfare states: this *normative* model of employment was the product of what was arguably the most profound, though highly gendered and racialized, mediation of the tension in capitalist labour markets surrounding the free circulation of labour power. But, while the SER was the norm for a rather lengthy period, the regulatory regime that brought it to dominance began to reach its limits in the 1970s, a process reinforced by the feminization of employment. In the next two decades, feminization not only connoted rising female labour force participation rates but three other central dimensions as well: namely, persisting sex segregation; continuing income and occupational polarization between women and men, and among women and men themselves; and growing casualization or the 'gendering of jobs.' One important outcome of these developments is that labour market actors such as the temporary help agency increasingly treat workers situated at the expanding margins of the labour market like commodities.

As this book has shown, the tendency to commodify labour power, always present in capitalist labour markets, intensifies with the decline of security and freedom in the wage relation: witness the erosion of the SER and the coincident spread of the TER beginning in the 1970s. Thus, its primary contribution lies in highlighting the persistence of an employment relationship throughout the twentieth century, albeit in different forms, where workers' labour power is acutely vulnerable to extreme forms of commodification. The various means by which states have managed the commodity status of labour power historically are widely documented; for example, the way that the Canadian state balanced the competing interests of capital and organized labour after the Second World War by extending an unprecedented level of security to a well-defined group of (largely male) workers through the wage relation, has received considerable scholarly attention. But there has been substantially less scrutiny of the persistence of precarious employment relationships like the TER and its precursors, especially their coexistence alongside the SER, even though their resilience is equally central to understanding labour power's commodity status under capitalism and its gendered underpinnings. While there is a tendency among scholars to characterize nonstandard forms of employment, such as temporary help work, as 'new' and the regulatory regime developing alongside them as breaking from the Fordist paradigm, the history and evolution of the TER demands a more nuanced understanding. Indeed, the central actors in the

TER have their roots in a pre-existing social formation, revealing that its contemporary manifestation is a product of both continuity and change and its most recent variant reflects the erosion of the SER as a *normative* model of employment and the feminization of employment norms.

This chapter recalls the evolution of the TER in Canada, harnessing the theoretical argument to the historical case study. It then addresses a central question raised by the book's findings: what are the prospects for improving the conditions of employment for temporary help workers? Specifically, what can unions and other social movement groups do to organize termporary help workers collectively?

The Evolving Temporary Employment Relationship

In the late nineteenth century, the TER did not exist in its present form. Nor did temporary help agencies. However, intermediaries such as padrones and general labour agents played a vital role in the Canadian labour market, one that prefigured the role of the 'classic' temporary help agency and its more mature incarnation in several crucial respects. Accordingly, the types of employment relationships engendered by the early private employment agency industry served as templates for the THI at its inception. Moreover, the poor conditions of employment endured by workers engaged by early private employment agents at the turn of the century share some striking similarities with those experienced by temporary help workers situated in the bottom tiers of the THI in the late 1990s.

Private employment agents of the late nineteenth and early twentieth centuries imported workers from abroad with the aim of serving the labour needs of the emerging capitalist class, who decried the shortage of agricultural and industrial workers. Although the agents' recruitment activities conflicted with the Canadian government's nation-building objectives, which involved treating the white British agricultural settler as the only 'desirable' type of immigrant, in reality they complemented its expansionary project. They allowed the government to advance modern labour market principles on the one hand, while still preserving age-old customs, habits, and practices that limited the mobility of a well-defined group of workers on the other.

The typical male worker engaged by private employment agents at the turn of the century was the Southern and Eastern European industrial or agricultural worker. In turn, many women recruited for domestic work by philanthropic agencies from 1900 onwards emigrated not only from Britain but also from continental Europe and the Caribbean. Hence, the profiles of these two groups of workers differed sharply from the image of the 'desirable' British agricultural settler and that of the 'mother of the nation.' Many of the workers recruited by private employment agents (both male and female) either came as 'guest workers' bound to work in railway construction, agriculture, or mining for the duration of their stay in Canada, or, by virtue of their occupation, were not fully protected as citizen-workers. A sizeable number had also signed contracts abroad that made them quasi-indentured labourers; although contracts of this sort were illegal in Canada at the time, agents and employers often used them to coercive ends and government officials largely overlooked abusive practices.

At the turn of the century, the Canadian state encouraged the formation of a class of Canadian-born free wage labourers with British roots. But, at the same time it relied heavily on exploited foreign-born labourers recruited by private employment agents to build an agricultural and industrial proletariat. As Chapter 2 documented, agents hired by steamship and railway companies were central to achieving these objectives and the Canadian state ignored their coercive practices until organized labour and organizations of immigrants took it to task. The success of early private employment agents rested on the highly racialized division of labour built into the nation-building process. In the early Dominion of Canada, the 'sons and daughters of the empire' enjoyed the full benefits and protections of the free wage labour market while the largely non-British immigrants and migrants engaged by private employment agents were often denied basic freedoms of mobility. Thus, the activities of private employment agents in this era support the historical link, as theorized by Miles (1987) and Satzewich (1991), between the process of racialization and forms of labour exploitation where labour power is recruited and exploited through various forms of political and legal compulsion.

Only when it became clear that groups of immigrant workers, opposition MPs, and organized labour were prepared to challenge the state in order to extend the benefits of free wage labour market to a more representative group of primarily male workers did the federal government begin to back away from its acceptance of these labour market entities. The most important turning point in this process occurred when the *Royal Commission Appointed to Inquire into the Immigration of Italian Labourers to Montreal* (1905) released its findings. Embarrassed by the graphic documentation of abuses, MPs began to introduce immigration legislation designed to restrict the activities of private employment agencies abroad as well as within and between provincial borders. Still, while a survey of reports documenting the implementation of such measures gives the impression that tough immigration legislation eliminated the most disreputable intermediaries from the Canadian labour market by the late 1910s, the findings of this book point to a more nuanced conclusion. They indicate that federal immigration legislation and early provincial employment agency acts prompted various segments of the industry to decline and others to take on new forms. They also suggest that the new types of private employment agencies thriving in the labour market towards the end of the first decade of the twentieth century – mainly those catering to the clerical sector – owed their success to the narrow group of workers that they recruited and placed in employment. By the late 1910s, the workers these agencies placed were not male immigrant workers in agriculture and industry or immigrant women domestic workers, but instead, young, well-educated, Canadian-born, middle-class women. For this reason, the agencies escaped criticism from the organized (male) labour movement, social reformers, and the immigrant communities that had objected to the practices of private employment agencies acting abroad and/or engaging immigrants.

An instructive example of a group of agencies thriving in from 1910 through 1920 were agencies run by typewriting companies in the Province of Ontario. These agencies recruited and placed young women typists and stenographers in businesses requiring clerical assistance on a temporary basis with the explicit objective of selling typewriter equipment. The agencies' existence provide both a historical and conceptual bridge between private employment agents operating at the turn of the century and the 'classic' temporary help agency. The emergence of these agencies and the corresponding decline of the more unscrupulous segments of the industry reveal that, although the form of state intervention into labour market relations changed drastically from the late 1800s until the 1930s, neither private employment agencies nor employment relationships resembling the TER disappeared from the labour market entirely. Instead, the state opted to address the perceived needs of a well-defined group of workers (i.e., largely white male breadwinners) by initiating some crucial restraints on the market circulation of labour power, while in turn still satisfying employers' demands for casual office workers by carefully delineating which groups of workers could be recruited and placed by private employment agencies. Consequently, at a conceptual level, by the end of the first quarter of the century the newest segment of the industry in Ontario and elsewhere effectively exchanged immigrant workers – whose cost to social reproduction was borne largely by the sending country – for women whose unpaid domestic labour contributed to producing and maintaining the population, but whose own social reproduction was presumed to depend upon the male wage. Simultaneously, the state shifted its stance away from accepting the highly racialized forms of labour recruitment and exploitation practised by private employment agents to tacitly accepting the feminization of the private employment agency industry.

Given the findings of Chapters 2 and 3, the connection between private employment agencies operated by typewriting companies and the 'classic' temporary help agency catering to the clerical sector in the post–Second World War period is quite apparent. There is also a striking resemblance between the young Canadian-born women first engaged by typewriting firms in the Province of Ontario and the white middle-class married women filling the ranks of the early Canadian THI. Under the hegemony of the ideology of domesticity, both sets of workers were considered secondary breadwinners, 'preferring' short-term paid employment where they were not required to make a commitment to a given employer. However, the married women working in the THI in the 1950s and 1960s had to contend with the accelerated rise of the SER as well as the explicit marriage bars that accompanied it. These women lacked the independence of the single women engaged by employment agencies run by typewriter companies because of their perceived 'natural' role in social reproduction. As well, legislative measures designed to exclude married women from specific sectors of the economy prevented them from circulating freely in the labour market. Given the wealth of scholarly literature on mechanisms designed to limit women's labour force participation in post–Second World War Canada, a substantial proportion of the married women initially working through the THI presumably participated in the labour market during the war but were expelled shortly afterwards. Ironically, by the end of this era, officials in the THI came to argue that temporary help agencies provided married women with a work life re-entry vehicle, what one prominent industry official pejoratively labeled a 'halfway house' for housewives.

On first reading, it seems counter-intuitive that the THI emerged as a formal entity in the labour market when the SER was rising to dominance, especially during a period in which the state was fairly successful at balancing the interests of capital and organized labour. Upon greater scrutiny, however, it is evident that the THI actually played a vital role in upholding this balance: it positioned the TER as a supplement to the SER. For this reason, the industry's very existence was important to the Canadian state; it helped to enable the government to cement the postwar compromise by introducing the SER while embracing other highly precarious forms of employment that represent the flip side of this employment relationship.

Although the Canadian state, following on the heels of other emerging capitalist welfare states, forged an accord between capital and organized labour after the Second World War, tensions between these actors persisted in the postwar era. Capital participated in the postwar compromise, committing employers to making key concessions to a well-defined group of workers, but it continued to have a stake in securing a consistent supply of casual workers. Organized labour was similarly vehement in its opposing demand for extending the SER to a broader group of workers outside core sectors of the economy; still, its historic support for the 'family wage' contributed to its uneasy relationship with the 'woman question,' leading various segments of the labour movement to passively accept state policies limiting married women's labour force participation. Consequently, it effectively turned a blind eye to the THI's strategy of targeting white middle-class married women as its chief workers and claiming employer status as a means of counteracting the predictable challenge that temporary help agencies were just like other private employment agencies.

In light of the demands of employers for casual clerical workers and the relative silence on the part of organized labour on the role and function of the THI, the Canadian state neglected the issue of regulating and monitoring temporary help agencies through the post–Second World War era. For example, at the provincial level most private employment agency acts failed to take the rise of the THI into account in the 1950s and 1960s. This regulatory vacuum is not surprising since the THI crafted a highly effective lobbying campaign from its inception into the 1970s, arguing that 'a temporary help service is an independent organization engaged in the business of providing its own employees to perform work, on a time basis for its customer firms' (Fromstein, 1978: 230). In contrast to its earliest precursors, or even its immediate forerunners, the 'classic' temporary help agency did not situate itself as a labour market intermediary. Instead, it posed as a labour-only contractor to its customers and as an employer to the (largely women) workers that it engaged. Given that it placed women workers almost exclusively in the clerical sector on a temporary basis, the temporary help agency did not

threaten the hegemony of the SER or the complex regulatory apparatus surrounding it; indeed, it reinforced it. For this reason, the THI's
strategy was very successful in the Canadian context. By the mid-1960s,
then, it had attained conditional legitimacy in the labour market,
escaping regulation. The TER and the so-called temporary help
formula became the newest manifestation of an old theme, and
feminization supplemented racialization as a means by which the THI
secured its workforce.

After the THI attained legitimacy by situating the TER as a necessary
supplement to the SER in the postwar era, the shape of the Canadian
labour market began to change dramatically. In the early 1970s, many
international and national developments contributed to undermining
the SER as the *normative* model of employment. At the national level, the
Canadian government moved away from its full-employment objective,
which was always rather tenuous and was never intended to include
women, towards embracing an anti-inflationary program that spurred
the rise and spread of non-standard forms of employment and the
feminization of the labour force. This set of developments opened up a
new space for the THI in the labour market, and, although the THI
continued to distance itself from other segments of the private employment agency industry, it also created a host of possible reconfigurations
for the industry. Not only had it survived the postwar era unaffected by
the norms surrounding full-time permanent employment, the THI
emerged from the 1960s with a bold new image, an image that was
sufficiently strong that the THI no longer had to rely on its prior mediating role to preserve the legitimacy of temporary help work. The THI
abandoned the role that it had played in the post–Second World War
labour market and began to situate the TER as an alternative, as opposed
to a supplement, to the SER, and one without an equivalent set of social
protections for temporary help workers. In this way, it built upon the
dramatic changes in the labour market, the exceptionally stable regulatory regime surrounding private employment agencies, the removal of
explicit marriage bars, and the diminishing force of the ideology of
domesticity.

At the level of industry strategy, in the post-1970 period temporary
help agencies shifted their emphasis away from supplying 'stop-gap'
workers to selling 'staffing services.' The larger aim behind this shift in
strategy was to appeal to a broader cross-section of workers, including
not only married women with family responsibilities but also workers
displaced from the SER and young people entering the labour market.

In turn, the THI began to sell its services as a way for employers to avoid employment-related responsibilities, including those related to hiring, dismissal, payroll, and the administration of benefits, as well as to increase their 'numerical flexibility.' By implication, the popular image of the 'Kelly Girl' became less central to driving the success of the THI even though the 'feminized' character of the TER remained. Indeed, the THI's transformation from a female-dominated industry to an industry where sex parity is emerging reveals the industry's ability to alter both its 'feminine' face and its role as a supplement to the SER, despite the powerful imagery that it initially relied on to secure legitimacy.

The THI adapted its strategy to suit shifting employment norms, to respond to the interventions of organized labour and to conform with the changing manner in which the state chose to balance the competing interests of capital and organized labour in the early 1970s. The distinct forms that its strategy took in countries such as Germany, where the THI successfully argued that its business involved 'lending out' employees, and Japan, where it characterized temporary help agencies as belonging to the 'worker-dispatching' business, versus Canada in the post-1970 period reveals its striking capability to adapt to different regulatory environments.

A particular variant of the TER persisted alongside the spread of other types of nonstandard employment relationships from the 1970s onwards, just as specific variations had endured from the turn of the century to the interwar years and in the post-Second World War era. However, in contrast to the two-and-a-half decades following the Second World War, when many advanced capitalist welfare states (including Canada) took significant measures to protect workers from market forces, the high degree of security and freedom associated with the wage relation began to contract; indeed, beginning in the early 1970s, states deregulated national labour markets and abandoned supranational measures originally designed to protect workers moving within and between borders. The decline of security and durability in employment relationships was most apparent for workers either expelled from the SER or from core sectors where the SER (and its associated package of protections) had prevailed since the Second World War; a key example here is the sharp decline of men's employment in Canadian manufacturing in the late 1980s and early 1990s. However, the transformation of the THI, particularly its emphasis on moving companies out of the business of 'managing labour,' exposes another dimension of this complex set of developments, offering insights into the future trajectory of employment relations and the changing mode of state intervention into labour relations.

The history and evolution of the TER in Canada reveals that there has always been dualism in the labour market. As numerous scholars have demonstrated theoretically and historically, dividing workers on the basis of ascriptive characteristics and their presumed roles in the sphere of social reproduction is central to the functioning of capitalist labour markets (Peck, 1996; Picchio, 1992; Rubery and Humphries, 1984). Still, with the erosion of the standard wage relation, evidenced by the decline of the SER and the feminization of employment, the newest manifestation of the TER offered by the THI threatens to exaggerate existing divisions in the labour market. At the micro-level, temporary help agencies are 'promising flexibility' to the workers that they engage, many of whom continue to be women, immigrants, and workers belonging to other marginalized groups, but they are 'delivering precariousness.' Moreover, when the persistently precarious character of the TER is examined in light of macro-level trends associated with the feminization of employment, the larger significance of its spread signals more than simply the extension of feminized employment relationships to a growing diversity of working people: if developments in the THI are indicative of broader changes in the labour market, then the spread of the TER signifies the feminization of employment *norms*.

Chapter 1 argued that the notion of the TER serves as both a descriptive and an analytic concept, because, on the one hand it demonstrates the persisting dualism in the Canadian labour market, and on the other hand, it reveals the expansion of precarious jobs at its expanding margins. With the case study complete, it is now possible to assert that the spread of the TER signals the growth of precarious forms of employment in the current period, particularly among women and immigrants,[1] and the extension of a highly unstable model of employment to workers in a growing number of sectors and occupations. The absence of a comprehensive regulatory framework surrounding the TER both in Canada and at a supranational level, and the growing evidence of state acceptance of the TER evident in the shift from welfare-oriented to workfare-driven social policy reinforces this conclusion.[2]

The spread of the TER in the late 1990s and its increasingly precarious character still underscores the fragile balance required to fulfil the maxim 'labour is not a commodity,' first etched into the ILO's founding charter and later used to limit the activities of private employment agencies in the labour market. Labour power is inevitably a commodity under capitalism, but its commodification comes into clearer view with the erosion of security and freedom in the wage relation. It is for this reason that temporary help workers, more than perhaps any other category of workers in the contemporary labour market, have the appearance of commodities. These workers, particularly women, immigrants, and other marginalized groups confined to the bottom rungs of the THI, are subject to a highly feminized and racialized variant of the TER, one whose precarious character will persist until the state and organized labour are moved to action.

Prospects for Organizing Temporary Help Workers

Like their predecessors, temporary help workers face considerable obstacles to resisting their substandard conditions of employment in the late 1990s. In the early part of the twentieth century, many workers engaged by private employment agencies confronted barriers to organization, because as immigrants and migrants they lacked full social citizenship rights. Rather than agitating for protections for these workers, core segments of the organized labour movement pursued an exclusionary strategy around the turn of the century – one that conformed with the highly racialized nation-building discourses espoused by the Dominion government – and even beyond, as it struggled to make the SER a norm. Similarly, from the interwar years until the early 1970s, temporary help workers experienced significant impediments to unionization since the THI successfully situated the TER as a 'supplement' to the SER. As a result, these predominantly white middle-class married women had virtually no access to the benefits first formally accorded to largely male blue-collar workers by Order in Council PC 1003. Here, too, most branches of organized labour took a relatively passive approach to the question of the THI, and they did not work to extend collective bargaining rights to workers engaged in nonstandard forms of employment. In the late 1990s, fundamental obstacles to organizing temporary help workers persist, due to the prevailing worksite-based regime of collective bargaining, where standard workers still benefit most from unionization. Temporary help workers are unquestionably a difficult group of workers to unionize within conventional structures since they work in multiple locations, have shorter job tenure than the standard worker, and belong to a wide array of occupational groupings. Yet, while it requires a paradigm shift at the level of union policy and state policy, the need to cultivate 'new' models for organizing workers falling outside the SER is quite compelling.

Given the continued existence of atypical employment relationships like the TER, it is instructive to conclude by examining the limits and possibilities of the prevailing regime of collective bargaining in Canada, where temporary help workers and other nonstandard workers are concerned, offering a preliminary typology of alternative models and addressing the pressing issue of organizing temporary help workers.

Collective Bargaining in Canada

The prevailing regime of collective bargaining in Canada has its origins in Order in Council PC 1003, a legislative instrument inspired by the American *Wagner Act* (1944), which brought the 'New Deal Model' of industrial relations to dominance in North America (Forrest, 1995; Gonick, Phillips, and Vorst, 1995; O'Grady, 1991; Russell, 1995). This regime introduced compulsory union recognition and the right to bargain collectively in Canada and was widely touted as a victory for organized labour. In substance, PC 1003 brought certification by cards or majority vote; exclusive bargaining-agent status defined by bargaining units; protection against 'unfair practices'; and enforceable obligations on employers to bargain in good faith (O'Grady 1991: 157). But despite its obvious merits, PC 1003 set considerable constraints on the bargaining process in Canada, limits that continue to exist.

The central distinguishing features of PC 1003 contributed to the emergence of a highly decentralized model of collective bargaining, one that is premised on the assumption that bargaining will not occur at a sectoral or regional level (see also Cameron, 1995: 165; O'Grady, 1991: 158). Not surprisingly, therefore, the regime of collective bargaining originally fostered by PC 1003 was highly gendered (Forrest, 1995; Fudge, 1993; D. MacDonald, 1998a, b). As Ann Forrest (1995: 140) notes: '[PC 1003] accorded rights to men (but not women) because it codified an "industrial model" of workers' rights. What emerged in the 1940s was a compromise designed to quell unrest among blue-caller workers in the mass-production and resource industries. As a practical matter, therefore, the promise of compulsory collective bargaining was made (only) to industrial workers and men.' Although it did not explicitly exclude women workers from coverage, this legislation was designed to serve the interests of male workers in industrial sectors, many of whom could not sustain single-breadwinner households at the time that it was enacted. Moreover, the narrow and gendered lenses through which labour relations boards have interpreted this legislation have contributed to a fragmented structure of collective bargaining, one that is premised on labour market segmentation rather than on solidarity between all workers. This narrowness has also perpetuated modes of dividing workers within unions, such as through preserving gender-biased seniority rules and creating separate bargaining units for part-time and full-time workers in substantially similar occupations.

Two structural features, in particular, limit the scope of collective bargaining in Canada: bargaining unit determination and the related presumption that collective bargaining will take place at the level of the worksite. In the Canadian context, the bargaining unit is the basic structural element of labour law relations (Fudge, 1993: 234). Provincial and federal labour relations boards determine bargaining units based on well-defined policies and principles. These policies relate to a range of criteria[3] that vary provincially, but the 'community of interest' criterion (and the legal tests that implement it) is of paramount importance in limiting the possibilities for organizing temporary help and other marginalized workers. The legal test for determining the 'community of interest' is significant, because in many respects it simply reflects employers' decisions about how to organize production, decisions that often capitalize by design on dividing workers on the basis of their ascriptive characteristics (e.g., age, race, sex/gender) and their relationship to the sphere of social reproduction.

As Fudge (1993: 233) notes, the test to determine the 'community of interest' in Ontario includes six narrow components: the nature of work performed; the conditions of employment; the skills of employees; administration; geographic circumstances; and functional coherence and interdependence. Thus, there are a number of structural constraints built into this test beyond its baseline assumption that individual worksites are considered 'natural' bargaining units. For example, the Ontario Labour Relations Board effectively uses these criteria to separate women employed in female-dominated workplaces from their male counterparts in similar occupations, a practice that adversely affects women's ability to attain comparable wages and conditions of employment to men in similar occupations (Ontario District Council of the International Ladies' Garment Workers Union and INTERCEDE, 1993). The well-entrenched policy of defining standard units of occupational distinctions compounds the consequences of this practice. The Ontario Labour Relations Board differentiates between a standard production unit and a standard office unit; except where office workers are located inside or adjacent to a plant, the board normally places office and production workers in different units (Fudge, 1993: 235). As well, most provincial labour boards have historically separated part-time and full-time workers, although this practice is changing slowly.[4] The exclusion of homeworkers from bargaining units covering garment workers inside factories is another example of how labour boards' bargaining unit policies isolate standard workers from nonstandard workers (Ontario District Council of the International Ladies' Garment Workers Union and INTERCEDE 1993). Citing case law in Ontario, Forrest (1986: 846) highlights the gender-biased assumptions of the board, whose long-time doctrine implied that most part-time workers not only choose to engage in this form of employment but also are secondary breadwinners: '[The practice of creating] separate units for part-time workers ... reflects the view that these workers generally do not share a community of interest with full-time employees. The former are "primarily concerned with maintaining a convenient work schedule which permits them to accommodate the other important aspects of their lives with their work and with obtaining short-term immediate improvements in remuneration rather than with obtaining life insurance, pension, disability, and other benefit plans; extensive seniority causes; and other long-term benefits." Accordingly, part-time workers will be segregated at the request of either party.' Predictably, the original reasoning behind this policy, which is still worthy of emphasis even though the policy is waning, mirrored a common rationale for labour market segmentation, identified in Chapter 1, where workers who are perceived to have access to alternative forms of subsistence are predominant in sectors and occupations characterized by limited prospects for job advancement.

Under Canada's regime of collective bargaining, the policies and practices associated with defining the 'community of interest' are clearly based on a narrow conception of which factors and indices should serve as the basis of workers' common interests. But beyond playing a role in fragmenting the labour force (as well as union membership) by gender, these policies limit the extent of union power as a whole by promoting certification among small bargaining units. Together, the assumption that individual work sites are 'natural' bargaining units, and the convention of separating standard and nonstandard workers, creates a number of well-documented consequences for unions, two of which are worthy of emphasis here. First, they make it extremely difficult for precariously employed workers, like the majority of temporary help workers, to overcome the hard-bargaining tactics of employers in the long run because they are isolated in small units (Forrest, 1986: 847; D. MacDonald,

1998a: 257). Second, combined with the exclusive representation rights first afforded under PC 1003, these practices perpetuate what Fudge (1993: 241–2) aptly labels a 'symbiotic relationship' between bargaining unit structure and trade union organization:

> Since the prize of exclusive representation goes to the first union which signs up the majority of employees in a proposed bargaining unit, unions tend to accept, rather than challenge, the labour-relations boards' standard units. Because unions are unwilling to take the risk of proposing new bargaining-unit structures, those structures which emerged during the major organizing drives for the 1940s through the 1960s (when only a few, unsuccessful, attempts were made to organize female-dominated sectors and occupations) are frozen in labour-board policy. *In this way, the institutional structures of unions reflect the labour-relations boards' policies regarding standard units. In fact, the boards' standard bargaining units create a profound incentive against the development of innovative organizing structures by trade unions* [my emphasis].

In other words, the twin assumptions that individual worksites are the ideal bargaining units and that standard and nonstandard workers are distinct 'communities of interest' have led unions to draw jurisdictional lines, in conformance with the customs and conventions of provincial labour boards. As a result, unions themselves have contributed to elevating one form of organizing workers over the range of mobilization practices that predated PC 1003, a mode of organizing that fails to take into account workers engaged in a wide range of employment relationships (Annunziato, 1990). This last point is particularly crucial because opening up a dialogue about the prospects for organizing temporary help workers involves first acknowledging that various elements within the labour movement have contributed to the rather unfortunate tendency to emphasize the organization of standard workers over nonstandard workers by focusing on the workplace as their primary site of struggle.

Just as the rise of nonstandard forms of employment undermines the effectiveness of prevailing labour legislation and regulations that take the SER as the norm, it also poses fundamental challenges to union structures, policies, and practices. The project of feminizing unions, in the positive sense of the term (i.e., making unions more accessible to women and responsive to their interests), has always been important. Women have long been marginalized within unions, their militancy

frequently underemphasized and their acts of resistance often misinter-
preted (Guard 1995), and relegated to insecure segments of the labour
market where unionization is virtually impossible: witness the historically
precarious character of temporary help work, where workers rarely benefit from basic collective bargaining rights. However, as evidenced by the
findings of Chapters 4, 5, and 6, this project is becoming even more
pressing with the feminization of employment norms. The restructuring
in the labour market that entails the feminization of employment 'not
only threatens our norm of the male worker with a dependent family, *it
threatens our norm of collective bargaining as the most suitable means of improving the terms and conditions of employment*' [my emphasis] (Fudge, 1993:
232). The feminization of employment translates into more exclusions
from existing collective bargaining legislation, forcing a larger number
of workers to rely on minimum standards legislation as their primary
source of protection under labour law. Correspondingly, intensifying sex
segregation and income and occupational polarization amounts to deepening the inherent biases in the existing regime of collective bargaining,
which encourages the separation of standard office units and production units. Thus, although labour boards are already inclined to separate
workers by occupation, the nature of the work performed, and the skill
of employees – with the aim of preventing fragmentation within bargaining units – the growing polarization in the labour market reinforces
these practices instead of breaking them down. Finally, the casualization
of employment or the appearance of more 'women's work' in the market
means that a shrinking percentage of workers are standard workers and/
or eligible for the comprehensive package of benefits and entitlements
associated with this SER, further narrowing the already limited scope of
collective bargaining.

The prevailing regime of collective bargaining in Canada, which organized labour struggled to secure, has served rather well its intended
targets: namely, mainly male workers in mass production, primary
(nonagricultural) and transportation sectors. However, due to its inherent biases, it never met the needs of workers excluded from the SER,
disproportionately women, immigrants, and Aboriginal people. Although
organized labour has, at many crucial junctures, attempted to extend
the net of collective bargaining in Canada, it has never successfully
addressed the structural problems inherent within it, with the unfortunate consequence of contributing to a system that protects standard
workers to the exclusion of other important groups of workers. For this
reason, union policies and practices require refinement and reorientation

to suit the needs of the expanding group of workers situated at the margins of the Canadian labour market.

Towards an Alternative Model

The difficulties encountered by organized labour in its attempts to address the needs of the growing number of marginalized workers in Canada and the United States has led a number of scholars to explore alternative models of unionism. In devising templates for adapting union policy to better represent the 'new majority' (i.e., women, immigrants and minority workers) (Cobble, 1993), many researchers embrace the notion of 'broader-based bargaining,' a shorthand for a range of mechanisms designed to enable unions to protect workers who are unable to organize under PC 1003 or the *Wagner Act* model of industrial relations.[5] Consequently, researchers are re-examining unconventional forms of unionization at the regional and local levels in the two countries and beginning to advance alternative modes of organizing workers that could be accommodated within existing structures.

Existing Models

Broader-based bargaining is not completely foreign to the Canadian system of collective bargaining even though the worksite-based unionism envisioned by the drafters of PC 1003 remains dominant. Indeed, as noted in Chapter 6, forms of province-wide bargaining exist in the construction industry in most provinces, and Quebec's *Collective Agreement Decrees Act* (1934) and the failed Baigent-Ready proposals in British Columbia provide examples of legislation that draw on such principles.

Quebec's *Collective Agreement Decrees Act* (1934) is the best-known example of legislation designed to encourage broader-based bargaining in Canada. A product of the Great Depression era, this act enables the provincial government to extend judicially some provisions of a collective agreement to both workers and employers in a particular location or sector who were not parties to the original agreement (D. MacDonald, 1998a; Schenk, 1995). This legislation was designed to reduce 'unfair' competition between different employers in the same region or in a specific sector by raising labour standards. Under this system, either employers or workers may apply to the minister of labour for the extension of key provisions of a collective agreement, including those related to wages, hours of work, and apprenticeships, to nonunionized firms in the same sector. In such circumstances, extension is conditional upon these provisions being 'voluntarily accepted' by a substantial percentage of the industrial sector, a rather imprecise measure,[6] and, once extension occurs, a committee composed of an equal number of employers and employees is responsible for enforcing the Decree (Schenk, 1995: 203).[7]

The model of broader-based bargaining advanced under the Quebec Decree System is particularly relevant to raising standards in small workplaces since it requires no formal certification before negotiations take place. Not surprisingly, therefore, a large number of economic sectors covered by Decrees are composed of highly competitive small- and medium-sized workplaces (Trudeau, 1998). As Chris Schenk (1995: 203) incisively notes, '[t]he strength of the Decree System is that it offers an intermediate between the decentralized model of PC 1003 and mandated multi-employer bargaining. In a context of the PC 1003 model of bargaining it provides a valuable mechanism for reaching unorganized workers in a particular sector.' However, aside from the fact that Decrees only cover about 6 per cent of Quebec's workers, the most significant weakness of the legislation is its undemocratic nature, the enormous discretionary powers it gives to the Ministry of Labour over both the introduction and enforcement of Decrees (D. MacDonald, 1998a: 276; Schenk; 1995: 205).

Although it never came to fruition, the *Baigent-Ready Report* (1992), which made recommendations for labour law reform in the province of British Columbia, also included proposals for broader-based bargaining certification and collective bargaining.[8] This report took the limits of the *Wagner Act* model of industrial relations as its point of departure and called for a form of sectoral certification. It recommended that 'unions at *small* enterprises [my emphasis] which have been historically under represented by trade unions be allowed to amalgamate their bargaining units for the purpose of bargaining jointly with their employers' (D. MacDonald, 1998a: 269).[9] Thus, it encouraged sectors composed of low-waged, precariously employed workers to bargain together through the introduction of one bargaining unit certification to cover all working people in a given sector or geographic area. It also allowed for the extension of sectoral agreements to new workplaces midway through the life of the collective agreement if the union could demonstrate sufficient support from additional locations within the sector, a feature of the proposal that became extremely controversial (270).

While the Baigent-Ready proposal was based on a more democratic set of principles than the Quebec *Collective Agreements Decrees Act*, it also had significant shortcomings, two of which are important to note. First, it focused exclusively on sectors rather than on groups of workers, which were historically underrepresented by unions, setting clear limits on the number of workers that would actually benefit from the legislation. Second, its stipulation that each workplace in a given sector could not employ more than fifty employees (or their equivalent) set unnecessarily strict criteria for certification. As Diane MacDonald (1998a: 274) argues in critiquing this proposal: '[t]o address the needs of the restructured labour market,' Baigent and Ready should have targeted 'both those who are employed in small workplaces (as set out in the Baigent/Ready proposal), and those employed in precarious or contingent forms of employment (e.g., temporary, contract and seasonal workers).' Had it been implemented, this legislation would not have covered temporary help workers moving within and between large firms in a given sector or between sectors in a specific geographical region. As well, unlike the Quebec Decree System, this model would not have allowed the terms of a collective agreement to be extended to non-union employees and employers.[10]

These models borrowed from the type of craft-based model of organizing workers that still prevails, at least to some extent, in the construction industry.[11] But, what is even more important for our purposes, the Baigent-Ready proposal and legislation facilitating broader-based bargaining, such as Quebec's *Collective Agreements Decrees Act*, also took direction from some uncommon or less well-established models of organizing workers designed to cultivate unionization (or collective representation of some sort) among workers in segments of the economy such as the service sector that are virtually impossible to organize under the present regime (Cobble, 1993; Wial, 1993). Because they attempt to move beyond the rather static models of worksite, enterprise, and industrial unionism dominant in both Canada and the United States since the postwar period, these 'new' models deserve serious scrutiny in devising a set of medium-term strategies for facilitating collective representation among temporary help workers.

A Typology of Models

Scholarly literature advancing 'new' models for organizing workers begins with the following basic premise: the worksite-based model of collective bargaining is outdated because it cannot accommodate workers that move from employer to employer and from industry to industry. This job-mobility path has always been common among women,[12] and is increasingly prevalent among low-wage service sector workers as well as other types of workers (including professionals) due to the growth of involuntary self-employment, contract work and, of course, temporary help work (Cobble, 1994: 286; Heckscher, 1988: 177; Wial, 1993: 670). However, after identifying the fundamental problem with the regime, scholars follow several distinct paths, examining and evaluating different models to suit distinct segments of the working population; the dominant scholarly trajectories borrow elements from associational, craft/occupational, and geographical unionism.

One trajectory advances a variant of 'unionism' that is reminiscent of a professional association rather than a union per se, geared to workers ranging from professionals confronting corporate restructuring to recently displaced workers seeking the type of representation they once enjoyed from a worksite-based union. This model, commonly referred to as 'associational unionism,' was first advanced by Charles Heckscher in his book *The New Unionism: Employee Involvement in the Changing Corporation* (1988). Heckscher constructs a model of decentralized representation built around workers' common identification with a sector, a profession, or any other basis of identity that is appropriate, including race, gender, ethnicity, and geography, rather than around a single employer or employment contract (9–11). His model resembles a service organization or political pressure group more than a traditional union. For Heckscher, associations should focus on the following: principles (e.g., professional excellence); internal education and participation; diverse forms of representation and service (e.g., the provision of benefits and training); pressure and negotiation tactics beyond the conventional strike; and 'extended alliances' with community groups and related organizations (188–90).

Heckscher's model of associational unionism, as well as other models borrowing from his proposals, has been sharply criticized both within union circles and among academics seeking to preserve union structures, not only because it eliminates exclusive representation on the basis of occupation, industry, employer, and worksite, but also, more crucially, because 'it dilutes the economic strength of workers' by de-emphasizing collective bargaining and introducing multilateral negotiations (Middleton, 1996; Wial, 1993: 689). If associational unionism, as it is conceived by Heckscher, is to serve as anything more than a transitional model of organizing, it has the potential to take the union out of the union structure. Still, as a transitional model of organizing and representing workers, this model deserves some consideration because it can offer a measure of representation to workers who are not attached to a single employer in either a clearly defined long-term employment relationship or based at a single workplace. A number of organizations representing marginalized workers in the United States, such as the Carolina Alliance for Fair Employment (CAFE), and, in Canada, the Toronto-based Homeworkers' Association run by UNITE (formerly the International Ladies' Garment Workers Union),[13] have taken some insights from this type of model in creating pre-union structures.

A second model of unionism that offers an alternative to the worksite-based model of unionism dominant in Canada and in the United States, but is quite distinct from associational unionism, is craft/occupational unionism. It is common in the construction industry and associated trades and it was once prevalent among waitresses and other food-service workers. Thus, it has considerable potential for workers with clearly defined occupational ties as well as for workers with a clear affiliation to a sector or a trade (Armstrong, 1993; Cobble, 1994; Middleton, 1996). Craft/occupational unionism was the dominant form of union structure in North America before the rise of mass production, and at present there is a growing movement to revive it to suit the needs of women, minorities and low-wage service workers, such as waitresses and janitors.[14]

As Dorothy Sue Cobble (1991, 1996) illustrates, craft/occupational unionism is characterized by four features. First, workers are organized based on a common sense of occupational identity[15] and loyalty to the trade/occupation rather than to the employer. Second, the union controls the labour supply in the occupation through administering a system based on hiring halls and closed shops. The hiring hall is of particular interest here because it takes over the role of the private employment agency by engaging in recruitment, placement, and monitoring workers' performance, as was the case with waitresses and as continues to be common among construction unions.[16] Third, benefits and entitlements are extended to workers on the basis of union membership instead of worksite affiliation. As a result, under a craft/occupational-based model, workers do not have job security at a particular worksite or with a specific employer, but the union, through the hiring hall, provides them with employment security across the industry or sector and employment benefits beyond job tenure. Fourth, the union controls occupational performance standards through 'peer management' and other measures, and in so doing shoulders responsibility for workers' performance and thereby contributes to building industry standards as a whole (Cobble, 1996: 345).

In the contemporary context, craft/occupational unionism offers an interesting prototype for service sector workers as well as for teachers and nurses whose needs cannot be met by either a traditional worksite-based union or a professional association. However, the primary critique of this model is that, on its own terms, it has limitations with respect to organizing the growing number of unorganized low-wage workers with limited occupational affiliations. As Wial (1993: 686) argues, 'it is not clear ... that the craft model of organization is applicable *in toto* to low-wage service workers today,' since these workers generally lack the occupational consciousness that has historically characterized craft unions. Although this critique has some merits, several variants of craft/occupational unionism themselves could offer a solution to the problem that Wial raises.

In the early twentieth century, before the New Deal model of industrial relations emerged, there were two transitional forms of craft unionism in Canada and the United States: federated craft unionism and amalgamated craft unionism (Wial, 1993; Savage, 1971). In a federated structure, craft unions in related fields, such as waitering and hotel services, came together to organize and bargain collectively but retained autonomy in other crucial respects, by, for example, running their own hiring halls, maintaining separate seniority rules, and operating apprenticeship and training programs exclusively for their own membership. In contrast, in an amalgamated structure workers in related occupations merged their separate craft unions into one larger union. Both amalgamated and federated structures provide templates that are potentially useful in adapting the prevailing regimes of collective bargaining to suit unorganized workers, especially given the concept of 'related' fields or occupations that they advance; indeed, the idea of 'related' fields has the potential to unite workers from a range of complementary occupational groupings, such as clerical workers, or even workers from a common industrial sector, such as garment and textile workers.[17]

Craft/occupational unionism offers even more potential if combined with a third model known as 'general geographical' unionism. Although it is outdated and therefore unsuitable for the current period on its own, it is instructive to describe what is meant by 'general geographical' unionism before examining the more relevant hybrid models that are emerging. Predictably, in its purest form, general geographical unionism involves organizing workers according to geography, without regard to their occupational location. The most salient historical example of general geographical unionism existed in western Canada in the early twentieth century. In this era, an entity known as One Big Union (OBU) organized miners, lumberjacks, and low-wage manufacturing workers in British Columbia and Alberta on a general geographical basis and eventually gained a foundation amongst similar workers in the western United States. The OBU developed an organization based on the dual understanding that workers were more mobile across occupations and sectors than geography and that worker solidarity would best flourish along geographical lines. Consequently, the OBU cut across craft and industrial lines by situating the local labour council as its basic organizational unit, although at times it relied on semi-autonomous divisions based on industry or occupational affiliation (Savage, 1971: 188). However, the OBU placed little emphasis on collective bargaining, relying on the general strike as its primary economic leverage point.[18] For this reason, it is an inappropriate model for addressing the challenges posed by the present regime of collective bargaining.

A fourth alternative to the prevailing model of collective bargaining is an amalgam of geographical and occupational unionism termed 'geographical associationalism,' a model still in its infancy. Geographical associationalism is more the product of several recent and highly successful struggles on the part of service workers than of academic theorizing. This model evolved from campaigns by janitors and hotel and restaurant employees, such as the Justice For Janitors Campaign launched by the Service Employees International Union (SEIU).[19] In advocating the hybrid notion of geographical associationalism, both Cobble (1991 and 1994) and Wial (1993) argue that pure occupational unionism is inappropriate for low-wage service workers because they frequently lack strong occupational consciousness. Indeed, they are skeptical of 'peer-based' enforcement of work standards for low-wage service workers, which usually results in including management in the union, because workers' primary workplace grievances tend to be directed towards their immediate supervisors. Instead of adapting conventional models of craft/occupational unionism, they each begin to advance alternatives. Wial's sketch involves a model whereby workers in a specific geographic region unite around loosely defined common occupational interests, based on the concept of 'related' occupations or industries in an attempt to introduce uniform wage and benefit structures on employers in that geographic area. Under this model, unions negotiate regional multi-employer collective agreements to limit wage and benefit competition, much like those recommended in the *Baigent-Ready Report* in British Columbia.

Certainly, this hybrid model makes valuable proposals for improving the conditions of nonstandard workers moving from worksite to worksite, particularly in a long-term sense, since it aims to bring wages out of competition, to create uniform and employer-financed portable benefits for workers, and to 'bring the bottom up' more generally. However, although few scholars have formally addressed the merits and shortcomings of 'geographical associationalism,' there are two fundamental flaws in this model: first, its failure to intervene at the level of controlling the labour supply, a major difference with conventional craft/occupational unionism; and, second, the absence of sufficient mechanisms for workplace representation in the model (Middleton, 1996). Because it neither attempts to control the labour supply to ensure that workers engaged in different types of employment relationships receive equal treatment (even as an interim measure), nor to introduce mechanisms designed to address workers' concerns at the level of the worksite, it offers few avenues for workplace representation (1996). This latter criticism is rather ironic given that the literature on broader-based bargaining attempts to distance itself from the worksite as the primary site of struggle. Still, some measure of worksite-based representation is necessary in order for geographical associationalism to be a viable model. Clearly, precariously employed workers (especially those who work alongside full-time and permanent employees) often have grievances against either their immediate supervisors or their individual employers that must be taken into consideration at the level of the worksite under any structure of unionism. A geographical/associational amalgam of this sort will not provide sufficient representation for such workers unless it takes workplace issues more seriously. There is an additional danger: in concentrating on securing multi-employer agreements that impose uniform conditions top-down in a given region or a particular sector to the exclusion of paying close attention to the nature and shape of the labour supply, rifts may develop between workers who have loyalty towards a single employer and those who move from worksite to worksite. As the history and evolution of the TER demonstrates, the present diversity in employment relationships is partly the product of employers' desires to segment work and divide workers. Therefore, it is crucial that whatever 'new' models of unionism workers and organized labour choose to adopt, they be attentive to the hierarchies generated by employers in their efforts to differentiate the labour supply and avoid reproducing unnecessary divisions.

Options for Organizing Temporary Help Workers

The broader-based models of unionism highlight the limits of collective bargaining as it presently operates in Canada and the United States. But what is more important, they also offer some valuable guidance on how best to cultivate collective organizing amongst temporary help workers, a project that necessitates further research and a dramatic shift in the political terrain if it is to come to fruition. Before introducing some proposals for developing mechanisms to organize and represent temporary help workers collectively, however, a caveat is in order. Even though this book's findings point to the need for collective representation among workers engaged by the THI, organizing temporary help workers is a monumental task. Furthermore, unions are obviously hesitant to organize temporary help workers, because in many instances the interests of temporary help workers are perceived to conflict with their existing membership. More importantly, temporary help workers are very difficult to locate and they require a mode of organization that transcends the employment relationship itself to include representation in recruitment and placement as well as between assignments. These types of structural and political obstacles make it difficult to achieve any form of collective representation within traditional union structures. Still, with such limitations in mind, insights may be drawn from associational, craft/occupational, and general geographical unionism as well as from the emerging hybrid of geographical associationalism.

Despite the very valid critiques of associational unionism, any effort to organize temporary help workers would likely first require an associational-type structure mirroring those currently serving homeworkers and domestic workers. Creating workers' associations would address the pressing need raised by temporary help workers for a forum for workers from the same region or even in the same temporary help agency. Indeed, temporary help workers are frequently isolated in different worksites, with their immediate 'peer group' usually composed of full- and part-time permanent workers, contract workers, or temporary workers engaged in bilateral employment relationships. Although developing this type of pre-union structure would be difficult because the THI is composed of so many small- and medium-sized agencies, one viable approach would involve launching several related associations simultaneously, based on loosely affiliated occupational and sector-based groupings; this strategy would take advantage of the substantial degree of specialization in the contemporary THI.

After this parallel pre-union structure is put into place, the second logical step would involve a two-pronged program aimed at making labour law and union policy more hospitable to temporary help workers, and facilitating broader-based bargaining. First, it would entail founding an umbrella association of temporary help workers (and their advocates) to lobby for changes that would make labour law (both minimum standards and collective bargaining legislation) more responsive to temporary help workers' needs. In advancing a program of legislative reform, many of the ideas introduced in Chapter 6, such as extending benefits beyond job tenure, ensuring equal treatment for temporary help workers, and delineating provisions for conversion, would be of assistance in improving minimum standards legislation. Similarly, the Quebec *Collective Agreement Decrees Act* and the Baigent-Ready proposal could serve as templates in developing proposals for broader-based bargaining to cover temporary help workers. Second, once these groupings become viable, creating nonprofit occupation- or sector-based or, preferably, union-run employment agencies based on a hiring hall model would become a genuine option. It is instructive to take inspiration from Cobble's (1994: 299) historical work here. In describing the merits of the hiring hall as an alternative to the private employment agency and arguing for modernizing this institution as a means of 'making postindustrial unionism possible,' she notes that

> Operating among waitresses, agricultural workers, garment workers, performing artists, janitors, teamsters, longshoremen, and many other groups, [non-profit employment agencies] raised wages in the local labour market, offered portable, high-quality benefits that did not penalize intermittent work force participation, and provided workers with control over their hours in work schedules without jeopardizing their employment security [at the turn of the century] ... *It is important to recognize that hiring halls have not been solely the creature of the building trades and other male-dominated occupations. Historically, they served the interest of women and minorities in a wide range of industries, including garment, agriculture and food-service* [my emphasis].

The significance of creating union-run agencies would be even greater for temporary help workers than other nonstandard workers engaged in bilateral employment relationships because establishing these entities would remove the for-profit intermediary (i.e., the temporary help agency) from the employment relationship altogether. Clearly, the central findings of this book, especially the overwhelming evidence that the TER is a precarious model of employment, underscore the merits of this type of proposal. Other studies that probe the practices of private employment agencies placing domestic workers give further credibility to this strategy. For example, Abigail Bakan and Daiva Stasiulis (1995) demonstrate that private domestic placement agencies not only continue to play a pivotal role in negotiating citizenship rights for migrant domestic workers, they also reproduce highly racialized practices and criteria in the recruitment and placement of female non-citizen domestic workers in Canadian households.

In addition to the obvious possibility of introducing government-run temporary help agencies, reminiscent of the type of public employment services advocated by the ILO at its inception, several models of nonprofit employment agencies are worthy of consideration, including agencies run by voluntary associations, worker cooperatives, and union-run agencies based on the hiring-hall model. It is not feasible to present a comprehensive review of the strengths and weaknesses of each model here.[20] However, establishing either worker cooperatives or union-run agencies would be best in the long term. Union-run agencies, in particular, would contribute to a larger strategy of modifying prevailing union policy and state policy to accommodate broader-based bargaining. Where it is impossible to create union-run agencies in either the short run or the long run, worker-run agencies have the capacity to offer benefits ranging from flexible scheduling, where desirable; variety in assignments; on-the-job training; and portable benefits. Where they already exist, agencies based on a worker cooperative model operate by collecting direct dues from worker members or by a fixed administrative fee charged to each customer; the most successful examples of worker-run agencies operate in a well-defined geographic area and confine themselves to a single sector (e.g., farm labour, domestic work, or landscape work) (Middleton, 1996: 557–9). The common problem with these agencies is that they require worker members to take considerable risks by staking their savings, as well as their job, on a single enterprise. Moreover, although their existence can enhance temporary help workers' conditions of employment, worker cooperatives are usually limited to exerting moral (rather than economic) pressure in calling for better labour standards, because they do not have recourse to the same type of economic sanctions as unions. In these respects, union-run agencies offer a much more suitable alternative since individual workers are not required to make such a significant investment in resources.

The creation of union-run temporary help agencies is also preferable to agencies whose operations are based on a worker cooperative model since it provides a much-needed opening for developing a hybrid of geographical and craft/occupational unionism and extending it to temporary help workers. Once a hiring hall exists, as was the case with waitressing until the 1960s and is still true of the construction industry, the union can intervene in creating industry-wide standards, require pre-hire agreements, set wage scales for temporary help workers that mirror those of full-time permanent workers, offer training and apprenticeship programs, and provide portable benefits. Furthermore, a union-run temporary help agency operating as an arm of a well-established union could contribute to breaking down artificial barriers between standard and nonstandard workers. For example, if the Office and Professional Employees International Union (OPEIU) opened an agency for workers destined for temporary office work in a geographic area where it has a stronghold, it could be highly successful.

Especially if it is twinned with a coherent program of legislative reform, which is unfortunately not on the horizon at present, the introduction of occupationally and sectorally based union-run temporary help agencies would advance the ultimate goal of broader-based bargaining. Indeed, their very existence would contribute to shifting the locus of organizing workers away from the worksite. What is even more important, if union-run temporary help agencies take a long-range view and struggle for parity wages and conditions of employment between standard and nonstandard workers, they have the potential to contribute to eliminating the TER as it presently exists, and therefore to reduce the force of the feminization of employment. The history and evolution of the TER demonstrates that the best prospect for improving the conditions of employment of workers situated at the expanding margins of the labour market is to adapt union and state policies and practices simultaneously.

Appendix A: Qualitative Methodology

The qualitative dimension of my research involved open-ended interviews; an observation at a local branch of a major international temporary help business; and observation at several orientation sessions for the Workfirst program.

Between June 1996 and August 1997, I conducted formal interviews with a total of twenty-four individuals, including ten temporary help workers, five branch managers, representatives from five client firms using temporary help workers, two industry officials and two participants at the International Labour Conference, June 1997 (Appendix B). With the exception of the two Workfirst participants, all the temporary help workers, client firms, and branch managers were contacted (using a snowball sampling) through the temporary help agency where I conducted the observation in December 1996. I sought interviews with temporary help workers of both genders in as wide an array of occupations as possible. I also deliberately chose to interview representatives of client firms from five different sectors. Similarly, I selected branch managers to interview, based on the specialty of the agency they represented. The rationale behind interviewing temporary help workers, managers, and representatives from client firms was to deepen existing understandings of the shape of the TER in practice. Thus, the interview questions were designed to probe the relationships between these three sets of actors and thereby expose the similarities and differences between the SER and the TER. Although all the formal interviews were based on interview schedules, the interviews themselves were open-ended.

I also collected demographic information about the participants based on Statistics Canada's *General Social Survey*. However, since several of the participants did not complete the demographic questionnaire, I only report the sex, occupation/type of work, and date that the interviews took place (Appendix B).

Most interviews were recorded, with the consent of the participants, and various segments of the interviews were transcribed. I also took notes during the interviews. As well, I took extensive fieldnotes to record the day-to-day operations of the temporary help agency where I undertook the branch observation, at the Eighty-Fifth International Labour Conference where I observed the adoption of the new convention on private employment agencies (No. 181), and at Workfirst orientation sessions (although these sessions were also taped). The fieldnotes were extremely valuable in reconstructing the daily operations of the THI and the interactions between agency personnel, temporary help workers, and client firms.

Appendix B: Interviews

Temporary Help Workers

T1   Type of work: administrative assistant
Sex: female
Date: 20 November 1996

T2   Type of work: computer programmer/graphic designer
Sex: male
Date: 9 December 1996

T3   Type of work: clerical worker,
Sex: female
Date: 10 December 1996

T4   Type of work: parts assembly
Sex: female
Date: 12 December 1996

T5   Type of work: executive secretary, small engineering firm
Sex: female
Date: 7 January 1997

T6   Type of work: sales representative (direct sales)
Sex: male
Date: 7 January 1997

T7   Type of work: customer service representative (call centre)
Sex: female
Date: 4 January 1997

T8   Type of work: equipment mechanic, pharmaceutical
            manufacturer
            Sex: male
            Date: 30 January 1997

T9   Type of work: marketing and sales assistant
            Sex: female (former social assistance recipient)
            Date: 17 January 1997

T10   Type of work: sales
            Sex: male (social assistance recipient)
            Date: 20 February 1997

Client Firms

C1   Type of organization: light manufacturer
            Position: human resources manager
            Sex: female
            Date: 11 December 1996

C2   Type of organization: telecommunications firm
            Position: human resources manager
            Sex: male
            Date: 16 December 1996

C3   Type of organization: bank (call centre)
            Position: human resources manager
            Sex: female
            Date: 11 March 1997

C4   Type of organization: pharmaceutical firm
            Position: human resources manager
            Sex: female
            Date: 13 February 1997

C5   Type of organization: heavy manufacturer
            Position: human resources manager
            Sex: female
            Date: 27 January 1997

Branch Managers

M1   Specialization of agency: bilingual clerical/light
           industrial/sales
           Sex: female
           Date: 6 December 1997

M2   Specialization of agency: materials handling/trucking/
           heavy industrial
           Sex: male
           Date: 11 December 1996

M3   Specialization of agency: sales/light industrial
           Sex: female
           Date: 7 January 1997

M4   Specialization of agency: general
           Position: representative of Workfirst broker
           Sex: male
           Date: 29 January 1997

M5   Specialization of agency: outplacement services,
           general labour and clerical
           Position: co-owner
           Sex: male
           Date: 29 January 1997

Industry Officials

I1   Sex: male
           Date: 29 January 1997

I2   Sex: male
           Date: 28 February 1997

ILO Officials

IL1   Position: employer representative
           Sex: male
           Date: 22 April 1997

IL2   Position: worker representative
             Sex: female
             Date: 27 June 1997

Personal Communication

Luc Desmarais, *Conseiller en development de politiques*, 22 May 1997
Elizabeth Majweski, Statistics Canada, 13 March 1998
Helen Moussa, World Council of Churches, 7 July 1997
Informant, Social Assistance Department, Regional Municipality of
    Peel, 17 June 1998

Notes

Introduction

1 The standard employment relationship typically entails 'the employment of workers for wages by another person or firm, where the worker has only one employer, works full time on the employer's premises and expects (or is expected) to be employed indefinitely' (Schellenberg and Clark, 1996: 2). Evolving in the post-Second World War period, this employment relationship 'incorporated a degree of regularity and durability in employment relationships, protected workers from socially unacceptable practices and working conditions, established rights and obligations, and provided a core of social stability to underpin economic growth' (Rogers and Rogers, 1989: 1).

  Still, even at its height the standard employment relationship was merely the *normative* model for employment, a model against which to measure all other forms of employment. It did not reflect the reality of all workers in advanced capitalist welfare states even in the postwar period. While scholars often claim that it was once the norm for most workers, the standard employment relationship represents a (white) male model. Women, immigrants, and people of colour largely lacked the social entitlements associated with the standard employment relationship at its height. Chapter 1 addresses the *normative* character of the standard employment relationship and its gendered underpinnings.

  In contrast, the temporary employment relationship normally entails a triangular relationship between a worker, a temporary help agency, and a client firm that violates all the central features of the standard employment relationship. The worker establishes occupational connections with several employers rather than one, is rarely party to an open-ended employment contract, and is often engaged in part-time or casual employment (Carré,

1992; ILO, 1997; Mangum, Mayall, and Nelson, 1985; OECD, 1995). Chapter 1 also describes the shape of the contemporary temporary employment relationship, and subsequent chapters trace its evolution.

2 At the end of the First World War, Part XIII of the Treaty of Versailles entrenched several principles designed to delineate fundamental workers' rights. Known as the 'workers' clauses,' these principles, which were subsequently modified and endorsed in the constitution of the International Labour Organization (ILO), included the affirmation that 'labour is not a commodity.' This principle suggested quite literally that 'workers should not have to pay for work'; ILO member states therefore used it to devise a framework for regulating the activities of fee-charging employment agencies, early precursors to the temporary help agency (ILO, 1992a, 1992b; ILO, 1997: 5; *Labour Gazette*, December 1919: 1425; O'Higgins, 1997). However, the maxim 'labour is not a commodity,' and the sentiments behind it, also gradually led many national governments to formally extend to workers the right to circulate freely in the labour market. Chapter 1 examines the significance of this maxim in depth.

3 The theoretical literature on segmented labour markets is quite extensive. Subsequent chapters draw primarily on 'third generation' Segmented Labour Markets Theory. This body of literature departs from early dual labour market models adopting a multicausal analysis of segmented labour markets. Unlike many first- and second-generation segmented labour market theorists, third-generation theorists distance themselves from neoclassical economic theory. Positing that, 'segmentation is the outcome of the contingent and dialectical interaction of several causal tendencies,' third-generation theorists are acutely sensitive to the relationship between institutional and social forces (Peck, 1996: 75). Thus, processes of social reproduction, actions of the state, and the struggles of labour and social movements are central to their understanding of the nature and origins of segmented labour markets (Picchio, 1992; Rubery, 1989; Rubery and Wilkinson, 1994).

4 While the Regulation approach is normally identified with the work of French political economists such as Michel Aglietta, Robert Boyer, and Alain Lipietz, this school of thought has become very diverse since its inception in the 1970s, and many other scholars, such as David Harvey (1989), Jane Jenson (1989b), and Bob Jessop (1990), have begun to use its tools. Chapter 1 critically engages with several theorists associated with the French Regulation School.

5 Prior to outlining specific methodologies, several caveats are in order. First, I deliberately chose the Greater Toronto Area as the site for my qualitative

research, since it is where the Canadian temporary help industry is most concentrated. Still, while regulations governing the conduct of private employment agencies and employment standards legislation are quite similar from province to province, the relationships between branch managers of temporary help agencies, customers, and temporary help workers may differ provincially or regionally. Second, it is impossible to attain a complete understanding of the experiences of workers in the temporary help industry by simply observing the workings of a temporary help agency. Hence, I draw on the combination of in-depth interviews, documentary analysis, and historical research to develop the clearest and most deeply textured picture possible of the industry in Canada. Third, I was fortunate to gain access to archival materials and primary statistical data (largely, but not exclusively, confined to the period between the mid-1970s and the mid-1990s) which contribute to presenting a clear picture of the growth of the temporary help industry and the spread of the temporary employment relationship in Canada in an international context. However, this book is not a comprehensive historical work; rather, it is a problem-centred, interdisciplinary study that is organized historically to capture the gendered character of shifting employment norms in the twentieth century in Canada.

6 Unfortunately, the Canadian government only began collecting data on the temporary help industry in the early 1970s, and data-gathering techniques still require improvement. As a consequence, the bulk of the data is derived from the *Survey of Work Arrangements* (1995) – made available through the *Data Liberation Agreement* between Canadian universities and Statistics Canada – the *Labour Force Survey*, and the *Survey of Employment Agencies and Personnel Suppliers*.

7 In subsequent chapters, I refer to the prototypical temporary help agency of the 1950s and 1960s, centred around the image of the 'Kelly Girl' (i.e., the young woman clerical worker presumed to be seeking some 'extra pocket money') as the 'classic' temporary help agency.

8 Readers will note that the discussion of organized labour's response to the rise and spread of the temporary employment relationship is limited in Chapters 4 and 5. This reflects the labour movement's inactivity on this issue from the post-Second World War era to the early 1990s, owing to the fact that unions had effectively agreed to the establishment of the standard employment relationship as a normative model of (white) male employment. As this book illustrates, the capital-labour entente, specifically its introduction of the standard employment relationship, had several trade-offs and consequences. The gendered rise of the temporary employment relationship was chief among them.

288 Notes to pages 14–15

Chapter 1: 'Labour Is Not a Commodity'

1 References to T, M, C, I, IL, and O refer to temporary help workers, agency managers, clients, industry officials, ILO officials, and Workfirst orientation leaders respectively. For example, T7 is a reference to the seventh temporary help worker interviewed (see Appendix B).

2 I place 'normative' in italics for two reasons. First, by characterizing these employment relationships as norms, or potential norms, I am avoiding sweeping generalizations about the character of employment in either the postwar era or the changing nature of employment at present. Second, I use the term as an interpretive device, helpful in examining the nature and form of prevailing employment trends.

Given that norms are 'conventions of behaviour and standards of value which exist independently of individuals and which exercise a *coercive* influence,' they encompass descriptive and prescriptive dimensions. They both mirror and construct reality (Holy and Stuchlik, 1983). Thus, this book does not engage the concept of the SER to represent a singular material employment relationship, or even the most common employment relationship in the postwar period, but as an ideal-type model upon which policies and practices pertaining to employment were based in the post-war period.

3 In this inquiry, I adopt Marx's definition of the terms 'labour' and 'labour power,' and I subscribe to his conception of the commodity form, understanding that 'to become a commodity a product must be transferred to another, whom it will serve as the use-value, by means of an exchange' (Marx, 1913: 41). For the sake of conceptual clarity and to highlight the significance of the ILO's usage of the term 'labour' in its founding charter, it is useful to clarify the distinction between labour and labour power at the outset.

For Marx, labour is the activity of work and labour power is the capacity to work, although many contemporary scholars elide the distinction between labour and labour power (Mandel, 1976: 50; Marx, 1976). Thus, labour power is what workers sell to employers in exchange for a money wage under capitalism. In conventional Marxist terms, it is a commodity whose use adds value to other commodities. The historical precondition for the appearance of labour power in the market is the emergence of the class of 'free wage labourers' that are free in a double sense: they have the legal right to dispose their labour power and they are free from the ownership of the means of production.

In advancing the maxim 'labour is not a commodity' in the early twentieth century, member states of the ILO attempted to consolidate the modern labour market. As the century progressed, however, the activities of member states and the ILO itself (based on this maxim) contributed to obscuring the 'peculiar' (as critical political economists describe it) commodity status of labour power and the important tensions that it gives rise to.

4 The debate over the nature of labour power as a commodity is rooted in the different assumptions of classical and neoclassical economists and critical economists. Classical and neoclassical economists often presume that labour is a commodity like all others (making an elision between labour and labour power), while critical economists (and other social thinkers) characterize labour power as a peculiar commodity because it is attached to the worker.

5 The labour market does not include people engaged in nonmarket activities such as the 'inactive' population, the hidden unemployed (i.e., the labour reserve) and the registered unemployed. However, it relies upon those engaged in nonmarket activities, especially women, youth and elders (who are presumed to have access to other forms of subsistence), to reproduce the labour supply.

6 Robert Miles (1987) and Vic Satzewich (1991) move even beyond Marx to assert that unfree labour is not only characterized by the absence of the wage relation and physical forms of compulsion but also by the imposition (usually by states) of politico-legal constraints affecting the labourer's ability to circulate freely within a given labour market. They define forms of unfree waged labour as occurring when 'the circulation of labour power as a commodity is subject to politico-legal constraints which restrict the individual's ability to determine the allocation of his or her labour power subject to the conditions of the labour market' (Miles, 1987: 32). Labour tenancy, contractual servitude and contract migrant labour are three examples (Miles, 1987: 170–76). Each of these forms of unfree waged labour involve the payment of a cash wage and imply a recruitment system based on individual free choice but economic compulsion is the primary determinant.

In this book, I draw on Miles and Satzewich's insights regarding unfree *waged* labour to highlight the lack of security and freedom in the wage relations of workers engaged in two variants of the TER. I also take direction from their compelling distinction between racialization and racism, and substantiate the historical link that they make between the process of racialization and 'forms of labour exploitation [not only slave labour] where labour power is not commodified (or only partially commodified) or is recruited and exploited primarily by means of political legal compulsion'

(Miles, 1987: 8). Miles (1982: 7) defines racism as 'an ideology which ascribes *negatively* [my emphasis] evaluated characteristics in a deterministic manner (which may or may not be justified) to a group which is additionally identified as being in some way biologically (phenotypically or genotypically) distinct.' In contrast, he defines racialization as 'a process of signification in which human beings are categorized into "races" by reference to real or imagined phenotypical or genetic differences' (Miles, 1987: 7). Thus, as Satzewich further suggests, the process of racialization 'can be said to occur even in the absence of the term "race" from discourse' (Satzewich, 1991: 50). Miles and Satzewich concur that although the processes of racism and racialization have been historically intertwined, the two concepts need to be analytically separated (Satzewich, 1991: 51). For a more detailed discussion on the relationship between unfree labour, both waged and unwaged, and temporary help work, see Vosko, 1998c.

7 Several scholars have illustrated that the origins of discussions surrounding deploying this maxim at the supranational level lie with the Irish political economist John Kells Ingram (O'Higgins, 1997; Shotwell, 1934). Ingram used it in his 1880 address to the British Trades and Labour Congress. Entitled 'Work and the Workman' and focused on the problem of wages, he made the following call to the congress:

> Our views of the office of the workman must also be transformed and elevated. The way in which his position is habitually contemplated by the economists, and indeed by the public, is a very narrow, and therefore a false, one. Labour [power] is spoken of as if it were an independent entity, separable from the personality of a workman. It is treated as a commodity, like corn or cotton – the human agent, his human needs, human nature, and human feelings, being kept almost completely out of view. Now there are, no doubt, if we carry our abstractions far enough, certain resemblances between the contract of employer and employed and the sale of a commodity. But by fixing exclusive, or even predominant, attention on these, we miss the deepest and truly characteristic features of the relation of master and workman – a relation with which moral conditions are inseparably associated. By viewing labour [power] as a commodity, we at once get rid of the moral basis on which the relation of employer and employed should stand, and make the so-called law of the market the sole regulator of that relation. (Ingram as cited in O'Higgins, 1997: 226)

In making these remarks, Ingram was clearly arguing that labour power is far too important for its price to be left exclusively to market forces. Therefore, its social character must be taken into consideration in determining wage levels and other measures central to the reproduction of the working population.

Building on his remarks, drafters of the articles pertaining to labour in the Treaty of Versailles, such as American trade union leader Samuel Gompers, lobbied to have this principle included in the 'Labour Charter.' It was based on their efforts that the ILO proclaimed the guiding principle that 'labour should not be regarded as merely a commodity or article of commerce' in its founding Constitution of 1919. (For further discussion on the life of John Kells Ingram, see O'Higgins, 1997; Shotwell, 1934.)

8 While the Regulation School is generally identified with the work of French political economists such as Aglietta, Boyer, and Lipietz, it has become very diverse since its inception in the 1970s. According to Jessop, it currently encompasses at least seven different schools and/or individual approaches, including the three variants of the French Regulation School, the Amsterdam School, the West German Regulationists, the 'Nordic models' group, and the American Radicals (Jessop, 1990: 155). This discussion refers primarily to the insights of the French Regulation theorists and their critics.

9 As indicated in the Introduction, this chapter draws primarily on the insights of third generation Segmented Labour Markets Theory, and is highly critical of early strands of Dual Labour Markets Theory.

10 In their book *No Easy Road* (1990), Ruth Pierson and Beth Light document how Canadian economists and other experts defined the concept of full employment after the Second World War. They develop a compelling argument suggesting that experts believed that full employment should translate into lower rates of labour force participation among women and other marginalized groups. To make this argument, they cite a study noting that:

> Full employment before and after the war is bound to be less than the highest level of employment attained during the war. At present [August 1943] there are probably hundreds of thousands of persons in gainful occupations who would not ordinarily be so employed. Such persons include (a) young people of both sexes who would otherwise be at school or college, (b) unmarried young women who would otherwise be living with their parents and assisting in purely household duties pending marriage, (c) young women already married who would otherwise be keeping house and rearing children, (d) older able-bodied women, single and widowed, who ordinarily depend on their relatives or live partly on their own means, (e) young war widows most of whom

will marry again and become homemakers, (f) married women who are
going out to work for patriotic reasons or to maintain their standard
of living in the face of higher taxes and living costs, and (g) persons
of advanced age who would ordinarily have retired or been laid off.
(D.C. MacGregor as cited in Pierson and Light, 1990: 256)

They interpret this checklist as a 'sweeping denial of women's right to
work' (256).

11 According to Leo Panitch and Donald Swartz (1988: 19), an 'unparalleled
shift in the balance of class power' took place in Canada in this period.
Labour unrest was so prevalent that one in three trade union members
engaged in strike action in 1943 alone.

12 Variously characterized as 'permeable' (Jenson, 1989b), 'exceptional'
(Albo, 1990), and 'specific' (Campbell, 1991), the Canadian variant of
Fordism rested on a limited, and, as history would demonstrate, tenuous
set of compromises between business, labour, and the state. While it was
shaped by the horrors of the Great Depression as well as prewar and wartime labour unrest in core male-dominated sectors, Canada's version of
Fordism was also profoundly affected by factors such as American ownership of the means of production in resource sectors, regional unevenness
in economic activity, federalism, and a reliance on export-led growth (Albo,
1990; Jenson, 1989b).

From the perspective of workers in core sectors of the Canadian
economy, Privy Council Order 1003 (February 1944) represented the
positive side of the Fordist compromise since it conformed with the sentiments behind the maxim 'labour is not a commodity' and the right of
association for both workers and employers enunciated in the constitution
of the ILO (1919). It amounted to the following gains for organized labour:
union recognition, standard wages, association rights, and collective bargaining rights at designated sites. On the downside, however, even though
P.C. 1003 and its successor (i.e., the *Industrial Relations Disputes Investigations
Act* of 1948) gave workers' rights permanency, these instruments still
secured capital's long-run dominant position by banning strikes during the
term of a collective agreement, constructing legitimate (i.e., 'reformist')
and illegitimate (i.e., 'radical') trade unionism, and encouraging labour
leaders to adopt a self-policing role (Panitch and Swartz, 1988: 22–3). For
the purposes of this study, what is even more central is that the legalistic
collective bargaining framework endorsed at both federal and provincial
levels, combined with Canada's lukewarm pledge to advance policies aimed
at full (male) employment, failed to improve conditions for workers outside designated sectors (Cameron, 1995; Campbell, 1991: 4–5; Fudge,

1991). Hence, the type of Fordist economic growth model adopted in Canada, and the policy measures emerging out of this model, provide insight into the range of forces perpetuating labour market inequalities in the postwar era. (For more detailed accounts of the merits and shortcomings of P.C. 1003 and the *Industrial Relations Disputes Investigations Act* (1948), see Albo, 1990; Finkel, 1995; Gonick, Phillips, and Vorst, 1995; McCrorie, 1995; Panitch and Swartz, 1988).

13 By highlighting the contribution of third generation Segmented Labour Markets Theory below, I do not intend to underplay the merit of arguments advanced by several contemporary critics of early Segmented Labour Markets Theory (particularly its 'dualist' and 'radical' variants) who emphasize the complexity of forces contributing to persistent inequalities in the postwar era (see, for example, Botwinick, 1993). Rather, I am drawing on the descriptive and causal insights of third generation theorists, in particular, to emphasize how employers use various forms of discrimination to preserve labour market inequality.

14 For example, they are quite useful in revealing how 'family wages' primarily became the reality in what early segmentation theorists label the primary labour market (M. MacDonald, 1982: 197).

15 Early works by Rubery (1978) and Rubery and Wilkinson (1994) are particularly effective in demonstrating that groups of organized workers act defensively to protect themselves from the competition of the external labour market, to obtain job security and higher wages, to the exclusion and possible detriment of those remaining in the unorganized sector. Indeed, although these scholars focus on the British case, their insights resonate in the Canadian context, where, in the post-Second World War period, married women were excluded from certain spheres of employment partly due to the actions of organized male workers (see, for example, Morgan, 1988; Pierson and Light, 1990). Chapter 3 further develops this observation.

16 Since the segmentation literature focuses on how '... the marginalization of women is similar to the marginalization of non-whites, youth, immigrants and rural/urban migrants in capitalism, and how this marginalization is necessary to the system' (MacDonald 1982: 189) and feminist work (especially feminist analyses of women as a reserve army) focuses on how women's relationship to capitalism differs from men's, they are suitable complements in probing how women's inequality relates to capitalism (Armstrong and Armstrong, 1994: 82–3).

17 The term 'flexibility' is normally deployed to describe two distinct, yet compatible, strategies linked to labour market restructuring.

It is used to refer to 'labour market flexibility' in discussions of economic policy measures that involve state deregulation in the labour market (see, for example, Stanford, 1996). 'Flexibility-enhancing' labour market policies contribute to weakening labour market regulations (such as those governing minimum wages, employment security, collective agreements, etc.), and hence facilitate the spread of precarious forms of employment. In referring to 'labour market flexibility,' here and elsewhere, I subscribe to this definition.

In the industrial relations literature, the term is also used to denote the rise of a new 'innovation-driven' production system known as 'flexible specialization,' and to designate a set of firm-level practices – including practices designed to facilitate 'numerical flexibility' (i.e., measures used by employers to alter the size of workforces to accommodate fluctuations in demand and to shift employment-related responsibilities such as the provision of benefits), 'functional flexibility' (i.e., practices that require workers to be capable of performing multiple tasks), and 'pay flexibility' – that are emerging alongside this 'new' system. Michael Piore and Charles Sabel (1984: 6) first advanced (and advocated) the notion of 'flexible specialization,' which involves reinventing and combining production techniques derived from both artisanal and mass production systems, advocating it as a means of halting the 'deterioration of economic performance' in Western industrialized countries originating in the early 1970s. Their work, as well as the subsequent work of John Atkinson (1988) on the flexible firm, has been highly criticized by feminist scholars who reject what is presented as the positive side of this strategy (i.e., that it has the potential to offer workers more variety in their work lives); they argue instead that defenders of flexible specialization de-emphasize the ongoing 'struggle between capital and labour in the workplace and the continual threat of the "degradation" of work and de-skilling of labour' (M. MacDonald, 1991: 180; see also Pollert, 1988) and overlook its highly gendered underpinnings (Jenson, 1989a; Vosko, 1998a; Walby 1989). Many also question whether the firm-level practices associated with flexible specialization are really 'new,' casting them as demarcating a complex material and ideological strategy that has strong prescriptive elements that are complementary to labour market deregulation (Pollert, 1988: 43).

18 The labels that these authors attach to shifts in the evolution of capitalism reflect their different interpretations of the nature of change. Scholars referring to neo-Fordism often emphasize continuity over change, those labeling the emergent regime of accumulation 'flexible accumulation' often examine the dynamic interaction of continuity and change, and those

proclaiming the arrival of post-Fordism tend to view change as most relevant.

19 In depicting how atypical employment contracts deviate from the employment contract associated with the SER, a study conducted by the ILO (1996: 42) illustrates that they 'may take the form of temporary employment contracts, offering no more security than would follow from one large order for work placed with a worker who is classified as self-employed. They may be part-time, leaving the worker with the need to find more than one such job in order to earn a full-time wage. The hours of work may even be unspecified with the worker being paid only when work is available and the business risk thus shifting from the employer to the employee, as it would if the employee were running a separate business.' The ILO study also demonstrates that these contracts are increasingly common in nations where law permits, and suggests that private employment agencies, especially temporary help agencies, that 'act as brokers or market-makers ... trading in contracts of short duration,' are growing up alongside them (ILO, 1996: 42).

20 To recall, this employment relationship involves three central actors: a temporary help agency that acts as the formal employer, a client firm that supervises workers' on-site, and a temporary help worker.

21 To begin with age distribution, only 10.7 per cent of workers aged 15 to 24 years were union members in 1997. This figure contrasts sharply with workers aged 45 to 54, 44.1 per cent of whom were union members in the same year; high union density ratios among older workers are a clear reflection of the aging blue-collar and public sector workforces (Akyeampong, 1997: 47–8). Regarding work arrangements and job tenure, a high percentage of unionized employees still held full-time, permanent jobs in 1997, although few unionized workers held temporary jobs or engaged in some type of flexible work arrangement. For example, the union density ratio for workers with job tenures of one to twelve months was only 12.9 per cent in 1997, a figure that is consistent with the low rates of unionization among temporary workers. Finally, even in the face of declining employment in the public sector, union density ratios were 72.5 per cent among public sector employees and only 21.9 per cent among private sector employees in 1997.

Combined with the rise and spread of the TER, and the dim prospects for organizing workers engaged in TERs, such as temporary help workers, these statistics suggest that union density may continue to stagnate or even decline in Canada in the near future. They also reinforce the magnitude of the challenge of organizing workers engaged in TERs, which Chapter 8 addresses at some length.

22 For a discussion of the tenor of the prevailing shift in class power, see Panitch and Swartz, 1988: chaps. 2–4.

23 To be clear, the aims of the ensuing discussion are twofold: first, to describe gendered global employment trends using the literature on feminization; and, second, to highlight several ambiguities (or problem areas) in this body of scholarship and identify a definition of feminization that deepens our understanding of the rise and spread of the TER. It is not my project in this book to assess (i.e., measure empirically) the relationship between global employment trends and developments in Canada.

24 While I use the term 'feminization' to label a particular group of gendered labour market trends, to be described below, I am cognizant of some of the potential drawbacks to this choice of terminology. In particular, I am aware of (and concerned about) the problem of associating women with what are largely a 'negative' set of labour market trends; this issue was raised, for example, in debates over the most appropriate way to label a phenomenon that came to be known as the 'feminization of poverty' in the late 1980s (see various contributions in Gordon, 1989).

Partly in response to this dilemma, several authors offer alternative means of describing prevailing (gendered) employment trends. Sylvia Walby (1997), for example, advances the notion of 'gender transformations' in the labour market to move away from a narrow discussion of sex-based trends and her earlier analysis of 'patriarchy at work.' Highlighting that both men and women are being affected by the important changes taking place in the labour market, Jane Jenson (1996) speaks of a new set of 'gendered employment relationships' and Jill Rubery (1998) adopts a similar emphasis in calling for a new 'gender contract' in OECD countries. Finally, in contrast to the preceding options, Pat Armstrong (1996) speaks of the creation of 'more *women's work* in the market,' with the express intention of preserving the importance of the variable sex in describing labour market trends. In this book, I take the middle ground. I retain the concept 'feminization' as the most suitable option for keeping both sex and gender at the centre of our understanding of contemporary labour market trends (global and national), and, at the same time, in tension with one another. In Chapter 5, I develop my conception of feminization in greater depth.

25 Prior to the publication of Standing's article, a group of scholars in the field of development studies were beginning to identify the gendered nature of international employment trends (Frobel, Heinrichs, and Kreye, 1980; Sanderson, 1985). However, they did not characterize these trends in terms of the global feminization of employment.

26 Henceforth, I will refer to Standing's thesis as the 'conventional thesis.'

27 Moreover, growing evidence suggests that feminization does not necessarily involve women's rising labour force participation rates. While accelerating rates of labour force participation among women initially correlated with the introduction of free trade and export-led growth strategies in many industrializing countries, many occupations that were formerly female dominated are now becoming male dominated because 'women tend to be disadvantaged in the processes of production which are capital-intensive and rely on skilled labour' (Joekes, 1987: 329). Hence, some scholars now use the term de-feminization to describe recent developments in specific countries, such as Singapore and Mexico (Joekes, 1987). Rather than weakening the force of the notion of feminization, however, evidence of so-called de-feminization points to the importance of understanding the gendered underpinnings of the process of employment change as well as its material effects, which may, but do not necessarily, include the substitution of women for men in formerly male jobs.

28 The work of Antonieta Barron (1994) on the Mexican vegetable sector is particularly instructive here. In the case of this sector, she demonstrates that with the emergence of export-led growth models in the 1970s, women initially entered this sector because few men were available for work and because land reforms were making families more reliant on the market.

29 To cite Barron (1994:141) once again, even in the increasingly female-dominated Mexican vegetable sector, sex-segregated job categories persist. For example, women continue to perform the labour-intensive task of picking, and, when local men are not available for packaging, employers often ship fresh vegetables to export-processing zones, where, paradoxically, both men and women work at this greater-skilled job.

Trends in Turkey also undermine the argument that declining sex segregation necessarily accompanies feminization. While there is evidence of women's rising participation rates in core manufacturing industries in Turkey, growing feminization is promoting intensified sex segregation since women's increased entry into the formal labour force is concentrated in historically female-dominated industries (Catagay, 1994). Nilufer Catagay (1994: 134) aptly notes, 'To the extent that the activities involved, such as knitting, embroidery, ready-made clothes production, are typically female dominated activities in the formal manufacturing sector, they do not represent a feminization of the type conceptualized by Standing via the substitution of women for men.' In a recent study on the British case, Rubery and Fagan (1994: 141) also report similar findings.

30 Katherine Ward (1994: 6) refers to a 'triple shift' in describing the impact

of global restructuring on women's work. She identifies formal labour force participation as the 'third shift' for women in industrializing nations, since most women perform informal waged work as well as domestic work before entering the formal labour force.

31 Notably, contrary to the conventional thesis, Boyd, Mulvihill, and Myles (1991: 427) suggest that women's mass entry into the labour force was marked by an increase in exclusively female work environments in the Canadian case; thus, women's numerical strength has not eroded traditional gender hierarchies.

32 Still, since patterns of feminization differ from country to country and from sector to sector, women's mass entry into the labour force cannot be traced to a specific year or decade.

33 The fact that women of colour represent a disproportionate percentage of workers in low-wage, labour-intensive manufacturing industries worldwide, such as clothing, textiles, and footwear, and ill-remunerated service work, such as domestic work, contributes to the racialized nature of income and occupational polarization (Arat-Koc, 1990; Armstrong, 1996: 35; Fernandez-Kelly and Garcia, 1989).

   On the question of differentiation among women and men by age, attributable largely to the nature of the employment relationship, see Vosko (2000).

34 The rise of this employment relationship reflects a grouping of trends that entails more than women's mass entry into the labour market; chief among them is the feminization of employment relationships, a development rooted in the enduring link between nonstandard employment relationships and so-called women's work, and the lack of fit between labour policies central to the occupational welfare state and these relationships (Vosko, 2000).

35 Few industries have endured this type of shift. Usually when men enter highly female-dominated industries in significant numbers, the industry's status is rising, and, when they exit, the industry is in decline (see, for example, Lowe, 1987).

36 Even though sex segregation persisted in the THI in the late 1990s, this trend does not undermine the claim that the type of feminization that is occurring in the Canadian labour market is leading more men to compete for jobs, particularly 'good' jobs, traditionally held by women. Nor does it reduce the force of the hypothesis that some men are facing downward harmonization and many women are enduring increasing economic pressures in the labour market. Rather, given the racialized character of employment in the THI, to be addressed in Chapter 5, persisting sex

segregation and the apparent preponderance of women, immigrants, and people of colour at the bottom end of the occupational hierarchy in the THI raises the following questions: Which men are competing for jobs stereotypically characterized as 'women's work,' particularly those characterized by low wages and limited security? To what extent does the hypothesis that prevailing labour market trends (precipitated by globalization) are leading to 'increasing control for a few, mostly white, men' reflect prevailing trends in a THI (Armstrong, 1996: 53)? This last question is difficult to address at an empirical level given the dearth of employment data disaggregated by race and immigration status. Still, an examination of the policies, practices, and processes at the intra- and inter-firm level in the THI brings us closer to a suitable response (see Chapter 5).

Chapter 2: Putting Workers in Their Place

1 The word 'padrone' literally means contract labour boss, and it is normally used to refer to labour market intermediaries or agents that exploit ethnic ties to promote the commerce of migration. In the context of this study, I follow the work of Robert F. Harney (1979) who uses the term as 'a convenient word for the chief intermediaries' involved in recruiting, transporting, and organizing a pool of immigrant and migrant labourers, not seen fit to be permanent agricultural settlers, to fill jobs at the bottom of the labour market.

2 These practices ranged from crafting contracts with highly exploitative terms and conditions to forcibly transporting immigrant and migrant workers to distant work sites. Bradwin (1972: 60) describes the abusive practices of employment agents transporting immigrant workers to work on the railway as follows: 'To protect themselves, the employment agents would sometimes dispatch the men that signed up with them for railway work in car lots, with two guards in charge. Separate coaches filled with navvies were sometimes attached to the regular trains on the Temiskaming Railway. The doors of the coaches bearing the labourers were locked for some hours while passing through the towns of the mining district ... During those particular years cases were not infrequent of men being handcuffed and thus manacled conveyed under guard to a camp, there to fill the terms of agreement for work for which they had engaged at an employment office.' This type of account underscores the unfree status of the many male workers (immigrant and migrants) hailing from Southern and Eastern Europe in this period.

3 While the composition of the female domestic workforce has changed

markedly over the last century, domestic workers continue to be devoid of many occupational protections to date. There is a rich body of literature addressing the intricacies of their marginal status in the labour market (see Arat-Koc, 1990; Bakan and Stasiulis, 1997; Silvera, 1983).

4 In referring to the ideology of domesticity, I follow feminist scholars such as Michele Barrett (1988) and Lenore Davidoff and Catherine Hall (1987), who use the term to describe and group ideologies that encourage women to occupy a specific location in the social division of labour, performing tasks associated with the domestic sphere. In the Canadian context, many women social reformers used these ideologies to secure women's participation in paid and unpaid domestic work, and, more broadly, to cement men's status as primary breadwinners in the late nineteenth and early twentieth centuries. Chapter 3 discusses ideologies of domesticity in greater depth.

5 By 1904 there were about 100 private employment agencies operating in Canada, and their numbers had grown to over 300 by 1913. Of these 300 agencies, Ontario had the largest number (97), followed by British Columbia (45), Manitoba (36), Alberta (32), and Quebec (26). These agencies recruited workers in Europe and the United States, where they collaborated with similar labour market entities (*Labour Gazette*, September 1904: 262; Wilgress, 1916: 21).

6 There is more documentation on the situation of male immigrant workers engaged by private employment agents than their female counterparts, since men's paid work rarely relegated them to the private sphere. As a result, the ensuing discussion focuses on abuses committed by private employment agents largely engaging male immigrant agricultural and industrial workers. Still, it is important to note that recent studies documenting the means through which immigrant women domestic workers came to Canada suggest that the practices of social reformers were remarkably similar to those of the private employment agents engaging male workers at the turn of the century (Arat-Koc, 1997; Bakan and Stasiulus, 1995, 1997).

7 The distinction between the general labour agency and the padrone is somewhat arbitrary, since in many instances both types of private employment agents/agencies furnished so-called gangs of workmen and individuals. As well, although general labour agencies normally operated domestically and padrones worked both domestically and abroad, usually within one ethnic enclave, it is not inconceivable that general labour agencies would have had ties to similar types of agencies (or even operated branches) abroad. Nor is it inconceivable that some general labour

agencies would have dealt with workers of a specific class, race, and/or ethnic background. What is most crucial to stress is that the padrones came under significant attack, in both Canada and abroad, since they were reputed to recruit and place 'foreigners.'

8 While there is considerable documentation of abuses committed by padrones and other private employment agents focusing on transatlantic recruitment and placement and/or engaging immigrants, evidence of ill-treatment by general labour agencies operating domestically and engaging Canadian-born workers is more sparse. Between 1900 and 1930, various issues of the *Labour Gazette* report on the outcome of court cases (instigated either by workers themselves or by government representatives on behalf of workers issuing complaints) where general labour agents were found in breach of municipal or provincial employment agency acts, the *Immigration Act* of 1910, and/or Privy Council Order 1028, which arose out of this act. The majority of charges relate to false promises of employment and exorbitant fee-charging, and the majority of complainants were male immigrant workers; although women workers were covered by the *Immigration Act* of 1910 and/or Privy Council Orders 1028 and 1064, as well as by most provincial and municipal legislation governing employment agencies (save Quebec where agencies recruiting and placing women only were exempt from legislation pertaining to private employment agencies), their experiences of abuse failed to generate significant attention in the media (see: *Labour Gazette*, November 1907: 212, December 1907: 696, February 1908: 1024). However, there is little evidence to suggest that general labour agencies were ever prosecuted, let alone convicted, under the *Alien Labour Act* of 1897.

9 From this point onwards, I refer to the *Royal Commission Appointed to Inquire into the Immigration of Italian Labourers to Montreal and the Alleged Fraudulent Practices of Employment Agencies* (1905) as the *Royal Commission Appointed to Inquire into the Immigration of Italian Labourers to Montreal* (1905).

10 Cordasco began to operate in the Canadian labour market around 1900. In many respects he represents the prototypical padrone in the Canadian context in this period, since he had strong ties with the railway and steamship companies that provided labourers to employers in seasonal industries in Canada's North and in sectors where permanent settlers did not want to work (see Harney, 1979).

11 There are striking similarities between the tone of this advertisement and those common in the contemporary THI.

12 For example, he organized a parade on 23 January 1906, where he was crowned 'King of the Workers.' On this occasion Cordasco 'was presented

with a crown, in shape not unlike that worn by the King of Italy, and this crown was publicly placed on his head ...' (*Labour Gazette*, June 1906: 1349).

13 Fees took the form of both direct fees to workers for placement and a commission that the customer paid to the private employment agent for the provision of workers, prefiguring the temporary help formula later adopted by the THI.

14 Indeed, in this period the anti-Chinese sentiment was particularly fierce in Western Canada, specifically Ralph Smith's home province of British Columbia, where 'gangs' of day labourers, first in canneries and mining and subsequently in railway construction, were largely composed of Chinese guest workers and immigrants.

Rather than solely directing their opposition to employers and labour market intermediaries, organized labour directed considerable hostility towards Chinese labourers, and in some cases supported their lack of access to citizenship status. As Kay Anderson (1991: 37) asserts,

> BC labourers came to view the Chinese, rather than their employers, as their most formidable enemy, and this disposition soon became a channel for the political protest of the province's labour. White workers – ignoring the demostrated willingness of early Chinese labourers to strike over job and pay dicrimination – believed that the 'Chinese' were endowed as a category with the capacity to undersell more deserving labour. They also felt strongly that the Chinese could be used by employers (as indeed they were) to break the strikes mounted by white labourers for higher pay and better working conditions ... For white labourers of British Columbia, then, just as for entrepreneurs, Chinese immigrants were somehow immediately beyond the body of eligible citizenry from the time they entered the province.

15 The final report of the *Royal Commission appointed to inquire into the Immigration of Italian Labourers to Montreal* (1905) forced the Laurier government to alter its stance on private employment agencies acting abroad, only partially satisfying Italian immigrants and the Trades and Labour Congress. They forced revisions to the *Alien Labour Act* of 1897, making it illegal to import immigrants under promise or offer of employment. However, these clauses only applied to the United States. Thus, steamship and railway companies were quite successful in their efforts to prevent the introduction of stronger legislation.

To the dismay of the Trades and Labour Congress, the Senate also eroded the bill designed to implement these changes after its initial passage through Parliament, so that penalties applied not only to those who induced immigration by misrepresenting conditions in Canada, but also to anyone who tried to discourage immigration to Canada (Avery, 1995: 254; *Labour Gazette*, October 1904: 365; *Senate Debates* 1904: 1223–30, as cited in Avery 1995: 253–4).

16 At this point, two federal acts already expressly prohibited any persons, company, or partnership from prepaying the transportation of any 'alien' or 'foreigner' under contract to Canada and provided harsh penalties for employment agents found guilty of making false representations to workers. However, the MPs claimed that this legislation was quite ineffective and ill-enforced (Canada, 1897, 1905).

17 Still others, while they did not object in principle to the use of replacement workers, objected to the lengths that some employers would go to break a strike, and to many of the practices of private employment agents operating abroad. In 1906 Mr Hance Logan, an MP from Cumberland, noted, 'I do not contest the right of any one, when there is any labour trouble, to get men to take the positions of the strikers; but on the other hand I do not believe that any one has the right to go on the other side of the line or to the old country and publish misleading advertisements and by false representations induce men [*sic*] to sell out everything and come out to this country in the belief that they would receive $18 a week' (Canada, May 1906: 2962).

18 The first free municipal labour bureau opened in Montreal in 1896 at the beginning of the period when the padrone system was reaching its height.

19 The *Municipal Act* of 1897 granted regulatory powers to councils of counties, townships, villages, and cities where there were fewer than 100,000 inhabitants and to commissions of police in cities with more than 100,000 inhabitants, and it made it mandatory for employment offices to keep a licence. The act also gave municipal authorities the power to set regulations regarding record-keeping, licensing fees (no more than $10 per annum), and fees to employers and workers. In 1903, the identical regulations were re-enacted in the *Consolidated Municipal Act* (*RSO*, 1903: 391).

20 No other provincial employment agency act addressed the two distinct types of placement until well on in the century. For example, Manitoba only acknowledged this in *An Act Respecting Employment Services* in 1950.

21 In the same year, Quebec amended the *Act respecting the Establishment of Employment Bureaus* (1914) to strengthen the licensing requirements so that a private bureau had to go through both the Ministry of Public Works and Labour and the chief factory inspector (Section 2520f). As well, the fee paid by workers was not to exceed $3. The act also set differential yearly licensing fees for private fee-charging bureaus located in regions where a

public bureaus existed ($200) and regions where they did not exist ($25) to strengthen the position of the emerging Public Employment Service (*Labour Gazette,* June 1914: 1421). As well, the minister was given the power to revoke licenses at any time.

In contrast to Ontario, none of Quebec's regulations applied to employment bureaus operating for women only, agencies that presumably catered to categories of workers such as domestic workers, clerical workers, and nurses (*RSQ*, 1914). This is a notable difference given that early temporary help agencies catering to the office sector targeted women almost exclusively.

22 The option of prohibition also became common in other provinces, such as Quebec and Manitoba during the period under study (*RSM*, 1924; *RSQ*, 1941). However, the era in which prohibition was allowable in Ontario was relatively short, particularly in contrast to Quebec, where the option of prohibition remained in place from 1941 until 1977, which was the last act where prohibitions are officially maintained (*RSQ*, 1941, 1977).

Other provinces, such as British Columbia and Alberta, opted for strict regulation and the prohibition of direct fees as opposed to giving the Lieutenant-Governor-in-Council the option of complete prohibition (*RSA*, 1919; *RSBC*, 1919).

23 In 1926 R.A. Rigg, director of the Employment Service Branch, of the Department of Labour, delivered a lengthy address to his department on 'Canada's Experience with Private Employment Offices,' where he condemned the private employment agency industry and suggested that the Employment Service of Canada should have a monopoly on placement and recruitment (*Labour Gazette,* April 1926). His remarks confirm that the federal government viewed the creation of a coordinated Public Employment Service as part of the solution to the problem of abuse among private employment agencies. The following is an excerpt from his conclusion:

> The private agency system stands condemned not only because it has resulted in crimes perpetrated against workmen but also because of the fact that it creates disorganization of plant arrangements and causes unnecessary labour turnover ... *There are very few services which the State can render to its citizens which are more important than that of providing a free national system of employment offices* ... [my emphasis] The sins of commission [i.e., fees] and the spirit of venality which controls the conduct of many [private employment] agencies, coupled with the inability of all of them as uncoordinated activities to so function as to meet successfully the needs of modern industry, have led the governments of Canada to indict them as being incapable of efficiently discharging the responsible duties attaching to employment service work. (335)

In coming to this forceful conclusion, Rigg identified several weaknesses in the private employment agency system, such as the lack of coordinating and clearance facilities and the inability of the system to render adequate service to the handicapped and young people. He also linked the fact that the system 'depends for its existence on fees collected either from employee or employee' to its 'malignant influence upon relations existing between employers and their workpeople' (*Labour Gazette*, April 1926: 334–5).

24 From this point forward, I shall refer to these labour market actors as 'private employment agencies' since the term 'fee-charging employment agency' has the potential to create confusion with respect to the issue of indirect fees, whereby the customer firm pays the private employment agency a set rate for remuneration and the administration of mandatory benefits, and thus the fee to workers is somewhat disguised. The nature of this indirect fee to the worker became a central subject of debate at both the international and national level with the emergence of the THI from the 1950s onward.

25 The extensive *Report of the Ontario Commission on Unemployment* (1916) prepared by T.W. Wilgress is the primary source of information in the ensuing discussion, since there is a dearth of material documenting the activities of private employment agencies operated by typewriter companies.

26 In sharp contrast to other spheres of women's employment, Canadian-born women dominated the clerical sector in this period. Thus, private employment agencies run by typewriting companies engaged them in large numbers. For example, one employment agency in Toronto with a total registration of 3,212 over an eighteen-month period placed 2,663 applicants from Toronto, 484 from outside Toronto, and only 65 from the 'Old Country' (Wilgress, 1916: 181).

27 Since they did not become a dominant force in the labour market until after the ILO adopted Convention No. 34, the role, function, and character of employment agencies run by typewriter companies, which were later known as 'ambulatory typing agencies,' did not receive international attention until well after the THI grew up in North America and Europe (ILO, 1966).

Chapter 3: 'Halfway Houses' for 'Housewives'

1 As established in Chapter 1, this norm is best epitomized by the SER.
2 Notably, when a significant number Canadian-born women returned briefly to domestic work during the Great Depression, most only accepted posi-

tions as live-out domestics, undeniably the most desirable type of domestic work. Their presence in the occupation made life even more difficult for immigrant women from Central and Eastern Europe, who endured the harshest working conditions (normally associated with live-in domestic work) due to the prevailing racialized gender division of labour (Barber, 1991: 19).

3 Organized labour's support for the male breadwinner norm in the 1940s was intricately tied to the evolution of what Andy Andras and Eugene Forsey characterized as the 'sheltered proletariat' that grew out of the post-war compromise (i.e., the sizeable group of primarily white male workers employed in large firms and benefiting from the collective bargaining rights prescribed under PC 1003) (Finkel, 1995). Organized labour made considerable gains in this era since blue-collar workers earned the right to 'lay claim to a respectability that had previously only been associated with skilled craftworkers' (Guard, 1995, 20). However, these gains led many of its more radical segments to abandon a wider political platform that involved seeking social justice for all working people and wealth redistribution among various segments of the working class as well as among women and men. For example, they led groups such as the Canadian Congress of Labour (CCL), which had called for maternity benefits and day nurseries for working mothers during the war, to abandon such issues in exchange for the patriarchal notion of the 'family wage' and the Trades and Labour Congress (TLC), which was always conservative when it came to women's issues, to remain divided over the issue of whether married women should be eligible for UI. As Finkel (1995: 62) notes: 'In large part union positions on these issues reflected a conservative, patriarchal vision of the social order: male breadwinners, defended by trade unions and state planning, were supposed to bring home sufficient wages to care for the needs of their families, in which wives restricted their labour to the domestic sphere and received no pay.'

After the Second World War, organized labour also demonstrated its ambivalence about married women's participation in the labour market through more covert means. For example, a number of the contracts negotiated following the war, such as those negotiated by the United Auto Workers, supported employers' marriage bars and included provisions that denied seniority rights to women workers (Sugiman, 1994: 47–58). Moreover, even when women overcame legislative barriers and participated alongside men in blue- and white-collar work, joined unions, and engaged in strike action, unions often invoked notions of 'feminine fragility,' highlighting women's supposedly reluctant labour militancy, as a strategic

means of gaining support (Guard, 1995). Segments of the union movement that boldly rejected discriminatory government policies and practices
and, hence, supported women's labour force participation as well as their
participation in unions were still uncomfortable with women's role in
militant forms of labour activism (Guard, 1995).

4 It also helps explain the absence of coordinated opposition to the growth
of the THI and the rise of the TER in these critical decades.

5 In English Canada, the main contributors to the reserve army of labour
debate were Margaret Benston (1969) and Patricia Connelly (1978). For a
synthesis of the contributions and the international debate, see Armstrong
and Armstrong (1990). See also Vosko (1998b) for a discussion of how the
reserve army concept applies to the THI and its workforce.

6 In many instances, economic necessity was the overriding reason that
middle-aged women, particularly married women, engaged in employment
during the Second World War. Referring to the efforts of the National
Selection Service, Phillips and Phillips (1983: 29) assert: 'The NSS's appeal
to women's patriotism was hardly necessary after a decade of depression. A
survey of women over thirty-five who were working (the least likely group to
be in the labour force) found that only 9 per cent were working out of
patriotism. The majority, 60 per cent, gave money as their reason.' Studies
by Joan Sangster (1995) and Veronica Strong-Boag (1994), which examine
women's continued attachment to the labour force after the war, provide
further evidence of the overwhelming economic necessity underpinning
their waged work.

7 As Jane Ursel (1992: 198) notes, this last measure represented a 'compromise between capital and labour in its most naked form – subsidizing a
wage system designed to ignore reproductive costs, only to perpetuate it.'
In an era when women's full-time, full-year employment was unwelcomed
by the state, the family allowance was a small wage for domestic labour,
which aimed to quell women's resistance to exclusionary policies and
practices (Armstrong and Armstrong, 1989: 69).

8 For example, program planners had tried, but failed, to obtain coverage for
domestic workers under protective labour legislation and social insurance
programs. As Ruth Pierson (1977: 96) indicates, this failure signaled, once
again, the government's unwillingness to give the 'occupation [of domestic
work] the legal protection and benefits which might have raised its status
and made it capable of providing a decent livelihood.' Consequently,
Canadian-born women continued to reject domestic work as a viable and
respectible occupation in the long run.

9 Under Regulation 5A of P.C. 5090, married women laid off because of

pregnancy were disqualified from UI for a period of two years after birth. As Ann Porter (1993: 129) aptly notes, 'it seems that pregnancy was still considered a voluntary state, and that women who chose to enter that condition were not deserving of an independent source of income security.'

10 I am grateful to Ann Porter for calling my attention to Office Overload's submission.

11 As evidenced by its remarks to the Commission of Inquiry into UI, Office Overload was already in the position of protecting its territory within the labour market by 1961. At this point, the Canadian THI had survived the period when it was most under threat through a carefully crafted strategy that is described in the next section of this chapter.

12 Upon its inception, Office Overload supplied the following set of office workers: stenographers, typists, file clerks, dictaphone operators, switchboard operators, receptionists, and bookkeepers.

13 Some of these early covenants provided for a penalty in the form of liquidated damages.

14 For example, in the Canadian context, Office Overload made public the wage scales that it used. In 1957 workers in Toronto earned the highest wages, which ranged from a $1.00 per hour for junior clerks to a $1.40 per hour for more experienced stenographers and bookkeepers. At this point, Office Overload claimed that its rates were higher than average, and it indicated that it 'billed [clients] about twenty-five percent more to cover the overhead and profit' (Hutton, 1957: 88).

15 For example, the Office Employees International Union passed a resolution at its annual convention in 1965 urging locals to negotiate clauses bringing temporary help workers under the provisions of the collective bargaining agreement (Moore, 1965).

16 Indeed, in the United States, the industry engaged in a long and protracted struggle to secure employer status, one that continues to date (Gonos, 1994). To attain legitimacy, the THI attempted to avoid being designated as a private employment agency, to be free from state regulation under legislation pertaining to private employment agencies and to be declared the employer of temporary help workers to satisfy the customer's desire to avoid employment-related responsibilities (Ricca, 1982).

17 For a discussion of this decision, see Gonos, 1995: 11–12.

18 These three points are derived from my comparative survey of national laws and practices governing the TER to be presented in Chapter 6 and several articles detailing the history of the legal status of the temporary employment agency in a range of national contexts (Gonos, 1995; Moore, 1965, 1975; Valticos, 1973; Vosko, 1997).

19 Regulations of this sort were even common in Canada, the United States,

the United Kingdom, and other countries that failed to ratify the original 'Convention Concerning Fee-Charging Employment Agencies' (No. 34).

20 Upon the adoption of Convention No. 96, some countries interpreted it to include temporary help agencies and/or ambulatory typewriting agencies and others did not, creating a split between member states that reached its height in 1966.

21 The level of ratification of Convention No. 96 peaked at 44 in 1972 (ILO, 1996: 126–7).

22 The director general's remarks also opened up the possibility for the re-emergence of private employment agencies as legitimate labour market entities, signaling perhaps the earliest shift within the ILO from a policy aimed at the gradual prohibition of all private employment agencies to a policy endorsing the noncompetitive coexistence of private employment agencies and public employment services.

23 The same is true in the United States where temporary help agencies were regulated through employment agency acts at the state level for a lengthy period after the Second World War. However, unlike in the Canadian context, by the late 1950s and early 1960s, the THI had already won the legal battle for formal employer status in several American states, including New York (1958) and California (1961) (Gonos, 1995: 15, 23). Hence, they became subject to the same legal treatment as other employers so long as there were no direct fees charged to the employee.

24 An Act Respecting Workmen's Employment Bureaus (1925) gave the Quebec Lieutenant-Governor in Council the power to close down all private employment agencies (RSQ, 1925). However, in 1941 the province invoked even more drastic changes: this act revoked all pre-existing regulations pertaining to private employment agencies and the government began to formally prohibit private employment agencies, although eventually exceptions were granted for charitable organizations, workers' councils, and other philanthropic private employment agencies (RSQ, 1941). It also ensured that all 'employees' (i.e., any person working under contract of lease and hire of work or of apprenticeship) could register free with employment bureaus (RSQ, 1941). These measures were even retained throughout the 1960s with the introduction of the Employment Bureaus Act (1964). Still, there is no evidence that the Quebec government ever applied them to temporary help agencies.

Chapter 4: From Stop-gap Workers to Staffing Services

1 Notably, with the shift towards 'staffing services,' the repackaged 'numerical flexibility' that the THI offered began to appeal to employers outside

relatively contained gendered and racialized segments of the labour market.

2 In this and subsequent chapters, I use the term 'feminization of the labour force' to refer to rising and/or consistently high rates of labour force participation among women. Thus, 'feminization of the labour force' and 'feminization of employment' are not used synonymously, although I do suggest that feminization of the labour force is a core facet of the feminization of employment.

3 As a result of the oil shocks, unprecedented sums of money were transferred from oil-consuming countries to oil-producing countries beginning in 1973. However, the transfer of resources to the oil-producing countries was too large for them to absorb; they could not take in enough imports to make up for the transfer of funds. Nor could most oil-consuming countries reduce their oil consumption sufficiently to eliminate their deficits or increase their exports sufficiently to cover the gap (Harvey, 1989: 142–3; Spero, 1990: 47).

4 In reforming UI and reducing public expenditures on social programs, the 1976 budget took its wisdom from a study prepared by the Economic Council of Canada entitled *People and Jobs* (1976). This study introduced the notion of a 'non-accelerating inflation rate of unemployment' (NAIRU) – an equilibrium rate of unemployment that could be maintained without creating inflationary pressures – and offered a 'new' definition of unemployment that revived the concept of 'voluntary' employment. 'Voluntary' unemployment was seen to be a result of social programs like UI, which made the pain of unemployment less onerous than in the past. It was believed to be more prevalent due to the shifting demographics of the workforce, which included rising labour force participation rates among women (Campbell, 1991: 18–19).

5 The AIP was composed of

- fiscal and monetary policies aimed at restraining growth in total demand and production at a rate consistent with declining inflation;
- government expenditure policies intended to limit the rate of increase in public service employment and the growth of public expenditures to or below the trend in the growth of the GNP;
- structural policies to deal with the special problems of energy, food, and housing, and to improve labour/management relations;
- a temporary prices and incomes policy that established controls over prices, wages, and other incomes for larger firms, and over wages and some prices in the government sector. (Canada, 1985: 308)

6 In this period, rising male unemployment and falling male participation rates primarily reflect the decline of manufacturing rather than competition from women (for an instructive discussion of the relationship between increasing unemployment among men and the type of feminization described by Standing (1989), see Cohen (1994)).

7 Data on the THI is collected through Statistics Canada's annual *Survey of Employment Agencies and Personnel Suppliers* (1993). Although this survey has existed since the early 1980s, it only provided data at the three-digit SIC (Standard Industrial Classification) level (i.e., for both employment agencies and personnel suppliers together) until 1984. As a consequence, disaggregated data (i.e., at the four-digit SIC level) on the size and shape of the THI has only recently become available.

8 Temporary help agencies constitute the largest component of the personnel supply services classification in the United States.

9 Confidentiality guidelines pertaining to the release of data from Statistics Canada prohibit direct reference to data on other provinces.

10 The performance of small agencies between 1987 and 1993 is indicative of the potential for growth and diversification in the THI. Small firms earning revenues between $250,000 and $499,999 doubled their revenue over this six-year period while firms with revenues of $2 million grew by 24 per cent (Hamdani, 1996: 89).

11 Agencies specializing in placing professional workers, such as nurses, computer technicians, or engineers, usually prefer to be called 'employment services.' However, Statistics Canada defines them as 'temporary help agencies' since they operate along the same lines as the temporary help agency.

12 It is increasingly common for temporary help agencies placing general labourers to hire on-site managers, contract workers whose wages are paid by temporary help agencies and work as supervisors on the premises of large customers. As will be discussed in the third section of the chapter (pp. 150–51), managers of temporary agencies often perceive the existence of an on-site manager, which is usually described as an extra service for good customers, as reinforcing the arm's-length legal relationship between the customer and the temporary help worker.

13 This figure is significantly higher than that derived from Statistic Canada's *Survey of Work Arrangements*, 1995, which found that women only represented 47.8 per cent of workers employed by temporary help agencies in 1995.

14 Sex-based data on personnel suppliers and employment agencies is only available at the three-digit level in Canada's *Labour Force Survey*. Thus, since

temporary help agencies only constitute approximately 80 per cent of all personnel suppliers (SIC 7712), it is conceivable that the percentage of women employed by personnel suppliers may be lower than the figure cited (Akyeampong, 1989: 43).

15 The question on job tenure in Statistic Canada's *Survey of Work Arrangements 1995* (1996) is outdated in that it uses the SER as its central reference point. At the outset of this survey, respondents are asked to identify a single employer. However, if the respondent names two employers, an agency and a customer, the interviewer is expected to name the temporary help agency as the employer to conform with the definition of employer in the survey (personal communication, Elizabeth Majweski, Statistics Canada 13 March 1998). Later in the survey, respondents are asked how long they have worked for their current employer. However, since temporary help workers often have difficulty identifying their employer, it is possible that survey results are a more accurate reflection of the average length of an assignment than of the length of a given worker's relationship with a temporary help agency. My research supports this hypothesis since many of the temporary help workers that I interviewed reported being on assignment for extended periods, and in such instances had particular difficulty identifying their employer (Chapter 5). If this hypothesis is correct, then the data on job tenure may actually suggest that the duration of temporary help assignments is also getting longer.

16 Still, as Chapter 5 reveals, an overwhelming majority of temporary help workers reported that they would prefer more hours in 1995.

17 In presenting average hourly wages in this industry, Statistics Canada reports mean wages. However, a more useful measure of the shape of hourly earnings in the THI might be the mode due to the increased occupational polarization in the industry.

18 The data presented in this section are derived from a branch observation conducted at a temporary help agency in December 1996 and open-ended interviews conducted with industry officials, agency managers, client firms, and temporary help workers. For further information, see Appendices A and B.

19 Much of the stability in the TER in the post-1970 period was related to the THI's success at retaining its 'special status' in the national context, attributable partly to the lack of coordinated opposition from organized labour and other segments of civil society, and the absence of new regulatory initiatives at the supranational level until the late 1990s.

At the national level, although most provinces revised, and some even repealed, their employment agency acts in the 1970s and 1980s, temporary help agencies still enjoyed de facto employer status. For example, although Ontario revised its *Employment Agency Act* in 1970, 1971, and 1980, it only altered procedures surrounding the revocation of licenses for permanent placement agencies (RSO, 1970 1980). Similarly, following developments in provinces decades earlier, Manitoba revised the *Act Respecting Employment Agencies* to prohibit fees in 1980, and it set new licensing regulations in 1987 (RSM, 1980). The most dramatic developments that took place at the provincial level in this period occurred in Alberta, where the government formally repealed the *Employment Agencies Act* in 1988, thereby removing all pre-existing measures such as those limiting fees to workers and mandating yearly licensing (RSA, 1988). In the early 1990s the THI also actively lobbied the provincial government of Ontario to change its *Employment Agencies Act*, but, although it was successful in obtaining a review of legislation which is still ongoing, the act remained in place in the late 1990s (Association of Professional Placement Agencies and Employment Staffing Services Association of Canada, 1996; Chapter 6).

At the supranational level, the ILO's 1966 ruling led to an impasse on the issue of private employment agencies that lasted over three decades. In the intervening years, a number of ILO member states and workers' organizations lobbied for the creation of an international labour convention dealing exclusively with temporary help agencies, but they were unsuccessful (ILO, 1994a: 8). Still, the International Labour Office continued to follow trends in the private employment agency industry. For example, it conducted a large cross-national study between 1988 and 1990 that charted the changing shape of the private employment agency industry. This study found eighteen different varieties of private employment agencies operating in the international labour market and discovered that the question that Sweden had initially posed regarding the scope of Convention No. 96 (Revised), with specific reference to ambulatory typewriting agencies engaging primarily women, was now relevant to a range of new kinds of private employment agencies (ILO, 1994a). Despite the findings of this study, ILO member states, employers, and workers were reticent even to discuss the issue of private employment agencies at a supranational forum until the early 1990s (see Chapter 6).

20 Not all temporary help agencies offer the same set of services. Nor do all temporary help workers have common experiences with recruitment and testing. Even though the THI is attempting to standardize the services provided by temporary help agencies, standardization is far from complete at present. For this reason, the set of staffing services described below is merely a sketch of the range of practices, policies, and proce-

dures that the THI calls 'staffing services,' limited by the parameters of this inquiry.

21 If a customer enters into a contract with the agency with the ultimate goal of hiring someone permanently, s/he also often signs a service contract for the recruitment of permanent staff. This agreement is a modified version of the service contract for the provision of temporary staff, which normally includes what is known as the '100 Day Guarantee.' Shaped much like a product warranty, this customer satisfaction clause not only guarantees the continuous employment of the successful candidate for 100 days from the commencement of employment, but also offers to replace the worker if the customer is not 'fully satisfied' (fieldnotes, 4 December 1996).

22 When I took the psychological test and attempted to select what I perceived to be the most desirable answers from the agency's perspective, the branch manager allowed me to examine my own evaluation. I found that, although I scored in the ninety-sixth percentile, this was not a good sign. Rather, the printout from the test stated: 'This applicant likely overstated her positive qualities' (fieldnotes, 5 December 1996).

23 According to one manager, the American THI leads the Canadian THI in the proportion of on-site supervisors that it provides because the volume of business is higher: 'We're behind the U.S. a couple of years [in the provision of on-site supervisors] ... [In the United States] larger clients are using more temporaries so there's more need [for on-site supervisors] than there used to be. It's nothing to find 500 temporaries on a site in the U.S. ... They're a dime a dozen down there' (M3). Such claims conform with the tenor of legal advice in trade journals designed for employers, where having an on-site manager and a clear service contract are cast as the means of maintaining an arms-length relationship with temporary help workers (Wymer, 1993).

24 I place 'new' in quotations here because this service is reminiscent of the pre-First World War era, when employment agents were involved in transporting workers to the work site.

25 Chapter 5 describes this agreement.

26 This finding is consistent with the findings of other studies on self-employment and independent contracting (Linder, 1991; Wymer, 1993).

Chapter 5: Promising 'Flexibility' and Delivering Precariousness

1 In an article entitled 'Part-Time Employment and Women: A Range of Strategies' (1996), which examines the different strategies pursued by states, unions, and women to shape employers' use of part-time workers,

Jane Jenson makes a similar claim about the changing nature of employment. She convincingly argues that 'a new set of gendered employment
relations is at the heart of the restructured economies' and that 'new
employment practices draw in some ways on existing discourses and practices of gender relations, depend in some ways on their having been altered, and are profoundly implicated in setting the new limits to gender
equality that are being constituted' (92). My findings parallel Jenson's
claims to a large degree; they especially reinforce her view that the new
structures of inequality in the labour market will 'clearly undermine any
strategy for generating gender equality that focuses exclusively on women
themselves ... until they [women] have access to better employment contracts' (97). However, our emphases differ somewhat. Jenson focuses her
discussion of part-time work on the gendered character of the emergent set
of employment relations. In contrast, I still retain the concept 'feminization,'
while emphasizing that the current casualization of employment amounts
to the 'gendering of jobs,' because, in the case of the THI, employers'
efforts to restructure employment relations still rest on policies and practices designed to maintain a considerable and well-defined proportion of
temporary help work as 'women's work.'

2 A key consequence of women's predominance in this type of service sector
employment in the 1970s and 1980s was that new legislative measures
designed to redress sex inequality in the labour market, such as pay equity,
employment equity, and other labour standards, offered few tangible
benefits for many women since they only applied to medium and large
workplaces and benefitted primarily standard workers (see, for example,
Bakker, 1991).

3 Many employment agreements also contain a separate clause indicating
that the temporary help worker is aware that s/he is entitled to accept or
reject assignments without penalty. However, workers and managers report
many unwritten penalties for refusing assignments.

4 The relegation of temporary help workers to coverage under minimum
standards legislation is the product of a 'segmented model of labour market
regulation' (Cameron, 1995; Fudge, 1991,1993). This model gives workers in
primary and secondary labour markets differential and unequal access to
legislative protections and social security benefits based on the problematic
assumption that workers belong to segments of the labour market that reflect
their breadwinner status. Thus, the marginal status of minimum standards
legislation relates primarily to its historic association with women workers
perceived to be secondary breadwinners and the strength of organized
(male) labour in core sectors of the economy (Vosko, 2000; chap. 8).

In describing the conditions of employment common among temporary help workers, this chapter takes the overwhelming evidence of the inferior status of minimum standards legislation as its point of departure.

5 Management and administration was the only occupational category where the average hourly wage for temporary help workers surpassed that of temporary workers engaged in bilateral employment relationships.

6 Based on the results of the *Survey of Work Arrangements, 1991*, Brenda Lipsett and Mark Reesor found that 73.2 per cent of all temporary workers were not unionized or covered by a collective agreement (Lipsett and Reesor, 1997: 47).

7 This worker's comments, and the experiences of other workers trained either as professionals or tradespeople, conform with the growing body of feminist scholarship that argues that 'skill recognition follows from the employment contract rather than the other way around' (Jenson, 1996: 5).

8 A male worker with considerable experience as a temporary help worker observed that 'if you are a man, and you're [clerical] temping, they all think that you're gay,' reinforcing the gender-based stereotypes about the THI (T2).

9 After praising the growing income and occupational polarization in the THI, one industry official made the following analogy to distinguish between the conditions of employment attached to light industrial and clerical work versus managerial and professional temporary help work: '[i]t's like the difference between fast food and fine dining' (fieldnotes, 2 December 1996).

Chapter 6: 'Flexible Workers,' Intractable Regulatory Regime

1 In their joint submission, ESSAC and APPA indicate that they are considering amalgamation, since 83 per cent of Ontario's ESSAC members are involved in permanent placement, and therefore hold licenses (APPA and ESSAC: 2). Given the THI's historic attempts to distance itself from the private employment agency industry, the possibility of a merger between these associations is a notable development.

2 A submission made by the Federation of Temporary Help Services (now known as ESSAC) to the Ontario Ministry of Labour in 1993 on the subject of 'Compliance with the *Occupational Health and Safety Act*' reflects the THI's desire for temporary help agencies to be treated differently from 'normal employers.' The federation argues that 'it is impractical to require the temporary help service's Joint Health and Safety Committee to oversee the service's temporary workers when they are on assignment at customers'

workplaces,' suggesting instead that supervision of this sort should be the responsibility of the temporary help agency's customers (Federation of Temporary Help Services, 1995: 6). Control and supervision of workers at the worksite normally fall within the responsibilities of employers. However, the THI wants temporary help agencies to be exempt from such responsibilities under provincial law; it wants agencies to be considered employers but still wants to retain their status as legitimate labour market intermediaries.

3 ESSAC's standard code of conduct, which must be posted in all member agencies, reads as follows:

Code of Ethics and Standards
 1. We recognize that our primary objective is to provide quality temporary services and will take steps to ensure that our employees are carefully selected and assigned to customers.
 2. We will treat with dignity and respect those applying for employment and those employed.
 3. We will, as employers, fulfill all the legal obligations to our employees and will provide equal employment opportunities on the basis of job qualifications and merit.
 4. We will provide leadership in the adherence to both the spirit and letter of all applicable human rights laws and regulations. We will not accept any order from any customer that is discriminatory in any way.
 5. We will not restrict the right of an employee to obtain permanent employment.
 6. We will not encourage or coerce an employee to leave an assignment before completion.
 7. We will observe the highest principles of honesty and fair practice in dealing with clients and employers and comply with all federal and provincial labour and employment laws and regulations.
 8. We will maintain and promote the highest standards of integrity in our advertising, sales promotions and public relations, avoiding any misrepresentation with respect to job description, job conditions, wages or services offered.
 9. We will recognize and fully respect the rights and privileges of competitors in the true fashion of the individual initiative and free enterprise and refrain from engaging in acts of unfair competition.
10. We will conduct our business in a manner designed to enhance the operation, image and reputation of the temporary help service industry and will ensure that all our employees are aware of this Code of Ethics and Standards and comply with this Code in all their activities.

4 The committee charged with this discussion resolved that a process of revising Convention No. 96 should pursue the following goals:

(1) Set the pattern for response to the dynamics of changing labour market functions and recall the role of its actors;

(2) Draw up general parameters to describe the main actors, namely the Public Employment Service and Private Employment Agencies, as well as the nature of the relationship both between themselves and their clients;

(3) Establish general principles and provide guidance that protect:

(I) labour markets against poor and unethical practices

(II) workers' interests including where the stability of industrial relations' systems might be affected by some practices of PREA (these principles should consider the concerns of some (but not all) Committee members with regard to triangular employment relationships, including contract labour, temporary work agencies, and staff-leasing arrangements);

(III) workers recruited in one country for work in another;

(4) Create environments that allow for the improved functioning of all employment agencies;

(5) Ensure that national governments would be free to determine how the above objectives would be met. (ILO, 1994b: 31–2)

5 Even in many countries where governments formally prohibited temporary help agencies under Part II of Convention No. 96, there is considerable evidence that the THI continued to operate either openly (and therefore bans were not enforced) or underground (Blanpain, 1993; Eklund, 1997).

6 When it is ratified by a country, a convention becomes a binding legal instrument. Hence, a country may be subject to sanctions if it does not fulfill its obligations under a given convention. In contrast, a recommendation is a nonbinding legal instrument. It normally serves to provide guidelines for implementing and/or deepening standards adopted in an associated convention. While there is a growing move to adopt recommendations on their own, a typical package of international labour standards in a given area includes both a convention and a recommendation.

7 For an in-depth discussion on the historic relationship between public employment services and private employment agencies, see Ricca, 1982, 1988.

8 Regarding the meaning of the exclusion clause contained in Article 2.4(a) of Convention No. 181, the Provisional Record of the 1997 discussion states, 'the proposed draft Convention was aiming at offering maximum

"ratifiability." Thus, as the convention gave legal recognition to PREA
(private employment agencies) – including TWA [temporary work agen-
cies] – it would not be possible for any country which banned TWA to ratify
the proposed draft Convention.' (ILO, 1997c: 5–6).

9 Article 5, on equality of opportunity and treatment in access to employment, builds on Convention No. 96 (Revised). Supported by both the
Workers' and Employers' delegates, the addition of this article follows from
the abuses documented by the International Labour Office in 1994 and
corresponds with the 'Discrimination (Employment and Occupation)
Convention' (No. 111) (ILO, 1997b). Article 5 had the support of the
Employers' Group for reasons including the desire to ensure that 'agencies
operated in line with ethical codes' existing at national and international
levels (ILO, 1997b: 4). Governments supported Article 5 since its antidiscrimination criteria were in conformity with national law and practice.
As a result, Convention No. 181 states that 'the Member shall ensure that
private employment agencies treat workers without discrimination with
respect to race, colour, sex, religion, political opinion, national extraction,
social origin, or any other form of discrimination covered by national law
and practice, such as age and disability' (ILO, 1997c: 4).

10 Articles directed at protecting migrant workers also follow from the general principles established through Convention No. 96 (Revised). Given
the historic record of abuses among private employment agencies acting
abroad and the recommendations of the ILO's Expert Committee on Migration, the need for effective protections for migrant workers was treated
as a priority in the new convention (ILO, 1997b: 53). While recognizing
that reserving these agencies for the exclusive use of nationals is not necessarily in the interests of migrants, member states, the Employers' Group
and the Workers' Group concurred on the need to address migrant
workers' rights within the new convention due to the prevalence of abuses
and malpractices among private employment agencies. Consequently, to
supplement much more comprehensive ILO instruments on this issue, an
article on migrant workers was added to the draft text and adopted unani-
mously. Article 8 requires member states to ensure adequate protection for
migrant workers recruited, placed, or *employed* by private employment
agencies and to provide penalties, including prohibition, for agencies
engaging in fraudulent practices (ILO, 1997c: 6).

11 Article 11 calls on member states to take the necessary measures to ensure
adequate protection for the workers employed by service providers in the
following areas: freedom of association, collective bargaining, minimum
wages, working time and other working conditions, statutory social security

benefits, access to training, occupational safety and health, compensation in case of occupational accidents or diseases, compensation in case of insolvency and protection of workers' claims, and maternity and parental protection and benefits (ILO, 1997c: art. 11). Article 12 enumerates the identical set of areas to the exclusion of freedom of association.

12 In discussing Article 12, the Employers' Group expressed the view that 'governments should not involve themselves in the employee/employer relationship,' stressing the need for 'flexibility in the relationship between the user enterprise and the private employment agency' (ILO, 1997b: 42). Taking exception to the word 'allocate,' it argued that protection in the field of occupational health and safety was the only area in which governments should allocate responsibility (42). In contrast, in its effort to retain the word allocate, the Workers' Group expressed its desire to make it perfectly clear who had responsibility in a given situation (42). It indicated that it was particularly concerned with the allocation of responsibility in cases where a worker was sent by a temporary work agency to a user enterprise. At the same time, the Workers' Group also noted that the instrument did not prescribe specific responsibilities to the parties concerned because this would potentially undermine existing national laws and practices. In the end, the governments accepted the Workers' Groups' amendments to both articles on the condition that between the user enterprise and the service provider, 'allocation was not intended to be exclusive, i.e., that responsibility could be shared' (43). Contrary to the position of the Employers' Group, governments supported the possibility of a divided employment relationship where service providers are concerned, and this is extremely significant.

13 The Employers' Group only accepted this paragraph on the condition that a subsequent amendment put forward by the Workers' Group be withdrawn. The amendment that the Employers' Group objected to provided for 'no less favourable' terms and conditions of employment for workers employed by private employment agencies than those applying to employees of either the user enterprise or enterprises in the same of similar branches of economic activity (ILO, 1997b: 52).

14 Examples are drawn from the following jurisdictions: Germany, France, Spain, Norway, Finland, Denmark, Sweden, Japan, Belgium, Luxembourg, and the European Community. These national and supranational jurisdictions were selected on the basis that they have legislation explicitly governing the TER and/or other triangular employment relationships.

15 Similarly, the German 'Act on Temporary Employment Businesses'

(Germany, 1985), the Spanish 'Temporary Work Agencies Act,' (Spain, 1994), the French 'Labour Code' (France, 1996, art. 124) and the Japanese 'Worker Dispatching Law' (Japan, 1987) all clearly define workers engaged by temporary help agencies as the employees of these firms.

16 Depending on the jurisdiction in question, the temporary help agency is variously labeled as a lending out business (Germany), a hiring out business (Sweden), a labour supply business (Denmark), a worker dispatching business (Japan) or a manpower contracting business (Finland).

17 In jurisdictions such as Germany, where the bilateral employment relationship continues to serve as the model employment relationship, temporary help agencies are said to be engaged in 'lending' rather than 'hiring out' workers. This is an important conceptual distinction aimed at reinforcing the temporary help agency's status as the principal employer (Dombois, 1989; Halbach et al., 1994: 212–213; Weiss and Schmidt, 1993: 114).

18 Although this definition of the business enterprise is accurate within most jurisdictions where legislation exists, Japanese legislation governing the activities of temporary help agencies does not specify that these firms supply workers on a temporary basis. Rather, the Worker Dispatching Law (1985) covers labour supply businesses more broadly, even though the majority of these businesses identify themselves as temporary help agencies. Japanese legislation does not mandate that these firms engage in so-called temporary placements. Goka (1997: 13) justifies the use of the term 'worker dispatching business' as follows: 'The term "worker dispatching business" is used in preference to "temporary employment agency" because some of the workers who are dispatched to client firms are employed by the dispatching agencies on the basis of regular full-time employment contracts of indefinite term.' In making this assertion, he acknowledges that Japanese companies increasingly rely on temporary help workers to minimize employment-related responsibilities (14).

19 The amount of precarity pay is determined on the basis of whether the employee is offered another assignment (Carré, 1994; Rojot, 1993).

20 However, Convention No. 181 does name maternity and parental benefits as central, two important areas of protection largely ignored in national legislation.

21 Obviously these type of guidelines, specifically pertaining to the TER, are absent at the provincial level in Canada since no province has yet defined areas where protection is necessary for temporary help workers or other workers engaged in triangular employment relationships. Still, the absence of guidelines for devising a legal test to determine the respective responsi-

bilities of the customer and the agency in Convention No. 181 will not assist provinces in establishing where protection is necessary or addressing the related problem of allocating responsibility.

22 The following proposals by no means represent an exhaustive list of recommendations. Rather, if adopted, these proposals would enable both Canada and the provinces to begin to give recognition to the precarious nature of the TER and move towards the establishment of an equivalent set of protections surrounding the TER as those linked to the SER.

23 At the International Labour Conference in June 1997, countries advocating regulating the TER held up France as a model (fieldnotes, 6 June 1997). The reason behind the idealization of the French model is that France has the most comprehensive regulatory framework in Europe and possibly in the world.

While full-time employment was the norm in France until the early 1970s, part-time, temporary, and other nonstandard forms of employment rose quite sharply beginning in the mid-1970s; one of the central reasons was that the government viewed the spread of these forms of employment to be preferable to high unemployment, which it largely attributed to women's rising labour force participation rates (Jenson, 1996: 99–100; Carré, 1994). Faced with these new conditions of employment, when the Socialists came to power in the early 1980s, they introduced protections for nonstandard workers through the Auroux Laws, making France one of the only countries to normalize the TER (Carré, 1994).

As Section 3 demonstrated, the formal protections accorded to temporary help workers in France are quite extensive. However, there is considerable evidence to suggest that extending standard benefits to workers engaged in TERs has not fully remedied the precarious character of temporary help work (and other types of work where triangular employment relationships are the norm) in France. Rather, as Jenson (1996) aptly notes with respect to part-time work, 'such an extension does not address other structures of inequality embedded in' non-standard forms of employment. In particular, she and others (Duffy and Pupo, 1992; J. White, 1993) have found that the extension of benefits to part-time, temporary, and other nonstandard workers by no means eliminates labour market segmentation or the gender division of labour in the domestic sphere. These arguments correspond with the argument presented in Chapter 5, which suggests that a range of factors and indices contribute to making temporary help work precarious. Thus, together with the evidence in preceding chapters, the case of France suggests that extending benefits to temporary help workers is only one limited means of remedying the precarious character of the TER.

24 This type of measure attempts to circumvent existing provisions in some provincial employment standards legislation, such as Ontario's *Employment Standards Act* (1990), (reg. 325, s.14), which mandate severance pay if a worker is dismissed after thirteen weeks of employment.

Chapter 7: 'No Jobs, Lots of Work'

1 A preliminary version of this chapter was first published in the *Canadian Review of Social Policy* (winter 1998: 42).

2 Scholars sympathetic to Regulation Theory associate workfarism with the decline of the Keynesian Welfare State and the rise of the Schumpeterian Workfare State. As Peck (1996: 191) notes, 'broadly speaking, these strategies promote innovation and structural competitiveness in economic policy (hence Schumpeter) and flexibility and competitiveness in economic policy (hence workfare).' In contrast, the findings of this study suggest that the emergence of workfare-driven social policies neither represent a radical break from past practices nor the emergence of a completely new state form. Rather, in the Canadian case, the state has historically deployed a range of strategies to move social assistance recipients off the welfare rolls; the primary distinguishing feature of the present period is that social assistance recipients no longer have the formal right to refuse work for welfare formerly accorded to all Canadians under the now defunct *Canada Assistance Plan*. This leaves considerable space open for intensifying the coercive nature of welfare. Correspondingly, temporary help agencies and their precursors have always targeted workers at the margins of the labour market, although to greater and lesser extents. What is unique about this era, at least in the province of Ontario, is that the government is not only accepting temporary help agencies as legitimate labour market entities, it is involving them in its own efforts to move social assistance recipients into the labour market and thereby positioning the TER as a viable alternative to the SER. Despite this caveat, this chapter borrows the term 'workfarism' from Jessop (1993) and Peck (1996), since it has considerable salience as a tool in describing and analyzing new directions in social policy.

3 The purpose of this chapter is to examine the Ontario government's role in legitimizing the TER through an analysis of Workfirst. For this reason, the ensuing discussion devotes only limited attention to situating the legal and policy framework of Ontario Works in the context of theoretical discussions about workfare. (For some useful theoretically-grounded discussions of workfare in Canada, see: Lightman, 1995; Sayeed, 1995; Shragge, 1997.) Nor does it examine the relationship between Ontario Works (and the

various programs that it is generating) and Canada's liberal welfare state regime. (For further discussion on Canada's unique status as a liberal welfare state, see Myles, 1988; K. Scott, 1996; see also Esping-Andersen, 1990 for a comprehensive typology of welfare state regimes.) Rather, the chapter takes Workfirst as a case study in probing the means by which the TER is attaining greater normative pre-eminence in Canada and the consequences of this development for workers at the margins of the labour market.

4 For a detailed description of the history of the *Family Benefits Act* (1967) and the General *Welfare Assistance Act* (1958), see also K. Scott, 1996.

5 Under the act, single mothers of children as young as three years of age may be required to participate in workfare.

6 Although the legislation facilitating the privatization of administration and delivery of programs falling under the *Ontario Works Act* is still open to a range of legal interpretations, sections 45, 46, 48, and 49 of the act allow the public administrator to 'delegate' its 'powers and duties' to third-party delivery agents (s.46).

7 Ernie Lightman's (1995) general definition of workfare conforms with the definition of 'pure workfare' offered here. Following Martin Rein, Lightman (154) argues that workfare is 'a coercive or restrictive [work incentive] strategy, which uses sanctions and requirements to induce labour market participation.' By his definition, workfare must satisfy two conditions, although the first is more critical than the second: first, it must be *mandatory*; and second, work or other approved activities (e.g., training, job search, apprenticeship, career counselling, etc.) must be done in *exchange* for, rather than in addition or as a supplement to, the welfare payment.

8 Still, as Patricia Evans (1995a) notes, social assistance has never been an 'entitlement' (i.e., an unconditional benefit) in Canada. Rather, 'need' and 'available resources' have been used to determine eligibility throughout the history of the Canadian welfare state; this is not surprising given that most provincial social assistance programs predate the emergence of the Keynesian Welfare State. In most provinces, social assistance recipients have also had to fulfill two work-related requirements to receive assistance: a work availability requirement and an employment preparation requirement (Evans, 1995a: 6).

  What differentiates 'new style' workfare programs from the types of obligations formerly existing at the provincial level in Ontario (i.e., before the introduction of Ontario Works) is that, to borrow from the insights of Lightman (1995), once again they reflect a 'coercive or restrictive strategy' that uses punitive sanctions and requirements to induce labour market participation. In this way, although they do not neatly conform with the second condition that Lightman attaches to his formal definition of workfare, these programs flow from the same type of work incentive strategy that he associates with workfare.

9 In this way, the employment placement programs falling under Ontario Works are not 'pure workfare,' although they do reflect a restrictive work incentive strategy given the penalties for nonparticipation to be described below.

10 While the stated objective of the employment placement stream is to place social assistance recipients in employment, labour standards legislation may not cover workfare participants since it is debatable whether they are the genuine employees of the firms in which they are placed (McCrossin, 1997: 144). In the case of Workfirst, the employment status of participants is further complicated by the existence of a triangular employment relationship associated with the TER.

11 From this point onward, this chapter shall refer to the social assistance recipients selected for Workfirst as 'participants.' I intentionally place the word participants in quotation marks because the Ontario government's usage of this term suggests that social assistance recipients have a degree of choice where participating in Workfirst is concerned, when this is, in fact, not the case. Rather, selected social assistance recipients are now obligated to take part in Ontario Works to continue to receive social assistance.

12 Upon reviewing the project, officials in the social assistance department recommended that the role of the broker be extended to placing 'employable social service recipients in temporary employment opportunities' and reporting to the social assistance department on their success (Human Services Committee, April 1998: 2). They proposed this change, in consultation with the broker, since it was determined that a direct relationship with the placement agency would 'result in the highest chance of being able to closely monitor client [i.e., 'participant'] compliance and the success of the project.' In May 1998, the Regional Municipality of Peel formally approved this change, altering the placement portion of the program by eliminating the continuous participation of other temporary help agencies. Thus, the responsibilities of the broker now include placing participants directly in employment, where possible.

13 According to the social assistance department, requiring 'participants' to register with temporary help agencies to maintain eligibility is ethical because 'The agency will be paid by the employer, not by the Region or the Broker, and will only place recipients in work that it believes is appropriate given the applicant's work experience and abilities. The Broker will not

receive a fee from the placement agencies' (Brief to the Human Services Committee, 30 January 1996: 3).

14 Obviously, it is not possible to measure, in any true sense, how much the social assistance department 'saves' by placing a given social assistance recipient into a job, because it is impossible to know whether the person in question would have found work on their own. Still, documenting the savings reported by the department provides important insights into how the municipality is measuring the effectiveness of the program.

15 The social assistance department stopped collecting data of this type after the first eight months of Workfirst. It now only collects data on the number of participants who are deemed unemployable, refuse job offers, or are placed on assignment through temporary help agencies (Human Services Committee, 6 May 1998). Unfortunately, no longitudinal data is available on 'participants' placed in employment.

16 The training component of Workfirst was originally the orientation session to be described below and then entailed two separate sessions designed to introduce 'participants' to the program, one with a caseworker and one with the broker.

17 Although Workfirst effectively redefines the conditions of eligibility for welfare by making registration with temporary help agencies mandatory for 'employable' social assistance recipients, the municipality's acceptance of the TER as an alternative to social assistance is not total. In the Regional Municipality of Peel, some policy-makers are still somewhat wary about both the reliability and the availability of temporary help work. Therefore, under Workfirst, social assistance recipients who gain access to temporary employment are not officially removed from the welfare rolls until they indicate to the social assistance department that their employment is 'ongoing' (General Welfare Assistance Policy Directive, 1 August 1996: 4).

18 It is important to emphasize here, once again, that municipal government officials do not *actually* deliver many of the mandated components of Workfirst. Although the content of all segments of the program is approved by the social assistance department, most of the core elements are contracted out to a third-party delivery agent (i.e., the broker). This practice undoubtedly affects the content and tone of certain dimensions of Workfirst since the broker has a different set of interests than the state. The point, however, is that when it comes down to the larger objective of perpetuating growth and expansion in the THI, their interests converge.

19 This section draws on interviews with participants, orientation leaders, and managers of temporary help agencies involved in Workfirst as well as fieldnotes from two orientation sessions that I observed.

The roles and responsibilities of the broker and the temporary help agencies have been combined since the research was conducted. As a result, the temporary help agency that formerly acted as the sole-service broker now administers the entire program. In other words, where possible it places social assistance recipients directly into temporary help work without involving other temporary help agencies. At present, the broker only requires workers to register with other temporary help agencies when it is unable to place them directly. Involving the broker in placement is a notable change for a range of reasons, but most centrally because it gives the broker a potential monopoly on placement. As well, the broker no longer conducts regular half-day orientation sessions with social assistance recipients. Rather, caseworkers and employment agency personnel orient social assistance recipients to Workfirst either individually or in small groups. However, the materials used in the orientation session and the approach initially adopted by the instructors are incorporated into the modified delivery of the program. Thus, it is still instructive to describe this session and the conditioning process inherent within it.

20 Social assistance recipients were first selected to participate in Workfirst by computer. Only those individuals excluded from Workfirst (i.e., people with disabilities, seniors, and sole-support parents with young children) and a control group of 15 per cent of 'employable' social assistance recipients were not selected for the program; the control group was established by the social assistance department in order to measure the success of the program after a predetermined period. Although computer selection is still occurring to date, there is no longer a control group since Workfirst has been deemed successful in achieving its stated aims (personal communication, informant from the Peel Social Assistance Department, 17 June 1998).

21 Social service caseworkers are now responsible for discussing the employment agency interview and placement process with 'participants.' However, the means by which caseworkers prepare participants for this process are virtually identical to the orientation session described here (personal communication, informant from the Peel Social Assistance Department, 17 June 1998).

22 At present, the broker continues to place 'participants' in either industrial or clerical work. In the brochure that participants are given about the program, they are instructed that they will be 'performing office or warehouse duties for various companies in the local business community' (Workfirst brochure, April 1998: 1). Reminiscent of the kind of placements common among employment agents operating in the labour market at the turn of the century, men are also instructed to report to the agency with

steel-toed boots, lunch, and bus fare, at either 6:45 a.m. or 3:45 p.m. (to account for shift work) in order to be available for standby positions.

Chapter 8: The Challenge of Limiting Labour Market Fragmentation

1 Indeed, for immigrants and people of colour, the process of racialization remains key to their location in the division of labour inside the THI and within the labour market as a whole.

2 This is not to suggest that temporary help workers are unfree wage labourers because most retain the formal right to circulate freely in the labour market. Workfirst 'participants' represent the key exception here since this group of social assistance recipients is bound by a restrictive and coercive work-incentive strategy that requires them to register with temporary help agencies and to accept whatever types of work they are offered or face punitive sanctions. In this way, their status in the contemporary labour market resembles that of the many immigrants and migrant workers engaged by private employment agents at the turn of the century.

3 Fudge (1993) and D. MacDonald (1998a) assert that the following principles form the basis for bargaining unit determination at the provincial/territorial level: the 'community of interest'; the practices or history of collective bargaining; the desirability of separating white- and blue-collar employees; the aversion to 'fragmentation' within bargaining units; agreement between parties; desires of employees; organized structure of the employees; geography; and traditional methods of unionization. Still, their case studies of Ontario and British Columbia suggest that the relative significance of each principle differs from one region to another.

4 In 1993 the NDP government in Ontario amended the *Labour Relations Act*, overcoming the Labour Relations Board's historic policy of separating part-time and full-time workers; however, with the election of the Tory government in 1994, this progressive change was reversed in Bill 7. Still, in a 1996 decision the Ontario Labour Relations Board indicated that 'it was not satisfied that assertions about the lack of community of interest between full-time and part-time employees ought to continue to be elevated to the level of a labour relations axiom' (Fudge, 1996: 256; *Caressant Care Nursing Home of Canada Ltd. v CUPE Local 2225.09* [1996] OLRB Report, September/October, 748.

5 See, for example, Cameron, 1995; Cobble, 1993; Fudge, 1993; D. MacDonald 1998b; O'Grady, 1991; Wial, 1993.

6 The vague language used in the act is 'preponderant significance and importance.'

7 Workers in the construction sector were excluded from the jurisdiction of the act in 1969, although the *Construction Industry Labour Relations Act of Quebec* also provides for judicial extension.

8 For a detailed critique of this proposal, see D. MacDonald, 1998a.

9 In the proposal, small workplaces included those with fewer than fifty full-time workers or the equivalent number of part-time workers.

10 In addition, it would have imposed a 'double majority system': the union with 'the requisite support at more than one work location within a sector could apply for certification of the employees at those locations,' but to be certified it would require majority support through a representation vote at *each location* and majority support among all the employees at the work locations where certification was sought (Schenk, 1995: 206). On the one hand, this cumbersome system could have had the effect of limiting the spread of sectoral bargaining, but on the other it would have ensured that sectoral agreements were not imposed top-down.

11 The craft-based model of collective bargaining operating in the construction industry in provinces such as Ontario, Quebec, and British Columbia is organized on closed-shop and hiring-hall arrangements, where construction unions provide training/ apprenticeship to workers, place workers in employment, and establish industry-wide standards, and therefore hold a monopoly over skills. For a discussion of the type of unionism operating in the construction industry in Canada historically, one that treats the case of British Columbia quite closely, see D. MacDonald, 1998b, chap. 3. Here, MacDonald makes a crucial link between forms of unionism dominant in the construction sector and broader-based bargaining proposals.

12 I follow Howard Wial (1993: 673–4) in adopting the term 'job-mobility' path. Wial defines a job-mobility path as 'a sequence of jobs through which workers move, with some regularity, according to a socially defined transitional structure.' He uses the term to demonstrate that job mobility is channeled through social relations among workers and employers and between workers and employers whether or not it occurs within a single firm or between firms. Preferable to the notion of a 'career-line,' the concept job mobility path is a useful term for describing the work histories of workers without well-defined occupational affiliations.

13 For detailed discussions of these models, please see Borowy, Gordon, and Lebans, 1993; Cameron and Mak, 1991; Fudge, 1997; Ontario District Council of the International Ladies' Garment Workers Union and INTER-CEDE, 1993.

14 Scholars who are associated with this movement take different approaches to adapting the craft/occupational model to suit these workers. Still, most

are quite critical of the existing literature, emerging largely from schools of management and business administration, which argues that unions must change course drastically if they are to accommodate the growing number of workers confronted with 'new' forms of work organization, and situates the 'professional association' as a suitable prototype. In criticizing common assumptions made in this literature, Dorothy Sue Cobble (1994: 292) puts forward the following forceful counterclaim, an assertion that is worth repeating here: '[T]he argument goes, if industrial unionism is obsolete, so is unionism per se. This historical amnesia hampers attempts to create new forms of collective representation. Postindustrial unionism does not need to be invented out of whole cloth: it can be re-assembled, re-shaped and extended from elements of past, and current institutional practice.'

15 Referring to the case of nurses, Pat Armstrong (1993) uses the complementary term 'vocational identity' to express a similar idea.

16 Citing the case of waitresses in the early twentieth century, Cobble (1991: 423) notes that '[t]hose desiring work had to meet the approval of the union dispatcher and were required to be fully qualified union members "in good standing." Unlike the employment agencies against which the union hiring halls competed, union-run agencies prided themselves on offering free service to workers and employers.'

17 Interestingly, even though he is critical of the craft/occupational model of unionism as an ideal-type, Wial (1993: 688) notes:

> The federated amalgamated craft structures could be applicable to low-wage service sector workers who remain within the loosely defined occupation or group of occupations for an extended period of time by the lack of strong occupational consciousness that the peer craft model requires. Food-service workers, for example, might move between any of the number of tasks related to the preparation, serving, and selling of food (e.g., short-order cooking, serving, cashiering). They do not typically have strong occupational consciousness with respect to any of the tasks or with respect to the 'food-service occupation' as a whole. These workers might find an amalgamated union structure desirable. For occupations that are more sharply differentiated from one another, but are still 'related' (e.g., a set of occupations that makes up part but not all of an industry, such as the non-professional occupations in health-care), a federated structure might be appropriate.

18 For a detailed description of the OBU and other forms of revolutionary unionism prevalent in the early part of the century, see Savage, 1971: pt. 2.

19 Originating in Silicon Valley, California, this campaign aimed to address

the needs of workers (in similar occupations) engaged by contractors to perform service work at different worksites. It involved eschewing contractor-by-contractor organizing and instead targeting building owners; the strategy of pursuing industry-wide minimum standards by targeting building owners was based on the rationale that these entities controlled the work. The end result of the campaign was the negotiation of a geographically defined master contract establishing standardized wages for all worksites in the region (for an extended examination of this campaign, see Middleton 1996).

20 For a detailed review of worker-run employment agencies currently operating in the United States, see Middleton (1996).

References

Abraham, K.G. (1990). 'Restructuring the Employment Relationship: The Growth of Market Mediated Work Arrangements.' *New Developments in the Labour Market.* Boston: Massachusetts Institute of Technology, 85.

Advisory Group on Working Time and the Distribution of Work. (1994). *Report of the Advisory Group on Working Time and the Distribution of Work.* Ottawa: Human Resources Development Canada.

Aglietta, M. (1979). *A Theory of Capitalist Regulation.* London: NLB.

Akyeampong, E.B. (1989). 'The Changing Face of Temporary Help.' *Perspectives on Labour and Income* (Summer): 43.

– (1997). 'A Statistical Portrait of the Trade Union Movement.' *Perpectives on Labour and Income* (Winter): 45.

Alberta. (1919a). 'An Act to Establish the Alberta Government Employment Bureau.' *Revised Statutes of Alberta,* c. 14.

– (1919b). 'An Act Respecting Employment Offices.' *Revised Statutes of Alberta,* c. 15.

– (1927). 'An Act Respecting Government and Other Employment Offices.' *Revised Statutes of Alberta,* c. 179.

– (1937). 'An Act to Amend and Consolidate the Employment Offices Act.' *Revised Statutes of Alberta,* c. 50.

– (1942). 'An Act Respecting Employment Offices.' *Revised Statutes of Alberta,* c. 22.

Albo, G. (1990). 'The "New Realism" and Canadian Workers.' *Canadian Politics: An Introduction.* Toronto: Broadview Press, 471.

– (1994). '"Competitive Austerity" and the Impasse of Capitalist Employment Policy.' In R. Milliband and L. Panitch (eds.), *Socialist Register 1994: Between Globalism and Nationalism.* London: The Merlin Press.

Anderson, J. (1989). 'The Structure of Collective Bargaining.' In J.C.

Anderson, M. Gunderson, and A. Ponak. *Union-Management Relations in Canada*. 2d ed. Don Mills, Ont.: Addison-Wesley: 209.

Anderson, K. J. (1991). *Vancouver's Chinatown*. Montreal: McGill-Queen's University Press.

Annunziato, F.R. (1990). 'Commodity Unionism.' *Rethinking* Marxism 3 (Summer): 8.

Arat-Koc, S. (1990). '"Importing Houswives": Non-Citizen Domestic Workers and the Crisis of the Domestic Sphere in Canada.' In Meg Luxton, Harriet Rosenberg, and Sedef Arat-Koc. *Through the Kitchen Window*. Toronto: Garamond, 81.

– (1997). 'From "Mothers of the Nation" to Migrant Workers.' In A. Bakan and D. Stasiulus (eds.), *Not One of the Family*. Toronto, University of Toronto Press, 53.

Archibald, K. (1970). *Sex and the Public Service*. Ottawa, Ministry of Supply and Services.

Armstrong, P. (1993). 'Professions, Unions or What?: Learning from Nurses.' In L. Briskin and P. McDermott. *Women Challenging Unions: Feminism, Democracy and Militancy*. Toronto: University of Toronto Press, 304.

– (1995). 'The Feminization of the Labour Force: Harmonizing Down in a Global Economy.' In M. Hessing, et al. (eds.), *Invisible*. Charlottetown: Gynergy, 368.

– (1996). 'The Feminization of the Labour Force: Harmonizing Down in a Global Economy.' In Bakker, I. (ed.), *Rethinking Restructuring: Gender and Change in Canada*. Toronto: University of Toronto Press, 29.

– (1997). 'Restructuring Public and Private: Women's Paid and Unpaid Work.' In S.B. Boyd (ed.), *Challenging the Public Private Divide: Feminism, Law and Public Policy*. Toronto: University of Toronto Press.

Armstrong, P., and H. Armstrong. (1975). 'The Segregated Participation of Women in the Canadian Labour Force, 1941–1971.' *Canadian Review of Sociology and Anthropology* 12 (4): 370.

– (1983). 'Beyond Sexless Class and Classless Sex: Towards Feminist Marxism.' *Studies in Political Economy* 10 (Winter): 7.

– (1984). 'More on Marxism and Feminism: A Response to Connelly.' *Studies in Political Economy*. 15 (Fall): 179.

– (1989). 'Taking Women into Account.' In J. Jenson, E. Hagen, and C. Reddy. *Feminization of the Labour Force: Paradoxes and Promises*. Oxford: Polity Press, 66.

– (1994). *The Double Ghetto* 3d ed. Toronto: McClelland & Stewart.

Association of Professional Placement Agencies of Canada and Employment Staffing Services Association of Canada. (1996). 'A Submission to the Ministry of Labour of Ontario with Respect to an Analysis of the Employment Agencies Act.'

Atkinson, J. (1988). 'Recent Changes in the Internal Labour Market in the UK.' In W. Buitelaar (ed), *Technology and Work*. Aldershot, England: Avebury, 133.

Avery, D. (1979). *Dangerous Foreigners: European Immigrant Workers and Labour Radicalism in Canada, 1819–1932*. Toronto: McClelland & Stewart.

– (1995). *Reluctant Host*. Toronto: McClelland & Stewart.

Axelrod, J. G. (1987). 'Employee Leasing and the Joint Employer Relationship.' *The Labor Lawyer* 3: 853.

Baigent, J., V. Spelling-Ready, and T. Roper. (1992). *A Report to the Honourable Moe Sihota, Minister of Labour: Recommendations for Labour Law Reform*. British Columbia: Ministry of Labour.

Bakan, A.B., and D.K. Stasiulis. (1995). 'Making the Match: Domestic Placement Agencies and the Racialization of Women's Household Work.' *Signs* 20 (2): 303.

– (1997). 'Foreign Domestic Worker Policy in Canada and the Social Boundaries of Modern Citizenship.' *Not One of the Family*. Toronto: University of Toronto Press, 29.

Bakker, I. (1989). 'Women's Employment in Comparative Perspective.' In J. Jenson, E. Hagen, and C. Reddy. *Feminization of the Labour Force: Paradoxes and Promises*. Oxford: Polity Press, 17.

– (1991). 'Pay Equity and Economic Restructuring: The Polarization of Policy?' In J. Fudge and P. McDermott (eds.), *Just Wages: A Feminist Assessment of Pay Equity*. Toronto: University of Toronto Press, 254.

Bakker, I., and K. Scott. (1997). 'From the Post-War to the Post-Liberal Keynesian Welfare State.' In W. Clement (ed.), *Understanding Canada: Building on the New Canadian Political Economy*. Montreal: McGill-Queen's University Press.

Barber, M. (1988). 'The Women Ontario Welcomed: Immigrant Domestics for Ontario Homes, 1870–1930.' In A. Prentice, and S. Mann Trofimenkoff (eds.), *The Neglected Majority: Essays in Canadian Women's History*. Toronto: McClelland & Stewart, 102.

– (1991). *Immigrant Domestic Servants in Canada*. Ottawa: Canadian Historical Association.

Barrett, M. (1988). *Women's Oppression Today: The Marxist/Feminist Encounter*. London: Verso.

Barrett, M., and M. McIntosh. (1980). 'The "Family Wage": Some Problems for Socialists and Feminists.' *Capital and Class* (11): 51.

Barron, A. (1994). 'Mexican Women Wage-Earners and Macro-economic

Policies.' In I. Bakker (ed.), *The Strategic Silence: Gender and Economic Policy.*
London: Zed Books, 137.

Belgium (1987). 'Loi sur le travail temporaire, le travail interimaire et la mise
de travailleurs a la disposition d'utilisers,' 24 January.

Benston, M. (1969). 'The Political Economy of Women's Liberation.' *Monthly
Review* 21, (September): 13.

Bezanson, K., and F. Valentine. (1997). 'Act in Haste ... The Speed, Scope and
Style of Policy Change in Ontario.' Ottawa: Caledon Institute of Social
Policy.

Birt, A. (1960). 'Married Women, You're Fools To Take A Job.' *Chatelaine,*
January, 12.

Blanpain, R. (1993). 'Belgium.' In R. Blanpain (ed.), *Temporary Work and
Labour Law of the European Community and Member States.* Deventer, Netherlands: Kluwer, 45.

Blanpain, R. (ed.), (1993). *Temporary Work and Labour Law of the European
Community and Member States.* Deventer, Netherlands: Kluwer.

Borowy, J., S. Gordon, and G. Lebans. (1993). 'Are These Clothes Clean? The
Campaign for Fair Wages and Working Conditions for Homeworkers.' In
L. Carty (ed.), *And Still We Rise: Feminist Political Mobilizing in Contemporary
Canada.* Toronto: The Women's Press, 233.

Booth, P. (1997). 'Contingent Work: Trends, Issues and Challenges for
Employers.' Ottawa: Conference Board of Canada.

Botwinick, H. (1993). *Persistent Inequalities.* Princeton: Princeton University
Press.

Bow, F.T. (1964). 'The Great Manpower Grab.' *Reader's Digest,* October, 9.

Boyd, M., M.A. Mulvihill, and J. Myles. (1991). 'Gender, Power and Post-
industrialism.' *Canadian Review of Sociology and Anthropology* 28: 4.

Bradwin, E.W. (1972). *The Bunkhouse Man: A Study of Work and Pay in the Camps
of Canada, 1903–1914.* Toronto: University of Toronto Press.

British Columbia. (1912). 'An Act Respecting Employment Agencies.' *Revised
Statutes of British Columbia,* c. 10.

– (1915). 'An Act to amend the "Employment Agencies Act."' *Revised Statutes of
British Columbia,* c. 23.

– (1919). 'And Act to repeal the "Employment Agencies Act."' *Revised Statutes
of British Columbia,* c. 26.

– (1980). 'Employment Standards Act.' *Revised Statutes of British Columbia,* c. 10.

– (1995). 'Employment Standards Act (Bill 29).' *Revised Regulations of British
Columbia,* pt. 2.

Broad, D. (1991). 'Global Economic Restructuring and the (Re)casualization
of Work in the Centre.' *Review.* 4 (Fall): 555.

– (1993). 'Towards The Hollow Society? Global Economic Restructuring and the (Re)-casualization of Labour in Canada.' PhD diss., Department of Sociology, Carleton University.

Brodie, J. (1994). 'Shifting the Boundaries: Gender and the Politics of Restructuring.' In I. Bakker, (ed.), *The Strategic Silence.* London: Zed Books, 46.

Bronstein, A. (1991). 'Temporary Work in Western Europe: Threat or Complement to Permanent Employment?' *International Labour Review* 130 (3): 291.

Butchtemann, C.F., and S. Quack. (1990). 'How Precarious is "Non-standard" Employment? Evidence for West Germany.' *Cambridge Journal of Economics* 14: 315.

Calliste, A. (1993). 'Race, Gender and Canadian Immigration Policy: Blacks from the Caribbean 1900–1932.' *Journal of Canadian Studies* 28 (4): 131.

Cameron, B. (1995). 'From Segmentation to Solidarity: A New Framework for Labour Market Regulation.' In D. Drache and A. Ranikin. *Warm Heart, Cold Country: Fiscal and Social Policy Reform in Canada.* Ottawa: Caledon Institute of Social Policy / Roberts Centre for Canadian Studies, 193.

Cameron, B., and T. Mak. (1991). 'Working Conditions of Chinese-Speaking Homeworkers in the Toronto Garment Industry: Summary of Survey Results.' Unpublished brief. Toronto: International Ladies Garment Workers' Union.

Campbell, R.M. (1991). *The Full-Employment Objective in Canada, 1945–85: Historical, Conceptual, and Comparative Perspectives.* Ottawa: Economic Council of Canada.

Canada. (1897). 'An Act to Restrict the Importation and Employment of Aliens.' *Revised Statutes of Canada.* 60–61, c. 11.

– (1903). 'An Act Respecting Cities and Towns.' *Revised Statutes of Canada,* c. 38, s. 424.

– (1905). *Royal Commission Appointed to Inquire into the Immigration of Italian Labourers to Montreal and the Alleged Fraudulent Practices of Employment Agencies.* Ottawa: Department of the Interior.

– (1905–06). 'An Act Respecting False Representations to Induce Working Turns Immigration.' *Revised Statutes of Canada.* 4–5 Edw. 7, c. 16.

– (1906). 'Immigration from the United Kingdom – False Representation.' House of Commons. *Debates,* 9 May.

– (1909). Civil Service Commission. *Annual Report.* Ottawa: C.H. Parmelee.

– (1913a). 'Privy Council Order 1028.' *Canada Gazette,* 25 October, 1239.

– (1913b). 'Privy Council Order 1064.' *Canada Gazette,* 25 October, 1239.

– (1918). 'Organization and Coordination of Employment Offices.' House of Commons, *Debates.* 23 April.

– (1918). 'An Act to Aid and Encourage the Organization and Co-ordination of Employment Offices (Bill 57).' *Revised Statutes of Canada.* 8–9 Geo. 5.

- (1937). 'The Employment Agencies Act.' *Revised Statutes of Ontario*, c. 248.
- (1985). *Royal Commission on the Economic Union and Development Prospects for Canada*. Ottawa: Ministry of Supply and Services.
- (1986). *Commission of Inquiry into Unemployment Insurance*. Ottawa: Ministry of Supply and Services.

Canadian Labour Congress. (1995). 'Brief to Working Group on Seasonal Work and U.I.'

Canadian Civil Liberties Organization. (1983). Letter to the Ontario Human Rights Commission.

Carolina Alliance For Fair Employment. (1994). 'Report on the Carolina Alliance for Fair Employment Greenville Temp School, 7–11 November 1994.' Unpublished.

Carré, F. (1992). 'Temporary Employment in the Eighties.' In V. duRivage (ed.), *New Policies for the Part-time and Contingent Workforce*. New York: M.E. Sharpe, 450.
- (1994). 'Policy Responses to Short-Term, Temporary and Part-Time Employment in France.' Washington: U.S. Department of Labor.

Catagay, N. (1994). 'Turkish Women and Structural Adjustment.' In I. Bakker (ed.), *The Strategic Silence: Gender and Economic Policy*. London: Zed Books, 46.

Civil Service Commission. (1908). *Annual Report, 1908*. Ottawa: C.H. Parmelee.

Cobble, D.S. (1991). 'Organizing the Postindustrial Work Force: Lessons from the History of Waitress Unionism.' *Industrial and Labor Relations Review* 44 (3): 419.
- (ed.), (1993). *Women and Unions: Forging a Partnership*. Ithaca, N.Y.: ILR Press.
- (1994). 'Making Postindustrial Unionism Possible.' In S. Friedman, R.W. Hurd, R.A. Oswald, and R.L. Seeber (eds.), *Restoring the Promise of American Labor Law*. Ithaca, N.Y.: ILR Press, 285.
- (1996). 'The Prospects for Unionism in a Service Society.' In C.L. Macdonald, and C. Sirianni (eds.), *Working in the Service Society*. Philadelphia: Temple University Press, 333.

Cohen, M. (1994). 'The Implications of Economic Restructuring for Women: The Canadian Situation.' In I. Bakker, (ed.), *The Strategic Silence: Gender and Economic Policy*. London: Zed Books/ North-South Institute, 103.

Commons, J. R. (1967). *Principles of Labor Legislation*. 4th rev. ed. New York: Augustus M. Kelley.

Connelly, P. (1978). *Last Hired, First Fired: Women and the Canadian Work Force*. Toronto: The Women's Press.
- (1983). 'On Marxism and Feminism.' *Studies in Political Economy* 12 (Fall): 153.

Cordova, E. (1986). 'From Full-Time Wage Employment: A Major Shift in the Evolution of Labour Relations?' *International Labour Review* 125 (6): 641.

Council of Europe. (1985). *Les entreprises de travail Interimaire generaux; problemes particuliers du travail interimaire transfrontalier legal ou illegal.* Strasbourg: Council of Europe.

Crompton, S. (1993). 'The Renaissance of Self-employment.' *Perspectives on Labour and Income* (Summer): 22.

Cunningham, N. (1991). 'Seduced and Abandoned: The Legal Regulation of Domestic Workers in Canada from 1867 to 1940.' Masters' thesis, Osgoode Law School and York University.

Cuthbert-Brandt, G. (1982). '"Pigeon-Holed and Forgotten": The Work of the Subcommittee on the Post-War Problems of Women, 1943.' *Histoire Sociale – Social History* X (29): 239.

Daenzer, P.M. (1997). 'An Affair between Nations: International Relations and the Movement of Household Service Workers.' In A. Bakan, and D. Stasiulus (eds.), *Not One of the Family.* Toronto: University of Toronto Press, 81.

Davidoff, L., and C. Hall. (1987). *Family Fortunes: Men and Women of the English Middle Class, 1780–1850.* Chicago: University of Chicago Press.

Department of Labour, (1900). 'The Trades and Labour Congress of Canada.' *The Labour Gazette* (3 October).

– (1901). 'The Trades and Labour Congress of Canada.' *The Labour Gazette* (October).

– (1902). 'The Trades and Labour Congress of Canada – Eighteenth Annual Convention.' *The Labour Gazette* (October): 228.

– (1904). 'Free Employment Offices in the United States and Foreign Countries.' *The Labour Gazette* (March): 944.

– (1904). 'Employment Bureaus and Agencies in Canada.' *The Labour Gazette* (September): 257.

– (1904). 'Twentieth Annual Convention of Trades and Labour Congress of Canada.' *The Labour Gazette* (October): 355.

– (1905). 'Trade and Labour Congress of Canada – Twenty-First Annual Convention.' *The Labour Gazette* (October): 41.

– (1906). 'Action by Parliament of Canada to Prevent Fraudulent Representations to Working Men.' *The Labour Gazette* (June): 1346.

– (1907). 'Dominion Government Employment Agencies for Immigrants.' *The Labour Gazette* (March): 1011–12.

– (1907). 'Dishonest Employment Methods.' *The Labour Gazette* (August): 212.

– (1907). 'Fraudulent Labour Agent Convicted of False Pretenses and Forgery.' *The Labour Gazette* (November): 212.

– (1907). 'Proceedings of Commission to Enquire into Methods to Induce Oriental Labourers to Emigrate to Canada.' *The Labour Gazette* (December): 695.

- (1908). 'Chinese Employment Agent Guilty of False Pretences.' *The Labour Gazette* (February): 1026.
- (1908). 'Fraudulent Employment Agents Convicted.' *The Labour Gazette* (February): 314.
- (1908). 'Fraudulent Employment Agent Convicted.' *The Labour Gazette* (March): 1161–2.
- (1908). 'Employment Agent Sent to Prison.' *The Labour Gazette* (March): 1165.
- (1909). 'Employment Agent's Commission.' *The Labour Gazette* (May): 1271.
- (1910). 'False Representations to Intending Immigrants to Canada.' *The Labour Gazette* (May): 1312.
- (1910). 'Quebec Legislation Affecting Labour.' *The Labour Gazette* (September): 1420.
- (1911). 'Conditions of Employment in Western Canada Employment Bureaus.' *The Labour Gazette* (March): 997.
- (1913). 'British Columbia Legislation Affecting Labour, 1912.' *The Labour Gazette* (April): 1103.
- (1913). 'Regulations for the Protection of Immigrants Seeking Employment through Employment Offices in Canada.' *The Labour Gazette* (May): 1275.
- (1914). 'Saskatchewan Legislation Affecting Labour.' *The Labour Gazette* (March): 1066.
- (1914). 'Violation of Immigration Regulation by Employment Agencies.' *The Labour Gazette* (May): 1359.
- (1914). 'Quebec Legislation Affecting Labour.' *The Labour Gazette* (June): 1420.
- (1914). 'Condition during October Affecting Women Workers in leading Industrial Centres.' *The Labour Gazette* (November): 570.
- (1915). 'Much Effective Work by Dominion, Provincial and Municipal authorities: Regulation of Private Employment Agencies.' *The Labour Gazette* (March): 1063.
- (1919). 'League of Nations International Labour Conference.' *The Labour Gazette* (December): 1425.
- (1926). 'Canada's Experience with Private Employment Offices.' *The Labour Gazette* (April): 331.
- (1932). 'League of Nations International Labour Organization: 16th Session of the International Labour Conference.' *The Labour Gazette* (May): 553.
- (1933). 'Unemployment Relief Expenditure – Ontario.' *The Labour Gazette* (May): 506.
- (1933). 'Annual Report of the Director of the International Labour Organization.' *The Labour·Gazette* (June): 622.

– (1933). 'League of Nations International Labour Organization: 17th Session of the International Labour Conference.' *The Labour Gazette* (August): 786.

– (1933). 'Trade Union Congress of Great Britain, 1933.' *The Labour Gazette* (October): 1007.

– (1934). 'Employment Conditions in Canada at the End of May, 1934: Reports of the Superintendents of the Employment Service.' *The Labour Gazette* (June): 542.

– (1935). 'Employment Offices Co-ordination Act.' *The Labour Gazette* (January): 16.

– (1935). 'Reports – British Ministry of Labour.' *The Labour Gazette* (June): 536.

– (1950). 'Employment Service Convention Ratified by Canada.' *The Labour Gazette* (July): 1158.

– (1950). 'International Labour Organization: 112th Session of the ILO Governing Body.' *The Labour Gazette* (July): 1657.

– (1960). 'Labour Standards Legislation Enacted in 1960.' *The Labour Gazette* 1049.

Doeringer, P., and M. Piore. (1971). *Internal Labour Markets and Manpower Analysis.* Boston: Lexington Heath.

Dombois, R. (1989). 'Flexibility by Law? The West German Employment Promotion Act and Temporary Employment.' *Cambridge Journal of Economics* (13): 359.

Duffy, A., and N. Pupo. (1992). *The Part-Time Paradox: Connecting Gender, Work, and Family.* Toronto: McClelland & Stewart.

Economic Council of Canada (1976). *People and Jobs.* Ottawa: Ministry of Supply and Services.

– (1990). *Good Jobs, Bad Jobs: Employment in the Service Economy.* Ottawa: Ministry of Supply and Services.

Eklund, R. (1997). 'A Look at Contract Labour in the Nordic Countries.' *Comparative Labor Law Journal* 18 (Winter): 229.

Elson, D. (1989). 'The Impact of Structural Adjustment on Women: Concepts and Issues.' In B. Ominiode (ed.), *The IMF, the World Bank and the African Debt.* London, Zed Books, 56.

Elson, D. (ed). (1995). *Male-Bias in the Development Process.* Manchester: Manchester University Press.

Epstein, E., and J. Monat. (1973). 'Labour Contracting and Its Regulation: I.' *International Labour Review* 107 (5): 451.

Esping-Andersen, G. (1990). *The Three Worlds of Welfare Capitalism.* Princeton: Princeton University Press.

European Community Commission. (1990a). 'Proposal for a Council Directive on Certain Employment Relationships with Regard to Working Conditions.' *Official Journal of the European Communities* 33(90/C224/04): 4.

– (1990b). 'Proposal for a Council Directive on Certain Employment Relationships with Regard to Distortions of Competition.' *Official Journal of the European Communities* 33(90/C224/05): 6.

– (1990c). 'Proposal for a Council Directive Supplementing the Measures to Encourage Improvements in Safety and Health at Work of Temporary Workers.' *Official Journal of the European Communities* 33(90/C224/06): 8.

Evans, P. (1988). 'Work Incentives and the Single Mother: Dilemmas of Reform.' *Canadian Public Policy* 14 (2): 125–36.

– (1995a). 'Linking Welfare to Jobs: Workfare Canadian Style.' *Policy Options*, 5 May.

Federation of Temporary Help Services. (1995). 'A Proposal to the Ministry of Labour of Ontario with Respect to Compliance with the Occupational Health and Safety Act.'

Fernandez-Kelly, M.P., and A. Garcia. (1989). 'Informalization at the Core: Hispanic Women, Homework, and the Advanced Capitalist State.' In A. Portes, M. Castells, and L.A. Benton (eds.), *The Informal Economy: Studies in Advanced and Less Developed Countries.* Baltimore: Johns Hopkins University Press, 242.

Finkel, A. (1995). 'Trade Unions and the Welfare State in Canada, 1945–1990.' In C. Gonick, P. Phillips, and J. Vorst. *Labour Gains, Labour Pains: 50 Years of PC 1003.* Winnipeg: Society for Socialist Studies/Fernwood Publishing, 59.

Forrest , A. (1986) 'Bargaining Units and Bargaining Power.' *Relations Industrielles/ Industrial Relations* 41 (4): 840.

– (1995). 'Securing the Male Breadwinner: A Feminist Interpretation of PC 1003.' In C. Gonick et al. *Labour Gains, Labour Pains: 50 Years of PC 1003.* Winnipeg: Society for Socialist Studies/ Fernwood Publishing, 139.

Fowler, E. (1996). *San'ya Blues: Laboring Life in Contemporary Tokyo.* Ithaca, N.Y.: Cornell University Press.

Fraser, N., and L. Gordon. (1994). 'A Geneology of Dependency: Tracing a Keyword of the U.S. Welfare State.' *Signs* 19 (21): 309.

France. (1972). 'Act No. 2 Respecting Temporary Employment.' Trans. in *ILO Legislative Series* (November–December): 35.

– (1996). *Code Due Travail.* Chap. 5. Dalloz: Strasbourg.

Fric, L. (1973). The Role of Commerical Employment Agencies in the Canadian Labour Market. PhD diss., Toronto: Department of Economics, University of Toronto.

Frobel, F., J. Heinrichs, and O. Kreye. (1980). *The New International Division of Labour.* London: Cambridge University Press.

Fromstein, M. (1978). 'The Socio-economic Roles of the Temporary Help Service in the United States Labour Market.' In E. Ginzberg (ed.), *Labour Market Intermediaries.* Conference proceedings. Washington: National Committee For Manpower Policy: 170.

Fudge, J. (1991). *Labour Law's Little Sister: The Employment Standard Act and the Feminization of Labour.* Ottawa: Canadian Centre For Policy Alternatives.

– (1993). 'The Gendered Dimension of Labour Law: Why Women Need Inclusive Unionism and Broader-Based Bargaining.' In L. Briskin and P. McDermott. *Women Challenging Unions: Feminism, Militancy and Democracy.* Toronto: University of Toronto Press: 231.

– (1995). 'Precarious Work and Families.' Working paper. Toronto: Centre for Work and Society, York University.

– (1996). 'Rungs on the Labour Law Ladder: Using Gender to Challenge Hierarchy.' *Saskatchewan Law Review* 60 (1): 237.

– (1997). 'Little Victories and Big Defeats: The Rise and Fall of Collective Bargaining Rights for Domestic Workers in Ontario.' In A. Bakan and D. Stasiulus (eds.), *Not One of the Family.* Toronto: University of Toronto Press: 119.

Galarneau, D. (1996). 'Unionized Workers.' *Perspectives on Labour and Income* (Spring): 43.

Gannage, C. (1986). *Double Day Bind.* Toronto: The Women's Press.

Gannon, M. (1978). 'An Analysis of the Temporary Help Industry.' In E. Ginzberg, (ed.), *Labour Market Intermediaries.* Conference proceedings. Washington: National Committee For Manpower Policy, 195.

Gannon, M.J. (1984). 'Preferences of Temporary Workers: Time, Variety, and Flexibility.' *Monthly Labour Review* (August): 26.

General Welfare Assistance Policy Directive. (1996). 'Ontario Works in Peel, Phase I: Workfirst,' PSS-O1–O11 (1 August).

Germany. (1972). 'An Act Respecting the Provision of Manpower as a Commercial Operation (Manpower Provision Act),' 7 August 1972. Trans. in *ILO Legislative Series* (November–December): 1.

Gill, S. (1993). 'Global Finance, Monetary Policy and Cooperation among the Group of Seven, 1944–1992.' *Finance and World Politics: Markets, Regimes and States in the Post-hegemonic Era.* Aldershot, England: Edward Elgar: 86.

Gill, S., and D. Law. (1988). *The Global Political Economy.* Baltimore: Johns Hopkins University Press.

Gilpin, R. (1987). *The Political Economy of International Relations.* Princeton: Princeton University Press.

Ginzberg, E. (ed.), (1978). *Labour Market Intermediaries.* Special Report No. 2. Conference proceedings. National Commission for Manpower Policy.

Goka, K. (1997). 'Country Study: Japan.' *Development of Private Employment Agencies and Government Policies*. Geneva: ILO.

Golden, L., and E. Applebaum (1992). 'What Was Driving the 1982–1988 Boom in Temporary Employment?' *American Journal of Economics and Sociology* 51 (4): 473.

Gonick, C., P. Phillips, and J. Vorst. (1995). *Labour Gains, Labour Pains: 50 Years of PC 1003*. Winnipeg: Fernwood Publishing.

Gonos, G. (1994). 'A Sociology of the Temporary Employment Relationship.' PhD diss., Dept. of Sociology, New Brunswick, NJ: Rutgers University.

– (1995). 'The Battle Over "Employer" Status in the Post-War U.S.: The Case of the Temporary Help Firm.' Paper presented at the annual meeting of the Law and Society Association, Toronto, June 1995.

Gordon, D.M., R. Edwards, and M. Reich. (1987). *Segmented Work, Divided Workers: The Historical transformation of labor in the United States*. Cambridge: Cambridge University Press.

Gordon, L. (1989). (ed.). *Women, the State and Welfare*. Wisconsin: University of Wisconsin Press.

Gottfried, H. (1992). 'In the Margins: Flexibility as a Mode of Regulation in the Temporary Help Service Industry.' *Work, Employment And Society* 6 (3): 443.

Gramsci, A. (1971). *Selections from the Prison Notebooks*. New York: International Publishers.

Guard, J. (1995). 'Womanly Innocence and Manly Self-Respect: Gendered Challenges to Labour's Postwar Compromise.' In C. Gonick, P. Phillips, and J. Vorst. *Labour Gains, Labour Pains: 50 Years of PC 1003*. Winnipeg: Society for Socialist Studies/Fernwood Publishing: 119.

Gunderson, M., L. Muszynski, and J. Keck (1990). *Women and Labour Market Poverty*. Ottawa: Canadian Advisory Council on the Status of Women.

Halbach, G., N. Paland, R. Schwedes, and O. Wlotzke. (1994). *Labour Law in Germany: An Overview*. Deventer, Netherlands: Kluwer.

Hamdani, D. (1996). 'The Temporary Help Service Industry: Its Role, Structure and Growth.' *Service Indicators, 2nd Quarter*. (Statistics Canada, cat. 63–016XPB): 73.

Hardy, C. (1991). *The Age of Unreason*. London: Random House.

Harney, R.F. (1979). 'Montreal's King of Italian Labour: A Case Study of Padronism.' *Labour/Le Travailleur* 4 (4): 57.

Harvey, D. (1989). *The Condition of Postmodernity*. Cambridge, Mass.:, Blackwell Press.

Heckscher, C.C. (1988). *The New Unionism: Employee Involvement in the Changing Corporation*. New York: Basic Books.

Henson, K. (1993). '"Just a Temp": The Disenfranchised Worker.' PhD Diss. Northwestern University.

Hepple, B. (1993). 'The United Kingdom.' In R. Blanpain, (ed.), *Temporary Work and Labour Law of the European Community and Member States.* Deventer, Netherlands: Kluwer.

Hobbs, M. (1993a). 'Equality and Difference: Feminism and the Defence of Women Workers during the Great Depression.' *Labour/Le Travail* 32: 201.

– (1993b). 'Rethinking Anti-Feminism in the 1930s: Gender Crisis or Workplace Justice?.' *Gender and Society* 5 (1): 4.

Hobson, B. (1990). 'No Exit, No Voice: Women's Economic Dependency and the Welfare State.' *Acta Sociologica* 33 (3): 235.

Hodgetts, J.E., W. McClosky, R. Whitaker, and V.S. Wilson. (1972). *The Biography of an Institution: The Civil Service Commission of Canada, 1908–1967.* Montreal & London: McGill-Queen's University Press.

Holy, L., and M. Stuchlik. (1983). *Actions, Norms and Representations: Foundations of Anthropological Inquiry.* Cambridge: Cambridge University Press.

Human Resources and Development Canada. (1994). *Improving Social Security in Canada: A Discussion Paper.* Ottawa: Ministry of Supply and Services.

Human Services Committee. (1996). 'Employment Placement Program Pilot Project – "Work First,"' Unpublished brief. 30 January.

– (1998). 'Social Assistance Division Workfirst Program: Recommendation.' Unpublished minutes (16 April).

– (1998). 'Ontario Works Activity Update.' Unpublished minutes (6 May).

– (1998). *Workfirst.*

Hutton, E. (1957). 'A New Way to Keep House and Hold a Job.' *Maclean's,* November, 19.

International Labour Organization (ILO). (1923). *International Labour Office: Official Bulletin.* 1 (April 1919–August 1920).

– (1932). *International Labour Conference: Record of Proceedings, 16th Session.* Geneva: International Labour Office.

– (1933a). *International Labour Conference: Record of Proceedings, 17th Session.* Geneva: International Labour Office.

– (1933b). *Employment Exchanges: An International Study of Placing Activities.* Geneva: International Labour Office.

– (1944). 'Future Policy, Programme and Status of the International Labour Organization.' Geneva: International Labour Office.

– (1949). *International Labour Conference: Record of Proceedings, 32nd Session, 1949.* Geneva: International Labour Office.

– (1966). 'Memorandum Sent by the International Labour Office to the Ministry of Health and Social Affairs of Sweden.' *International Labour Office: Official Bulletin.* 49 (3): 390.

– (1992a). *International Labour Conventions and Recommendations 1919–1991.* Geneva: International Labour Office, 145–6.

- (1992b). *Constitution of the International Labour Organization and Standing Orders of the International Labour Conference.* Geneva: International Labour Office.
- (1994a). *The Role of Private Employment Agencies in the Functioning of Labour Markets.* Report No. 6. Geneva: International Labour Office.
- (1994b). 'Sixth Item on the Agenda: The role of Private Employment Agencies in the Functioning of Labour Markets' (Report of the Committee on Private Employment Agencies). International Labour Conference: *Provisional Record.* 81st Session. Geneva: International Labour Office.
- (1996). *List of Ratifications by Convention and by Country.* Report 3 (pt. 2). Geneva: International Labour Office.
- (1997). *World Employment Report, 1996/97.* Geneva: International Labour Office.
- (1997a). *Revision of the Fee-Charging Employment Agencies Convention No. 96 (Revised), 1949* Report 4 (pt. 1). Geneva: International Labour Office, 6.
- (1997b). 'Fourth Item on the Agenda: Revision of the Fee-Charging Employment Agencies Convention No. 96 (Revised), 1949' *Provisional Record, 85th Session of the International Labour Conference.* Geneva: International Labour Office.
- (1997c). *Text of the Convention Concerning Private Employment Agencies, 85th International Labour Conference.* Geneva: International Labour Office.
- (1997d). *Text of the Recommendation Concerning Private Employment Agencies, 85th International Labour Conference.* Geneva: International Labour Office.
Jacobsen, P. (1993). 'Denmark.' In R. Blanpain (ed.), *Temporary Work and Labour Law of the European Community and Member States.* Deventer, Netherlands: Kluwer.
Japan. (1987). 'Worker Dispatching Law.' (English translation). Geneva: International Labour Office.
Jenson, J. (1986). 'Gender and Reproduction: Or, Babies and the State.' *Studies in Political Economy* 20 (9): 9.
- (1989a). 'The Talents of Women, the Skills of Men.' In S. Wood (ed.), *The Transformation of Work?* London: Unwin Hyman: 141.
- (1989b). '"Different" but Not "Exceptional": Canada's Permeable Fordism.' In *Canadian Review of Sociology and Anthropoloty* 26 (1): 69.
- (1996). 'Part-Time Employment and Women: A Range of Strategies.' In I. Bakker, (ed.), *Rethinking Restructuring: Gender and Change in Canada.* Toronto: University of Toronto Press: 92.
Jenson, J., E. Hagen, and C. Reddy. (eds.), (1989). *Feminization of the Labour Force: Paradoxes and Promises.* Oxford: Polity Press.
Jessop, B. (1990). 'Regulation Theories in Retrospect and Prospect.' *Economy and Society* 19 (2): 153.

– (1993). 'Towards a Schumpeterian Workfare State? Preliminary Remarks on Post-Fordist Political Economy.' *Studies in Political Economy* 40 (Spring): 7.

– (1995). 'Towards a Schumpeterian Workfare State in Britain? Reflections on Regulation, Governance and Welfare state.' *Environment and Planning* 27: 1613.

Joekes, S. (1987). *Women in the World Economy: An INSTRAW Study.* New York: Oxford University Press.

Johnson, L.C., and R.E. Johnson. (1982). *The Seam Allowance: Industrial Home Sewing in Canada.* Toronto: Alger Press.

Joray, P.A., and C.L. Hulin. (1978). 'A Survey of the Socio-Economic Aspects of Temporary Work in the United States.' Lexington, Virginia: International Institute for Temporary Work.

Katz, S. (1951). 'Why Wives Are Out to Work.' *Maclean's*, 9 May.

Kealey, L. (ed.). (1974). *Women at Work, 1850–1930.* Toronto: Women's Educational Press.

Keith, W. (1960). *Chatelaine,* Letter to the editor. 'Married Women, You're Fools to Take a Job.' January, 148.

Kellor, F. (1915). *Out of Work: A Study of Unemployment.* New York, G.P. Putnam's Sons.

Kirby, S., and McKenna, K. (1989). *Experience, Research, Social Change: Methods from the Margins.* Toronto: Garamond Press.

Koniaris, T.B. (1993). 'Greece.' In R. Blanpain (ed.), *Temporary Work and Labour Law of the European Community and Member States.* Deventer, Netherlands: Kluwer.

Krahn, H. (1995). 'Non-standard Work on the Rise.' *Perspectives on Labour and Income* (Winter): 35.

Labour Force Survey. See Statistics Canada.

Labour Gazette. See Department of Labour.

Laflamme, R., and D. Carrier. (1997). 'Droits et conditions de travail des employes des agences de location de main-d'oeuvre.' *Relations Industrielles/Industrial Relations* 52 (1): 162.

Leach, B. (1993). '"Flexible" Work, Precarious Future: Some Lessons from the Canadian Clothing Industry.' *Canadian Review of Sociology and Anthropology,* 30 (1): 64.

Lee, E. (1997). 'The Declaration of Philadelphia: Retrospect and Prospect.' *International Labour Review* 33 (4): 467.

Legal Agreement (Workfirst). (1996). 'The Regional Municipality of Peel and Duggan and Harvey and Associates Inc.' (31 July).

Lenskyj, H. (1981). 'A "Servant Problem" or a "Servant-Mistress Problem?": Domestic Service in Canada, 1890–1930.' *Atlantis* 7 (1): 3.

Lewis, J. (1993). 'Women, Work, Family and Social Policies in Europe.' In J. Lewis (ed.), *Women and Social Policies in Europe.* London: Edward Elgar Publishing.

Lightman, E.S. (1995). 'You Can Lead a Horse to Water, But ...: The Case against Workfare in Canada.' In J. Richards, A. Vining et al. (eds.), *Helping the Poor: A Qualified Case for 'Workfare.'* Toronto: C.D. Howe Institute.

Linder, M. (1992). *Farewell to the Self-Employed: Deconstructing a Socio-Economic and Legal Solopsism.* New York: Greenwood Press.

Lindsay, C. (1995). *Women in the Labour Force.* 3d ed. Ottawa: Statistics Canada.

Lindstrom-Best, V. (1986). '"I Won't Be a Slave": Finnish Domestics in Canada, 1911–1930.' In *Looking into My Sister's Eyes: An Exploration in Women's History.* Toronto, Multiculturalism Historical Society of Ontario, 32.

Lipsett, B., and M. Reesor. (1997). *Flexible Work Arrangements: Evidence from the 1991 and 1995 Survey of Work Arrangements.* Ottawa: Human Resources and Development Canada.

Low, W. (1996). 'Wide of the Mark: Using "Targeting" and Work Incentives to Direct Social Assistance to Single Parents.' In J. Pulkingham and G. Ternowetsky (eds.), *Remaking Canadian Social Policy.* Vancouver: Fernwood Press, 188.

Lowe, G. (1980). 'Women, Work and the Office: The Feminization of Clerical Occupations in Canada, 1901–1931.' *Canadian Journal of Sociology* 5 (4): 361.

– (1987). *Women in the Administrative Revolution: The Feminization of Clerical Work.* Toronto: University of Toronto Press.

Luxembourg. (1994). 'Loi du 19 mai 1994 portant réglementation du travail intérimaire et du pret temporaire de main-d'oeuvre.' *Recueil De Legislation* 42: 740.

Luxton, M. (1990). 'Two Hands for the Clock: Changing Patterns in the Gendered Division of Labour in the Home.' In M. Luxton, H. Rosenberg, and S. Arat-Koc. *Through the Kitchen Window: The Politics of Home and Family.* 2d ed. Toronto: Garamond Press, 39.

MacDonald, D. (1998a). 'Sectoral Certification: A Case Study of British Columbia.' *Canadian Labour and Employment Law Journal* 5: 243.

– (1998b). 'The New Deal Model of Collective Bargaining and the Secondary Labour Market.' PhD diss., Department of Law, Policy and Society, Northeastern Illinois University.

MacDonald, M. (1982). 'Implications for Understanding Women in the Labour Force of Labour Market Segmentation Analysis: Unanswered Questions.' In N. Hersom, and D.E. Smith. *Women and the Canadian Labour Force.* Ottawa: Social Sciences and Humanities Research Council, 167.

– (1991). 'Post-Fordism and the Flexibility Debate.' *Studies and Political Economy* (Autumn): 177.

Macpherson, M.E. (1945). 'Working Mothers.' *Chatelaine* (August): 68.

Mandel, E. (1976). 'Introduction.' In K. Marx. *Capital.* Vol. 1. New York: Penguin.

Mangum, G., D. Mayall, and K. Nelson. (1985). 'The Temporary Help Industry: A Response to the Dual Internal Labour Market.' *Industrial and Labor Relations Review* 38 (4): 599.

Manitoba. (1924). 'An Act to Establish Government Employment Bureaus.' *Revised Statutes of Manitoba*, c. 67.

– (1950). 'An Act Respecting Employment Services.' *Revised Statutes of Manitoba*, c. 15.

– (1954). 'An Act Respecting Employment Services.' *Revised Statutes of Manitoba*, c. 72.

– (1980). 'An Act Respecting Employment Services.' *Revised Statutes of Manitoba*, c. E100.

Marron, K. (1997). 'Scientific temps for hire.' *The Globe and Mail.* Toronto: B1.

Marx. K. (1913). *A Contribution to the Critique of Political Economy*. Chicago: C.H. Kerr.

– (1976). *Capital.* Vol. 1. New York: Penguin.

Maslove, A., and G. Swimmer. (1980). *Wage Controls in Canada, 1975–1978*. Montreal: Institute for Research on Public Policy.

McCrorie, A. (1995). 'PC 1003: Labour, Capital, and the State.' In C. Gonick, P. Phillips, and J. Vorst. *Labour Gains, Labour Pains: 50 Years of PC 1003.* Winnipeg: Society for Socialist Studies/Fernwood Publishing, 15.

McCrossin, S. (1997). 'Workfare or Workhouse? Occupational Health and Safety under Ontario Works.' *Journal of Law and Social Policy* (Fall): 140.

McFarland, J., and R. Mullaly. (1996). 'NB Works: Image vs. Reality.' In J. Pulkingham and G. Ternowetsky (eds.), *Remaking Canadian Social Policy*. Vancouver: Fernwood Press, 202.

Middleton, J. (1996). 'Contingent Workers in a Changing Economy: Endure, Adapt or Organize?' *New York University Review of Law and Social Change* 22: 557.

Miles, R. (1982). *Racism and Migrant Labour*. London: Routledge.

– (1987). *Capitalism and Unfree Labour: Anomaly or Necessity?* New York: Tavistock.

Ministry of Community and Social Services. (1996). 'Program Guidelines for Early Implementation of Ontario Works' (August).

– (1997). 'The Ontario Works Act.' Communique, 12 June.

Mitter, S., and S. Rowbotham. (1994). *Dignity and Daily Bread: New Forms of Economic Organizing*. London: Routledge.

Moore, M.A. (1965). 'The Legal Status of Temporary Help Services.' *Labor Law Journal* (October): 620.

– (1975). 'Proposed Federal Legislation for Temporary Labour Services.' *Labor Law Journal* (December): 767.

Morgan, N. (1988). *The Equality Game: Women in the Federal Public Service, 1908–1987.* Ottawa: Canadian Advisory Council on the Status of Women.

Mouat, J. (1995). *Roaring Days: Rossland's Mines and the History of British Columbia.* Vancouver: UBC Press.

Muckenberger, U. (1989). 'Non-standard Forms of Employment in the Federal Republic of Germany: The Role and Effectiveness of the State.' In G. Rogers, and J. Rogers (eds.), *Precarious Jobs in Labour Market Regulation: The Growth of Atypical Employment in Western Europe.* Belgium: International Institute for Labour Studies: 267.

Myles, J. (1988). 'Decline or Impasse? The Current State of the Welfare State.' *Studies in Political Economy* 26 (Summer): 73.

National Council on Welfare. (1997). *Another Look at Welfare Reform.* Ottawa: Ministry of Government Works and Services.

Nova Scotia. (1920). 'An Act Respecting Employment Agencies.' *Revised Statutes of Nova Scotia,* c. 13.

O'Connor, J. (1993). 'Gender, Class and Citizenship in the Comparative Analysis of Welfare State Regimes: Theoretical and Methodological Issues.' *British Journal of Sociology* 44 (3): 501.

Ocran, A. (1997). 'Restructuring Public and Private: Women's Paid and Unpaid Work.' In S.B. Boyd (ed.), *Challenging the Public Private Divide: Feminism, Law and Public Policy.* Toronto: University of Toronto Press.

Offe, C. (1985). *Disorganized Capitalism: Contemporary Transformations of Work and Politics.* Cambridge, Mass.: MIT Press.

O'Grady, J. (1991). 'Beyond the Wagner Act, What Then?' In D. Drache, (ed.), *Getting on Track.* Montreal and Kingston: McGill-Queen's Univeristy Press: 153.

O'Higgins, P. (1997). '"Labour Is Not a Commodity" – An Irish Contribution to International Labour Law.' *Industrial Law Journal* 26 (September): 225.

Ontario. (1897). 'The Municipal Act: An Act Respecting Municipal Institutions.' *Revised Statutes of Ontario,* c. 223.

– (1903). 'Consolidated Municipal Act.' *Revised Statutes of Ontario,* c. 19.

– (1914). 'An Act Respecting Employment Agencies.' *Revised Statutes of Ontario,* c. 38.

– (1917). *Revised Statutes of Ontario: An Act respecting Private, Voluntary and Municipal Employment Bureaux,* c. 37.

– (1927). *Revised Statutes of Ontario: An Act Respecting Employment Agencies,* c. 56.

– (1950). 'The Employment Agencies Act.' *Revised Statutes of Ontario,* c. 114.

– (1970). 'The Employment Agencies Act.' *Revised Statutes of Ontario,* c. 146.

- (1980). 'Employment Agencies Act.' *Revised Statutes of Ontario,* c. 136.
- (1990). 'Employment Agencies Act.' *Revised Statutes of Ontario,* c. E. 13.
- (1990). 'Employment Agencies Act (Regulation 320).' *Revised Regulations of Ontario.* 485.
- (1996). *Revised Regulations of Ontario: General Welfare Assistance (Regulation No. 537).* Ontario: Ministry of Labour.
- (1996). *Program Guidelines for Early Implementation of Ontario Works/Guidelines for the Devlopment of Business Plans for Early Implementation of Ontario Works.* Ontario: Ministry of Community and Social Services.
- (1998). 'An Act to Prevent Unionization with Respect to Community Participation under Ontario Works Act, 1997.' *Revised Statutes of Ontario,* c. 17.
Ontario District Council of the International Ladies' Garment Workers Union and INTERCEDE. (1993). *Meeting the Needs of Vulnerable Workers: Proposals for Improved Employment Legislation and Access to Collective Bargaining for Domestic Workers and Industrial Homeworkers.* Toronto: February.
Ontario Federation of Labour. (1998). 'Bill 22. Prevention of Unionization Act' (Ontario Works). Presentation to the Standing Committee on Justice (16 June).
Ontario Social Safety Network. (1998). *Social Safety News* 19 (April).
Organization of Economic Cooperation and Development. (1993). *The OECD Employment Outlook.* Paris: OECD.
- (1994). *The OECD Jobs Study: Facts, Analysis. Strategies.* Paris: OECD.
- (1995). *OECD Employment Outlook, 1995.* Paris: OECD.
Panitch, L. (1976). *Wages, Workers and Controls: The Anti-Inflation Program and Its Implications for Canadian Workers.* Ottawa: New Hogtown Press.
Panitch, L., and D. Swartz. (1988). *The Assault on Trade Union Freedoms: From Consent to Coercion.* Toronto: Garamond Press.
Parker, R.E. (1994). *Flesh Peddlers and Warm Bodies: The Temporary Help Industry and Its Workers.* New Jersey: Rutgers University Press.
Peck, J. (1996). *Work Place: The Social Regulation of Labor Markets.* New York: The Guildford Press.
Phillips, E., and P. Phillips. (1983). *Women and Work: Inequality in the Labour Market.* Toronto: Garmond.
Phizacklea, A., and C. Wolkowitz. (1995). *Homeworking Women: Gender, Racism and Class at Work.* London: Sage Publications.
Picchio, A. (1981). 'Social Reproduction and Labour Market Segmentation.' In J. Rubery, and F. Wilksinson. *The Dynamics of Labour Market Segmention.* London: Academic Press.
- (1992). *Social Reproduction: The Political Economy of the Labour Market.* Cambridge: Cambridge University Press.

Pierson, R. (1977). '"Home Aide": A Solution to Women's Unemployment After WWII.' *Atlantis* 2 (2): 85.

– (1990). 'Gender and the Unemployment Insurance Debates in Canada, 1934–1940.' *Labour/Le Travail* 25 (Spring): 77.

Pierson, R., and B. Light. (1990). *No Easy Road: Women in Canada 1920s to 1960s.* Toronto: New Hogtown Press.

Piore, M., and C. Sabel. (1984). *The Second Industrial Divide: Possibilities for Prosperity.* New York: Basic Books.

Polanyi, K. (1957). *The Great Transformation.* Boston: Beacon Press.

Polivka, A.E., and T. Nardone. (1989). 'On the Definition of "contingent work."' *Monthly Labour Review* (December): 9.

Pollert, A. (1988). 'Dismantling Flexibility.' *Capital and Class* 34 (Spring): 42.

Porter, A. (1993). 'Women and Income Security in the Post-War Period: The Case of Unemployment Insurance, 1945–1962.' *Labour/Le Travail* 31 (Spring): 111.

– (1996). 'Feminism and Fordism: A Critique of the Regulation Approach.' Paper presented to the Learned Society Conference, June 1996.

Quebec. (1903). 'An Act Respecting Cities and Towns.' *Revised Statutes of Quebec.* 3 Edw. 7, c. 38.

– (1914). 'An Act respecting the Establishment of Employment Bureaus.' *Revised Statutes of Quebec.* 4 Geo. 5, c. 21.

– (1925). 'An Act Respecting Workmen's Employment Bureaus.' *Revised Statutes of Quebec.* c. 99.

– (1941). 'An Act Respecting Employment Bureaus.' *Revised Statutes of Quebec.* c. 161. s.8.

– (1964). 'Employment Bureaus Act.' *Revised Statutes of Quebec.* c. 147.

– (1968). 'Labour and Manpower Department Act.' *Revised Statutes of Quebec.* c. 43.

– (1977). 'Employment Bureaus Act.' *Revised Statutes of Quebec,* c. b10.

Ramirez, B. (1986). 'Brief Encounters: Italian Immigrant Workers and the CPR, 1900–1930.' *Labour/ Le Travail* 17 (Spring): 9.

– (1991). *On The Move: French-Canadian and Italian Migrants in the North Atlantic Economy.* Toronto: McClelland & Stewart.

Rashid, A. (1993). 'Seven Decades of Wage Changes.' *Perspectives on Labour and Income* (Summer): 9.

Revised Regulations of British Columbia (RRBC). See British Columbia.

Revised Statutes of British Columbia (RSBC). See British Columbia.

Revised Statutes of Canada (RSC). See Canada.

Revised Statutes Manitoba (RSM). See Manitoba.

Revised Statutes of Ontario (RSO). See Ontario.

Revised Statutes of Quebec (RSQ). See Quebec.

Ricca, S. (1982). 'Private Temporary Work Organizations and Public Employment Services: Efforts and Problems of Coexistence.' *International Labour Review* 121 (2): 141.

– (1988). 'The Changing Role of Public Employment Services.' *International Labour Review* 127 (1): 19.

Roberts, B. (1976). 'Daughters of the Empire and Mothers of the Race: Caroline Chisholm and Female Emigration in the British Empire.' *Atlantis* 1 (2): 106.

– (1988). *Whence They Came: Deportation from Canada, 1900–1935.* Ottawa: University of Ottawa Press.

– (1990). 'Ladies, Women and the State: Managing Female Immigration, 1880–1920.' *Community Organization and the Canadian State.* Toronto: Garamond Press, 109.

Rodrigues-Sanudo, F. (1993). 'Spain.' In Blanpain, R. (ed.), *Temporary Work and Labour Law of the European Community and Member States.* Deventer, Netherlands: Kluwer.

Rogers, G., and J. Rogers (eds.), (1989). *Precarious Jobs in Labour Market Regulation: The Growth of Atypical Employment in Western Europe.* Belgium, International Institute for Labour Studies.

Rogers, J.K. (1995). 'Experience and Structure of Alienation in Temporary Clerical Employment.' *Work and Occupations* 22 (2): 137.

Rojot, J. (1993). 'France.' In R. Blanpain, (ed.), *Temporary Work and Labour Law of the European Community and Member States.* Deventer, Netherlands: Kluwer: 91.

Rubery, J. (1978). 'Structured Labour Markets, Worker Organization and Low Pay.' *Cambridge Journal of Economics* 2: 17.

– (1989). 'Precarious Forms of Work in the United Kingdom.' In G. Rogers, and J. Rogers (eds.), *Precarious Jobs in Labour Market Regulation: The Growth of Atypical Employment in Western Europe.* Belgium: International Institute for Labour Studies, 49.

– (1994). 'Internal and External Labour Markets: Towards an Integrated Analysis.' *Employer Strategy and the Labour Market.* Oxford: Oxford University Press, 38.

– (1998). 'Women for the Labour Market: A Gender Equality Perspective.' Working paper prepared for the OECD. Paris: Organization for Economic Cooperation and Development. October.

Rubery, J. and C. Fagan. (1994). 'Does Feminization Mean a Flexible Labour Force?' In R. Hyman, and A. Ferner (eds.), *New Frontiers in European Industrial Relations.* Cambridge, Mass.: Blackwell, 140.

Rubery, J., and J. Humphries. (1984). 'The Reconstitution of the Supply Side of the Labour Market: The Relative Autonomy of Social Reproduction.' *Cambridge Journal of Economics* 8: 331.

Rubery, J., and F. Wilkinson. (1981). 'Outwork and Segmented Labour Markets.' In F. Wilkinson (ed.), *The Dynamics of Labour Market Segmentation.* London: Academic Press, 115.

– (1994). *Employer Strategy and the Labour Market.* Oxford: Oxford University Press.

Ruiz, L. V. (1992). 'Home Work: Towards a New Regulatory Framework?' *International Labour Review* 131 (2): 197.

Russell, B. (1995). 'Labour's *Magna Carta?* Wagnerism in Canada at Fifty.' In C. Gonick, P. Phillips, and J. Vorst. *Labour Gains, Labour Pains: 50 Years of PC 1003.* Winnipeg: Society for Socialist Studies/Fernwood Publishing, 177.

Sanderson, Steven. (1985). *The Americas in the New International Division of Labour.* New York: Holmes Meier.

Sangster, J. (1995). 'Doing Two Jobs: The Wage Earning Mother, 1945–1970.' In J. Parr, (ed.), *A Diversity of Women.* Toronto: University of Toronto Press, 98.

Satzewich, V. (1989). 'Unfree Wage Labour and Canadian Capitalism: The Incorporation of Polish War Veterans.' *Studies in Political Economy* 28 (Spring): 89.

– (1991). *Racism and the Incorporation of Foreign Labour: Farm Labour Migration to Canada since 1945.* London: Routledge.

Savage, M.D. (1971). *Industrial Unionism in America.* New York: Anro & *The New York Times.*

Sayeed, A. (ed.). (1995). *Workfare: Does It Work? Is It Fair?* Montreal: The Institute for Research on Public Policy.

Schellenberg, G. and C. Clark (1996). 'Temporary Employment in Canada: Profiles, Patterns and Policy Considerations.' Ottawa: Canadian Council on Social Development.

Schenk, C. (1995). 'Fifty Years after PC 1003: The Need For New Directions.' In C. Gonick, P. Phillips, and J. Vorst. *Labour Gains, Labour Pains: 50 Years of PC 1003.* Winnipeg: Society for Socialist Studies/Fernwood Publishing: 193.

Scott, J. (1988). *Gender and the Politics of History.* New York: Columbia University Press.

Scott, K. (1996). 'The Dilemma of Liberal Citizenship: Women and Social Assistance Reform in the 1990s.' *Studies in Political Economy* 50 (summer): 1.

Seavey, D., and R. Kazis. (1994). 'Skills Assessment, Job Placement, and Training: What Can Be Learned from the Temporary Help Staffing Industry?: An Overview of the Industry and a Case Study of Manpower, Inc.' Jobs for the Future, Washington: U.S. Department of Labor.

Shea, C. (1990). 'Changes In Women's Occupations.' *Canadian Social Trends* (Autumn): 21.

Shotwell, J. T. (ed.), (1934). *The Origins of the International Labour Organization.* Vol. 1. New York: International Labour Office.

Silvera, M. (1983). *Silenced.* Toronto: Sister Vision Press.

Spain. (1994). 'Temporary Work Agency Act, 1944.' *Boletin Oficial del Estado* 131: 17408–12.

Spencer, B.G., and P.C. Featherstone. (1970). *Married Female Labour Force Participation: A Microstudy.* Canada: Dominion Bureau of Statistics.

Spero, J. E. (1990). *The Politics of International Economic Relations.* 4th ed. New York: St. Martin's Press.

Standing, G. (1989). 'Global Feminization through Flexible Labour.' *World Development* 17 (7): 1077.

Stanford, J. (1996). 'Discipline, Insecurity and Productivity: The Economics behind Labour Market "Flexibility."' In J. Pulkingham, and G. Ternowetsky (eds.), *Remaking Canadian Social Policy.* Vancouver: Fernwood Press, 130.

Statistics Canada. (1993). *Survey of Employment Agencies and Personnel Suppliers.* Ottawa: Statistics Canada, cat. no. 63–232.

– (1995). *Survey of Payroll, Employment Earnings and Hours.* Ottawa: Statistics Canada, cat. no. N. 72.002.

– (1995). *General Social Survey.* Ottawa: Statistics Canada.

– (1996). *Labour Force Survey.* Ottawa: Statistics Canada, Cat. no. 71-220XPB.

– (1996). *Survey of Employment Agencies and Personnel Suppliers.* Ottawa: Statistics Canada, cat. no. 63–232.

– (1996). *Survey of Work Arrangments, 1995.* Ottawa: Statistics Canada, cat. no. 71M0013GPE.

Strong-Boag, V. (1994). 'Canada's Wage Earning Wives and the Construction of the Middle Class, 1945–1960.' *Journal of Canadian Studies* 1: 5.

Sugiman, P. (1994). *Labour's Dilemma: The Gender Politics of AutoWorkers in Canada, 1937–1979.* Toronto: University of Toronto Press.

Tapin, J. R. (1993). 'Agences de Placement Temporaire.' Quebec: Bureau du Travail.

Tiano, S. (1994). 'Maquiladora Women: A New Category of Workers?' In K. Ward, (ed.), *Women Workers and Global Restructuring.* Ithaca, N.Y.: ILR Press.

Treu, T. (1993). 'Italy.' In R. Blanpain, (ed.), *Temporary Work and Labour Law of the European Community and Member States.* Deventer, Netherlands: Kluwer.

Trudeau, G. (1998). 'Temporary Employees Hired through a Personnel Agency: Who Is the Real Employer?' *Canadian Labour and Employment Law Journal* 5: 359.

U.S. Bureau of Labor Statistics. (1995a). 'New Data on Contingent and Alternative Employment Examined by BLS.' Washington: U.S. Department of Labour.

– (1995b). 'New Survey Reports on Wages and Benefits for Temporary Help Services Workers.' Washington: U.S. Department of Labor.

– (1995c). 'Occupational Compensation Survey: Temporary Help Supply Services, United States and Selected Metropolitan Areas, November 1994.' Washington: U.S. Department of Labour.

U.S. Department of Labor. (1995). *Report on the American Workforce*. Washington: U.S. Department of Labor.

U.S. Department of Labor. (1996). LABSTAT Series Report. Series EEV80736302. Washington: Bureau of Labor Statistics.

Ursel, J. (1992). *Private Lives, Public Policy: 100 Years of State Intervention in the Family*. Toronto: The Women's Press.

Valticos, N. (1973). 'Temporary Work Agencies and International Labour Standards.' *International Labour Review* 107 (1): 43.

Veldkamp, G., and K. Raesten. (1973). 'Temporary Work Agencies and Western European Social Legislation.' *International Labour Review* 107 (2): 117.

Vosko, L. F. (1995). 'Recreating Dependency: Women and UI Reform.' In D. Drache, and A. Ranikin (eds.), *Warm Heart, Cold Country*. Toronto: Caledon Press, 213.

– (1996). '*Irregular* Workers, *New* Involuntary Social Exiles: Women and UI Reform.' In J. Pulkingham, and G. Ternowetsky. *Remaking Canadian Social Policy: Social Security in the Late 1990s*. Toronto: Fernwood Press, 265.

– (1997). 'Legitimizing the Triangular Employment Relationships: Emerging International Labour Standards from a Comparative Perspective.' *Comparative Labor Law and Policy Journal* 19 (Fall): 43–77.

– (1998a). '"Regulating Precariousness": The Temporary Employment Relationship under the NAFTA and the EC Treaty.' *Relations Industrielles/Industrial Relations* 53 (1): 123.

– (1998b). 'Workfare Temporaries: Workfare and the Rise of the Temporary Employment Relationship in Ontario.' *Canadian Review of Social Policy* 42 (Winter).

– (1998c). 'No Jobs, Lots of Work: The Gendered Rise of the Temporary Employment Relationship in Canada, 1897–1997.' PhD diss., York University.

– (2000). 'Gender Differentiation and the Standard/Nonstandard Employment Distinction: A Geneology of Policy Interventions in Canada.' In D. Sukan (ed.), *From Differentiation to Inclusion*. Toronto/Montreal: University of Toronto Press, University of Montreal Press. Forthcoming.

Walby, S. (1989). 'Flexibility and the Changing Sexual Division of Labour.' In S. Wood (ed.), *The Transformation of Work*. London: Unwin Hyman, 127.

– (1997). *Gender Transformations*. London: Unwin Hyman.

Ward, K. (1994). *Women Workers and Global Restructuring*. Ithaca, N.Y.: ILR Press.

Weiss, M., and M. Schmidt. (1993). 'Germany.' In R. Blanpain, (ed.), *Temporary Work and Labour Law of the European Community and Member States*. Deventer, Netherlands: Kluwer: 121.

White, J. (1980). *Women and Unions*. Ottawa: Canadian Advisory Council on the Status of Women.

– (1983). *Women and Part-time Work*. Ottawa: Canadian Advisory Council on the Status of Women.

– (1987). *Current Issues for Women in the Federal Public Service*. Ottawa: Canadian Advisory Council of the Status of Women.

– (1993). *Sisters and Solidarity: Women and Unions in Canada*. Toronto: Thompson Education Publishing.

Wial, H. (1993). 'The Emerging Organization Structure of Unionism in Low-Wage Sources.' *Rutgers Law Review* 45 (Spring): 671.

Wilgress, W.T. (1916). *Report of the Ontario Commission on Unemployment*. Toronto: Legislative Assembly of Ontario.

Wymer, J.F. (1993). 'Contract Employees: Yours, Mine or Ours?' *Employee Relations Law Journal* 12 (2): 247.

Index

Note: Page numbers followed by 't' indicate a table.

Studies in Comparative Political Economy and Public Policy

Editors: Michael Howlett, David Laycock, Stephen McBride, Simon Fraser University

This series is designed to showcase innovative approaches to political economy and public policy from a comparative perspective. While originating in Canada, the series provides attractive offerings to a wide international audience, featuring studies with local, sub-national, cross-national, and international empirical bases and theoretical frameworks.

Editorial Advisory Board:

Published to date: